# Impact of Mobile Payment Applications and Transfers on Business

Thaisaiyi Zephania Opati
*Riara University, Kenya*

Martin Kang'ethe Gachukia
*Riara University, Kenya*

A volume in the Advances in Finance, Accounting, and Economics (AFAE) Book Series

IGI Global
DISSEMINATOR OF KNOWLEDGE

Published in the United States of America by
IGI Global
Business Science Reference (an imprint of IGI Global)
701 E. Chocolate Avenue
Hershey PA, USA 17033
Tel: 717-533-8845
Fax: 717-533-8661
E-mail: cust@igi-global.com
Web site: http://www.igi-global.com



Library of Congress Cataloging-in-Publication Data

Names: Opati, Thaisaiyi Zephania, 1979- editor. | Gachukia, Martin Kang'ethe, 1979- editor.
Title: Impact of mobile payment applications and transfers on business / Thaisaiyi Zephania Opati and Martin Kang'ethe Gachukia, editors.
Description: Hershey, PA : Business Science Reference, [2020] | Includes bibliographical references and index. | Summary: ""This book explores the impact of mobile money transfer and its impact on social, corporate, micro, and macro policies concerning the aggregated economy and individual households as a whole within an economy"--Provided by publisher"-- Provided by publisher.
Identifiers: LCCN 2019039185 (print) | LCCN 2019039186 (ebook) | ISBN 9781799823988 (hardcover) | ISBN 9781799823995 (paperback) | ISBN 9781799824008 (ebook)
Subjects: LCSH: Electronic funds transfers. | Mobile commerce. | Economic development. | Financial services industry.
Classification: LCC HG1710 .I548 2020 (print) | LCC HG1710 (ebook) | DDC 332.1/78--dc23
LC record available at https://lccn.loc.gov/2019039185
LC ebook record available at https://lccn.loc.gov/2019039186

This book is published in the IGI Global book series Advances in Finance, Accounting, and Economics (AFAE) (ISSN: 2327-5677; eISSN: 2327-5685)

British Cataloguing in Publication Data
A Cataloguing in Publication record for this book is available from the British Library.

# Advances in Finance, Accounting, and Economics (AFAE) Book Series

ISSN:2327-5677
EISSN:2327-5685

Editor-in-Chief: Ahmed Driouchi Al Akhawayn University, Morocco

**MISSION**

In our changing economic and business environment, it is important to consider the financial changes occurring internationally as well as within individual organizations and business environments. Understanding these changes as well as the factors that influence them is crucial in preparing for our financial future and ensuring economic sustainability and growth.

The **Advances in Finance, Accounting, and Economics (AFAE)** book series aims to publish comprehensive and informative titles in all areas of economics and economic theory, finance, and accounting to assist in advancing the available knowledge and providing for further research development in these dynamic fields.

**COVERAGE**

- Comparative Accounting Systems
- Bankruptcy
- E-Accounting
- Interest Rates and Annuities
- Evidence-Based Studies
- Fiscal Policy
- Ethics in Accounting and Finance
- Risk Analysis and Management
- Applied economics
- Taxes

IGI Global is currently accepting manuscripts for publication within this series. To submit a proposal for a volume in this series, please contact our Acquisition Editors at Acquisitions@igi-global.com or visit: http://www.igi-global.com/publish/.

The Advances in Finance, Accounting, and Economics (AFAE) Book Series (ISSN 2327-5677) is published by IGI Global, 701 E. Chocolate Avenue, Hershey, PA 17033-1240, USA, www.igi-global.com. This series is composed of titles available for purchase individually; each title is edited to be contextually exclusive from any other title within the series. For pricing and ordering information please visit http://www.igi-global.com/book-series/advances-finance-accounting-economics/73685. Postmaster: Send all address changes to above address. 

## Titles in this Series

*For a list of additional titles in this series, please visit:*
*https://www.igi-global.com/book-series/advances-finance-accounting-economics/73685*

***Handbook of Research on Social and Economic Development in the European Union***
Yilmaz Bayar (Uşak University, Turkey)
Business Science Reference • © 2020 • 614pp • H/C (ISBN: 9781799811886) • US $295.00

***Avatar-Based Models, Tools, and Innovation in the Digital Economy***
Vardan Mkrttchian (HHH University, Australia) Leyla Gamidullaeva (Penza State University, Russia) and Ekaterina Aleshina (Penza State University, Russia)
Business Science Reference • © 2020 • 288pp • H/C (ISBN: 9781799811046) • US $195.00

***Monetary Policies and Independence of the Central Banks in E7 Countries***
Hasan Dinçer (İstanbul Medipol University, Turkey) and Serhat Yüksel (İstanbul Medipol University, Turkey)
Business Science Reference • © 2020 • 286pp • H/C (ISBN: 9781799816430) • US $195.00

***Handbook of Research on Creating Sustainable Value in the Global Economy***
Ulas Akkucuk (Boğaziçi University, Turkey)
Business Science Reference • © 2020 • 562pp • H/C (ISBN: 9781799811961) • US $295.00

***Applied Econometric Analysis Emerging Research and Opportunities***
Brian W. Sloboda (University of Phoenix, USA) and Yaya Sissoko (Indiana University of Pennsylvania, USA)
Business Science Reference • © 2020 • 270pp • H/C (ISBN: 9781799810933) • US $195.00

***Examining the Relationship Between Economics and Philosophy***
Ilkben Akansel (University of Bartin, Turkey)
Business Science Reference • © 2020 • 333pp • H/C (ISBN: 9781799810377) • US $205.00

***Comparative Approaches to Old and New Institutional Economics***
Ilkben Akansel (Bartin University, Turkey)
Business Science Reference • © 2020 • 380pp • H/C (ISBN: 9781799803331) • US $240.00

*For an entire list of titles in this series, please visit:*
*https://www.igi-global.com/book-series/advances-finance-accounting-economics/73685*

IGI Global
DISSEMINATOR OF KNOWLEDGE

701 East Chocolate Avenue, Hershey, PA 17033, USA
Tel: 717-533-8845 x100 • Fax: 717-533-8661
E-Mail: cust@igi-global.com • www.igi-global.com

# Editorial Advisory Board

# Table of Contents

# Detailed Table of Contents

With the government spending huge amounts on making digital payments successful, the reports indicate that the rate of penetration is not as rapid as it is supposed to be. Many third parties are entering into the payment sector with alternative payment systems at retail sector. This study is based on the literature available on the consumer behaviour theory of planned behaviour (TPB). The purpose of the research is to test the relationship between the trust-based factors and the antecedents of the behavioural intention to use electronic payments by the users. Presently, the research question that has been concentrated on is to study the impact of trust on the attitude and intention to use electronic payments in India. The objective of the study is to examine the role of trust in technology adoption model. The findings indicated that trust acts as a significant determinant of consumer adoption of digital payments in India. Therefore, in order to find the answers to the research question, the study has been conducted among the users of electronic payments.



Lenders employ AI and algorithms in analyzing the potency for loan advancement. AI and algorithms are seen as efficient, and banks seem to be adopting or exploring the AI applications and algorithms to manage risk and cut bottom line cost, thus replacing costly, laborious, and repetitive activities along the value chain. The chapter offers practical solution to the practitioners and stakeholders on identifying customers associated with consumer risky default behaviors. It then advises on how to deal with these issues and what banks should employ to curb risky borrowing behavior.



Digitalization of payments related to education has played a significant role in driving the fourth agenda of the Sustainable Development Goals (SDG) aimed at providing free, equitable, and quality primary and secondary education to children by 2030. Since the launch of mobile money transfer (MMT) technologies by Safaricom in Kenya in 2007, many providers have developed a range of services to ensure efficient, transparent, and sustainable means of paying for school and college fees. This has led to enhanced teacher-student interaction times, reduced absenteeism, improved security in handling money, and made it easier for families to save, plan, and educate their children. This chapter reviews key success cases of countries and institutions that have digitalized payments and other education services to empower disadvantaged communities.

The chapter explores financial exclusion, its causes, and consequences in society. The chapter found that the existing discrepancy in financial inclusion between the developed and developing world is driven by financial exclusion that makes it difficult for financial service providers to expand outreach to the poor at affordable prices. The chapter aims to investigate the role of mobile financial service design and development in dealing with financial exclusion. It was found that mobile financial services are promoting financial inclusion in various markets. However, few studies have been undertaken on the benefits of mobile financial services in dealing with the high rates of financial exclusion. The chapter recommended that to achieve financial inclusion, there is need for mobile financial services providers to take into account customer experience through the ease of using the phone interface. The chapter concluded that there is need for scholars in the fields of finance and economics to conduct research in the areas of mobile financial services and their role in society.



Though the digital loan industry is still in its diapers, the unprecedented growth of it is a concern to many stakeholders within the financial industry. In fact, the emerging apprehensions arising out of the process of lending, distribution, and use of the digital loans have become a cause for consumerism and consumer advocacy within this new emerging product category. Of great apprehension are issues relating to regulation, consumer privacy, and loan processing among others. With this regard, a survey was carried out in Nairobi County, Kenya with over 500 questionnaires being sent through email to respondents who fall within the middle-class category. A convenience sampling method was adopted for the study, and 243 were answered and returned. A further analysis was done given the objective of the study was to examine consumer and ethical concerns arising out of sale and marketing of digital loans. This chapter examines consumer issues arising out of the digital loan applications and addresses what the industry needs to do. It recommends the way forward in dealing with these issues.

The theft of public revenues is a daily ethical failing associated with corruption in African countries. Yet many government sectors and agencies in Africa have failed to use ICTs to create the required culture of transparency. What do recent literature and empirical research findings reveal about solutions to these problems? Thus, the primary focus of this chapter is to conduct an extensive literature review on how electronic payment programs can be used as an anti-corruption strategy in Africa. Given the complex nature of corruption, the focus in this proposed chapter is to understand how other developing countries like Malaysia have successfully used electronic payment programs to reduce corruption and improve national accountability. A critical review of the observed ambiguity in the contemporary definition of corruption from different cultures in Africa will be reviewed. The ambiguity of the true commitment of African power elites in fighting corruption will also be examined with alternative solutions from existing literature.



Despite Kenya having over 40 banks, only three banks are accessible to the residents of Kibera Slum. Kibera Slum is located on the outskirts of Nairobi and is home to approximately 0.75 million people. A majority of the population in Kibera Slum comprises of either unemployed or casually employed adults whose income levels are considerably low, making it impossible for many of them to operate formal bank accounts. However, the evolution of mobile money technologies has made financial inclusion and innovation possible for Kibera Slum residents. The mobile-banking facility known as M-Pesa enables mobile money remittances and has an outstanding record of financial inclusion and innovation. The objective of this research was therefore to examine financial inclusion and innovation in the Kibera Slum. The study used self-administered questionnaires to answer to two objectives. The study found out that M-Pesa services are accessible and widely used in Kibera Slum. The study also found that M-Pesa business is rated average as a source of income to M-Pesa agent. Ultimately, the study observed that financial inclusion and financial innovation are prevalent in Kibera Slum. These findings have significant implications: the study sheds light on the fact that the slum dwellers have embraced the use of M-Pesa services as a platform to access financial services, establishing

# Foreword

Technological advances continue to disrupt virtually every sphere of life. Technology gave birth, for example, to Mobile Money Transfer (MMT) which has dictated a new wave of change on how business is being conducted globally. According to a GSMA Report on the "State of the Industry Report on Mobile Money (2018)," the MMT sector is on a rapid growth trajectory with more than 866 million registered accounts in 90 countries and a whopping $1.3 billion transacted daily. MMT applications now offer innovative solutions like processing and issuance of digital loans through Artificial Intelligence techniques, and within the shortest time ever.

Undeniably, consumer behavior has changed drastically in recent times following the mainstreaming of MMT services. Consumers are now adopting the culture of heavily relying on their mobile phones for almost all transactions, from checking account balances, transferring of money from one account to another, transfer to mobile platforms, payments, among others. It signals a major shift on how transactions and access to money is undertaken, as well as the emergence of a sub-culture within banking sector, particularly when it comes to accessing credit (loans) through digital platforms, without stepping into a physical bank. Many business entities are currently embracing this key innovation by default, acknowledging how MMTs have redefined the flow of money globally. These innovations are considered to offer inclusivity features among the marginalized societies and in particular, women in Africa.

Certainly, since the launch of M-Pesa in Kenya, the evolution of MMT services has seen similar products sprouting around the world in such places as Afghanistan, Philippines, Tanzania, Uganda, China and Malawi, among others, in order to facilitate business transactions and reach more clients. However, the policy and legal frameworks appear to be serving as hindrances to this innovative culture. This is because many governments, and by extension, business entities are wary of ethical, cultural, money laundering and regulation issues that could, or have been considered to handicap the MMT industry. As such in some jurisdictions, it is left to the mobile money users to be more prudent to protect themselves against malpractices and crimes that bedevil the industry.

These challenges within the legal and regulatory framework are becoming a setback in providing a conducive environment for MMTs to thrive. Though MMT has increased the velocity of money in circulation and cut down on the transaction speeds, consumer, and indeed business concerns abound. MMTs have been accused of becoming a conduit of digital crime creating a monumental challenge for law enforcers and regulators like Central Banks especially in countering money laundering and such other vices. Suffice to note, the risk associated with MMTs is enormous given the viability, visibility and integrity of these systems online. It calls for a concerted effort to enforce a tighter risk management regime to deal with cybercrimes, as well as ethical and system issues in order to protect consumers, businesses, and integrity of economic systems.

It is the high time therefore that all stakeholders come to the table to discuss and synchronise efforts to fully understand the intricacies of the MMT sector - which has become integral to most economies, conduct research, and set in place the policies, structures and mechanisms to ensure that the immense benefits of Mobile Money Transfer systems are not eroded by the actions of those that would wish to use the "darkness" of the cyberworld to advance crimes and other vices. This is indeed a wonderful and monumental step in the right direction.

*Robert Gateru*
*Riara University, Kenya*

# Preface

Since M-PESA, the first African mobile money platform, was launched by *Safaricom* in Kenya in 2007, the growth of mobile money transfer (MMT)has adopted a quantum leap in growth in certain developing countries. For instance 96 percent of households currently outside Nairobi [Kenya] have at least one M-PESA account (Logan, 2017). This adoption is significant and is currently changing and upsetting the financial landscape of these nations where the MMT has been adopted.

Agrawal (2009) defines mobile money transfer as the use of a mobile phone in order to transfer funds between banks or accounts, deposit or withdraw funds, or pay bills or use of a mobile device to purchase items, whether physical or electronic. Accordingly, Orozco (2003) illuminates that MMT service is an aspect of a broader concept emerging in the electronic payment and banking industry referred to as Mobile banking. Irrefutably the double-digit growth of MMT in Africa has been credited to the progression of the platform beyond peer-to-peer mobile payments to include paying for shopping, utility bills such as school fees, water, rent and electricity, receiving dividends, and diaspora remittances. This trend has led Logan (2017) to admit that the impact of MMT to poverty reduction a definite result of improved financial behavior – by facilitating easier transactions and safer savings – and changes in the occupational choice of users. This trend has forced corporates to adopt mobile money linkages and transactions to maintain their market share heavily due to consumer convenience posed by MMTs. For instance, Kenya Power a power utility company in Kenya estimates that 80 per cent of the utility's 654,953 pre-paid customers buy electricity tokens through mobile money platforms. Kenya Airways, the Kenyan national carrier has adopted mobile money payments now make up one per cent of total air ticket sales in 2015 .Without a doubt the as the World Bank (2009) notes the primary function of MMT services has been to reduce the costs of making payments from one individual to another, especially across large distances .

Adam and Walker (2015) posits that as a result mobile money tends to increase the macroeconomic stability of the countries contrary to popular expectations that it would destabilize the conduct of monetary policy in those countries. For instance M-PESA as part of economic expansion and customer convenience the transaction costs in Kenya has significantly reduced for instance, during its launch the average distance to the nearest bank was 9.2 kilometers, eight years later in 2015 the average distance to the nearest M-PESA agent was a mere 1.4 kilometers (Logan, 2017). MMT tends to increase the velocity of money in circulation because it cuts the transactions and time costs of making retail payment prompting efficiency of transactions desired by customers (Nampewo & Opolot, 2016).

MMTs triumphs in Africa have been tried and tested and they are being replicated around the world. Recent inventory by the social venture credit SMS suggests that that there are at least 23 distinct MMT, operating or pending in 20 countries following the success of MPESA (Pulver, & Gunnar, 2009). These places include Greenfield deployment in Indonesia launched in 2009 and the SMART Communications' Island Activations Program in the Philippines. M-PESA like infrastructure was even adopted by the leading Afghan mobile network operator, Roshan, anticipate building an M-PESA-like infrastructure in Afghanistan by end of 2010 (Pulver & Gunnar, 2009). Mobile money users are able to form more diverse risk-sharing networks, it's not surprising that users, compared with non-users, tend to receive more remittances from more people (Logan, 2017). Kamukama and Tumwine (2012) notes that the proliferation of mobile payments may disadvantage commercial banks by weakening their liquidity positions but they are now adopting the same platform to do business efficiently

MMT is vital in enabling households to lift themselves out of extreme poverty (Logan, 2017). The innovations in the financial sector, including mobile money, have been shown to have statistically significant positive long-run effects on money velocity in Uganda (Nampewo & Opolot, 2016).

The intention of the authors of this book is to bring to the fore an in-depth assessment on the impact of mobile payment applications and transfers on business and customers; keenness has to be drawn on how the emergent area of mobile money technology has changed relationships in business organizations and consumers. Mobile payment applications have spawned the world over and have been adopted to varied business needs and settings particular to Sub-Saharan Africa. The advent of MMT has had a significant impact and has borne a momentous stride on business entities and the general economic systems although with a considerable resistance due to complacency in use of cash and card systems; security assurance in mobile transactions, underlying risks associated to innate ability to data privacy. The impact of mobile payment applications and transfers on business and customers is therefore current and appealing to all stakeholders whether in the Telcom industry, management, mobile money operators as well as policy analysts; all will find this book being a valuable tool for career development, practitioners and academics.

The book makes concerted effort to ensure authenticity and authority of the different cases, data and chapter designs. It covers a wide coverage both in geographical and in-depth cases, overarching themes relating to application of artificial intelligence, design and development of mobile financial services, MMTs and global money remittances, consumerism and in the wake of digital loans, financial crimes, money laundering and terrorism financing, mobile and electronic payments in deterring corruption, ethics in mobile banking and financial inclusivity of women in the wake of alleviation of poverty and promotion of sustainable development goals.

## ORGANIZATION OF THE BOOK

**Chapter 1**: The chapter reviews the growth of mobile money transactions (MMTs) and their effect on international remittances and financial inclusion. Given the novelty of MMTs, its adaptation ballooning effect, there is need to interrogate its impact around the world exclusively on international remittance beyond Sub-Saharan Africa. The chapter avers that with increased confidence in its use, international humanitarian agencies and governments are employing MMTs to reach out to citizenry through Government to People (G2P) as well as People to Government (P2G) payment platforms. The chapter is conceptualized on the emergent themes emanating from the World Bank data under the G20 financial inclusion indicators in 60 countries with remarkable MMT per 100,000 adults. Emergent findings from the data indicates of MMT benefits to small countries such as the Pacific Island Countries, benign economic policies under West African countries, increased uptake of cash and voucher transfers through humanitarian support and the pursuit of cashless economy through mobile wallets. Essentially the growth of MMTs is currently viewed as leap-frog strategy to the low- and middle-income countries embracing MMTs in promoting the sustainable development goals.

**Chapter 2:** This chapter takes an empirical approach to deliberate on the pivotal role trust plays in promoting digital payments. Using the Indian government as a case, the chapter explicitly highlights how digital payments can be utilized by exchequer to dispense billions of cash when dealing with macro- economic issues. It highlights how the Indian government has been successful in expending funds through digital payments. However limited by mediating factors of trust, the chapter gives an image of low penetration. Myriads of third parties still in the process of adopting these modes as an alternative within the retail industry. Conclusively the chapter clearly identifies the mediating role of trust using technology adoption model (T.A.M). The findings cement the fact that trust acts as a significant determinant of consumer adoption of digital payments.

**Chapter 3:** The chapter scrutinizes the current functionality of Artificial Intelligence and algorithms as an enabler of businesses in examining customers to avoid the pitfalls of engaging risky customers. The need to develop systems which are invasive free and customer friendly to endear customers to such AI and Algorithms applications are profound in this chapter. The chapter indicates the role of AI and Algorithms to be decisive in dealing with the vice of money laundering -a chief predicament for the financial services and banking industry mostly faced at the global level. Lastly the chapter contributes further insights to banks profitability potential in application of AI and algorithms in taking over repetitive tasks from bank employees; autonomous AI software(s) could be instrumental reducing the demand for less skilled labor and increase the adeptness of the remaining bank workforce.

**Chapter 4:** Digitalization of payments related to education has also played a remarkable role in driving the fourth agenda of the Sustainable Development Goals (SDG) aimed at providing free, equitable and quality primary and secondary education to children by 2030. This chapter advances the thesis of mobile money transfer (MMT) technologies' application in advancing access of education to the vulnerable. MMT industry with intent of providing nourishing and critical success factors within the education sector has led to many providers to develop a variety of services that ensure efficient, transparent and sustainable means of paying for school and college fees. The chapter draws the attention to MMT facilitation of enhanced teacher-student interaction times, reduced absenteeism, improved security in handling money and made easier for families to save, plan and educate their children. This chapter seeks to review key success cases of countries and institutions that have digitalized payments and other education services to empower disadvantaged communities. The chapter consequently exposes the role that MMT has played in achieving the fourth SDG on education for all children. It ultimately brings to the fore the pervasive need and comprehensive acceptance of centralized information management by the government and all education stakeholders to achieve these goals.

**Chapter 5:** This chapter reviews the financial exclusion-inclusion agendum, its causes and consequences in the society. The ingredients posits existing discrepancy in financial inclusion between the developed and developing world, and this wedge is driven by financial exclusion that makes it difficult for financial service providers to expand outreach to the poor at affordable prices. The chapter then suggests a framework to be adopted in investigating the role of mobile financial service design and development in dealing with financial exclusion. Largely, mobile financial services are seen to be involved in promoting financial inclusion in various markets across Africa. The necessity of mobile financial services in combating the high rates of financial exclusion cannot be underemphasized. It advises financial inclusion need to be more evident, and mobile financial services providers to consider customer experience through the ease of using the phone interface.

**Chapter 6:** With exponential rise of the cost of credit to individuals and small-scale businesses, the concerns are rife on what to do to curtail the runaway behavior of lenders. The unprecedented growth of the expensive digital loans has led to uneasy stay to many stakeholders within the financial industry. This chapter presents emerging apprehensions arising out of the process of lending, distribution and use of the digital loans have become a clarion call for consumerism and consumer advocacy within this new emerging product category. Of great apprehension are issues relating to regulation, consumer privacy, and loan processing among others. With evidence from over 200 questionnaires submitted by respondents who fall within the middle-class populace, the difficult questions must be answered. This chapter identifies large consumers' concerns arising out of the digital loan applications and addresses what the industry needs to do to herness the nascent but blooming digital loan product category.

**Chapter 7:** The daily theft of public revenues is a failing vice associated with the corrupt in place of authorities in African countries. The chapter highlights the failure of many government sectors and agencies in Africa to employ the use ICTs to create the required culture of transparency. What do recent literature and empirical research findings reveal about solutions to these problems? The prime focus of this chapter through the extant literature review on how electronic payment programs can be used as an anti-corruption strategy in Africa. The study proposes a peer to peer approach by benchmarking with other developing economies like Malaysia on how the use of electronic payment programs have successfully reduced and mitigated corruption and improve national accountability. A critical review of the observed ambiguity in the contemporary definition of corruption from different cultures in Africa is as well reviewed within the pages of this chapter and plausible solution made.

**Chapter 8**: The chapters delves in the interrogation of the sea of financial inclusion among slum dwellers in Africa (those earning less than a dollar a day). With the invention of MMTs financial inclusion has become a reality to many even among the poor of the poorest within the borders of Sub-Sahara Africa countries. This chapter revisits the role played by a business entity – Safaricom – and its world-renowned innovation M-pesa in facilitating financial inclusion. The case captures *Kibera* slum [Nairobi –Kenya] -one among the largest slums in Africa -with a population of 0.75 million majority of whom are either unemployed or casually employed persons an anathema to formal banking sectors due to their meagre pay (KNBS, 2018). The chapter delves into mannerism and issues relating to restoration of the dignity of slum dwellers by offering them financial inclusion through MMT given that more 40 corporate banks have shunned such jurisdictions doted with informal settlements.

**Chapter 9:** This chapter deals with elephant in the room – ethical issues cutting across creeds, culture and nationality that have plagued MMT while at its introduction stage of product life cycle. It highlight theories associated and concepts that tag along with the MMTs innovations and addresses the ethical issues relating to mobile money transfer in Kenya, given that Kenya is considered the cradle of MMT services. With the exponentially growth of mobile money transfer industry in Kenya, gray areas relating transaction, integrity and conduct unbecoming of traders and customers have emerged. In both formal and informal sectors of the Kenyan economy despite a plethora of advantages, MMT has its ethical demerits incidentally some leaning towards the integrity of national security e.g. terrorism financing and money laundering. The chapter seizes the moment to sensitize readers on various issues ethical issues associated with MMT and front homemade solutions to tackle unethical conduct.

**Chapter 10:** This chapter take on the dicey menace of financial crime, money laundering and terror financing that has become a challenge to the security apparatus world over. The gravity of these issues convened by the chapter have been downplayed in recent years. These financial crimes have now making major headways within the MMT industry in the financial sector transaction space. It delves into how the MMT has stirred a hornet nest and consequently been plagued myriad of financial crimes having been reported over the past decade. It behooves stakeholders to stay vigilant and stay abreast of development of robust financial securities in this space in order to deter crime and customer distrust.

**Chapter 11:** One of the challenges MMT has superlatively addressed is the alienation of women within the financial system spectrum. It is notable that since the inception of M-Pesa services women especially within the Sub Saharan Africa region have not been left behind. Teething challenges have risen primarily due to illiteracy among this women but not because of financial exclusion. This chapter examines a host of challenges that require the immediate attention of the stakeholders to raft in measures and delink the alienation of women from this progressive financial movement. The chapter suggests a way forward and behooves the concerned parties to reduce the operational risks arising, create new channels of communication and accompanying standards, and security protocols in a bid to safeguard these women against any unforeseen malpractices. It concludes that financial regulators need expanded resources to train and build the capacity to oversee MMTs.

**Chapter 12:** The book is concluded with this chapter examining the adoption of mobile application and its impact on business through the lens of cyber security. The chapter projects the marketing facets of the adoption of MMTs and MPAs chronically through the attributes of security, ease of use, service availability and risk are some of the main factors contributing to the adoption of mobile payment application. The chapter then proposes a model and examines these affect factors encouraging the adoption of Mobile Payment Application with a strong link to business' outputs in Pakistan through the mediating role of cyber security.

## SUMMARY

Currently many businesses are using these applications worldwide, therefore the need to adopt such business practices to make it more successful. Enhanced service with better availability is important in the adoption of MMTs and ultimately influence the business enterprises positively and profits northwards. Undeniably whatever the appropriate scope and location for supervision of new instruments and channels, it is clear that financial regulators need expanded resources to train and build the capacity to oversee fast-moving technology. The regulators should focus on making a secure infrastructural arrangement to boost the user trust and consumer adoption of electronic payment systems and contact-less payments. On the same front governments must come up with sound policies and guidelines to see to it that the mobile money transfer services operate smoothly. This needs to be implemented expeditiously. It is essential for the regulatory bodies to work on the strong structural assurances and stringent regulations for promoting safer online environment. MMTs have as well promoted the reduction of cost of remittance of funds largely poised with increased infrastructure costs with the large cost savings of MMTs operating as embedded software within the mobile phone systems, this has led to the increased number of remittance corridors in comparison to the country corridors that traditional remittance channels have taken. Infrastructure on which these products are rolled out need to reach even the remotest communities of every country.

## REFERENCES

Adam, C., & Walker, S. E. J. (2015). *Mobile Money and Monetary Policy in East African Countries*. University of Oxford. Available at https://www.researchgate.net/publication/318393870_

Agrawal, B. (2009). Gender and Forest Conservation: The Impact of Women's Participation in Community Forest Governance. *Ecological Economics*, *68*(11), 2785–2799. doi:10.1016/j.ecolecon.2009.04.025

Kamukama, N., & Tumwine, S. (2012). Mobile money services: A liquidity threat to Uganda's commercial banks. *African Journal of Accounting, Economics, Finance and Banking Research*, *8*(8), 33–46.

Kenya National Bureau of Statistics (KNBS). (2018). *Economic Survey report.* Available at https://www.knbs.or.ke/download/economic-survey-2018/

Logan, S. (2017). *Regulating mobile money to support scale-up.* International Centre of Growth Synthesis brief. Available at https://www.theigc.org/wp- content/uploads/2017/10/Mobile-money-synthesis-brief-.pdf

Nampewo, D., & Opolot, J. (2016). Financial Innovations and Money Velocity in Uganda. *African Development Review, 28*(4), 371–382. doi:10.1111/1467-8268.12218

Nampewo, D., Tinyinondi, G.A., Kawooya, D.R., & Ssonko, G.W. (2016). Determinants of private sector credit in Uganda: the role of mobile money. *Financial Innovation, 2*(13), 1-16.

Orozco, M. (2003). *Worker Remittances: an international comparison.* Working Paper commissioned by the Multilateral Investment Fund, Inter-American Development Bank. Retrieved from http://www.iadb.org/exr/prensa/images/RemittancesInternational.pdf

Pulver, C., & Gunnar, C. (2009). *Mobile Money What Makes a Successful Mobile Money Implementation? Learnings from M-PESA in Kenya and Tanzania for the Unbanked.* Available at https://www.semanticscholar.org/paper/Mobile-Money-What-Makes-a- Successful-Mobile-Money-Camner-Pulver/a2d5914b5fb87b0b7a6433c69421e126f7b83125

World Bank. (2009). *China: From Poor Areas to Poor People – China's Evolving Poverty Reduction Agenda: An Assessment of Poverty and Inequality in China.* World Bank Report 47349-CN, East Asia &Pacific Region: Poverty Reduction & Economic Management Department. Washington, DC: World Bank.

# Acknowledgment

The editing and publishing of this book is a statement of conceived teamwork and hard work conceived behind the scenes. Consequently, we would like to appreciate the following team for being instrumental aiding the completion of this book. First and foremost we like to appreciate Blessings Suzzanna Thaisayi (Kenya Medical Training Center [K.M.T.C ], Nairobi-Kenya) and Doxa Omwami Thaisaiyi for their support, dedication and sacrifice in seeing the fruition of editing and publishing this book. We convey our sincere appreciation to Dr. Mutuma Michubu (Kenyatta University), Dr. Beatrice Matiri – Maisori (Riara University), Dr. Job Omangwa (Kenyatta University), Dr. Olayemi Abdullateef Aliyu, (Toi Ohomai Institute of Technology,), Dr. Julius Otundo (Riara University), Dr. Alice Kande Gakuo (Commission of University Education), Dr. Albert Juma (La Trobe University, Australia Dr. Olouch J. Olouch (Jomo Kenyatta University of Agriculture and Technology),Dr. Samuel Ekundayo (Eastern Institute of Technology, New Zealand) Phanice Ambusti (Presbyterian University of East Africa), Rogers Kinoti (Riara University), Dr. Palak Kanojia (Hansraj College, University of Delhi), Dr. Margaret Njeru (Riara University), and Dr. Dennis Ouma (Kaimosi University College) for the support and advice that freely flowed during the editing phase of this book. We also take time to single out work of David Alidadi Opati of KEMRI as a research assistant in data collection for selected chapters within the domain of digital lending. We also feel indebted to Marion Amukunzi (School of Journalism -Raira University) for her critical role in editing some of the chapters contained in this book. Lastly our heartfelt gratitude goes to Prof Gateru Robert, the Vice-Chancellor, Riara University, for his advice and continual support during inception, editing and publishing of this book.

# Chapter 1
# Mobile Money Transfer:
## Reshaping Remittances and Bridging Financial Inclusion in Africa and Beyond

**Martin Gachukia**
https://orcid.org/0000-0001-9597-9933
*Riara University, Kenya*

## ABSTRACT

*The chapter reviews the growth of mobile money transactions (MMTs) and their effect on international remittances and financial inclusion. The novelty of MMTs is its widening adaptation beyond Sub-Saharan Africa with increased confidence in use of MMTs by international humanitarian agencies and governments in reaching out to citizenry through government-to-people (G2P) as well as people-to-government (P2G) payment platforms. The chapter is conceptualized on the emergent themes emanating from the World Bank data under the G20 financial inclusion indicators in 60 countries with remarkable MMTs per 100,000 adults. Emergent findings from the data indicates of MMT benefits to small countries such as the Pacific Island countries, benign economic policies under West African countries, increased uptake of cash and voucher transfers through humanitarian support, and the pursuit of cashless economy through mobile wallets. In essence, the growth of MMTs is currently viewed as leap-frog strategy to the low- and middle-income countries embracing MMTs in promoting the sustainable development goals.*

DOI: 10.4018/978-1-7998-2398-8.ch001

## INTRODUCTION

Remittances in general to Low and Middle Income Countries (LMICs) have surpassed Foreign Direct Investments (FDIs) flows since 2015 (Dilip Ratha, De, Kim, Seshan, & Yameogo, 2019); diaspora remittances have thus been characterised as an important source of external financing to social development and financial inclusion (Reisen, Fulgencio, Stam, & Otieno, 2016). Remittances are largely understood as person-to-person funds transfers largely from diaspora to persons and households in least and developing nations largely for social economic development. However the cost of sending remittances in Sub-Sahara Africa remains to be the highest at 9.3 percent compared to other remittance corridors as well as against the global average of 6.9 percent, this has been attributed partly to the lack of adequate remittance infrastructure amongst the poorest countries and rural areas (IFAD, 2017; Dilip Ratha et al., 2019).

Remittance service providers traditionally have included banks, Money Transfer Operators (MTOs) national post offices; recent entrants to the remittance channels have included the various forms and variations of Mobile Money Transfers (MMTs). According to Ratha et al., (2019), banks have the highest charges at 10.9 percent followed by MTOs and Post offices respectively attracting 7.7 and 5.5 percent charges. As of 2017, MMTs transactions for remittance of $200 via mobile money stood at 1.7 percent which was a reduction by 40 percent in the preceding year (GSMA, 2019c).

This chapter seeks to explore the MMTs landscape and its impact in facilitating remittances and promotion of financial inclusion largely in Africa and beyond to other low- and middle-income developing economies. The assessment is largely to voice the position that MMTs hold and command as critical player of remittances to the LMIC regions as compared to the established remittance providers who have been in place prior to the dawn of MMTs service platform. This chapter reviews pertinent literature on MMTs corroborated with data from World Bank on under the G20 Financial inclusion indicators on the mobile money transactions per 100,000 persons as well as well as the Global System for Mobile Communication Association (GSMA) data. The findings are largely oriented to MMTs facilitation to the economy of African countries and other low income countries with low Gross Domestic Product (GDP) representation as well as countries that are under humanitarian assistance due forcefully displaced persons (FDP) due to war and conflict, harsh climatic conditions, forces of nature are amongst other challenges in which the role of MMTs to those economies and their households has been appraised as an enabler to their resilience.

The chapter is structured as follows: a general cursory view of diaspora remittances while drawing on the unique parallels between the traditional remittances channels vis a vis the adoption of MMTs following the germane success of the mobile money platform in Kenya (M-Pesa) that rolled-out in 2007 and its subsequent mobile payment spin-off platforms globally. This section is followed by a review of the MMTs transaction with five thematic patterns in Africa and beyond are highlighted together with the factors enabling the rapid growth of MMTs; finally this chapter draws its conclusion from the emergent themes, trends and challenges.

## DIASPORA REMITTANCES IN MOBILE MONEY TRANSFER CONTEXT

Remittances to LMICs in 2018 reached $529 billion (Ratha et al., 2019) with the total value of mobile facilitated international transactions in the same period standing at $4.3 billion (GSMA, 2019b). While the general understanding on remittances is understood as person-to-person (P2P) funds transfers largely from diaspora to persons and households in least and developing nations largely for social economic development, the nuance of this definition to mobile money remittances is in this context further improved; the enriched understanding of mobile money enabled remittances follows the transaction of low value peer-to-peer (P2P) international transfers that are delivered or terminated to a financial account on a mobile phone (GSMA, 2017). This definition embraces the multifaceted nature to which mobile money transfers are linked from the remittance senders who may on one hand may not be holding a mobile money enabled account but are enabled to transfer funds through different financial media such as bank accounts, MTOs and postal offices. Remarkable to this nuance is the termination point where a mobile phone is accessed both as an interface detailing the transactions and as an account to the remitted funds.

Unique to remittance of funds through the banks, MTOs, and national postal offices is the understanding of a remittance corridors or remittance markets which specifies the remittance flow between an originating country or region and a receiving country or region. An originating or sending corridor as specified by the World Bank is understood as a country with a GDP of above $18,000 and net remittance sending countries with a per capita below $18,000; sending countries being countries with net remittance receivers with a GDP below $18,000 (IFAD, 2017), this for example allows a country like Tanzania to be both a sending country due to her being a net remittance sending country while also being a net receiver since its GDP is below $18,000.

According to the World Bank classification, there are 48 sending corridors/ countries and 105 receiving corridors/countries that remit funds through banks, MTOs, and National Postal Offices. In contrast to the main remittance channels there are 184 unique corridors for MMTs as outlined by GSMA in a survey carried out in 2017 within the larger 35 World Bank remittance sending corridors and 40 remittance receiving countries (GSMA, 2018a); this proportion indicates a huge potential in scaling up the MMTs sector largely in LMICs and a wider option to which P2P remittance persons can use while leveraging on the mobile phone infrastructure in addition to the 690 million registered accounts across 90 countries making MMTs the leading payment platform in the digital economy largely shared by LMICs. Unique to the MMTs remittance channels is the absence of United States as a remitting channel which in exclusion of MMT remittance has one of the highest remittance recipients and could be a plausible option for many migrant workers from nations that have been characterised as MMTs recipient channels such as in Ghana, Guatemala, Kenya, Nigeria, Pakistan, Philippines and Somalia.

## REVIEW OF THE MMTS TRANSACTION PATTERNS IN AFRICA AND BEYOND

Based on GSMA survey in 2017, MMTs remittance corridors were found to depict unique characteristics that are explored in this chapter. The geographical representation of countries or remittance corridors that are involved in MMTs remittances internationally follows that there are set of corridors in MMTs, namely countries/corridors that can only send, countries/corridors that can only receive and countries/corridors that can send as well as receive MMTs funds. Countries with the ability to send and receive include, Benin, Burkina Faso, Côte d'Ivoire, Kenya, Malawi, Mali, Niger, Philippines, Rwanda, Senegal, Tanzania, Togo, Uganda and Zambia. Countries that can only receive international remittances as MMTs include Madagascar, Mozambique, Nigeria, Pakistan, Philippines, Romania, Samoa, Somalia, Sri Lanka, Tonga, Zimbabwe, Burundi, DRC, Ecuador, El Salvador, Fiji, Ghana, Guatemala, Indonesia and Lesotho. Countries that can only send to but not receive MMTs remittances as shown in maroon colour include Malaysia, Qatar, South Africa and Singapore (GSMA, 2018a).

Increased sending and receiving corridors have significantly increased the number of mobile money products. In December 2018, P2P transfers accounted for $12.6 trillion with 59.6 percent of this amounts being transferred under Sub-Sahara Africa while South Asia and East Asia Pacific accounted for 20.3 and 18.5 percent respectively.

*Figure 1. Mobile money usage in various products in USD for December, 2018*

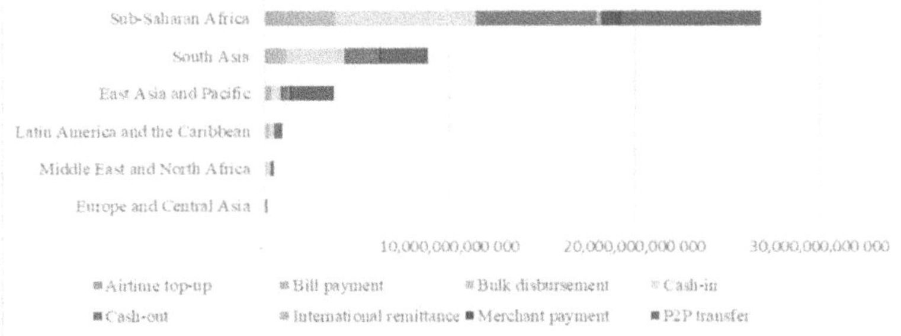


*Figure 2. Global mobile money transactions by value in US Dollars*

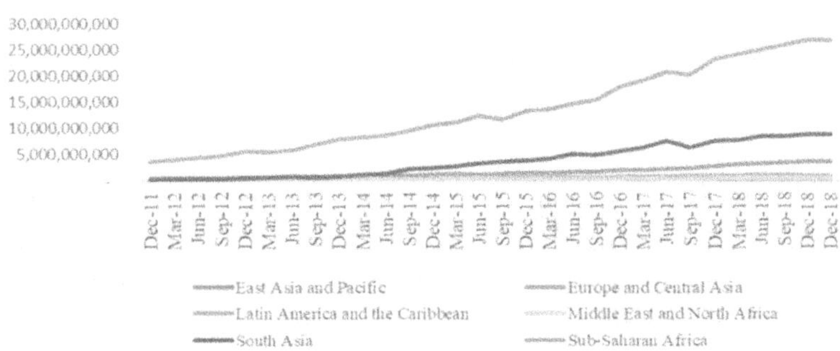


In all the eight MMT transactional products categories monitored by GSMA in 2018 on Airtime/talk-time top-up, bill payments, bulk disbursement, cash-in, cash-out, international remittances, merchant payment and P2P transfers, Sub Sahara Africa accounted for at least 59.6 percent in each of these product categories with the highest trading products being witnessed in merchant payments at 87.2 percent and bills payment at 74.7 percent. Noteworthy is the increased confidence in Business to Business (B2B) users of mobile money transfers or mobile application networks interface in bulk payment disbursement, bill payments and merchant payment respectively for the same period traded at $2.6, 2.3 and 1.6 trillion.

Globally, as represented in Figure 2 global mobile money transactions in Sub-Saharan Africa, South Asia and East Asia and Pacific have continually grown since 2011, in particular South Asia surpassed East Asia and Pacific from 2013 to 2018 with these two regions holding 21 and 9 percent share of the $40.8 billion transacted in 2018 with the 65 percent being taken up by Sub-Sahara Africa.

*Figure 3. Mobile money transactions per 100,000 adults*

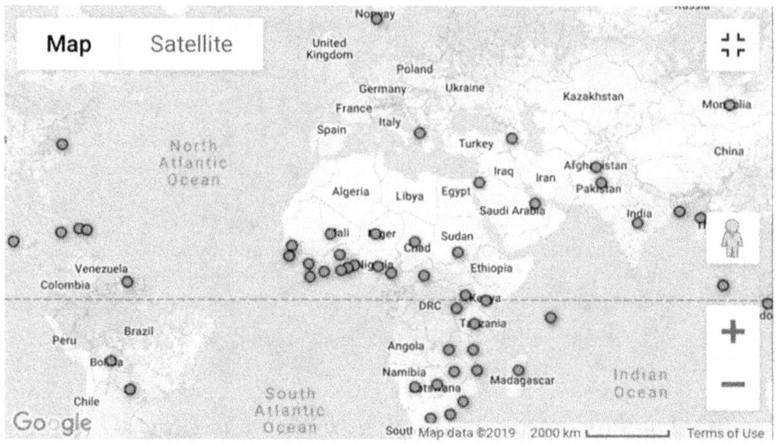


## Global Emerging Patterns From MMTs Data Per 100,000 Adults: Selected Region/Countries

Increased number of mobile money transactions per 100,000 adults as per the World Bank data on the G20 financial inclusion data depicts a unique set of patterns that are despite being descriptive of MMTs in the globe they outline strong themes on the trends that MMTs are currently taking in the globe and provide significant inferences to this chapter. East-African region dominates the mobile money transactions cumulatively from 2011 to 2017 collectively under the larger Sub-Saharan region, the first nine countries that rank highest with close to 20 million transaction per 100,000 adults are Kenya, Uganda, Zimbabwe, Tanzania, Rwanda, Ghana, Côte d'Ivoire, Burkina Faso, Mali and Botswana as depicted with the red dot in Figure 3.

Other than the Sub-Saharan countries, non-African leading ten countries include Bangladesh, Philippines, Solomon Islands, Norway, Cambodia, Bolivia, Pakistan, Mongolia, Guyana, and Samoa as depicted in Figure 4. In total the G20 financial inclusion data of mobile money transactions per 100,000 adults includes 6 countries with a range of transactions in a country being above 19 million as in Kenya to about 200 transactions witnessed in Central African Republic. The transactions being the annual cumulative transaction data for years 2011 to 2017.

A number of emerging business models, themes and inferences are depicted from the pattern of the 60 countries that have been highlighted demonstrating various trajectories highlighting on financial inclusion, support of the MMTs infrastructure and the benign policies advocated across certain regions and the globe in promotion of sustainable development goals and synergies aimed at reduction of remittance

*Figure 4. Non-Sub-Saharan countries with higher MMTs per 100,000 adults*

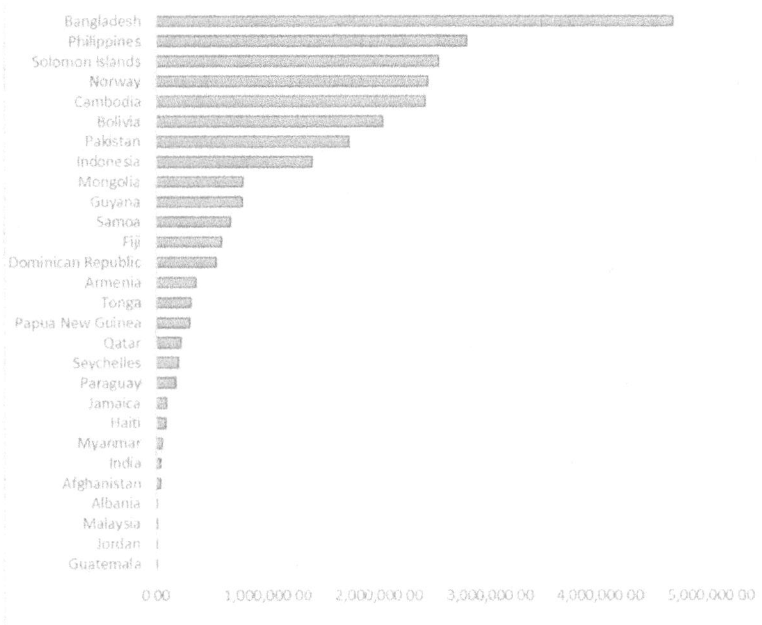


charges as well as nurturing potential trends towards cashless societies managed under mobile wallets. The themes discussed here include:

## MIRAB Miracle to Pacific Island Countries (PICs) Through MMT Remittances

New Zealand economists Bertram and Watters (1985) characterised the unique attributes that are found in small Pacific Island Countries in the 1980s namely Fiji, Papua New Guinea, Samoa, Tonga, Kiribati, Cook Islands, French Polynesia and Oceania with large reliance on foreign aid and overseas remittances and hence the Migration, Remittance, Foreign Aid & public Bureaucracy model (MIRAB). Characteristic of this region the number of people living outside of their countries of origin was noted to be more than 60 percent over the past 14 years (2000-2013) (Ratha, Eigen-Zucchi, Plaza, Wyss, & Yi, 2013) and is considered to be the second highest charged remittance region in the traditional remittance channels namely banks, MTOs, and National Postal Offices remittance after Sub-Saharan region. Specifically, its noted that in the first quota of 2017 remittance from the Australian corridor to Samoa stood at 14.4 percent while receiving money to Tonga from

Australia in the same period was at 11.1 percent far much higher than the average global percent of 7.4 (Ratha et al., 2019).

The MMTs in the Pacific region largely in Fiji, Tonga and Samoa are characterised as recipient corridors and a rich blessing to the MIRAB remittance model largely to the migrant remitters to their households as well as to the government. As per the G20 financial inclusion data the cumulative total of transactions per 100,000 persons from 2011 to 2017 stood at 588,164 for Fiji, 672,574 for Samoa and 312,200 for Tonga. This growth is currently witnessed from the partnership between Digicel a Mobile Money operator and KlickEx a digital service provider in remittances which has translated the traditional cash-to-cash remittances into digital channels (GSMA, 2018a). Digicel money transfer launched respectively to Fiji in mid-2010 and in Tonga and Samoa in 2011, during this time the cost for transferring New Zealand $200 ranged between 1 to 27 percent with an average of about 14 percent, KlickEx was the cheapest with 1 percent, Digicel at 4 percent and Melie Mei Langi at 8.5 percent, at this time also Western Union was charging 14 percent (Connell, 2015). It is evident that the role MMTs to the MIRAB region has currently supported the larger populace of migrants living outside the MIRAB region but are depended upon by their households for support.

## Interoperability of Border Remittances Models in West Africa

The second unique theme discerned from the G20 financial inclusion data is in the net effect realised in Interoperability of accounts in West Africa. Interoperability of accounts refers to the interconnectedness of several product portfolios of accounts. In mobile money transaction framework, interoperability of accounts is understood as the interconnection of use in mobile money transfers between P2P, Mobile account to Bank account, Bank account to Mobile account (Bourreau & Hoernig, 2016; GSMA, 2016). This form of interoperability is referred to as *account to account (A2A) interoperability.*

While domestic remittances have been largely transacted under P2P channels, the potential for international remittances under A2A other than providing a platform for various MMOs rides on a stronger integration and business process that relies on real-time, secure transactional processing with a managed prefunded settlement and reconciliation accounting system. A2A interoperability amongst mobile money operators in Africa have largely been ventured by MTN, Orange, Airtel and M-Pesa; these Mobile Money Operators (MMOs) having satisfactorily covered the P2P MMTs segment are in a phased out approach are increasing furthering a corroborative foothold by moving to the upper echelons of international remittances; with such efforts the growth share of Africa's Mobile money footing has been experienced beyond the home countries that the MMOs have operated from, with the increased MMT presence through MMOs interoperability operators have witnessed collaborative arrangements with the established international MTO channels such as Western Union, Money Gram and World Remit to offer mobile money as the primarily receiving channel from the developed economies. Scharwatt and Williamson (2015) documents that by 2015 there were 60 such partnerships but often these partnerships have been handicapped due customers opting for certain channels that may not be offered within the partnership coverage between the MTOs and the MMOs due to higher negotiation and commercial terms of brokering new customer centric channel partnerships.

GSMA currently documents eight exclusive mobile money to mobile money operator interoperable models currently in African. The models include Tigo Rwanda and Tigo Tanzania; Safaricom Kenya and Vodacom Tanzania; MooV Benin and MooV Togo; Airtel Zambia, Airtel Rwanda and Airtel DRC; Orange Côte d'Ivoire, Orange Mali and Orange Senegal; Orange Côte d'Ivoire and Airtel Burkina Faso; MTN Côte d'Ivoire and MTN Benin; and MTN Côte d'Ivoire and MTN Burkina Faso; MooV Côte d'Ivoire, the latter 5 models are all based in West Africa (GSMA, 2016; Scharwatt & Williamson, 2015).

The remarkable growth of the five West African regional/international remittance channels have been attributed to the synergies and a cohesive Francophone market, common currency, and central bank, the Banque Centrale des Etats de l'Afrique de l'Ouest commonly known as the BCEAO. Other than these synergies that have been considered to be benevolent escalators and accelerators to the interoperability arrangement the region has developed further from the common economic block West African Economic and Monetary Union (WAEMU) that provides a common economic and monetary unity amongst member countries that include Togo, Senegal, Niger, Mali, Guinea-Bissau, Côte d'Ivoire, Burkina Faso and Benin. Côte d'Ivoire happens to be the leading mobile money market with 4 of the A2A interoperability models already specified under MTN, MooV and Orange MMOs and according to the World Bank is also the highest remittance corridor to Burkina Faso in Sub-Saharan Africa.

Other than the success achieved by West Africa's A2A interoperability, in November 2018 mobile money operators MTN and Orange the current largest mobile money players in Anglophone and Francophone Africa jointly launched a continent wide mobile wallet interoperability (MoWaLi) to its members, the service which is also open to other mobile money service providers in Africa, banks, MTOs, and other financial service providers. The uniqueness to Mowali's concept is that it's a mobile money sector owned and industry governed payment platform commercially designed to mobile money. This model is taunted to bring down significantly costs of providing mobile money services largely to the low income customers due to economies of scale and cost of recovery business model with the visionary aim of

*Figure 5. Sub-Saharan regions mobile money transactions by value in USD*

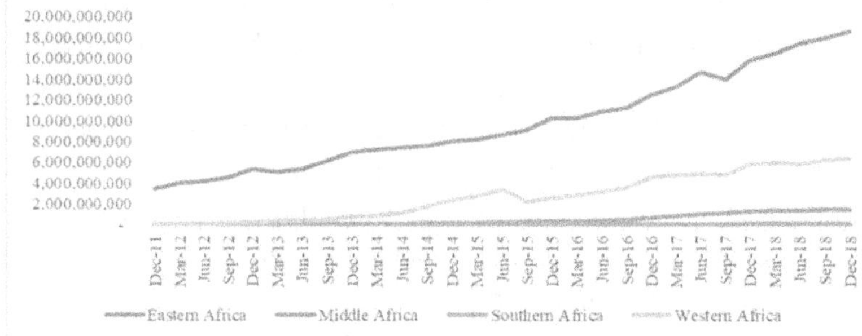


capturing the 396 million mobile money accounts across Africa (GSMA, 2019b). The model is also believed to promote growth of MMTs in West Africa as the most upcoming region in terms of monetary policies, common currency, as well as having the highest number of interoperable MTO initiatives.

Other than the Sub-Saharan region, interoperability in Latin America is well crystallised with the Bolivian case where Tigo money and MTO partnered with the Bolivian private bank (ASOBAN); this association collectively links with the ASOBAN 16 membership banks as opposed to negotiating bilaterally with individual banks. Tigo's application approval to use ASOBAN's independent company, the Clearing and Settling Chamber administrator (ACCL) allowed for the mobile wallet to bank account (A2B) and bank account to mobile wallet (B2A) interoperability (GSMA, 2018b). While this model of Mobile money to banks interoperability was strategic to Tigo, it however appears to be asymmetrically disadvantaged to Tigo since the latter pays fees both for initiating and receiving fees through ACCL switch. Overall, Mowali commercial model structured purely by MTOs and governed by the MTOs seems the best approach and circumvents similar handicaps as witnessed in Tigo Money in Bolivia.

## Growth of Voucher for Cash-Assistance (VCAs) in Humanitarian Aid

The potential of mobile money use in humanitarian assistance to forcefully displaced persons (FDP) due to war, harsh climatic conditions, forces of nature such as in earthquakes and hurricanes has been phenomenal. It continues to be much more apparent with international humanitarian agencies such as World Food Programme (WFP), Mercy corps and Oxfam being in the forefront in applying this service. Reasons behind embracing this technology in humanitarian circumstances relate to ease of transferring high volumes and high value transactions with increased safety and speed and coupled with the secure identification systems and documentation trails (GSMA, 2019a); success case Haiti documents this advantage.

Haiti's Mobile Money Initiative in 2010 brought about the increased use of MMTs platforms in place. The MMT platform was also applied in Haiti following the prolonged drought of 2013-2016 that culminated in the El Nino of 2016 where WFP provided food assistance through cash transfers in support of the 270,660 people affected (European Union, 2019) through Digicel a mobile phone e-transfer technology. By 2016 Haiti's remittance monetary value represented close to a quarter of the country GDP at 24.7 percent (GSMA, 2018a; IFAD, 2017). In Myanmar, while remittances contribute to 5 percent of its GDP with migration being witnessed in the one-way corridor to Thailand (IFAD, 2017) there has been no noticeable gender gap between men and women account ownership as based on the Global Findex report on measuring financial inclusion and fintech revolution similar findings are found with Cambodia in East Asia (Demirguc-Kunt, Klapper, Singer, Ansar, & Hess, 2018).

## Mobile Money Platforms Enabling G2P and P2G Payments

Government-to-people (G2P) and People-to-Government (P2G) payment platforms continue to demonstrate various governments' confidence and effectiveness of digital payments and commensurately influence their citizenry into embracing digital payments both to governments as in P2G and from governments through G2P. In reference to the G20 financial inclusion indicators specifying countries with above 100,000 mobile transactions per year and in corroboration with GSMA mobile money deployment tracker, different governments have embraced a three pronged approach to G2P and P2G transactions; some governments have applied the first prong of using both the G2P and P2G, other governments of whom form majority, have applied the second prong by use of P2G platforms to largely collect taxes, payment of government bonds, fines, levies amongst other chargeable services offered by the governments and the third prong has been embraced the G2P platform where governments together with other government affiliated agencies which are largely humanitarian, have adopted the MMT system for bulk payments by way of dispersing payments, vouchers to the elderly or displaced persons.

Six Countries that are currently using both the G2P and P2G platforms have so far been identified as Cameroon, Ghana, Madagascar, Pakistan, Philippines and Uganda, strikingly, other than Madagascar, Pakistan, Philippines, the other three countries have MTN Mobile Money as the mobile transaction operator. The majority of the countries totalling to 14 are running P2G platforms these include Cameroon, Côte d'Ivoire, Ghana, Guinea, Guyana, Kenya, Madagascar, Pakistan, Philippines, Rwanda, Sri Lanka, Tanzania, Uganda and Zimbabwe, significant share of the MTOs in the P2G platform is taken up by MTN Mobile Money, Orange Money,

Airtel Money, Tigo and M-Pesa. Lastly, G2P countries have to a majority been conducting humanitarian aid in parts of their countries through the MMT channels, these countries have included Afghanistan, Bangladesh, Botswana, DRC, Eswatini, Ghana, Guinea Bissau, Haiti, Madagascar, Malawi, Nigeria, Pakistan, Philippines and Uganda.

## Going Cashless Economy in Norway With Mobile Wallets

Based on the G20 financial inclusion indicators specifying countries with above 100,000 mobile transactions per year, Norway stands out as an outlier, a Nordic country in the developed economies with a significant number of over 2.45 million transactions. The rationale for the presence of Norway in this research proposes the continued growth in harnessing the promotion of cashless societies largely in the advanced economies. According to GSMA (2018a), Norway is amongst the 35 remittance sending countries with no live mobile money services but offering mobile money partnerships with remittance service providers. According to Deloitte, (2019) this country is considered to have the highest number of cashless transactions per capita with the least Automated Teller Machines (ATM) withdrawals. In P2P payments this report accounts for cash payments constituting 15 percent, while 80 percent of funds being transferred via phone app or mobile wallet (58%) and mobile bank or online bank (22%).

Rise of mobile P2P payment providers has been favoured largely in advanced economies since majority of customers connect or pair their payment cards or a number of bank account(s) to the mobile wallet apps and the requirement to complete the transactions is largely relied only with the use of a mobile number or email address of the recipient. The uptake after the launch of Vipps mobile wallet app in Norway in May 2015 for instance is reported that more than 300,000 downloads were witnessed in the month. The significant increase and visibility of Norway's transactions under the G20 financial inclusion data is largely then attributed to more than 100 Norwegian banks adopting the Vipps app as well as the increased adoption of mobile wallet apps after the successful launch of Apples first mobile app in 2014 followed by Samsung and Android. According to Rolfe (2018) Norway ranked 2$^{nd}$ globally in mobile wallet usage by country at 42 percent, second to China at 47 percent, other countries that rank in the top ten list include United Kingdom (24%), Japan (20%) Australia and Colombia at 19%, United States and Singapore having 17 percent of the share and Canada and Austria closing the list at 16 percent.

## CONCLUSION

The burgeoning growth of MMTs in Africa and beyond and its continued uptake as an international remittance channel for more than decade can no longer be considered as a start-up. From the foregoing sections a number of factors can be stylised regarding this growth; these factors include the maturation of the Mobile money transfer establishment to many regions beyond the ideation period of 2007 with the launch of M-pesa, currently the proof of concept on the MMT reality is well founded with a myriad mobile payment platform spin-offs. MMTs have as well promoted the reduction of cost of remittance of funds largely poised with increased infrastructure costs with the large cost savings of MMTs operating as embedded software within the mobile phone systems, this has led to the increased number of remittance corridors in comparison to the country corridors that traditional remittance channels have taken. Financial inclusion has also been witnessed with MMTs with the readily evidence of reduced cost of transactions, increased ability to sending smaller denominations through P2P transfers as well as settling bills, inclusion of the unbaked masses previously side-lined by gender has also been reduced. In a large scale transactions, MMTs have permitted for interface with larger financial channels such as banks and MTOs.

This chapter also coagulates the evidence of the role of MMTs in the financial inclusion promotion policy agenda for LMICs; with support of initiatives such as MoWali infrastructure the goal of reducing significantly the charges for international remittances can be achieved. Further, with the 184 unique remittance corridors channels for MMTs within the larger 35 World Bank remittance sending corridors and 40 remittance receiving countries a huge potential in scaling up the unique MMTs remittance corridors sector can largely promote MMTs as the leading payment platform in the digital economy largely shared by LMICs.

## REFERENCES

Bertram, I. G., & Watters, R. F. (1985). The MIRAB Economy in South Pacific Microstates. *Pacific Viewpoint*, *26*(3), 497–519. doi:10.1111/apv.263002

Bourreau, M., & Hoernig, S. (2016). *Interoperability of mobile money: International experience and recommendations for Mozambique*. Retrieved from https://www.theigc.org/wp-content/uploads/2017/01/Hoernig-et-al-2016-Final-Report.pdf

Connell, J. (2015). Samoa and Tonga: Migration and Remittances in the Twenty-first Century. In W. H. Khonje (Ed.), *Migration and Development: Perspectives from Small States* (pp. 122–181). London: Commonwealth Secretariat. Retrieved from https://books.google.com.mx/books?id=CJhlsrSuIMUC&pg=PA3&vq=%22en+ella.+II.+Preparar+al+trabajador+para+ocupar+una+vacante+o+puesto+de+nueva%22&hl=es&source=gbs_selected_pages&cad=2#v=onepage&q=%22en

Deloitte. (2019). *Chasing Cashless? The Rise of Mobile Wallets in the Nordics*. Retrieved from https://www2.deloitte.com/content/dam/Deloitte/dk/Documents/financial-services/Downloads/Chasing_Cashless-The_rise_of_Mobile_Wallets_in_the_Nordics.pdf

Demirguc-Kunt, A., Klapper, L., Singer, D., Ansar, S., & Hess, J. (2018). *The Global Findex Database 2017: Measuring Financial Inclusion and the Fintech Revolution*. Washington, DC: World Bank. doi:10.1596/978-1-4648-1259-0

European Union. (2019). *EU Cash Compendium 2019: Doing More Cash, Better*. Retrieved from https://ec.europa.eu/echo/sites/echo-site/files/eu_cash_compendium_2019.pdf

GSMA. (2016). *The Impact of Mobile Money Interoperability in Tanzania: Early data and market perspectives on account-to-account interoperability*. GSM Association.

GSMA. (2017). *Licensing Mobile Money Remittance Providers: Early Lessons*. GSM Association. Retrieved from https://www.gsma.com/mobilefordevelopment/wp-content/uploads/2017/02/GSMA_Licensing-mobile-money-remittance-providers_Early-lessons-1.pdf

GSMA. (2018a). *Mobile Money Competing with Informal Channels to Accelerate the Digitisation of Remittances*. GSM Association. Retrieved from https://www.gsma.com/mobilefordevelopment/programme/mobile-money/competing-with-informal-channels-to-accelerate-the-digitisation-of-remittances

GSMA. (2018b). *Mobile Money Interoperability in Bolivia: A case study for Latin America.* GSM Association. Retrieved from https://www.gsma.com/mobilefordevelopment/programme/mobile-money/mobile-money-interoperability-in-bolivia-a-case-study-for-latin-america

GSMA. (2019a). *Mobile Money enabled Cash aid Delivery: Essential Considerations for Humanitarian Practitioners.* GSM Association. Retrieved from http://www.cashlearning.org/downloads/essentialconsiderationsforusingmobilemoney.pdf

GSMA. (2019b). *State of the Industry Report on Mobile Money 2018.* London: GSM Association. doi:10.1002/9781118290743.wbiedcs023

GSMA. (2019c). *The Mobile Economy 2019.* GSM Association. Retrieved from https://www.gsma.com/r/mobileeconomy/

IFAD. (2017). Sending Money Home: Contributing to the SDGs, One Family at a Time. *International Development Fund for Agricultural*, 60. Retrieved from https://www.ifad.org/documents/38714170/39135645/Sending+Money+Home+-+Contributing+to+the+SDGs%2C+one+family+at+a+time.pdf/c207b5f1-9fef-4877-9315-75463fccfaa7

Ratha, D., De, S., Kim, E. J., Seshan, G., & Yameogo, N. D. (2019). Migration and Movement: Recent Developments and Outlook. *Migration and Development Brief*, (31), 1–29. doi:10.1016/B978-0-12-409548-9.10596-2

Ratha, D., Eigen-Zucchi, C., Plaza, S., Wyss, H., & Yi, S. (2013). Migration and Remittance Flows: Recent Trends and Outlook 2013–2016. *Migration and Development Brief*, (21), 1–29. Retrieved from http://scholar.google.com/scholar?hl=en&btnG=Search&q=intitle:Migration+and+Remittance+Flows:+Recent+Trends+and+Outlook,+2013-2016#0

Rolfe, A. (2018). *The Rise of Digital and Mobile Wallet: Global usage statistics from 2018.* Payments Cards & Mobile. Retrieved from https://www.paymentscardsandmobile.com/mobile-wallet-global-usage-statistic/

Scharwatt, C., & Williamson, C. (2015). *Mobile Money Crosses Borders: New Remittance Models in West Africa.* GSM Association. Retrieved from https://www.gsma.com/mobilefordevelopment/wp-content/uploads/2015/04/2015_MMU_Mobile-money-crosses-borders_New-remittance-models-in-West-Africa.pdf

Van Reisen, M., Fulgencio, H. T., Van Stam, G., & Otieno, A. (2016). mMoney Remittances: Contributing to the Quality of Rural Health Care. In AfriCOMM (pp. 1–17). Academic Press.

# Chapter 2
# Impact of Trust on Customer Adoption of Digital Payment Systems

**Palak Kanojia**
https://orcid.org/0000-0001-9118-157X
*Hansraj College, University of Delhi, India*

**Madan Lal**
https://orcid.org/0000-0002-6357-5464
*Department of Commerce, Delhi School of Economics, University of Delhi, India*

## ABSTRACT

*With the government spending huge amounts on making digital payments successful, the reports indicate that the rate of penetration is not as rapid as it is supposed to be. Many third parties are entering into the payment sector with alternative payment systems at retail sector. This study is based on the literature available on the consumer behaviour theory of planned behaviour (TPB). The purpose of the research is to test the relationship between the trust-based factors and the antecedents of the behavioural intention to use electronic payments by the users. Presently, the research question that has been concentrated on is to study the impact of trust on the attitude and intention to use electronic payments in India. The objective of the study is to examine the role of trust in technology adoption model. The findings indicated that trust acts as a significant determinant of consumer adoption of digital payments in India. Therefore, in order to find the answers to the research question, the study has been conducted among the users of electronic payments.*

DOI: 10.4018/978-1-7998-2398-8.ch002

## INTRODUCTION

According to a whitepaper by MasterCard Advisors, *"around 85% of all retail payment transactions are done with cash, which equates to 60% of retail transaction value"* (Thomas, Jain, & Angus, 2013). The Indian government is developing the centralized Aadhar-based payment infrastructure to boost the success of digital payment system; however, the reports indicate that the rate of penetration is not as rapid as it is supposed to be. From the point of financial inclusion, India lags behind China and Kenya with 35%, 64% and 42% of the population banked respectively. The payment system in India is highly dominated by cash, with less than 0.1% C2C payments being done digitally (Bill & Melinda Gates Foundation, 2013). India has just begun to move towards cashless economy and is at the inception stage where the economy has shifted away from cash but at quite a slow pace in the last five years. The conditions in the market are not conducive enough to boost the pace towards cashless economy in India and thus it lags behind many other countries (Thomas, Jain, & Angus, 2013).

Banking system in India is highly concentrated in the large cities having high mobile network penetration in urban areas, whereas rural areas have low mobile penetration and banking system reach (Bill & Melinda Gates Foundation, 2013). There is a huge gender gap in the adoption of electronic payments in India. The World Bank data on global financial inclusion shows that females have been less accommodating in case of digital means of payments in their lifestyles (The World Bank, 2014). The World Bank data on financial inclusion clearly depicts the status of education and its impact on the usage of financial technology in India. Lower education levels may lead to lack of awareness of the financial technologies, their benefits and their know-how. This may create a strong resistance towards adoption of the digital payments. Wide proliferation of mobile technology is a prerequisite for adoption of mobile payments by the customers (Mallat & Tuunainen, 2008).

According to 2011 GEAR report, India scored 56.1 in the overall performance and Indian government ranked 36 among the 62 countries in the adoption of electronic payments. India attained quite a low score and rank in most of the categories. India ranks 47 in the category infrastructure and 54 in socio-economic context (Economist Intelligence Unit, 2012). However, India has jumped to the twenty eighth rank in 2018 global index ranking. It has been categorised an intermediate in adoption and ranks above compared to China and Kenya in the same category with 48 and 54 rank respectively (The Economist Intelligence Unit, 2018). Growth in adoption of financial technology by consumers worldwide is evident of bright future of digital payments all. As per the statistical data published, seventy five percent of the consumers "globally have adopted some form of money transfer and/or payment service" (Cherowbrier, 2019). China is the top most country having the highest transaction value of US $1,570,194 million made via digital payments in the world. Relatively, India and Kenya are making a slow growth in digital payment transactions valued at US $64,787.3 million and US $2295.8 million respectively. However, payments based on mobile technologies have been adopted more rapidly by consumers from developing countries than those from developed nations. On the other hand, there are stark differences in the rate of adoption within the country itself. There's a rapid growth of digital payment acceptance in urban India whereas rural India still lags behind. Though research claims that advancement of payment technologies have positive influence on rural areas of South India, the gap between urban and rural markets still persists (Balaji & Vijayakumar, 2018).

The last few years have witnessed a manifold increase in cyber attacks on banks' security systems throughout the world. There were cases of e-payment validation website of bank being hacked, filching of $5 million from the 9000 customers of Tesco Bank in U.K., theft of bitcoins of value of $65 million from Hong Kong digital currency exchange etc. (Singh, 2016). Security in mobile wallets is a greater issue currently, thereby restricting the customers to trust the mobile phone as a payment device. Even the most popular mobile payment applications lack the security features and hence are exposed to financial frauds. The research studying the security levels and issues have demonstrated that mobile payments applications are vulnerable to issues like weak authentication system, information leakage and storing preferences on the device which leads to impersonation, phishing, recovering passwords and frauds and even the PINs are feeble against the attacks (Reaves, Scaife, Bates, Traynor, & Butler, 2015). The mobile wallets, payment applications and mobile banking in India use only the basic layers of security which are mostly the device based security layers, most of the smart-phones which are using android have only basic security layers and are not meant for secure payments. In India, the mobile wallets and payment applications lack the hardware security which makes the confidential data of users vulnerable to cyber attacks and financial scams (Times of India, 2016).

In the early stages of interaction with the technology, trust plays a very significant role thereby considerably affecting the adoption and usage of electronic payment systems (Simpson, 2007). Initial hesitation needs to be overcome through diffusion and reducing inertia (Creehan, 2018). Trust can be defined in terms of credibility of a brand, integrity of the company and confidence of a customer in the brand or the product. Trust is imperative not only for the adoption of a new product or technology but also for the brand stickiness. Customer relationship management is possible through trust being in the picture, as relational marketing efforts will eventually lead to customer loyalty only if trust exists in the relationship of the brand and customer (Rizan, Warokka, & Listyawati, 2014).Therefore, trust plays an important role in customer retention and online experience.

This study is based on the literature available on the consumer behaviour theory of planned behaviour (TPB). Technology adoption model (TAM) has been taken as the foundation of the proposed model. Theory of reasoned action defined the attitude from the affective and evaluative dimension (Ajzen & Fishbein, 1977). Another construct which influences behaviour intention is subjective norm referring to the perception of an individual on the basis of what do the people important to him or her think with regard to performance of the behaviour in question. Further, theory of planned behaviour (Ajzen, 1991) revealed additional construct perceived behavioural control referring to variables impeding the adoption process; internal factors of control refer to self-efficacy and external factors of control referring to facilitating conditions and negative user experience. Davis, (1989) proposed the technology adoption model (TAM) with the two major constructs perceived usefulness and perceived ease of use impacting the attitude and behavioural intention to use a system. The objective of the study is to study the role of trust in attitude and intention to adopt electronic payment systems. The purpose of the research is to test the relationship between the trust-based factors and the antecedents of the behavioural intention to use electronic payments by the users. Presently, the research question that has been concentrated on is what is the impact of trust on the intention to use electronic payments? To find the answers to this question, the study has been conducted among the users of electronic payments.

## REVIEW OF LITERATURE

The diffusion of innovations theory unleashed the adoption of technology being a multi-variate process with relative advantage, complexity, compatibility, trialability and observability being the perceived attributes impacting the rate of adoption. The theory majorly focuses on how innovation is communicated. It was proposed that communication channels, behavior, change agents' efforts and adopters' personal innovativeness impacts the rate of adoption significantly (Rogers, 1983). Technology adoption model (TAM) found the constructs which impact the user adoption of information technology. A new scale to measure the impact of the variables namely perceived usefulness and perceived ease of use on user adoption or acceptance of technology was developed (Davis, 1989). UTAUT model proposed that adoption process is a developmental one which is a resultant of external as well as cognitive, emotional and contextual aspects (Straub 2009). The study which formulated Unified Theory of Acceptance and Use of Technology (UTAUT) model which is an extension of TAM, including constructs from other models but trust has not been studied in the hugely combined model of UTAUT (Venkatesh, Morris, Davis, & Davis, 2003). Theory of planned behaviour suggests that the behavioural beliefs have a significant relationship with the attitude towards behaviour (Ajzen, 1991). This study is widely based on the foundations of Technology adoption model (TAM) and the theory of planned behaviour and hence we have derived the following constructs from early researches.

## Perceived Usefulness

Davis (1989) defined perceived usefulness as the individual's perception that the technology in question will enhance the performance or help to achieve the expected results. The concept of perceived usefulness is similar to the perceived attribute of relative advantage in the theory of diffussion of innovations by Rogers (1983). Perceived usefulness significantly impacts the behavioural intention to use mobile banking (Luarn & Lin, Toward an understanding of the behavioral intention to use mobile banking, 2005). Lin (2011) studied the impact of perceived relative advantage on the adoption and usage of mobile banking. Customer's perception of relative advantage is the perceived benefit of adoption of a new technology over the previous technology in the context of perceived usefulness. In their study Venkatesh, Morris, Davis, & Davis (2003) measured performance expectancy with perceived uselfuness being one of the components. Attitude of both adopters and non-adopters in the case of online tax filing and payment system in Taiwan was influenced significantly by perceived usefulness (Hung, Chang, & Yu, 2006).

**H1:** Perceived usefulness has a positive influence on customer adoption of digital payment systems

## Perceived Ease of Use

Davis (1989) defined perceived ease of use as the individual's perception that the technology in question will be easy to use and understand. The measurement of perceived ease of use is the contrary of perceived attribute of complexity in the theory of diffussion of innovations by Rogers (1983). In their study Venkatesh, Morris, Davis, & Davis (2003) measured effort expectancy with perceived ease of being one of the components, because the perception of degree of efforts required to use a technology impacts the rate of adoption. Higher the degree of effort required to adopt a technology lower will be the perceived ease of use and hence, the intention to adopt and use will be adversely impacted. Perceived ease of use is one of the determinants of behavioural intention to use mobile banking in the study of Gu, Lee, & Suh (2009). Perceived ease of use significantly impacts intention to adopt electronic payments (Luarn & Lin, 2005). Perceived ease of use was found to be impacting intention directly while assessing the IT usage in the study by Taylor & Todd (1995); mobile banking (Luarn & Lin, 2005); adoption of IT innovation

(Moore & Benbasat, 1991); use of personal computers (Thompson, Higgins, & Howell, 1994); adoption of NFC mobile credit card (Tan, Ooi, Chong, & Hew, 2014); adoption of internet banking in Hong Kong (Yiu, Grant, & Edgar, 2007). Perceived ease of use was found to be most significant factor for the users of mobile banking services (Jeong & Yoon, 2013).

**H2:** Perceived ease of use has a positive influence on customer adoption of digital payment systems

## Trust

Interpersonal trust in a communication is a function of perceived credibility, reliability and intentions of the communicator (Giffin, 1967). According to Sheppard & Sherman (1998), integrity, concern and benevolence are the qualities of trustworthiness forming deep dependence between two parties based on the perceived risks involving misdemeanour, cheating, abuse and neglect. This gives a clear dimension to perceived trust. The study of trust has been used in innumerable researches like interpersonal communication, organization, socialization, strategic management, corporate relationships as well as in personal relationships. The variation in nature of the context leads to the fact that trust is a multi-dimensional concept.

*Trust is an expectancy of positive (or non-negative) outcomes that one can receive based on the expected action of another party in an interaction characterized by uncertainty. (Bhattacharya, Devinney, & Pillutla, 1998)*

Individuals having certain dispositions in terms of motives and expected outcomes are more likely to enter the relationships. As the trust develops leading to perceived security, tendency to enter the relationship increases. Hence, trust plays an important role in the early stages of relationship while determining the likelihood of entering the relationship (Simpson, 2007). Many third parties are entering into the payment sector with alternative payment systems at retail sector. Behavioural intention of consumers to use and adopt the technology has many determinants, but in the case of electronic payments trust seems to be the most imperative. As the Indian retail payment sector is highly dominated by cash in volume, the role of trust becomes more important in order to digitize the retail payments. Trust brings a competitive advantage to the e-commerce firm which intends to enhance the online buying experience (Kotha, Rajgopal, & Venkatachalam, 2004). Consumers' trust is essential for customer loyalty; given the relational marketing tactics trust makes it possible to gain customer loyalty especially in the case of retail banking (Rizan, Warokka, & Listyawati, 2014).

Presence of big players in the market and security issues are the important factors impacting adoption of mobile payments (Mallat & Tuunainen, 2008). Institution-based trust ensures that there are certain structures in place conferring the trust which can be formal procedures or informal norms of a practice (Tschannen-Moran & Hoy, 2000). Structural assurances refer to the safety covers provided by the payment firms to the users in the form of regulations, legal protection, guarantees and ethics charter. Structural assurances act as antecedent to trust and presence of strong structural assurances positively impacts the intention to use electronic payments (Gu, Lee, & Suh, 2009). Lin (2011) claimed that knowledge-based trust including perceived competence, perceived benevolence and perceived integrity positively impact the attitude of customers toward adopting or using mobile banking. Luarn & Lin (2005) proved in their study that perceived credibility has a positive impact on behavioural intention. Perceived credibility meaning that individual perceives the electronic payment system as secure having least or no privacy threats. A few studies have observed a significant relationship between trust and attitude towards online banking (Al-Somali, Gholami, & Clegg, 2009); m-payment in virtual social networks (Liébana-Cabanillas, Sánchez-Fernández, & Munoz-Leiva, 2014). The purpose of the research is to test the relationship between the trust-based factors and the antecedents of the behavioural intention to use electronic payments by the users. Trust negatively affects the perceived risk which further impacts the behavioural intention to use internet banking negatively (Kesharwani & Bisht, 2012). Trust has been seen as the bridging ties in tourism technology adoption referring to confidence in the reliability of others as an important construct which determines that how much an individual will be willing to share his or her information (Lee, Cho, & Hwang, 2013). Therefore, it becomes immensely critical for the firms to create a trustworthy relationship with the users in case of electronic payments.

**H3:** Trust has a positive influence on customer adoption of digital payment systems

## Adoption (Attitude and Behavioural Intention)

Ajzen (1991) argued that attitude towards the behaviour impacts the behavioural beliefs. Attitude is the degree of favourableness or unfavourableness of behaviour. Prior studies have validated attitude as a significant construct in the prediction of behavioural intention to adopt or use mobile banking (Lin 2011); online tax services (Hung, Chang, & Yu, 2006); online banking (Yaghoubi & Bahmani, 2010); online grocery buying (Hansen, Jensen, & Solgaard, 2004); electronic document management system (Hung, Tang, Chang, & Ke, 2009); online banking in Saudi Arabia (Al-Somali, Gholami, & Clegg, 2009); internet banking in Hong Kong (Cheng, Lam, & Yeung, 2006); mobile payments in virtual social network (Liébana-Cabanillas,

*Figure 1. Proposed model*

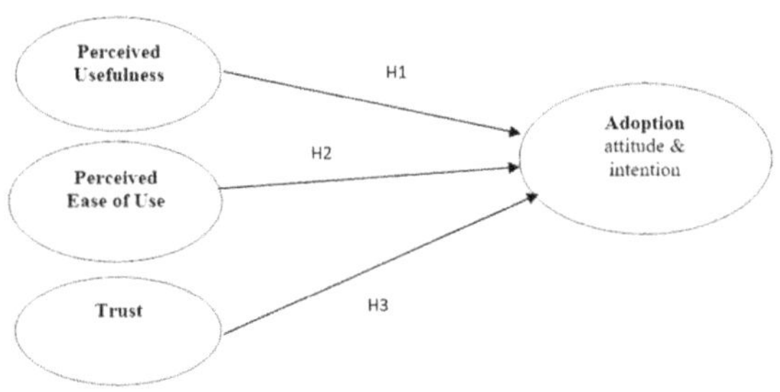


Sánchez-Fernández, & Munoz-Leiva, 2014); childhood behaviours (Trafimow, Brown, Grace, Thompson, & Sheeran, 2002).

In our study, the behaviour concerned is the adoption or usage of digital payment systems. The study by Venkatesh, Morris, Davis, & Davis (2003) claimed that behavioural intention directly impacts the usage of technology and attitude has no significant role to play in it. Positive attitude toward adoption is positively related to the behavioural intention to adopt or use digital payment systems (Lin, 2011). Lee, Cho, & Hwang (2013) in their study proved that attitude toward technology use has a significant relationship with the intention to use which further influences the final adoption decision of the individual. Attitude toward e-government services was found to be influenced by perceived usefulness, perceived ease of use and trust significantly (Hung, Chang, & Yu, 2006). Integrating the theory of planned behaviour (TPB) and technology adoption model (TAM) we have included both attitude and behavioural intention in the single construct to measure adoption of electronic payments systems (Yaghoubi & Bahmani, 2010).

## Impact of Demographic Factors

Wang, Dou, & Zhou (2008) suggested that the magnitude of effect of consumption attitude on new product adoption is highly influenced by the demographic characteristics of the consumers. An Indian study conducted the demographic research on adoption of digital wallets by the consumers found occupation and age to be significant factors affecting adoption of e-wallets (Rathore, 2016). The study conducted by Laukkanen & Pasanen (2008) in Finland among the customers of a bank found age and gender to be highly significant factors differentiating between the users. The literature suggested that customers of young age are more likely to use the digital payments. Age being an important demographic factor may impact the usage of digital payments. Customers of older age are more likely to restrict themselves to use the technological solutions for payments and hence they are unwilling to use the digital payments (Bertrand & Ahmad, 2014).

**H4a:** There is a significant difference in adoption of digital payment systems for male and female users

**H4b:** There is a significant difference in adoption of digital payment systems for users from different age groups

## RESEARCH METHOD

Based on the available literature on trust and technology adoption, variables were defined and item pools were created. A five point likert scale was constructed to measure the constructs. After conducting the pilot study, expert opinions were sought to make the required changes in wordings and structure and the questionnaire was finalised. The data has been collected from the people residing in the urban areas of India via online survey via convenience sampling method. The respondents are the users of electronic payments and have used digital payments in the past three months of filling questionnaire. The survey was made available to respondents via online link, which was opened from 18th June till 31st July 2017. The questionnaire was completed by 459 respondents. Out of 459 responses received, 414 responses were found to be usable. The responses were checked for unengaged responses and after the case-wise deletion of one case rest 413 cases were found usable for the further analysis.

The sample consisted of electronic payment users residing in urban areas of India. Out of 413 respondents, 202 were male and 211 female users. 42.9% of respondents are young with below 25 years of age and 54.5% between 25 to 50 years. All the respondents are literate and around 98.5% of the total respondents owning bank account.

Three constructs were hypothesized to influence the attitude and behavioural intention of users towards electronic payment systems. The researchers generated a multi-item scale on the basis of review of literature, prior research and relevant measures. Statistical procedure like assessment of item and scale reliability was used to validate measures. The psychometric properties of the final measures were assessed by exploratory analysis and cronbach's alpha.

## Perceived Usefulness

*Table 1. Demographic profile of respondents*

| Demographics | Frequency n=413 | % |
|---|---|---|
| Gender | | |
| Male | 202 | 48.9 |
| Female | 211 | 51.1 |
| Other | 0 | 0 |
| Age | | |
| Below 25 years | 177 | 42.9 |
| 25 to 50 years | 225 | 54.5 |
| Above 50 years | 11 | 2.7 |
| Income | | |
| Below Rs. 10,000 | 148 | 35.8 |
| Rs. 10,000-Rs. 50,000 | 148 | 35.8 |
| Above Rs. 50,000 | 117 | 28.3 |
| Education | | |
| Received upto 12th standard | 58 | 14 |
| Graduate | 98 | 23.7 |
| Post-graduate | 201 | 48.7 |
| Other | 56 | 13.6 |
| Occupation | | |
| Student/Unemployed | 162 | 39.2 |
| Self-employed/Business | 19 | 4.6 |
| Professional | 54 | 13.1 |
| Service/Employee | 178 | 43.1 |
| Own Bank Account | | |
| No | 6 | 1.5 |
| Yes | 407 | 98.5 |

*Table 2. Perceived usefulness (items adapted)*

| | | | |
|---|---|---|---|
| **Perceived Usefulness (PU)** | **(Davis, 1989)** | **PU1** | Using digital payments would enable me to make transactions more quickly. |
| | | **PU2** | Using digital payments would improve the process of doing transactions or the way payments are made. |
| | | **PU3** | Using digital payments would help in making banking transactions more efficiently. |
| | | **PU4** | Using digital payments would make it easier to do banking transactions. |
| | | **PU5** | Using digital payments would be more convenient for me. |

*Table 3. Perceived ease of use (items adapted)*

| | | | |
|---|---|---|---|
| **Perceived Ease of Use (PEOU)** | **(Davis, 1989); (Moore & Benbasat, 1991)** | **PEOU1** | Learning to operate digital payments is easier for me. |
| | | **PEOU2** | I find it easy to make transactions using digital payment systems. |
| | | **PEOU3** | My interaction with digital payment system is clear and understandable. |
| | | **PEOU4** | I find the digital payment system to be flexible to interact with. |
| | | **PEOU5** | It would be easy for me to become skilful at using the digital payment system. |

## Perceived Ease of Use

The study adapted the measures of perceived ease of use from prior research from Davis (1989) and Moore & Benbasat (1991). The five-item scale of perceived usefulness exhibits a very high reliability ($\alpha = 0.9$). Table 3 exhibits the items operationalised to measure perceived ease of use.

## Trust

Because there is little empirical research which examines the trust of users in electronic payments, we developed new scale for the antecedents of trust. The antecedents of trust include the three aspects namely integrity, credibility and structural assurances. The study adapted the measures of perceived ease of use from prior research. The

*Table 4. Trust (root constructs and items adapted)*

| | | | | |
|---|---|---|---|---|
| **Trust (TRUST)** | **Perceived integrity** | **(Lin, 2011)** | **INT1** | I think that Digital payment firms are reliable and will keep their commitments. |
| | | | **INT2** | I think that Digital payment firms provide unbiased and true information about banking transactions. |
| | **Perceived Credibility** | **(Luarn & Lin, 2005)** | **CRE1** | Using digital payment systems would not disclose my personal information. |
| | **Structural Assurances** | **(Gu, Lee, & Suh, 2009)** | **STRA1** | I feel safe conducting transactions electronically because the payments service provider will protect me. |
| | | | **STRA2** | I feel safe conducting transactions electronically because of the statements of guarantees and ethics charter of payment service provider. |

five-item scale of trust exhibits a high reliability ($\alpha = 0.887$). Table 4 exhibits the root constructs and items operationalised to measure trust.

*Attitude and Behavioural Intention.* The antecedents of adoption include attitude of users towards electronic payment systems and their behavioural intention to use digital payments. The study adapted the measures of attitude and behavioural intention from prior research. The two-item scale of attitude and the three-item scale of behavioural intention exhibits high reliability with $\alpha = 0.84$ and 0.85 respectively. The five item scale representing attitude and behavioural intention altogether exhibit even higher reliability with cronbach's $\alpha = 0.875$. Table 5 exhibits the root constructs and items operationalised to measure adoption of digital payment systems.

The test of assumptions was done in order to check for multicollinearity, exploratory factor analysis was performed, confirmatory factor analysis was done and finally partial least squares structural equation modeling (PLS-SEM) was run to test the proposed hypothesis and goodness of fit of the proposed model. On the basis of results and discussion, the study attempts to make recommendations for managerial implications of the research.

*Table 5. Adoption of digital payment systems (root constructs and items adapted)*

| | | | | |
|---|---|---|---|---|
| **Adoption (ADOPT)** | **Attitude toward using digital payment systems** | **(Lin, 2011)** | **AT2** | I like making transactions using digital payment systems |
| | | | **AT3** | The digital payment system makes the process of payments more enjoyable. |
| | **Behavioural Intention** | **(Venkatesh, Morris, Davis, & Davis, 2003)** | **BI1** | I would use the digital payment system in the near future. |
| | | | **BI2** | I intend to use the digital payment system in the next 6 months |
| | | **(Lin, 2011)** | **BI3** | I believe it is worthwhile for me to adopt digital payments |

*Table 6. KMO and Bartlett's Test*

| | | |
|---|---|---|
| **Kaiser-Meyer-Olkin Measure of Sampling Adequacy.** | | .938 |
| **Bartlett's Test of Sphericity** | **Approx. Chi-Square** | 5596.015 |
| | **Df** | 190 |
| | **Sig.** | .000 |

## RESULTS AND DISCUSSION

To determine the factors influencing the adoption of electronic payments, an exploratory factor analysis was performed. The data was screened for unengaged responses, using the case-wise deletion one case was deleted with no missing values, rest of the responses were fit for further analysis. A principal component analysis for the 20 items of the scale, using varimax with Kaiser normalization method of rotation. The KMO measure verified the sampling adequacy for the analysis KMO=0.938 (table 6), Bartlett's measure is significant ($p<0.001$). Table 7 represents the factor loadings after rotation. In the table of rotated component matrix where we have extracted and retained 4 factors using the extraction method of principal component analysis shows the items that cluster on the same factor suggesting that Factor 1 represents trust, factor 2 represents perceived ease of use, factor 3 represents

*Table 7. Rotated component matrix*[a]

| | Component | | | |
|---|---|---|---|---|
| | 1 | 2 | 3 | 4 |
| cre1 | .849 | | | |
| stra1 | .838 | | | |
| stra2 | .821 | | | |
| int1 | .725 | | | |
| int2 | .622 | | | |
| peou1 | | .794 | | |
| peou3 | | .783 | | |
| peou2 | | .724 | | |
| peou4 | | .704 | | |
| peou5 | | .668 | | |
| pu2 | | | .786 | |
| pu4 | | | .753 | |
| pu3 | | | .750 | |
| pu1 | | | .633 | |
| pu5 | | .408 | .622 | |
| bi1 | | | | .825 |
| bi2 | | | | .785 |
| bi3 | | | | .773 |
| at2 | | | | .636 |
| at3 | | | | .591 |

Extraction Method: Principal Component Analysis.
Rotation Method: Varimax with Kaiser Normalization.

a. Rotation converged in 6 iterations.

perceived usefulness and factor 4 represents attitude and intention to use indicating the adoption of electronic payments by the respondents.

The reliability of the overall scale is quite high with Cronbach's alpha being 0.940, while each construct namely, perceived usefulness, perceived ease of use, perceived trust, attitude and behavioural intention subscales of the scale all had high reliabilities, all having cronbach's alpha above 0.8 (table 8).

*Table 8. Reliability statistics*

| Factors/ Components | Cronbach's Alpha | Cronbach's Alpha Based on Standardized Items | N of Items |
|---|---|---|---|
| Overall | .940 | .943 | 20 |
| Factor 1 (Trust) | 0.887 | 0.886 | 5 |
| Factor 2 (PEOU) | 0.900 | 0.901 | 5 |
| Factor 3 (PU) | 0.884 | 0.884 | 5 |
| Factor 4 (Attitude and Intention) | 0.875 | 0.878 | 5 |

*Figure 2. Measurement model (CFA)*

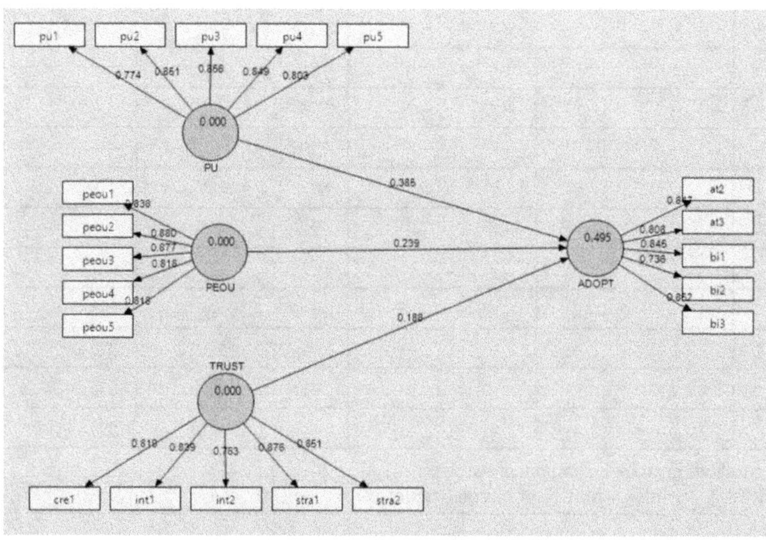


## CONFIRMATORY FACTOR ANALYSIS (MEASUREMENT MODEL)

Test of assumptions was conducted to check for multi-collinearity. The variance inflation factor (VIF) are low for all the independent variables, along with tolerance statistic higher than 0.2. Therefore, the multi-collinearity does not exist among the independent variables. The proposed research model (figure 1) was analysed using SmartPLS 2.0, a PLS structural equation modelling tool which assessed the psychometric properties of the measurement model. In order to specify relationships,

*Table 9. Cross loadings*

| | ADOPT | PEOU | PU | TR |
|---|---|---|---|---|
| **at2** | **0.8466** | 0.5724 | 0.5793 | 0.4754 |
| **at3** | **0.8078** | 0.536 | 0.5528 | 0.467 |
| **bi1** | **0.8445** | 0.4681 | 0.5168 | 0.3855 |
| **bi2** | **0.7356** | 0.407 | 0.4509 | 0.2962 |
| **bi3** | **0.8618** | 0.5205 | 0.5621 | 0.4723 |
| **peou1** | 0.5227 | **0.8383** | 0.5322 | 0.3802 |
| **peou2** | 0.5608 | **0.8797** | 0.6817 | 0.4582 |
| **peou3** | 0.5262 | **0.8768** | 0.6008 | 0.5066 |
| **peou4** | 0.4959 | **0.8184** | 0.5831 | 0.5052 |
| **peou5** | 0.4982 | **0.8175** | 0.6196 | 0.4699 |
| **pu1** | 0.5239 | 0.5467 | **0.7738** | 0.3766 |
| **pu2** | 0.5547 | 0.5377 | **0.8507** | 0.4397 |
| **pu3** | 0.5561 | 0.6181 | **0.8561** | 0.4731 |
| **pu4** | 0.5335 | 0.6138 | **0.8493** | 0.4169 |
| **pu5** | 0.5303 | 0.6365 | **0.8034** | 0.4429 |
| **stra1** | 0.4412 | 0.4777 | 0.451 | **0.8756** |
| **stra2** | 0.4332 | 0.4561 | 0.4143 | **0.8514** |
| **cre1** | 0.3629 | 0.3385 | 0.3513 | **0.8195** |
| **int1** | 0.4669 | 0.5051 | 0.4595 | **0.8388** |
| **int2** | 0.4342 | 0.4701 | 0.4681 | **0.7626** |

confirmatory factor analysis was conducted on the data. PLS algorithm was run on the model with the indicators using path weighing scheme.

Standardised factor loading estimates are above 0.7 as highlighted cells in the table 9 indicate outer loadings. According to criteria by Chin (1998), cross loading indicators with higher loadings in their respective latent variables are higher than with other loadings confirm that there is discriminant validity (Hair, Black, Babin, & Anderson, 2015).

In the table 10 (overview), AVE estimates of all the constructs are above 0.5 indicating that convergent validity exists. All constructs exhibit higher construct reliability i.e. cronbach's alpha is above 0.7 indicating convergence. Communality of all constructs higher than 0.4 indicates that the sample size for the model is adequate. Composite reliability of all constructs is high i.e. above 0.7, all of the constructs having composite reliability above the ideal threshold of 0.9 indicate high internal consistency. Using the Blindfolding module with 7 iterations on SmartPLS

*Table 10. Overview (AVE, $R^2$, $Q^2$, $f^2$)*

| | AVE | Composite Reliability | R Square | Cronbach's Alpha | Communality | Redundancy | Construct cross validated redundancy (Q square) | Construct cross validated communality (f square) |
|---|---|---|---|---|---|---|---|---|
| ADOPT | 0.6733 | 0.9113 | 0.4955 | 0.8784 | 0.6733 | 0.1584 | 0.3245 | 0.5071 |
| PEOU | 0.7167 | 0.9267 | 0 | 0.9009 | 0.7167 | 0 | | 0.7166 |
| PU | 0.6844 | 0.9155 | 0 | 0.8842 | 0.6844 | 0 | | 0.6843 |
| TR | 0.6897 | 0.9173 | 0 | 0.887 | 0.6897 | 0 | | 0.6898 |

generated results gave us the indication of the predictive quality and accuracy of the proposed model.

Stone Geisser Indicator (Q square) or construct cross validated redundancy output in table 6 of the endogenous variable (0.3245) is above zero (0) indicating towards predictive validity and relevance of the model. Cohen's indicator (f square) or construct cross validated communality of value above 0.35 exhibit a large effect size indicating the usefulness of each construct for the model adjustment. Table 10 indicates that all the constructs are important for the model adjustment with communalities above 0.35. Hence, $Q^2$ and $f^2$ indicate the model is accurate and the constructs are important for the model adjustment. Goodness of Fit evaluates the general adjustment of the model and calculated as the geometric mean of median $R^2$ and mean weighted of AVE. A value above 0.36 is considered adequate. Thus, calculating the geometric mean, we obtained the GoF value as 0.58515, indicating that our model has an adequate adjustment.

## STRUCTURAL EQUATION MODEL

From the structural model we find that the portion of variance explained by the structural model is large enough for the endogenous variable. A high $R^2$ of ADOPT' (49.55%) represents that the respondents are more likely to have favourable attitude and behavioural intention to use electronic payment systems further. To test the significance of cited relations a re-sampling technique (for 1000 samples) was applied through bootstrapping module using the Missing value algorithm with individual changes for sign changes. Bootstrapping results in table shows the values referred to on the Student t-test. Table 11 indicates that all of the values of the cited relations are above the referenced value of 1.96 thereby resulting in null hypotheses ($H_O$) of all the cases being rejected. Figure 3 shows the structural model results indicating the beta path coefficients in the expected directions and their statistical significance.

*Table 11. Bootstrapping results (student T-test), P-value and Path coefficients*

| | Original Sample(O) | Sample Mean(M) | Standard Deviation (STDEV) | Standard Error (STERR) | T Statistics (\|O/STERR\|) | P value | Path coefficients |
|---|---|---|---|---|---|---|---|
| PEOU -> ADOPT | 0.2386 | 0.2486 | 0.1153 | 0.1153 | 2.0693 | 0.01957** | 0.2386 |
| PU -> ADOPT | 0.3847 | 0.3789 | 0.1149 | 0.1149 | 3.3488 | 0.000443* | 0.3847 |
| TRUST -> ADOPT | 0.1878 | 0.1941 | 0.0884 | 0.0884 | 2.1249 | 0.017095* | 0.1878 |

*significant at p<0.05
**significant at p<0.01

*Figure 3. Structural model (path coefficients)*

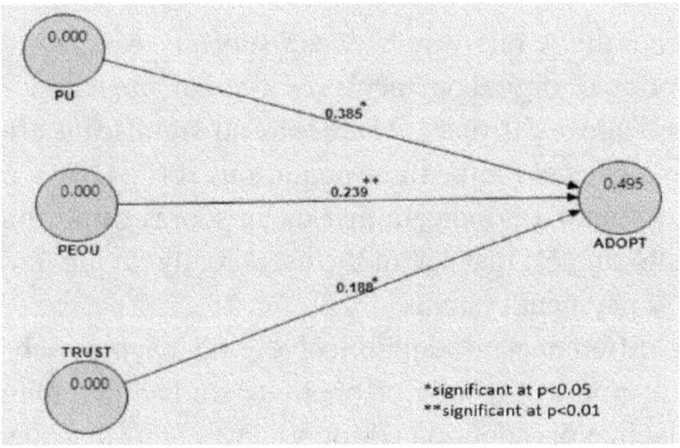


Perceived usefulness has a positive influence (beta= 0.305, $p < 0.01$) on the adoption (attitude and behavioural intention). Perceived ease of use has a positive influence (beta= 0.259, $p < 0.01$) on the attitude. Trust has a positive influence (beta= 0.134, $p < 0.05$) on the customer adoption of digital payment systems.

## COMPARISON OF GROUPS BASED ON GENDER AND AGE FOR ADOPTION OF DIGITAL PAYMENT SYSTEMS

An independent-samples t-test was conducted to compare adoption of digital payments for male and female users. Levene's test revealed that the variances are homogeneous. There was a significant difference in the scores for male users (M=21.03, SD=3.434) and female users (M=20.30, SD=3.553); t (411)=2.11, p = 0.035. These results suggest that gender has a significant influence on the adoption of digital payment systems. Specifically, our results suggest that male users are likely to adopt to digital

*Table 12. Hypotheses conclusions*

| Alternate Hypotheses | Finding | Conclusion |
|---|---|---|
| H1: Perceived Usefulness has a positive influence on adoption of digital payment system | Yes: Significant (beta= 0.385, $p < 0.05$) | Supported |
| H2: Perceived Ease of Use has a positive influence on adoption of digital payment system | Yes: Significant (beta= 0.239, $p < 0.01$) | Supported |
| H3: Trust has a positive influence on adoption of digital payment system | Yes: Significant (beta= 0.188, $p < 0.05$) | Supported |
| H4a: There is a significant difference in adoption of digital payment systems for male and female users | Yes: Significant ($p < 0.05$) | Supported |
| H4b: There is a significant difference in adoption of digital payment systems for users from different age groups | Not Significant | Rejected |

payments more rapidly. A one-way between subjects ANOVA was conducted to compare the adoption of digital payments for users of age below 25 years, between 25 to 50 years and above 50 years. There was no significant effect of age on the adoption at the p>.05 level for the three conditions [$F(2, 410) = 2.011$, $p = 0.135$]. Value of p greater than 0.05 indicate that mean scores of all three categories are same. These results suggest that age of the users really do not have an effect on the adoption of digital payment systems.

A significant difference in adoption of digital payments between male and female users correspond to results of previous studies claiming that gender has a significant influence on adoption. Prior studies claim that there are significant differences between men and women on the behavioural intention to use or accept a technology. Also, the male users are more likely to adopt and use mobile banking services as compared to their female counterparts (Laukkanen & Pasanen, 2008). The study contradicts from the results of prior studies stating that older individuals resist the usage of technology (Charness & Boot, 2009). Results from qualitative analysis confirm the same that age has no impact on the acceptance of electronic payment systems (Al-Somali, Gholami, & Clegg, 2009).

From the above results, it can be concluded that perceived usefulness, perceived ease of use and trust were found to be influencing the attitude and behavioural intention positively towards the digital payment systems. Therefore, it can be said that if there is an increase in trust of user, it is more likely to influence the positive attitude of user towards the electronic payments and intention to use will increase and vice-versa. Thus, the hypothesis (H3) is holds true in the study. It can be concluded from the results that in order to stimulate a positive attitude and intention to use alternative payment systems, the firms need to induce the potential users to trust the systems, technologies and payment firms. Financial technology industry shall take steps to ensure higher credibility, integrity and strong structural assurances to generate trust among the users.

## IMPLICATIONS

Merely introducing the mobile payments is not enough, ensuring secure infrastructure and development of safe technologies is the responsibility of payment firms and the government. Security issues and lack of privacy of transaction data might lead to doubts in the minds of customers (Mallat & Tuunainen, 2008). According to Rizan, Warokka, & Listyawati (2014), an indirect impact of consumer trust is greater on the customer loyalty. When customers trust the bank for their well being and perceive the bank as a genuinely interested partner, then the relational marketing efforts generate customer loyalty. For a digital consumer, trust becomes more important when the customer shares his or her personal details over the network while making an electronic transaction. The mere concept of data privacy and online frauds shook the trust in electronic payments. The payment firms need to assure credibility by ensuring secured transactions over internet. The attitude of customers towards the e-payments can be turned from negative to positive and their intention to adopt and use electronic payment systems might become higher if trust of the users is preserved. There has been a linear relationship between trust and behavioral outcomes with differing effects of gender, age, personalities and culture.

There are numerable antecedents of trust but till now no single robust technique has been developed to measure the trust. IT artifacts like website design, previous online transactions; text and contextual content; empirical methods like field interviews, surveys, experiments, analytical models and neuroscience information systems are some of the solutions available today which closely measure and analyze trust and its impact on attitude toward technology usage and behavioral intention to transact in online environments (Gefen, Benbasat, & Pavlou, 2008). Borst & Creehan (2017) suggested technology can be used to build consumer trust at three levels. Firstly, trust need to be bulid on the institutional stage, secondly customer should trust the product or the underlying payment system and thirdly the customer should be able to trust herself which might be indicated as self-efficacy. According to Qualcomm's statement, none of the mobile wallets in India are secure. The prime reason is that the mobile wallets lack the secured hardware level security systems and there are no specific regulations or security standards in case of mobile payment systems. The guidelines on the security standards have been left on the virtue of the best judgment of the system provider and this ambiguity provides an escape to service providers of payments. Central bank needs to review and modify the policy framework in different spheres. The legal and regulatory framework should be re-examined in depth, market conditions should be monitored and infrastructural arrangements must be re-evaluated for the implementation of the innovative systems. Conforming to technical and international standards such as data security, data formats and device certification requirements should be on the priority list (Reaves, Scaife, Bates, Traynor, & Butler, 2015; Times of India, 2016).

To support the country in building an ecosystem for electronic consumer payments, policies must be formulated converging several macro-economic factors like ease of making transactions, innovation in the payment methods, investment in payment infrastructure, access to electronic payment systems and most importantly cultural factors like credibility and integrity of payment firms (Thomas, Jain, & Angus, 2013). India needs to work towards reducing the size of informal economy since the government's policies have not been successful in integrating the informal economy and e-payment security has not yet been achieved with staggering number of e-payment frauds in recent years (Economist Intelligence Unit, 2012). A more promotional effort is highly required to push UPI payments to overcome the challenges faced due to initial distrust in alternative payment systems and for successful diffusion of digital payments (Creehan, 2018). Though digital payment adoption among Indian consumers has shown some progress in last couple of years, there is a need to push the acceptance of digital payment systems by merchants too especially with reference to mobile payments.

## LIMITATIONS AND SCOPE OF FURTHER RESEARCH

The limitation of the study is that it focuses only on adopters' perception and we have considered only the users of electronic payments who have experienced the e-payments. The perceptions of non-adopters are equally important to understand the antecedents of perceived behavioral control and factors acting as barriers to technology adoption but in this study their opinions have not been taken into consideration. Secondly, users primarily belong to urban cities and there can be impact of socio-cultural background on the adoption rate. Due to paucity of time and resources, the sample size is restricted to 414 responses. Though the sample size is adequate for drawing upon inferences on the basis of statistical analysis, contrary to it making a generalization is on the basis of sample is difficult. With the help of literature and prior research in trust, we have developed the scale for measuring trust, which will be helpful in future research and provides theoretical framework to measure trust in online environments and technology. So far, the robust measurement scales to measure the degree of trust in online environment has not yet been developed sufficiently. There is a possibility that neuroscience in information system might offer a potential solution in future. The study calls for further research in neuroscience marketing to develop technologies for measuring the trust in electronic space. Therefore, trust-building techniques need to be researched intensely in future for the managerial implications so that companies can gain trust of the users and increase the adoption rate of technologies especially financial technologies.

## CONCLUSION

Theoretical contribution of this study is proposed to test the trust based variables in the technology adoption relevant in Indian context. The research focuses on the development of theoretical framework that will help the organizations in the industry like payment firms and service providers to resolve trust issues with the Indian users and build a more credible user experience. The study suggests that trust is a pre-requisite for making electronic payment systems more trust-worthy so that the users consider electronic payment systems acceptable. With the growing need to combat the security risks, it is essential for the regulatory bodies to work on the strong structural assurances and stringent regulations for promoting safer online environment. Data security and risk management are the core issues that need to be resolved immediately. With the operational risks on rise, the cases like fraud, data theft and illegal payments have increased. Hence, the regulatory framework should focus on making a secure infrastructural arrangement to boost the user trust and consumer adoption of electronic payment systems and contact-less payments. Therefore, it is essential for the regulatory bodies to work on the strong structural assurances and stringent regulations for promoting safer online environment.

## REFERENCES

Ajzen, I. (1991). The Theory of Planned Behavior. *Organizational Behavior and Human Decision Processes*, *50*(2), 179–211. doi:10.1016/0749-5978(91)90020-T

Ajzen, I., & Fishbein, M. (1977, September). Attitude-Behavior Relations: A Theoretical Analysis and Review of Empirical Research. *Psychological Bulletin*, *84*(5), 888–918. doi:10.1037/0033-2909.84.5.888

Al-Somali, S. A., Gholami, R., & Clegg, B. (2009). An investigation into the acceptance of online banking in Saudi Arabia. *Technovation*, *29*(29), 130–141. doi:10.1016/j.technovation.2008.07.004

Balaji, R. P., & Vijayakumar, D. T. (2018). Diffusion of Digital Payment System in Rural India. *Global Journal of Management and Business Research: G, 14*(4), 29-32.

Bertrand, S., & Ahmad, K. (2014). *Mobile payments: Finally ready to take off?* Bain & Company.

Bhattacharya, R., Devinney, T. M., & Pillutla, M. M. (1998, July). A Formal Model of Trust Based on Outcomes. *Academy of Management Review, 23*(3), 459–472. doi:10.5465/amr.1998.926621

Bill & Melinda Gates Foundation. (2013, September). *Fighting Poverty Profitably: Transforming the economics of payments to build sustainable, inclusive financial systems.* The Gates Foundation's Financial Services for the Poor program. Bill & Melinda Gates Foundation. Retrieved from www.gatesfoundation.org: https://docs.gatesfoundation.org/Documents/Fighting%20Poverty%20Profitably%20Report%20Full%20Appendices.pdf

Borst, N., & Creehan, S. (2017, December 5). *Banking: How Technology Can Build Trust for the Newly Banked.* Retrieved from Federal Reserve Bank of Francisco Web Site: https://www.frbsf.org/banking/asia-program/pacific-exchanges-podcast/how-technology-can-build-trust-for-the-newly-banked/

Charness, N., & Boot, W. R. (2009, October). Aging and Information Technology Use: Potential and Barriers. *Current Directions in Psychological Science, 18*(5), 253–258. doi:10.1111/j.1467-8721.2009.01647.x

Cherowbrier, J. (2019, November 1). *Statistics: Global consumer fintech adoption rates 2015-2019, by category.* Retrieved from Statista Web Site: https://www.statista.com

Creehan, S. (2018, February 28). *Pacific Exchange Blog: India's Digital Payments: Growing Consumer Trust, but Merchants Needed.* Retrieved from Federal Reserve Bank of San Francisco Web Site: https://www.frbsf.org/banking/asia-program/pacific-exchange-blog/indias-digital-payments-growing-consumer-trust-but-merchants-needed/

Davis, F. D. (1989, September). Perceived Usefulness, Perceived Ease of Use, and User Acceptance of Information Technology. *Management Information Systems Quarterly, 13*(3), 319–340. doi:10.2307/249008

Economist Intelligence Unit. (2012). *2011 Government E-Payments Adoption Ranking.* Economist Intelligence Unit Limited. Retrieved from http://graphics.eiu.com/upload/eb/Visapayments.pdf

Gefen, D., Benbasat, I., & Pavlou, P. A. (2008, Spring). A Research Agenda for Trust in Online Environments. *Journal of Management Information Systems*, *24*(4), 275–286. doi:10.2753/MIS0742-1222240411

Giffin, K. (1967). The Contribution of Studies of Source Credibility to a Theory of Interpersonal Trust in the Communication Process. *Psychological Bulletin*, *68*(2), 104–120. doi:10.1037/h0024833 PMID:6065581

Gu, J.-C., Lee, S.-C., & Suh, Y.-H. (2009). Determinants of behavioral intention to mobile banking. *Expert Systems with Applications*, *36*(9), 11605–11616. doi:10.1016/j.eswa.2009.03.024

Hair, J. F., Black, W. C., Babin, B. J., & Anderson, R. E. (2015). *Multivariate Data Analysis* (7th ed.). Noida, India: Pearson Education Limited.

Hansen, T., Jensen, J. M., & Solgaard, H. S. (2004). Predicting online grocery buying intention: A comparison of the theory of reasoned action and the theory of planned behavior. *International Journal of Information Management*, *24*(6), 539–550. doi:10.1016/j.ijinfomgt.2004.08.004

Hung, S.-Y., Chang, C.-M., & Yu, T.-J. (2006). Determinants of user acceptance of the e-Government services: The case of online tax filing and payment system. *Government Information Quarterly*, *23*(1), 97–122. doi:10.1016/j.giq.2005.11.005

Jeong, B.-K., & Yoon, T. E. (2013, January). An Empirical Investigation on Consumer Acceptance of Mobile Banking Services. *Business and Management Research*, *2*(1), 31–40. doi:10.5430/bmr.v2n1p31

Kesharwani, A., & Bisht, S. S. (2012). The impact of trust and perceived risk on internet banking adoption in India. *International Journal of Bank Marketing*, *30*(4), 303–322. doi:10.1108/02652321211236923

Kotha, S., Rajgopal, S., & Venkatachalam, M. (2004, April). The Role of Online Buying Experience as a Competitive Advantage: Evidence from Third-Party Ratings for E-Commerce Firms. *The Journal of Business*, *77*(S2), S109–S133. doi:10.1086/381639

Laukkanen, T., & Pasanen, M. (2008). Mobile banking innovators and early adopters: How they differ from other online users? *Journal of Financial Services Marketing*, *13*(2), 86–94. doi:10.1057/palgrave.fsm.4760077

Lee, B. C., Cho, J., & Hwang, D. (2013, July). An integration of social capital and tourism technology adoption—A case of convention and visitors bureaus. *Tourism and Hospitality Research*, *13*(3), 149–165. doi:10.1177/1467358414522055

Liébana-Cabanillas, F., Sánchez-Fernández, J., & Munoz-Leiva, F. (2014). The moderating effect of experience in the adoption of mobilepayment tools in Virtual Social Networks: The m-Payment Acceptance Model in Virtual Social Networks (MPAM-VSN). *International Journal of Information Management, 34*(2), 151–166. doi:10.1016/j.ijinfomgt.2013.12.006

Lin, H.-F. (2011). An empirical investigation of mobile banking adoption: The effect of innovation attributes and knowledge-based trust. *International Journal of Information Management, 31*(3), 252–260. doi:10.1016/j.ijinfomgt.2010.07.006

Luarn, P., & Lin, H.-H. (2005). Toward an understanding of the behavioral intention to use mobile banking. *Computers in Human Behavior, 21*(6), 873–891. doi:10.1016/j.chb.2004.03.003

Mallat, N., & Tuunainen, V. K. (2008). Exploring Merchant Adoption of Mobile Payment Systems: An Empirical Study. *e-Service Journal, 6*(2), 24–57. doi:10.2979/esj.2008.6.2.24

Moore, G. C., & Benbasat, I. (1991, September). Development of an Instrument to Measure the Perceptions of Adopting an Information Technology Innovation. *Information Systems Research, 2*(3), 192–222. doi:10.1287/isre.2.3.192

Ngugi, B., Kamis, A., & Tremaine, M. (2011, Summer). Intention to Use Biometric Systems. *e-Service Journal, 7*(3), 20-46.

Parasuraman, A., & Grewal, D. (2000). The Impact of Technology on the Quality-Value-Loyalty Chain: A Research Agenda. *Journal of the Academy of Marketing Science, 28*(1), 168–174. doi:10.1177/0092070300281015

Rathore, H. S. (2016, April). Adoption of digital wallet by consumers. BVIMSR's. *Journal of Management Research, 8*(1), 69–75.

Reaves, B., Scaife, N., Bates, A., Traynor, P., & Butler, K. R. (2015). *Mo(bile) Money, Mo(bile) Problems: Analysis of Branchless Banking Applications in the Developing World. In 24th USENIX Security Symposium* (pp. 17–32). Washington, DC: USENIX Association. Retrieved from https://www.usenix.org/conference/usenixsecurity15/technical-sessions/presentation/reaves

Rizan, M., Warokka, A., & Listyawati, D. (2014). Relationship Marketing and Customer Loyalty: Do Customer Satisfaction and Customer Trust Really Serve as Intervening Variables? *Journal of Marketing Research & Case Studies, 2014*, 1–12. doi:10.5171/2014.724178

Rogers, E. M. (1983). *Diffusions of Innovations* (3rd ed.). London: The Free Press Collier Macmillan Publishers.

Sheppard, B. H., & Sherman, D. M. (1998, July). The Grammars of Trust: A Model and General Implications. *Academy of Management Review*, *23*(3), 422–437. doi:10.5465/amr.1998.926619

Simpson, J. A. (2007, October). Psychological Foundations of Trust. *Current Directions in Psychological Science*, *16*(5), 264–268. doi:10.1111/j.1467-8721.2007.00517.x

Singh, S. (2016, December 20). As India braces for digital payments future, how secure are banks from cyber attacks? *Economic Times*. Retrieved 2016, from Economic Times: http://economictimes.indiatimes.com/tech/internet/as-india-braces-for-digital-payments-future-how-secure-are-banks-from-cyberattacks/articleshow/56073576.cms?from=mdr

Straub, E. T. (2009, June). Understanding Technology Adoption: Theory and Future Directions for Informal Learning. *Review of Educational Research*, *79*(2), 625–649. doi:10.3102/0034654308325896

Tan, G. W.-H., Ooi, K.-B., Chong, S.-C., & Hew, T.-S. (2014). NFC mobile credit card: The next frontier of mobile payment? *Telematics and Informatics*, *31*(2), 292–307. doi:10.1016/j.tele.2013.06.002

Taylor, S., & Todd, P. (1995). Assessing IT Usage: The Role of Prior Experience. *Management Information Systems Quarterly*, *19*(4), 561–570. doi:10.2307/249633

The Economist Intelligence Unit. (2018). The 2018 Government E-Payments Adoption Ranking (GEAR). *The Economist*.

The World Bank. (2014). *Global Findex (Global Financial Inclusion Database)*. Development Research Group, Finance and Private Sector Development Unit: World Bank. Retrieved 2016, from databank.worldbank.org/data/reports.aspx?source=global-findex-(global-financial-inclusion-database)

Thomas, H., Jain, A., & Angus, M. (2013, September). *Cashless Journey*. MasterCard Advisors. Retrieved from MasterCard Web site: https://newsroom.mastercard.com/wp-content/uploads/2013/09/Cashless-Journey_WhitePaper_FINAL.pdf

Thompson, R. L., Higgins, C. A., & Howell, J. M. (1994). Influence of Experience on Personal Computer Utilization: Testing a Conceptual Model. *Journal of Management Information Systems*, *11*(1), 167–187. doi:10.1080/07421222.1994.11518035

Times of India. (2016, December 13). *None of mobile payment apps in India fully secure, warns Qualcomm.* New Delhi, India: The Times of India. Retrieved 2016, from http://timesofindia.indiatimes.com/business/india-business/None-of-mobile-payment-apps-in-India-fully-secure-warns-Qualcomm/articleshow/55967778.cms

Trafimow, D., Brown, J., Grace, K., Thompson, L. A., & Sheeran, P. (2002, Autumn). The Relative Influence of Attitudes and Subjective Norms from Childhood to Adolescence: Between-Participant and Within-Participant Analyses. *The American Journal of Psychology, 115*(3), 395–414. doi:10.2307/1423424 PMID:12221916

Tschannen-Moran, M., & Hoy, W. K. (2000). A Multidisciplinary Analysis of the Nature, Meaning, and Measurement of Trust. *Review of Educational Research, 70*(4), 547–593. doi:10.3102/00346543070004547

Venkatesh, V., Morris, M. G., Davis, G. B., & Davis, F. D. (2003, September). User Acceptance of Information Technology: Toward a Unified View. *Management Information Systems Quarterly, 27*(3), 425–478. doi:10.2307/30036540

Wang, G., Dou, W., & Zhou, N. (2008). Consumption attitudes and adoption of new consumer products: A contingency approach. *European Journal of Marketing, 42*(1/2), 238–254. doi:10.1108/03090560810840998

Yaghoubi, N.-M., & Bahmani, E. (2010, September). Factors Affecting the Adoption of Online Banking An Integration of Technology Acceptance Model and Theory of Planned Behavior. *Journal of Business and Management, 5*(9), 159–165.

Yiu, C. S., Grant, K., & Edgar, D. (2007). Factors affecting the adoption of Internet Banking in Hong Kong—Implications for the banking sector. *International Journal of Information Management, 27*(5), 336–351. doi:10.1016/j.ijinfomgt.2007.03.002

# Chapter 3
# Employing Artificial Intelligence and Algorithms in the Digital Lending Industry:
## Measuring and Managing Risky Consumer Behaviour

**Thaisaiyi Zephania Opati**
https://orcid.org/0000-0001-5470-8600
*Riara University, Kenya*

## ABSTRACT

*Lenders employ AI and algorithms in analyzing the potency for loan advancement. AI and algorithms are seen as efficient, and banks seem to be adopting or exploring the AI applications and algorithms to manage risk and cut bottom line cost, thus replacing costly, laborious, and repetitive activities along the value chain. The chapter offers practical solution to the practitioners and stakeholders on identifying customers associated with consumer risky default behaviors. It then advises on how to deal with these issues and what banks should employ to curb risky borrowing behavior.*

## INTRODUCTION

Credit loans are considered to be a cornerstone of the banking industry. Consequently the lending process starts with bringing a borrower onboard, collecting information about the borrower, then validation with the help of various documents to decide the amount of credit or loan to be approved on the precise interest rates. Ideally the

DOI: 10.4018/978-1-7998-2398-8.ch003

banking industry operates within a very sensitive environment -supremely relaying on information to run its business. However when information about the customer seeking for loan is not perfectly blended with the process, then these banks find themselves with a lot of non-performing loans. The challenge among the lending institutions has been identifying this lot of customers with defaulting tendencies before they even borrow. Essentially the consumer behavior patterns have been less predictable in the past due to insufficient tools to analyze them, but with the newly embraced computing approaches highly capable of extracting meaning from imprecise data and detecting trends that are too complicated to be discovered by either humans or other conventional techniques (Metawa, Hassan & Elhoseny 2017), the ground is slowly shifting to the industry players favour.

Kaya's (2019) opines that the banking industry is a data driven commerce, therefore such data is essentially the artery of which the industry links to almost all truncations lines, from traditional deposit taking and lending to investment banking and asset management. Parenthetically Vedapradha and Hariharan (2018) gave the impression that as a result, most banks employ a large number of indices that are used in the predictive analysis. This means that the loan sector is particularly keen on analyzing its potential loan customers to safe guard the business from shocks of losses and non-performing loans. Every loan is then considered by a highly dimensional vector of loan characteristics including; credit score, collateral, interest rate, loan balance, loan purpose, loan age and size, payment history, and location (Metawa, Hassan, & Elhoseny 2017). Chopde, et al (2012) avers that these lenders tend to classify applicants dependent on characteristics of the borrower (such as age, education level, occupation, marital status and income), the repayment performance on previous loans and the type of loan.

Kenya has served as a cradle of Mobile Money Transfer (MMT) innovations prompting Kaffenberger and Chege (2016) to admit the presence of more than 20 digital lenders credit has focused on financial inclusion -one of the most progressive in the developing world. However world over, financial institutions face a number of complications from lax credit standards for borrowers and counterparties, poor portfolio risk management, or a lack of attention to changes in economic or other circumstances that can lead to a deterioration in the credit standing of a bank's counterparties (Chopde, et al 2012). Giftedly the banking industry has placed a premium that such decisions should be made using the huge and substantial data available to them. Indeed the processing time of the traditional brick and mortar players has served to analyze a large number of variables and a variety of diverse cases related to different customers (Shorouq, Yaseen & Elrefae 2010) concludes. This exertion on the banks is being taken off the industry through the digital loans advancement. The evolution of digital banking platforms through innovations has phenomenally surged the uptake of loans and bolstered financial inclusivity among the poor. These loans are creating opportunities by offering increased liquidity to household, small business loans and capital for entrepreneurs (Kaffenberger & Chege 2016).

Vedapradha and Hariharan (2018) perceive that, the ever increasing the demand for consumer credit has led to the stiff competition within and without the financial industry. Consequently, credit managers have to innovate machines and methods to handle analysis of credit data to save time and reduce errors. Superlatively IT focuses on amplification, simultaneous causality, and multi-dimensional trust that are evident in improving research on mobile banking payments (Donner & Tellez, 2008). Rao (n.d) highlighted that the main steps of credit risk assessment are: training on the customer's history data (including default and non-default customers) to get the model, so as to get the potential relationship between customer defaults and customer attributes. Exceptionally, these technological advances of the neural networks have been particularly applicable to risk management and forecasting within the banking industry (Huang et al., 2004; Limsombunchai et al., 2005). Therefore financial institutions and lending organizations such as banks may avoid the perpetual risk of loss while granting credits (Chopde, et al 2012) to customers.

Krishna, Goyal and Joshi (2012) points out that in India, the biggest challenge in the entire banking industry is to decide how much money should be lent to a specific customer. Disturbing concerns then lie in identifying a customer with risky behaviors with higher degree of accuracy and actually identify this customer at earliest opportunity. Undeniably many banks have gone into financial distress due to the non-performing loans from risky customers. With the digital loan most of which are unsecured, the challenge appears monumental.

For Alexandre and Eisenhart (2013), digital business has become disruptive to incumbent financial services providers and has the potential to foster broad transformation through improved efficiency and simplified access. Unmistakably, Kaya, (2019) narrates that this autonomous data management through AI -essentially devoid of human involvement- consequently proposes great opportunities for banks to improve speed, accuracy and efficiency. Kaffenberger and Chege (2016) antedate that many digital loans users appreciate the convenience and speed of accessing a loan from their phone, and that digital credit is a safer option than informal moneylenders.

Vedapradha and Hariharan (2018) avers that most banks are on the mission of developing AI capabilities to gain the competitive edge to achieve betterment in speed, accuracy, cost effective-efficiency and customer satisfaction. It is logical to conclude that Information technology is highly successful when applied in the area of business process re-engineering to ensure business sustainability by creating an edge over other entities in the market (Attaran, 2004).

*Figure 1. KCB Bank Mobile loans advances (Billions) vs NPL (%)*
*Source KCB reports (2014-2018)*

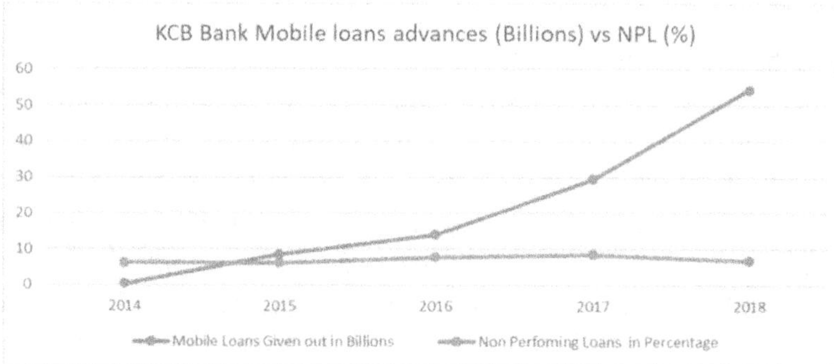


## DIGITAL LENDERS

Vedapradha and Hariharan (2018) opine that banks play a significant role in the economic development of any nation. These institutions that influences in implementation of regulatory policies to monitor economic activities and economic growth which can be possible only with the sophisticated technology enabled solutions (Hariharan. & Jebasingh, 2016).

Chopde, et al (2012) reveal that the large volume of loan portfolios also implies modest improvements in scoring accuracy that has resulted in significant savings for financial institutions. Commercial banks have become the major players in MMT business in Kenya, (World Bank, 2003) by providing loans to their customers, but they have been for years neglecting low-income users, whose ironical embrace of digital lending has grown to be phenomenal. Nevertheless at the advent of digital or mobile money lenders has changed the tide of the industry inducing the big players within industry to adopt MMT after neglecting that part of the market who have no collateral to ask for loans for years. These groups have been a gold mine for the digital lenders who employ artificial intelligence in gathering information about their capability and their willingness to repay advanced loans. Incidentally Kaffenberger & Chege (2016) reveal that while Kenya is at the forefront of digital credit growth, other countries have followed suit, these includes Tanzania with 10 lenders, and the number is growing and soon Uganda will launch an M-Shwari equivalent. With improved infrastructure, data mining etc. have redefined the banking operations with the help of machine intelligence (Vedapradha and Hariharan 2018), the banking industry is set to another quantum leap. Kaya, (2019) reveals that large volume of information, once cleaned and structured (i.e. big data), is at the core of data-driven decision-making.

Kaffenberger and Chege (2016) tips that digital markets are moving faster than regulations in most jurisdictions. Quite frankly though, digital credit has proven beneficial to consumers but possible risks that must be mitigated against through legislation are not being addressed by law and policy makers. Though algorithms tend to process information at much faster rates, it also contributes to the accuracy of their decision-making but other developments such as the laws governing these nascent industries are wanting to say the least.

The industry is still at its nascent stage, therefore FinCo Net (2018) hints that most of the digital loan products identified were established between 2012 and 2015 (36 products) and a further 16 were less than a year old or still in the planning stages of development. This provides a valid reason of dragging legal and operating framework. Irrefutably the mainstream of digital offerings were offered in one country only – of the 68 products identified, only two are offered in multiple countries: L-Pesa in Kenya, Tanzania and Uganda, and Mkopo Rahisi (Tala) in Kenya and Tanzania. The EPAR report noted that this geographic concentration may be due to partnerships or identity verification requirements (FinCo Net 2018). There has been lack of access to a wider set of financial options for many especially among the low income earners as Haggblade et al., (2007) explains, and consequently this has birthed the growth for informal channels of accessing credit for socially and privately profitable investment projects (Kirui, 2013) especially the digital lending apps. Nevertheless this hype is building up and creating opportunities for these products. Thanks to mobile loans there is a spike in household liquidity, small business loans for entrepreneurs (Kaffenberger & Chege 2016).

The novel methods and technologies for assessing creditworthiness have been attributed to digitalisation process. Customers then find it easy to borrow given that there is more access to consumer data than ever before (FinCoNet, 2018).) AI has been the missing link in financial industry. Rao, (n.d) discloses that AI intelligence model in credit risk assessment becomes an eye opener in decision-making tree, case-based reasoning, artificial neural network, support vector machine, etc. In Kenya, models that use mobile phone apps, mobile money wallets, and payroll lending, as well as through a range of provider types, including banks, mobile network operators, and even savings and credit cooperative organizations (SACCOs) are visible (Kaffenberger & Chege (2016). The use of these new technologies and alternative data tends to allow for more accurate and sophisticated credit scoring, and improve overall credit risk management (FinCoNet, 2018).

## TRADITIONAL WAYS OF ANALYZING LOAN CONSUMERS

Chopde, et al (2012) highlights that originally, the decision-making of accepting or rejecting a client's credit by financial institutions especially banks have commonly executed via judgmental techniques and/or credit scoring models. These included 3C's, 4C's or 5C's which are character, capital, collateral, capacity and condition (Chopde, et al 2012). It is easy to note that FinTech lenders discriminate approximately one-third less than lenders overall in terms of pricing. This means that FinTech lenders are motivated in removing discrimination arising from face-to-face interactions between originators and borrowers.

Breiman, (1994) underscored the significance of meta-algorithm to improve classification or regression models in terms of stability and classification accuracy in lending. Thus any system expending the use of data mining for credit risk analysis ideally enables any financial institution to reduce the manual errors involved in the same. Consequently Credit Risk Analysis is a theorem process of identifying the risk involved in granting a loan to a customer (Chopde, et al 2012). Such strategies help to reduce the variance and helps avoid over fitting. This means the prediction accuracy is improved by aggregating many models rather than building one high capacity model. The challenge has always been how to increase the assessment of loan applicants and in some cases credit scoring or predictive models to classify the risky applicants has been employed from time to time. Metawa, Hassan and Elhoseny (2017) insists that objective and constraint functions of bank profit maximization are nonlinear and sometimes non convex which can be costly to evaluate using traditional methods.

Evidently, credit risk analysis (finance risk analysis, loan default risk analysis) and credit risk management is imperative to any financial institutions which provide loans to businesses and individuals. Vedapradha and Hariharan (2018) reveal that applying big data analysis to collect information about their customers' information like income, work profile, personal details, and credit worthiness so as to offer various banking products through ATMs like loan facility is essential. Once enough data is available, the analysis model should ready to use this data to reach a decision regarding the customer's credit worthiness. Without a doubt, this decision making process is perceived to be quick and saves time and resources for the financial institution. In some cases decision trees and artificial neural network are utilized and are considered to be among the popular techniques to vet the applicants. The user has to accept the terms and conditions post verification through registered mobile number but misjudgment is unavoidable. Several techniques have been traditionally used to ascertain the credit worthiness of a client asking for a loan. Indeed the goal of each of these techniques is to reduce the misjudgments. If we

*Figure 2. Four loan management critical areas*

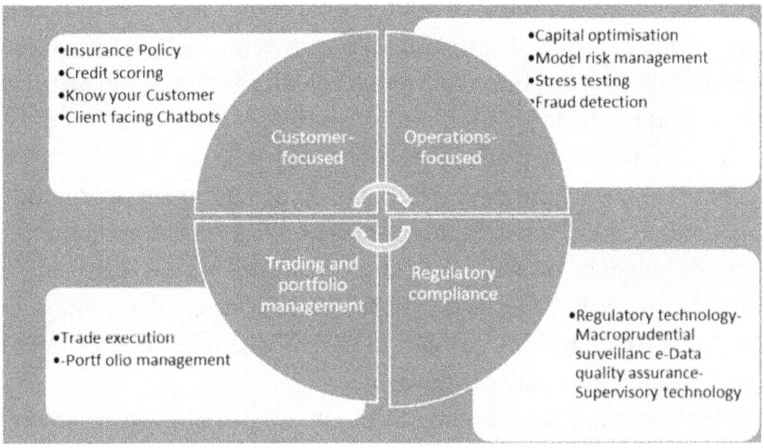


can completely eradicate it we can classify the customers directly and reduce loss for the financial institutions.

However, most of them are focused on either credit scoring - to determine whether the applied customer is eligible to get the required loan - (Ghodselahi & Amirmadhi, 2011; Marque et al., 2013), or portfolio selection (Berutich, Francisco, Luna, & Quintana, 2016; Lwin, Qu, & MacCarthy, 2017; Saborido, Ruiz, Bermúdez, Vercher, & Luque, 2016) aiming to choose the optimum stocks that maximize the customer profit. These includes techniques include;

## Credit Score

Ideally credit score has been used to estimate the risk factors of defaulting among customers. Malhotra and Malhotra, (2003) disclose that a set of credit scoring models have been used over time to analyze and correctly classify loan applications. Ideally the system determines the financial strength of the borrowers by approximating the probability of default and reducing the risk of non-payment to an acceptable level. Chopde, et al (2012) underscores that the goal of a credit scoring model is to categorize credit hopefuls into two classes: the "good credit" class that is likely to honor its financial obligation and the "bad credit" class that should be denied credit due to the high possibility of defaulting on the financial obligation. As a result Vedapradha and Hariharan (2018), intimates credit scoring is extensively used as a technique to benefit financial institutions in evaluating the likelihood for a credit applicant to default on the financial obligation and decide whether to grant credit or not. This precise judgment of the credit worthiness of applicants allows financial institutions to increase the volume of granted credit while minimizing possible losses.

The perception that has been created is that with the rise of digital banking the concept of credit score has been totally challenged. Kaffenberger and Chege (2016) are excited by the thought of the convenience and speed of accessing a loan from their phone, insisting that digital credit can be a safer option than informal moneylenders. This development cast doubts on development or continuous use of credit score method. Ideally the credit score which is a three digit numeric summary of entire credit behavior of a person can be instrumental in analyzing customers behavior for the benefit of the business. In recent times, the evolution of banking technology has enabled a quick resolution to be made regarding a credit history of a person while lending for any purpose.

Rao, (n.d) points out that according to this potential relationship, the classification model can be obtained to predict whether a new user will default. The disability of these traditional credit score methods is their ineptness of commercial banks to understand large amounts of information that should only reveal useful knowledge to improve decision-making. In some cases credit score has been also been used to detect delinquent customers. Patently modern bank managers face a challenge of being flooded with data, this poses a challenge of sifting through the tones of data to extract practical information to enforce this knowledge in their decisions (Mitchell &Pavur, 2002).

## Banking Scoring System

The banking credit scoring is one of the oldest method of reducing the credit risk on loan applications. The system determines the financial strength of the borrowers by approximating the probability of default and reducing the risk of non-payment to an acceptable level. As a result customers are required to give specific data so that the haziness of normal banking is removed. The credit scoring essentially employs a model of using a set of variables to determine creditworthiness of similar loan applications, a combined credit score can be calculated relative to the value of each variable (Tafti & Nikbakht, 1993).

The contestation with the credit scoring system lies in the connation that it cannot allay the subjective fears of the human factor; this means as Malhotra and Malhotra, (2003) found out that an individual eventually makes a decisions of applications that have scores between the accepted scores and rejected scores (Shorouq et al 2010). Undeniably the effect of these scores are compared to a cutoff point. If the score surpasses the set limit, the application is approved; otherwise it is rejected (Tafti and Nikbakht, 1993). However the inconsistencies in credit scoring models have been observed to dampen the quality of effectiveness to the lending risk assessment practice in some sectors. Shorouq et al (2010) believe that credit scoring models can serve as tool in loan pricing, loan monitoring, determining the amount of credit, credit risk management and the assessment of loan portfolio risks. Limsombunchai et al. (2005) argues that it's widely acceptable and thus many consumer lending institutions such as credit cards and mortgage lending tend to use it. However, as Walker et al., (1995) insists scoring consumer credits have short comings of having the inability to discriminate loan applicants due to the complexity of the data and as a matter of fact some scoring systems do not work in practice and become overtaken by change.

## Statistical

Conventional statistical techniques have been used to analyze whether to approve the loan or not, and are still in use but they are more difficult to use within the current context. Generally, linear discriminant analysis and logistic regression are two popular statistical tools to construct credit scoring models. Other techniques are decision trees, neural networks, Bayesian classifier, SVM, kernel networks etc. (Chopde, et al 2012). Breiman, (1994) believes that a meta-algorithm can improve classification or regression models in terms of stability and classification accuracy in machine learning. Among other statistical methods, Z-scores can be calculated, for instance they focus on the average amount of daily geopolitical news for a topic in the recent past and see what proportion of all geopolitical news is consumed by that topic (Kaya 2019), and then calculate risk factor for that jurisdiction. While Banks tend to use conventional statistical techniques to approve or reject loan applications the current situation is more difficult to make a call. Different from the statistical model, the artificial intelligence model does not need the assumption of variable distribution, and can get knowledge directly from the training data set. Furthermore it tends to reduce the variance and helps to avoid overfitting. Ideally the prediction accuracy can be improved by aggregating many models rather than building a high capacity model. Kaya (2019) continues to report that if a particular political event is receiving attention that is greater than two standard deviations more than normal, it is marked as an 'outlier' event. Furthermore last few decades has seen banks rely on the personal assessment of loan risks or on statistical methods to predict the default of loans instead of using a standardized evaluation tool. Though the available tools such as statistical models such as discriminant analysis and logistic regression were picked, they usually assume multivariate normality and homoscedastic and these assumptions are often debased in the real world banking data (Giang, 2005; Huang et al., 2004).

Templeman and Moniz (2019), through the Deutsche Bank Research report (2019) indicates a pertinent weakness with the statistical analysis. The reports says that no system can precisely forecast geopolitical insinuations all the time, but with tools like Alpha-Dig, an unprejudiced measure can assist investors in notoriously difficult times to understand the situation thanks to advancement in AI.

## Use of Credit Reference Bureau

While the introduction of Credit Reference Bureau (CRB) has greatly altered the behavior of compliance, it has not helped to identify risky customers entirely. Central Bank of Kenya (2009) highlights that CRBs act as financial intermediaries within the financial infrastructure, facilitating information exchange among lenders, allowing lenders to supplement their information with that from other lenders so that credit decisions are made from the best possible point of information. Unfortunately CRB has more to do with the enforcing repayment and feebly identifying risky customers but it is being used to punish the non-compliant customers rather than use this analysis to identify the customer risk margin. In many jurisdictions and within a legal context, CRBs have been given the obligation to collect, manage and disseminate borrower's information to the lenders, for the lenders to make accurate information when decisions are being made on credit worthiness of an applicant (Gikonyo, 2014). This mean that there is need for banks to further enhance their use of CRBs to go beyond using CRBs as a mechanism for curbing default and actually using the information contained therein to enhance their competitiveness (Wachira-Keriri, 2012). However CRBs are facing more credibility issues including abuse of data amongst players in the banking industry specifically in the context of competition, i.e. poaching of customers, the complexity of updating and sharing live data on current loans using the core banking systems, weak legal system governing the implementation of the full file information sharing.

Muiruri, (2019) reveals that Central Bank of Kenya is concerned over the differing formulas of credit scoring by the three licensed bureaus and are outlining plans for the creation of a central server for financial technology firms to facilitate the submission of client-credit information. Adding slat to injury the poor perception by consumers where the primary objective of credit information sharing is viewed as a punishment for defaulters and a debt recovery tool is causing a lot of apprehension.

World Bank (2019) study provides evidence that in India, the Credit reference Bureau is known as CIBIL - (Credit Information Bureau (India) Limited- an authority to issue credit score to the person by referring his base history of credit throughout years. This means that CRB should then gather information that includes credit accounts, loans bankruptcies and late payments and this information can be obtained from any source such as banks, SACCOs and utility companies (Gikonyo,

2014). However fears of a public backlash by consumers where full file information sharing is viewed as a breach of confidentiality thus a hindrance to CRB operations.

CBK (2009) reports that CRB act as financial intermediaries within the financial infrastructure, to expedite information exchange among financial institutions and thus allowing these lenders to supplement their information with that from other institutions to further credit decisions made from the best possible information. Gikonyo, (2014) perceives that reliable information gathered by CRBs has to be appropriate and all-inclusive on the repayment habits and current data of loan applicants and generally for any individuals who have at one time or another used the financial system to transact. In India Digital Companies make use of CIBIL to weigh credit score of potential lender as a base platform for lending (Anand, 2019). Nevertheless it is in the public domain that the use of CRBs by banks has been to get information about customer information rather than using CRBs to guide them on pricing of loan facilities and reducing their reliance on collateral (Wachira-Keriri, 2012).

## PERFORMANCE OF BAD LOANS IN KENYA

The performance of bad loans in Kenya has been a concern for many within the industry sector. These bad loans arise from risky customers who borrow and may be unwilling or not able to repay. To sort out this mess the Kenyan government through ministry of Information and communication has encouraged the adoption of IT related solutions to be to make banks and financial institutions competitive and have a global reach, penetrate more markets. This means the need to use Artificial Intelligence or algorithms to identify and weed out risky customers. Figure 3 clearly shows the growth of Non-performing loans regime despite having instituting Credit and Reference Bureaus in the Kenyan financial market.

## APPLICATION OF ARTIFICIAL INTELLIGENCE IN DIGITAL LOANS

The financial sector became one of the early adopters of utilizing AI technologies to seek to surge profitability margins (Kaya, 2019). This means that the innovation of AI has become a better way of managing risky customer. The predominant viewpoint of risk management is that it is not only a critical practice to ensure compliance with internal as well as regulatory standards but also a valuable business practice (KCB Bank 2015). Artificial intelligence is being perceived as a panacea though it is a branch of computer science that focus on creating intelligent machines (Vedapradha

*Figure 3. Performance of bad loans in Kenya*

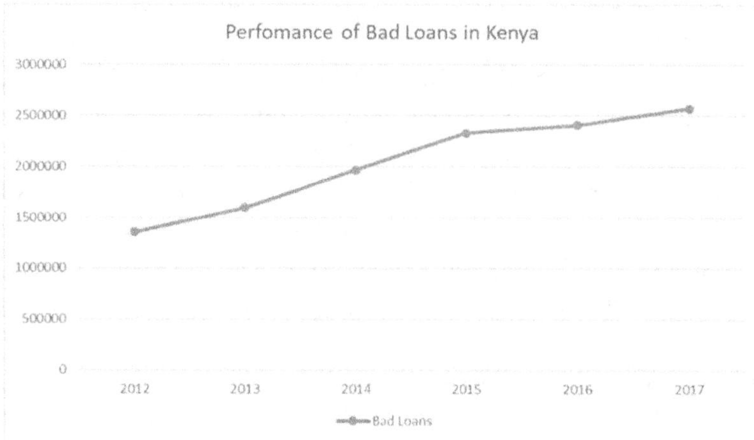


*Figure 4.*

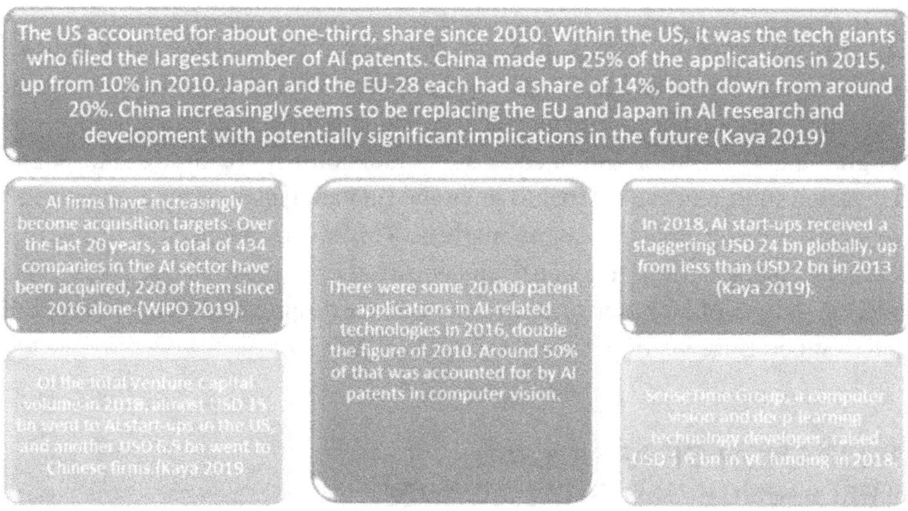


& Hariharan 2018) to determine certain decisions. At this juncture it is important to note that the introduction of Credit Reference Bureau (CRB) has greatly altered the behavior of compliance but does not help in identify risky customer to the highest degree. CRB has more to do with the enforcing repayment and weakly identifying risky customers but it is mostly used to punish the non-compliant customers rather than use this analysis to identify and risky customer risk margin.

Customer behavior is predicable with better tools of analysis it as such Kaya (2019) explains that AI is also being tested in KYC (Know Your Customer) processes to verify the identity of clients. This is the very reason why mobile money lenders have adopted the use of artificial intelligence which has been employed to determine whether giving a loan to a client will result in bad loans. Without a doubt bad loans have had a significant effect on banks performance and many of them at first were not willing to lend money to applicants who were of low income bracket or did not have collateral concerned. Kaya (2019), makes it known that within European continent, Germany, France and the UK are the leaders in experimentation and in the implementation of AI as such it has led to amplification of AI global competition with the European Commission proposing Nine Euro billion budget to fund AI-related projects between 2021 and 2027

In Kenya KCB has adopted the use of the Risk Management function which is apparently driving risk intelligence as a business enabler (KCB Bank 2015). As a matter of fact, Limsombunchai et al., (2005) disclose that A.I technologies have proved to be a fruitful investment in the banking industry, such as neural networks for their ability to assist in improving the quality of credit decisions to reduce credit risk. A.I is a significant step forward in the digitalisation and transformation of modern businesses. It refers to computers' capability to acquire and apply knowledge without programmers' intervention (Kaya, 2019). Ideally credit risk is reduced by limiting the asymmetrical information challenges and enables the public to be aware of the benefits of having a positive credit history (Gikonyo, 2014). Behavioural credit scoring is also being applied to agricultural businesses, with a view to increasing lending to this vital sector. The tools used in assessment of risks for new products enable KCB to formulate strategies to mitigate risks (KCB Bank 2015)

Artificial intelligence of neural systems and networks are able to identify complex patterns as crucial to predictions (Zhang, 2004) of behavior. AI refers to the ability of computer programs to acquire and apply knowledge without human intervention and involvement. This implies that computers can access cognitive skills similar to humans. This results in immense efficiency gains for firms and their clients alike (Kaya, 2019).

Digital lenders in India use customize models and industry best practices along with the existing customer data to automate the lending decision making process. Limsombunchai et al., (2005) opines that technological advances of the neural networks have been particularly applicable to risk management and forecasting within the banking industry (Huang et al., 2004).

*Figure 5. Global patent application status*

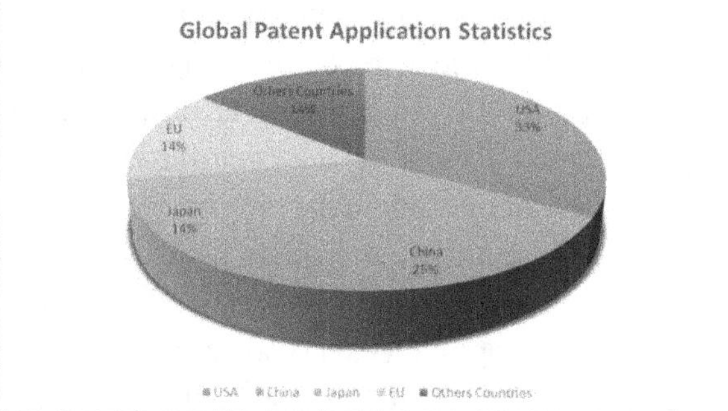


This growth of the mode is greatly due to the customer's mobile phone-based data, such as call and SMS records, mobile money transaction history and social media data, to determine a credit score and loan amount (Kaffenberger & Chege 2016). Kaya, (2019) hints at AI systems being able to observe the world, analyse the information autonomously, draw conclusions and take appropriate actions and ideally learning from their aforementioned decisions and, depending on the level of accuracy, improve their performance over time.

Limsombunchai et al., (2005) disclose that AI technologies have proved to be a fruitful investment in the banking industry, such as neural networks, save for their ability to assist in improving the quality of credit decisions to reduce credit risk. (Kaya, 2019). Since its lucrativeness is envied everywhere, investors have been lining up to be part of the great change. Going forward, AI has been able to engross USD 24 bn in investments globally in 2018, portending a twelvefold increase since 2013 with USA start-ups receiving the most attention, followed by China, which has already outpaced European AI counterparts start-ups (Kaya, 2019). Evidently AI system tends to give any bank or now mobile lenders a competitive advantage within the jurisdiction in which they operate in leading to a higher performance for that matter. Bartlett et al (2019) opines that with algorithmic credit scoring, the nature of discrimination changes from being primarily concerned with human biases – racism and in-group/out-group bias – to being primarily concerned with illegitimate applications of statistical discrimination, a handicap that was visible in the past cases.

In examining who qualifies for a loan, banks face the dilemma of identifying the likelihood of a customer's default, this is, most crucial and imminent vulnerability in lending. Nevertheless a proficient credit manager should be at vantage point to be able to make the right call, though there is a chance of missing some critical elements. This affirms that such analysis completely eliminates the risk of improper

*Box 1.*

| Tala Mobile loans,<br>To evaluate creditworthiness of a customer, Tala offers a smartphone app that would-be borrowers download onto their cell phones. This app gives Tala access to a range of data, from basic biographical information to the number of people loan applicants contact on a daily basis. Tala can see the size of the applicant's network and support system. The data even reveal where the applicant goes during the day, whether she demonstrates consistency, like making a daily call to her parents, and whether she pays her bills on time.<br>The revelation: a person's routine habits are more meaningful than traditional credit scoring. Once approved, a borrower can get money downloaded onto her smart phone in two minutes. On loans that average \$50 with an interest rate of 11%, Tala has logged a repayment rate of better than 90%. To date it has loaned almost \$20 million to more than 150,000 people. On revenue of \$1.5 million in the last year, it had a profit of more than \$500,000. One can download the app and answer eight questions that revolve around demographic and location data while this is being done Tala is working out a scoring for the potential client. The send a loan offer.<br>Once the client accept you, they get the capital directly into their mobile wallet. Eighty-five percent of customers get cash in their wallet in two minutes. Tala is opened 24 hours a day and customer can request capital and get it in under two minutes at four in the morning. Tala at first had default rate of 50% to 60% according to Siroya: the CEO of Tala Mobile once the organization built the AI model default rate went down to less than 10%.<br>*Source ; Susan Adams (2019). How Tala Mobile Is Using Phone Data To Revolutionize Microfinance. Forbes Magazine Trep Talks - Forbes' education coverage available at* https://www.forbes.com/sites/forbestreptalks/2016/08/29/how-tala-mobile-is-using-phone-d |
|---|

decision making as it happens in the regular practice in traditional lending. This then introduces the factual use of algorithms. In financial services, AI promises great efficiency gains and potential revenue increases and it is currently is being tested for real-time identification and prevention of fraud in online banking as well as in know-your-customer (KYC) processes. (Kaya, 2019).

## Artificial Intelligence at Work

Zhang, (2004) and Huang et al., (2004) posit that artificial neural networks possess the capabilities of capturing nonlinear and complex relationships and are considered promising techniques in classification problems relating to borrowing. Unlike the old-fashioned statistical and mathematical programming techniques such as discriminant analysis, linear and logistic regression, have demonstrated their ability to overcome different challenges in financial research areas, especially in banking loan portfolio optimization (Eletter, Yaseen, & Elrefae, 2010; Ghodselahi & Amirmadhi, 2011; Marque, Garci, & Nchez, 2013; Nazari & Alidadi, 2013). While banks are by large still experimenting with AI technologies rather than fully implementing them in their processes, many of the digital loan providers have made AI part of their core business (Kaya, 2019).

## Use of Algorithms

Though the available tools such as statistical models like discriminant analysis and logistic regression were picked, they usually assumed multivariate normality and were homoscedastic and these assumptions are often debased in the real world banking data (Giang, 2005; Huang et al., 2004). In US Consumer lending is changing rapidly, with loan origination becoming almost exclusively algorithmic (Bartlett et al 2019). Khandani, Kim and Lo (2010), reported the large number of decisions involved in the consumer lending business makes it necessary to rely on models and algorithms rather than human discretion, and to base such algorithmic decisions on ‘‘hard” information, e.g., characteristics contained in consumer credit files collected by credit bureau agencies. Kaya (2019) beefs up this notion by proposing that AI algorithms should check the probability of clients' credit card transactions in real time and compare new transactions with previous amounts and locations and identify fraudulent activities on credit cards and subsequently block the transactions discerned as risky.

Rao, (n.d) jubilates that in the credit risk assessment, especially when the problem of credit risk assessment is a nonlinear model, the performance of the A.I model is often better than the statistical model. Bruckner, (2018), avers that algorithms tend to bring the so-called “credit invisibles” into the credit markets by using non-traditional credit measures. AI algorithms can be developed to produce extremely refined investment strategies that guarantees high velocity data to outsmart the competition and enhancing value to the customers (Vedapradha & Hariharan (2018).

The consumer behavior patterns have been less predictable in the past due to insufficient tools but with A.I and algorithms the predictability of individual behavior in not only guarantee but estimated at higher degree of accuracy. Algorithmic loan origination is not, however, just a feature of FinTech companies, Bartlett et al (2019), studied 2,098 largest mortgage lenders (inclusive of all the big banks) over the 2012-2018 period, finding that as of 2018, 45% of them offer complete online or app-based loans. Kaya (2019) further hints at AI algorithms being in a position to scan client documents and evaluate the reliability of the information provided by comparing it with information from the internet. This means that as management of customer data appears to be prominent area, the application of AI is constantly progressing (Vedapradha &Hariharan, 2018), this means that as these algorithm fish out for inconsistencies, they raise a red flag and a more detailed KYC check by bank personnel is performed (Kaya, 2019). Additionally, other qualities comprise of dependability, confidence in source, appropriateness, correct recipient and use of correct channels to convey the information (Bocij et al, 2008).

In Kenya to access Branch, O-Kash loans, for example, users download an app from the Google play store and link the app to their social media accounts (Kaffenberger & Chege 2016). Vedapradha and Hariharan (2018) insist that artificial Intelligence is now being used as a cognitive application in functional areas of business along with investment and compliance sectors of financial services industry. Kaya (2019) reports subsequently that banks are also exploring AI such data from legal documents or annual reports, for example, and to extract important clauses, this AI tools then create models independently after observing the data and back testing to learn from their previous mistakes to improve accuracy.

These loans apps use algorithms to analyze these data and determine a credit score and loan size. Saida and Tala are two other examples of app-based lenders using mobile phone data to determine loan sizes (Kaffenberger & Chege 2016). EPAR found that common data used for credit scoring included previous digital credit loans, mobile money transactions and balance information, social media data, and mobile phone activity ((FinCoNet, 2018). Successively, Zhang, (2004) and Huang et al., (2004) admit that artificial neural networks have the innate capabilities of capturing nonlinear and complex relationships are considered promising techniques in classification of problems relating to such. Kaya (2019) brings in a new dimension of chatbox a part of AI technologies. These are digital assistants that interact with clients by text or voice and aim to address their requests without the involvement of a bank employee Kaya (2019). In Kenya Safaricom has developed a voice option an algorithm to identify the owner using his/her voice to counter fraudulent activities.

Shachmurove, (2002) postulates that ideally algorithms are strategically utilized to scrutinize relations among economic and financial phenomena, forecasting, generating time series, optimization and decision making. With the utilization of customer's mobile phone-based data, such as call and SMS records, mobile money transaction history and social media data, to determine a credit score and loan amount (Kaffenberger & Chege n.d), the artificial intelligence gives a near perfect prediction on default and risky behavior. And Kaya (2019), concludes that though not directly linked to the digital banking industry elsewhere robo-advisors are being utilized to enable full automation in certain asset management services and online financial planning tools that help customers make more informed consumption and saving decisions

The use of non-traditional data such as social media data and phone activity adds another dimension to creditworthiness assessments, and enables consumers who may be excluded under traditional assessments to access credit. (FinCoNet, 2018). Though there are several methods to update the weights and combine the individual classifiers (Vedapradha and Hariharan 2018), Dwoskin, (2015) reveals that the digital credit provider postulate that even subtle behaviour like deciding to add last names into one's phone contact list can indicate an increased likelihood of loan repayment.

Kavitha (2016) has proposed an improved risk evaluation version of Multidimensional Risk prediction clustering Algorithm to determine the good and bad loan applicants whether they are applicable or not. Vedapradha and Hariharan (2018) claim that using boosting algorithm is a game changer in that industry in that it gives all credit applicants the same weight. After a classifier is built, the weight of each applicant is changed according to the classification given by that classifier. Then, a second classifier is built using the reweighted training sample (Vedapradha and Hariharan 2018). The entire A.I decision-making process has to be compliant with regulatory and supervisory rules and fully transparent and while it may also cancel out some efficiency gains, the involvement of human programmers and overseers might be a solution to reduce issues around the opaqueness of some A.I algorithms (Kaya, 2019). This procedure is typically repeated several hundreds of times. The final classification of a credit applicant is a weighted average of the individual classifications over all classifiers (Vedapradha & Hariharan 2018). Dobbie, Liberman, Paravisini and Pathania (2018) examined data from a high-cost creditor in the UK and found substantial bias against immigrant and older loan applicants when measured using long-run profits.

## REGULATIONS

Due to the novelty of mobile money businesses, it is not surprising that many are quick to raise issues around consumer protection; the emphasis on the data digitization component of mobile money especially contributes to concerns regarding consumers. Bartlett et al (2019) admits that Algorithmic decision-making can reduce face-to-face discrimination in markets known to be prone to implicit and explicit biases. The challenge is that it can also lead to unintended discrimination (Barocas & Selbst, 2016) to customers seeking loan services.

Regulation has become a thorny issue with Dzokoto and Appiah (2012) showcasing that in Ghana persisting government regulations are not openly encouraging the mobile financial services inclusion and the educational barriers. Bartlett et al (2019) has revealed every extra basis point of interest charged on a home loan due to discrimination costs minorities $165 million per year in extra payments in the USA. Such practices may not be legal but loop holes within the sector may be propagating this behavior among the industry players. Micro-mobile links lending to future payrolls and will lend up to 50% of a borrower's monthly salary. This model is similar to payday lending in the United States, which often results in a debt cycle where the high-fee, short-term nature of the loans, means customers must continue borrowing to pay off previous loans and associated fees. Kaya, (2019) grieves that these exploited gaps in regulatory measures around data privacy and concerns regarding cybersecurity might be a hindrance to the full utilization of AI within the banking or the highly regulated nature of banking may blot out some efficiency gains of AI.

Bartlett et al (2019) explain that in business terms, any strategic pricing that causes disparate impact, even inadvertently, is discrimination in the eyes of the law. Brynjolfsson & Hitt, (2000) specify that investments on the technology are very huge in quantum and its effects must be clearly considered before implementation. The merits of such applications are intangible in nature and productivity can be valued in connection with economic value of the information technology.

Bartlett et al (2019) however laments lenders have been unfortunately accused using algorithms in discriminating against minorities in USA. Kaya, (2019) posits that a solution to this concern is the adoption of rapid implementation of AI technologies, because it has been cited as pivotal in fighting insistently weak profitability and to remaining competitive such that studies disclose AI has a significant positive impact on European banks' return on assets (ROA). Though sadly within the traditional banking sector, loan providers can use proxy variables that yield an incongruent impact on minority applicants, this applies where the creditor can demonstrate that these variables have a legitimate business necessity (Bartlett et al 2019). In fact if used well and labour productivity is increased, AI technologies could structurally reduce costs in the banking sector (Kaya, 2019) despite the ethnic background. As Bartlett et al (2019) posit that courts have indicated a legitimate business should necessitate the act of scoring credit risk and efforts to use proxy variables that produce a disparate impact for other purposes, including lenders' earning of higher profit margins, should not be employed . Irrefutably global business calls for solutions offered at global level to be assimilated with A.I intelligence to create a unified framework or policies in the areas like crypto currency, customized hacking at personal level legally, automation of business models etc (Erdélyi & Goldsmith, 2018). As matter of fact in business terms, any strategic pricing that causes disparate impact, even inadvertently, is discrimination in the eyes of the law (Bartlett et al., 2019).The development of neural networks has been a game changer in terms of their applicability to business settings. As such the final loan portfolio selection necessitates a solution of a high-dimensional nonlinear program and is computationally challenging (Elhachlouf, Guennoun, & Hamza, 2012; Sefiane & Benbouziane, 2012) but should be done in a more ethical way.

It is true that while the borrowers usually "consent" to the use of their data for calculating loans, it is questionable on whether they read the full terms and conditions, It is further doubtful that they understand exactly what data about them and their phone use will be used by the lender. In Kenya digital lenders' information has not been readily available leaving a number of them outside the scope of the credit database heightening consumer overleveraging risks (Muiruri, 2019). Other data-related policies could affect customers as well, such as how much data providers retain after calculating the loan amount, how long they hold it, how safely they store it and who would be liable if the data were accessed by an unauthorized party or otherwise used in a way that can harm the customer.

Vedapradha and Hariharan (2018) indicates that in Risk Assessment the large volumes of complex data are involved in due diligence, risk assessment, monitoring that facilitates effective lending practices. Ideally business strategies and technology are integrated and are needed to revamp the business model based on the core competencies to address the research account executives in offering direct interface from the business units directly (Chester, 1994). However many of these lenders are unregulated, lending outside the purview of current regulation. The services generally offer (relatively) small-value, short-term loans (Kaffenberger & Chege 2016).

## IMPEDIMENTS TO THE USE OF ARTIFICIAL INTELLIGENCE IN BANKING

The fact that AI impacts bank profitability means that it might help European banks to address one of their core problems of recent years: persistently weak profitability. Disclosure is very important such that legally in USA, the disclosure provisions of the act also means that if an AI tool rejects a bank account or loan application, the client has the right to know the logic involved in this decision. This means the open communication.

When it comes to human intervention, the programmers might be required to fully comply with these and many other data privacy rules, however, this is not an ideal situation for AI to thrive. It seems more as a setback for the expected efficiency gains of AI. A.I simulated in financial institutions are aiming at having least human intervention and have the system run the queries and make decisions.

Potentially malicious manipulation of big data in the financial institutions makes the adoption if AI an uphill task. Hackers are known to flood systems with fictitious data such as fake social media accounts, websites and news to influence AI decision-making. Malevolent issues are bound to intensify with the continuous use of AI and algorithm.

Regrettably any observer or customer will get the picture that AI – and especially neural networks – have opaque reasoning and function as black boxes. This means that there is need to increase customer or users understanding and the perception to increase trust into the system. It implies that the inability of customer to visualize and understand AI patterns will be construed to be lack of transparency for the financial solution provider. What aggravates the complexity of the problem is the fact that AI algorithms update themselves over time and become more connected.

It is important to remember that AI predictions and decisions might be very close to those of humans in the end. Unlike humans though, AI by its nature is unable to communicate its reasoning.

While credit information has revolutionized the issuance of loans, deepening inclusion, traditional lenders are yet to fully leverage on available credit information in comparison to their fin-tech counterparts (Muiruri, 2019).It is somewhat difficult at this early stage of AI diffusion in banking to assess the potential operational risks and associated costs for banks which might stem from the increased use of AI.

## CONCLUSION

The rapid proliferation of these digital loans have raised apprehensions particularly how they work (which are problematic to keep up within the hurriedly growing market), the ways clients are essentially using the products, consumer protection disputes and risks such loans might raise for borrowers Notwithstanding the consequences of loan portfolio range resolutions, the compromise between risky loans with higher returns or safe loans with inferior returns has not received nearly as much consideration as the equity portfolio selection decisions. While mobile money is at the crossroads of mobile communications and financial services, its power in distribution and marketing is actually disguised under a technology facade. Traditional lenders that compete with marketplace lenders will need to adapt to the market entrants and market conditions, perhaps adopting certain marketplace lender technologies and practices.

In addition, marketplace lending has not been through an entire economic cycle, and rising interest rates or the onset of a recession will likely reveal certain strengths and weaknesses of marketplace lending. Rather than being the apple of discord between financial inclusion and financial integrity, digital loans are actually helping to reduce dependency on cash, (a common enemy of both financial inclusion and financial integrity, generates data (instrumental to the health and growth of both financial inclusion and financial integrity) and accelerating the development of accounts, (which are the backbone of financial inclusion and financial integrity). AI has demonstrated to be decisive in dealing with the vice of money laundering -a chief predicament for the financial services and banking industry mostly faced at the global level.

The mobile lending is still a very young "industry" however; the first services were only launched commercially in the Philippines less than ten years ago and mobile money is becoming a reality at scale so far only in East Africa. So the potential is there, but it still needs to be realized without fail. The technology allows the bank to avert potential money laundering activity by analyzing internal, overtly accessible and transactional data within customer's wider grid. AI might contribute to bank profitability by taking over repetitive tasks from bank employees, autonomous AI software is could be instrumental reducing the demand for less-skilled labour and increase the adeptness of the remaining bank workforce and as a crucial step employee recompense customarily signifies a gigantic portion of banks' cost base.

FinTech lenders are using pricing strategies and data analytics that nonetheless produce discriminatory pricing meaning that that even if algorithmic lending can reduce discrimination relative to face-to-face lenders, it is insufficient to eliminate discrimination in loan pricing. Definitely the variance between noble and bad data can be recognized by considering whether or not it has some or all of the traits of information quality. There is very little question regarding the importance of consumer protection, and there are a number of regulatory issues to address on the demand side. For example, ensuring that terms and conditions as well as retail tariffs are published and available seems very sensible.

## Implications to Managers

The subjective fears of the human factor have been a cause of concern in giving out loans; this means that whenever individual decisions are made, the accepted scores and rejected scores may not be entirely true because of the emotive decisions. While the introduction of Credit Reference Bureau (CRB) has greatly altered the behavior of compliance within the banking industry ideally does not help in identifying the risky customer. The act has been fruitful in facilitating information exchange among lenders thus allowing managers in financial institutions to supplement their information with that from other lenders so that credit decisions are made from the best possible information. The challenge is that CRB focuses on enforcing repayment and identifying risky customers but succinctly it is used mostly to punish the non-compliant customers rather than use this analysis to identify the customer risk margin. Ideally the CRB was embraced by the financial sector to identify risky customer and set the stage for safeguards however, there are complaints of abuse of data amongst players in the banking industry in the context of competition, i.e. poaching of customers and the complexity of updating and sharing live data on current loans using core banking.

The adoption of AI decision-making can reduce face-to-face perspicacity in jurisdictions that are known to be prone to implicit and explicit biases. There is need for managers to offer solutions that are assimilated with artificial intelligence to create a unified framework or policies in the areas like crypto -currency, automation of business models and payment platforms. Managers should carefully ensure things are done in a more ethical way that questionable issues within A.I and algorithms are totally avoided.

The borrowers usually “consent” to the use of their data for calculating loans, however, this has been done in a questionable way and it is doubtful whether they understand exactly how their data and mobile phone information will be used by the lender. In Kenya some of the digital lenders have been accused of using consumer data such as accessing their mobile number contacts and calling them to ensure a loan is paid. These has been construed by many as breach of privacy and in future such may lead to litigations against MMT providers. Many of these lenders are unregulated, it behooves the government then to institute legislation to control operations of these Mobile lenders. Lack of legislation of MMT has led to over exploitation of customers and therefore the need for institutions to tread with care so as not to be run out of business due to their unethical practices and illegalities.

Still, AI’s and algorithms potency and impact on the profit margins within the financial institutions should not be underestimated. There needs to be more incentives and support for the banks to adopt the rapid and robust AI technologies for them to remain relevant and competitive.

Lastly adoption of AI should be encouraged but managers need to employ a human face to it. There is need for human interface to understand that sometimes computer generated output need a human face to circumvent the face-to-face discrimination prone to implicit and explicit biases. The use of Artificial Intelligence as cognitive applications in functional areas of business along with investment and compliance sectors of financial services should serve to shoulder the business from bad loans. Looking forward, regulatory framework along data privacy and the highly regulated nature of banking should clear the way to remove obstacles for the AI implementation. Managers must understand that consumer behavior patterns have been opaque and less probable in the past due to unsatisfactory tools but with Artificial intelligence and algorithms the predictability of individual behavior in not only guaranteed but estimated at higher degrees of accuracy. Managers must learn to embrace such to the advantage of the business and not to the detriment of the digital loan customers.

## REFERENCES

Ahmad & Amirmadhi. (2011). Application of Artificial Intelligence Techniques for Credit Risk Evaluation. *International Journal of Modeling and Optimization*, *1*(3).

Alexandre Claire and Eisenhart Lynn Chang. (2013) Mobile Money as an Engine of Financial Inclusion and Lynchpin of Financial Integrity. *Washington Journal of Law, Technology & Arts*, *8*(3). Available at https://digitalcommons.law.uw.edu/cgi/viewcontent.cgi?article=1178&context=wjlta

Arnold, D., Dobbie, W., & Yang, C. S. (2018). Racial bias in bail decisions. *Quarterly Journal of Economics*. Available at https://www.princeton.edu/~wdobbie/files/racialbias.pdf

Attaran, M. (2004). Exploring the relationship between information technology and business process reengineering. *Journal of International Management*, *41*(5), 585–596. doi:10.10160378-7206(03)00098- 3

Barocas, S., & Selbst, A. (2016). Big Data's Disparate Impact. *California Law Review*, *104*, 671–732.

Bartlett. (2019). *Consumer-Lending Discrimination in the FinTech Era*. Available at https://faculty.haas.berkeley.edu/morse/research/papers/discrim.pdf

Berutich, J. M., Francisco, L., & Quintana, D. (2016). Robust technical trading strategies using GP for algorithmic portfolio selection. *Expert Systems with Applications*, *46*, 307–315. doi:10.1016/j.eswa.2015.10.040

Breiman, L. (1994). *Bagging predictors. Tech. rep. 421*. Department of Statistics, University of California.

Bruckner, A. M. (2018). The Promise and Perils of Algorithmic Lenders' Use of Big Data. *Chicago-Kent Law Review, 93*(1).

Brynjolfsson, E., & Hitt, L. M. (2000). Beyond Computation: Information Technology, Organizational Transformation and Business Performance. *The Journal of Economic Perspectives*, *14*(4), 23–48. doi:10.1257/jep.14.4.23

Chester, A. N. (1994). Aligning Technology with Business Strategy. *Research Technology Management*, *37*(1), 25–32. doi:10.1080/08956308.1994.11670951

Chopde, K., Pratik, G., Paras, K., Niharika, M., & Pramila, M. C. (2012). A Study of Classification Based Credit Risk Analysis Algorithm. *International Journal of Engineering and Advanced Technology*, *1*(4).

Dobbie, W., Liberman, A., Paravisini, D., & Pathania, V. (2018). *Measuring Bias in Consumer Lending*. doi:10.3386/w24953

Donner, J., & Tellez, C. A. (2008). Mobile banking and economic development: Linking adoption, impact, and use. *Asian Journal of Communication*, *18*(4), 318–332. doi:10.1080/01292980802344190

Dwoskin, E. (2015), Lending Startups Look at Borrowers' Phone Usage to Assess Creditworthiness. *Wall Street Journal*. Available at https://www.wsj.com/articles/lending-startups-look-at-borrowers-phone-usage-to-assess-creditworthiness-1448933308

Dzokoto, V. A., & Appiah, E. (2012). Making Sense of Mobile Money In *Urban Ghana: Personal, Business, Social And Financial Inclusion Prospects*. Available at https://www.imtfi.uci.edu/files/docs/2014/dzkoto_final_report_feb2014.pdf

Eletter, S., Yaseen, S., & Elrefae, G. (2010). Neuro-based artificial intelligence model for loan decisions. *American Journal of Economics and Business Administration*, *2*(1), 27–34. doi:10.3844/ajebasp.2010.27.34

Elhachlouf, M., Guennoun, Z., & Hamza, F. (2012). Stocks portfolio optimization using classification and genetic algorithms. *Applied Mathematical Sciences*, *6*(94), 4673–4684.

Erdélyi, O. J., & Goldsmith, J. (2018). *Regulating Artificial Intelligence Proposal for a Global Solution*. Paper presented at the AAAI/ACM Conference on Artificial Intelligence, Ethics and Society.

FinCo Net. (2017). *Report on the Digitalisation of Short-term, High-Cost Consumer Credit*. Available at http://www.finconet.org/Digtalisation-Short-term-High-cost-Consumer- Credit.pdf

Giang, H. (2005). Using neural network in predicting corporate failure. *Journals of Social Science*, *1*, 199–202.

Haggblade, S., Hazell, P., & Reardon, T. (2007). *Transforming the Rural Nonfarm Economy: Opportunities and Threats in the Developing World*. Baltimore, MD: Johns Hopkins University Press.

Huang, W. (2004). Forecasting foreign exchange rates with artificial neural networks: A review. *International Journal of Information Technology*, *3*, 145-165.

Kaffenberger & Chege. (2016). *Digital Credit in Kenya: Time for Celebration or Concern?* Available at https://www.cgap.org/blog/digital-credit-kenya-time-celebration-or-concern

Kavitha, K. (2016). Clustering loan applicants based on risk percentage using K-means clustering techniques. *International Journal of Advanced Research in Computer Science and Software Engineering*, *6*(2), 162–166.

Kaya, O. (2019) Artificial intelligence in banking a lever for profitability with limited implementation to date. *EU Monitor Global financial markets*. Retrieved from https://www.dbresearch.com/PROD/RPS_EN-PROD/PROD0000000000495172 / Artificial_intelligence_in_banking%3A_A_lever_for_pr.pdf

KCB Bank. (2015). *KCB Bank Financial Reports 2015*. Available at https://kcbgroup.com/wp- content/uploads/2019/05/KCB-Group-Integrated-Report-and-Financial-Statements- 2018.pdf

Khandani, A. E., Kim, A. J., & Lo, A. W. (2010). Consumer credit-risk models via machine-learning algorithms MIT Sloan School of Management and Laboratory for Financial Engineering, United States. *Journal of Banking & Finance*, *34*, 2767–2787. doi:10.1016/j.jbankfin.2010.06.001

Khandani, A. E., Kim, A. J., & Lo, A. W. (2010). Khandani, Kim and Lo (2010), Consumer credit-risk models via machine-learning algorithms. *Journal of Banking & Finance*, *34*(11), 2767–2787. doi:10.1016/j.jbankfin.2010.06.001

Kirui Oliver, K. (2013). Impact of Mobile Phone-Based Money Transfer Services in Agriculture: Evidence from Kenya. *Quarterly Journal of International Agriculture*, *52*(2), 141-162.

Krishna, Krishna, & Vijay. (2012). Indian Banking Industry: Challenges and Opportunities. February 2012. *Global Business and Management Research: An International Journal*, *3*(1), 18–28.

Limsombunchai, V., Gan, C., & Lee, M. (2005). An analysis of credit scoring for agricultural loans in Thailand. *American Journal of Applied Sciences*, *2*(8), 1198–1205. doi:10.3844/ajassp.2005.1198.1205

Lwin, K. T., Qu, R., & MacCarthy, B. L. (2017). Mean-VaR portfolio optimization: A nonparametric approach. *European Journal of Operational Research*, *260*(2), 751–766. doi:10.1016/j.ejor.2017.01.005

Malhotra, R., & Malhotra, D. K. (2003). Evaluating consumer loans using neural networks. *Omega*, *31*(2), 83–96. doi:10.1016/S0305-0483(03)00016-1

Marque, A., Garci, V., & Nchez, J. (2013). A literature review on the application of evolutionary computing to credit scoring. *The Journal of the Operational Research Society*, *201364*(9), 1384–1399. doi:10.1057/jors.2012.145

Metawa, N., Hassan, M. K., & Elhoseny, M. (2017). Hassan, Mohamed Elhoseny Genetic Algorithm Based Model for Optimizing Bank Lending Decisions. *Expert Systems with Applications*, *80*, 75–82. doi:10.1016/j.eswa.2017.03.021

Mitchell & Pavur. (2002). Using modular neural networks for business decisions. *Manage.*, *40*, 58-63. Doi:10.1108/00251740210413361

Mohammed, H. A., & Tafti, E. N. (1993). Neural Networks and Expert Systems: New Horizons in Business Finance Applications. *Information Management & Computer Security*.

Nazari, M., & Alidadi, M. (2013). Measuring credit risk of bank customers using artificial neural network. *Journal of Management Research*, *5*(2), 17–27. doi:10.5296/jmr.v5i2.2899

Nupur, A. (2019). *Will It Backfire? Why Indian lenders are giving loans to risky customers with low credit scores*. Available at https://qz.com/india/1641387/indian-banks-nbfcs-fintech-firms-are-looking-over-cibil- scores

Rao, Y. (n.d.). *Big Data Algorithm Applied to Credit Risk Assessment Model.* School of Finance, Dongbei University of Finance and Economics. DOI doi:10.5013/IJSSST.a.17.42

Saborido, R., Ruiz, A., Bermúdez, J., Vercher, E., & Luque, M. (2016). Evolutionary multi- objective optimization algorithms for fuzzy portfolio selection. *Applied Soft Computing*, *39*, 48–63. doi:10.1016/j.asoc.2015.11.005

Sefiane, S., & Benbouziane, B. (2012). Portfolio selection using genetic algorithm. *Journal of Applied Finance and Banking*, 2(4), 143–154.

Shachmurove, Y. (2002). The Behavior of Secondary European Stock Markets to Positive and Negative Shocks. *International Journal of Business.*

Shorouq. (2010). Neuro-Based Artificial Intelligence Model for Loan Decisions. *American Journal of Economics and Business Administration, 2*(1), 27-34.

Templeman & Moniz. (2019). *Quantify geopolitical risk with alpha-DIG.* Deutsche Bank Research.

Vedapradha, R., Hariharan, R., & Shivakami, R. (2019). Artificial Intelligence: A Technological Prototype in Recruitment. *Journal of Service Science and Management*, *12*(03), 382–390. doi:10.4236/jssm.2019.123026

Vedapradha, R., & Ravi, H. (2018). Application of Artificial Intelligence in Investment Banks. *Review of Economic and Business Studies, 11*(2), 131–136. doi:10.1515/rebs-2018-0078

Wachira-Keriri. (2012). *Competitive Advantage of the Use of Credit Reference bureaus By Commercial Banks In Kenya* (Master's dissertation). The University of Nairobi.

Walker, R. F., Haasdijk, E. W., & Genets, M. C. (1995). Credit Evaluation Using a Genetic Algorithm. *Iin Intelligent System for Finance and Business. John Wiley and Sons.*

World Bank. (2003). *Reaching the Rural Poor: A Renewed Strategy for Rural Development.* Washington, DC: Author.

World Bank. (2019). *Credit Reporting Knowledge Guide 2019.* Available at documents.worldbank.org/curated/en/262691559115855583/pdf/Credit-Reporting-Knowledge-Guide-2019.pdf

Zhang, G. P. (2004). Neural Networks in Business Forecasting. Idea Group Inc. doi:10.4018/978-1-59140-176-6

# Chapter 4
# Impact of Mobile Money Transfer on the Education Sector in Sub-Saharan Africa:
## A Review

**Albert Juma**
*La Trobe University, Bundoora Campus, Melbourne, Australia*

## ABSTRACT

*Digitalization of payments related to education has played a significant role in driving the fourth agenda of the Sustainable Development Goals (SDG) aimed at providing free, equitable, and quality primary and secondary education to children by 2030. Since the launch of mobile money transfer (MMT) technologies by Safaricom in Kenya in 2007, many providers have developed a range of services to ensure efficient, transparent, and sustainable means of paying for school and college fees. This has led to enhanced teacher-student interaction times, reduced absenteeism, improved security in handling money, and made it easier for families to save, plan, and educate their children. This chapter reviews key success cases of countries and institutions that have digitalized payments and other education services to empower disadvantaged communities.*

DOI: 10.4018/978-1-7998-2398-8.ch004

## INTRODUCTION

The United Nations Sustainable Development Goal (SDG) number four aims to provide free, equitable and quality primary and secondary education by 2030. In many sub-Saharan Africa (SSA) countries, secondary education is not free and, despite there being 'free' primary education in some countries, there remains non-tuition costs like uniform, books, examination, meals and sports that must be met by parents. These non-tuition costs make up to 56% of household's education budget (Braniff, 2016). For example, most average Kenyan families spend about 11% of their monthly expenditures on education (Collins, Cojocaru, & Zollmann, 2015). Many families are not able to meet the expenses of taking their children to secondary schools leading to low transition rates.

Countless families in SSA depend on donations from relatives and sponsors to meet the financial obligations of educating their children. Since the introduction of mobile money services in Kenya in 2007 by Safaricom, a wide range of products have been developed to digitalize financial services and provide the unbanked community from the low-income backgrounds with manageable options to transact in flexible modes without necessarily having to open a bank account. The benefits accrued as a result of these developments are undeniable and range from saving time, improving livelihoods, efficiency, transparency, traceability, security and good relationships between parents, students and learning institutions.

Mobile money transfer (MMT) technology is a payment system that is linked to a mobile phone and allows an account holder to store money, transfer to other accounts or transact in many ways. This was initiated to allow customers to make person to person (P2P) transfers digitally without the need for a bank account or wire transfer (Suri, 2017). Consumers have been able to save money, pay bills, make person-to-business (P2B) payments, receive payments like salaries or wages and receive government-to-person (G2P) services – and vice versa.

In order to transact, a client must first register with an agent using government-issued identification documents. The client deposits money into their account by giving the amount to the agent, who enters it into the system using their business mobile phone. The client receives a notification SMS (Short Message Services) within a few seconds indicating the amount deposited and the new balance. They can then use the SIM (Subscriber Identification Module) card menu to transfer any amount from their available balance to a different account or make payments for any services. Since the advent of mobile money in Kenya by Safaricom in 2007, it is now possible to pay for almost any services via mobile money through a wide range of platforms developed by telecommunication companies and banks.

Several countries such as Cote d'Ivore, Uganda, Guinea, Mauritius, Tanzania, Kenya and Rwanda have well developed person to government (P2G) payment platforms for tax collection, school fees payment and for health services using MMT (GSMA, 2017). Innovative ideas and initiatives have been developed around MMT to enhance easy and efficient operation in many sectors for instance in agriculture where farmers accept payments via MMT in Uganda, promoting clean energy use through pay-as-go models in most East African countries, prepaid water utilities in Niger, as well as humanitarian services for refugees in Kenya and Uganda (GSMA, 2018). New products and apps are being established every year to diversify the market and meet the needs of different customer cohorts.

This aim of this review is to highlight the adoption of MMT for fee payment in the education sector and how this has contributed to improved access to financial inclusion and access to education. The background will highlight the scenario in terms of education status based on published reports and how costs related to education are met as well as an overview of the penetration rate of mobile money in the region. The impact of digitalization of fee payment systems on the education sector is then presented with a focus on the main models that successful countries like Kenya and Cote d'Ivore have implemented to improve efficiency in payments. Other models adopted by other countries are also discussed.

# BACKGROUND

## Mobile Money Transfer Technology

The first patent on mobile payment method to facilitate payments and transactions between registered members was filed in 2000 (USA Patent No. US 2002/0073027 A1, 2000). Since then, MMT technology has seen progressive adoption, development, innovation and persistent growth over the years. The main mobile money services involved in MMT are sale/purchase of airtime, payment of bills/invoices and remittances (Shrier, Canale, & Pentland, 2016). The state of industry report on mobile money indicates that in 2018, there were 262 live mobile money deployments in 90 countries; a 20% increase from the previous year (GSMA 2018). In addition, SSA region holds the largest percentage of the global subscribers at 45.6% followed by South Asia at 33.2%, East Asia and Pacific at 11%, Middle East and Northern Africa (MENA) region at 5.6%, Latin America and Caribbean region at 3.1 and lastly Europe and Central Asia at 1.4% (Pasti, 2018).

The invention of MMT technologies has seen an increase in the rate of financial inclusion among unbanked communities in SSA. GMSA (2018) indicates that with more than 866 million registered accounts transacting over $1.3 billion each day, the scale of MMT is continuing to grow. GSMA (2018) indicates that in 2017, MMT contributed 7.1% to the GDP across SSA and by 2022 the mobile economy is expected to contribute over 7.9% while the total number of mobile money transactions increased between 14.4% and 17.9%. East Africa remains the leader in mobile users with 56.4% of the total but both West and Central Africa regions have shown rapid uptakes of up to 30.9% and 9.7%, respectively (GSMA, 2017). International Telecommunication Union [ITU] (2016) indicates that several MMT providers have digitalized payments and created options for transparent, efficient and accountable ways to manage transactions by individuals, institutions and governments. In developed economies like the United States and Europe, mobile payments are linked to existing bank accounts, unlike developing and emerging economies where mobile payment can be stand-alone products (Aron, 2018).

The growth and economic impact of MMT is prominent in developing countries because it offers an alternative and less costly route for financial inclusion especially for the low-income earners. The global development of new telecommunication products and expansion of information and communication technologies (ICT) has been a key driver to the innovations in MMT technologies. In many countries, the rate of adoption and penetration is commensurate with the rate and extent of telecommunication and ICT advancement and connectivity. For example, the expansion of MMT in Kenya has been attributed to the rapid growth in the ICT sector which saw an increase from 10% to 22% in 2017 (Makena, 2019).

On the other hand, the inception of M-Pesa services has been linked to the 14% per capita real income growth and 3.4% of total factor productivity growth in Kenya between 2006 and 2013 (Beck, Pamuk, Ramrattan, & Uras, 2014). MMT methods are now used for payments in almost all sectors by businesses and government institutions besides domestic transactions. With continued technological developments and access to cheaper mobile phones, more countries are reviewing their policies to enhance regulatory structures that provide a healthy environment for the MMT services to continue expanding.

## Education in Sub-Saharan Africa

Recent data indicates that the world is likely to miss the target of free and equitable education for all children by the expected date of 2030. It is projected that 4 in 10 children will still not complete their secondary education by 2030 (UNESCO, 2019). One major contributor to this trend is that the number of trained teachers in SSA has been declining because most countries hire teachers on contracts. Training, recruiting and retaining highly qualified teachers is crucial in promoting quality education. Unfortunately, most countries have not invested more in improving the quality of education as much as they are raising enrolments, resulting in overcrowded classes and hence demoralized teaching staff. Antoninis and Montoya (2019) report that as much as literacy rates are steadily improving globally, by 2030, about 20% of youths and 30% of adults in low-income countries will still not be able to read.

Close to 263 million children, adolescents and youths aged between 6 and 17 years old are out of school partly due to location and poverty issues, especially for secondary education. In sub-Saharan Africa almost 60% of youths between the ages of about 15 and 17 are not in school (UNESCO, 2016). Considerable progress in attainment of the fourth sustainable development goal (SDG) on education has been reported due to increase in enrolment rates in developing nations of over 91% by 2015 with the greatest growth recorded in SSA regions (UNDP, 2015). Despite this improvement, many children are still out of school as their families struggle to meet the cost of education in many countries where it is not free.

In most, if not all, sub-Saharan countries, students must pay for their education in terms of tuition and related fees to complement the insufficient funding from the governments (UNESCO Institute for Statistics 2011). The conventional mode of paying fees involves students or their parents depositing money in the school's bank account or purchasing a banker's cheque, which they bring to the school bursar or account officer to enter into the school records and issue a receipt as proof of payment. In some cases, the student must pay in cash or kind at the school (Njeri, 2018; Collins, Cojocaru, & Zollmann, 2015). This pattern has seen the students and school administrations encounter difficulties in keeping consistent records, issues with transparency, theft by the accountants or bursars and sometimes the students themselves, loss of cash through burglary from external thugs among many other challenges that come with handling large sums of cash.

In countries where primary education is free, parents still pay for other expenses like books, uniform, meals, supplies, sports and exam fees. In many sub-Saharan countries, secondary education is not free, leading to sharp drops in enrolments after primary education (Braniff, 2016). For instance, in Uganda, the cost of sending a child to primary school is $ 111-184 and to secondary school is $ 207-600 yet 38% of the population live under the poverty line of $ 465 per year (Vital Wave, 2014). The report indicates that 42% of secondary school dropouts are mainly due to lack of school fees.

Since the rollout of free primary education in Kenya in 2003, gross enrolments into secondary schools and University admissions have skyrocketed. For example, between 2003 and 2012, secondary school enrolment rates grew strongly from 43% to 67% while university admissions jumped by 28% between 2013 and 2014, with higher numbers registered in following years (Clark, 2015). Despite the increase in school and university enrolments, government funding for education in Kenya has not changed concomitantly. For example, government expenditure on education in 2017 was only 5.2% of GDP (UNESCO, 2019).

Furthermore, schools' opening schedules in most countries do not always coincide with times when families earn money, making it difficult to meet fee requirements in time. Most families also depend on relatives and sponsors to support with fee expenses, extending the strain in funding education to the wider community. For an average family in Kenya, a good amount of their monthly expenses goes to education. Even with the free basic education, there are additional expenses for materials, food, extra payments for teachers and exams, and several other costs that add up, making it more expensive than it was before it became 'free' (Collins, Cojocaru, & Zollmann, 2015). School fees are the major expense for most households and an important cause of concern and anxiety.

## DIGITALIZATION OF PAYMENTS IN the EDUCATION SECTOR

Digitalization of financial services using MMT technology has introduced flexible and user-friendly options for planning, saving and paying for daily expenses by most of the unbanked communities in developing countries. Different academic and government institutions have adopted a range of models for covering educational expenses. This has led to many benefits to the governments in terms of developing and accessing detailed databases, to telecommunication companies which develop new products for the growing market, school's improvement on their financial management capabilities and parents to save on travel and queuing time by making payments with a few buttons on the phone.

MMT technology started in Kenya in mid 2000s with sub-Saharan Africa accounting for over 52% of all live mobile money services by 2017. Mobile money has provided significant reduction in transaction costs, improvements in convenience, security, traceability, increased savings, and time taken for the transaction, hence reduced poverty rates (Suri, 2017). Digitalization of financial transactions may not resolve many of the complex reasons that keep children from attending school, but there is potential to help those families who struggle with the cost of education by providing them with better tools that can help them save, plan and make education payments without losing productive time or selling assets prematurely (Braniff, 2016).

Mobile and digital finance innovations have had positive impact on education by providing students and their families a range of options to plan, save and manage the way they meet educational expenses throughout the year. Parents can now pay instalments throughout the school term, save the time they would spend traveling and queuing at the bank to make deposits and schools are able to track payments and make transactions for services with ease. Different governments, learning institutions and service providers have adopted varied models of implementing mobile money applications for fee payments.

## Penetration of Mobile Money Technologies in Sub-Saharan Africa

A report by GSMA (2018) indicates that the mobile money industry added a record 143 million registered customers and saw over $1.3 billion transactions each day in 2018. This progress was a result of increased smartphone adoption in emerging markets that expanded the customer base giving providers an opportunity to diversify their services and products to meet the demand. The main contributors to the transactions were bulk disbursements and bill payments. The impact of emerging markets on the penetration of mobile money in SSA has resulted in providers moving towards making payments as platforms that will integrate a wider range of products and services to individuals and businesses (Pasti, 2018).

In SSA, over 60% of adults have mobile money accounts. The growth in the number of registered accounts, active accounts and transaction volume increased by 13.6%, 13.6% and 11.8%, respectively in 2018 (Pasti, 2018). The Eastern Africa region has the most developed mobile money market with about 19 times as many mobile customers as in the Southern Africa context where the sector is still budding. As the market in Southern Africa matures, there has been increased growth rate of 29% in 2015-2016 providing opportunities for investment. The banking sector is also penetrating the market through their agent networks and partnerships with telecommunication companies, which are the main drivers of mobile money (Du, 2019). The mobile money market is now open and countries in SSA are reviewing and implementing new regulations to open their economies to technological trends in the continent

In Kenya, Central Bank reported that mobile money transactions in 2018 stood at $38.5 billion having increased by 10% from 2017, which translates to $108 million mobile cash transactions per day. The value of mobile transactions was equivalent to 44% of the country's GDP demonstrating the role of MMT in the economy (Rolfe, 2019). Major sectors like financial institutions, health, agriculture, retail and wholesale traders have integrated mobile money payments into their financial systems due to their convenience and ease of operation. The growth trajectory is expected to remain strong due to increased access to affordable smartphones, competition between service providers and growth of online shopping (Rolfe, 2019). Kenya has remained the leader in mobile money technologies and enjoys a very wide range of options for transactions and a market that is open to new service providers.

The three most populated countries in Africa, Nigeria, Egypt and Ethiopia, have great potential to change the mobile money market but they have had limited availability and low rates of financial inclusion. In Nigeria and Egypt regulatory frameworks have limited the number of service providers hence the low levels of investment in the sector, while in Ethiopia insufficient internet connectivity, lack of consumer trust and financial literacy have been the major bottle necks. In 2018, there have been changes in the regulations and financial inclusion strategies in these countries to open up the market for adoption of mobile money services and products with over 110 million accounts expected to be opened in the next five years (Pasti, 2018). This signals the continued growth of mobile money industry in Africa over several decades to come.

Many studies have shown the impact of mobile money penetration in SSA especially the benefits enjoyed by inclusion of the unbanked communities. Economic stability of households through improved financial management and planning has promoted living standards and given the low-income individuals an opportunity to meet most of their financial demands with reduced constraints. For example, a detailed study on the economic impact of mobile money in rural areas has reported decreased vulnerability to hunger shocks and an increase in remittances received by rural households, which acted as an informal insurance to manage risks between them and their urban migrants (Batista & Vicente, 2013). Migrants can send money to their family members cheaply and fast to meet living costs such as education, health care, accessing government services and investing (World Bank: Press Release, 2018). Despite increased adoption of mobile money by most countries in SSA, their remains a significant gender gap between male and female customers mainly due to cultural influence and lifestyle.

## Adoption of Mobile Money for Education Related Payments

Mobile transactions have been adopted by businesses, governments and corporate institutions to streamline financial management processes and enhance efficiency in service delivery. In Kenya for example, public schools have been the last government institutions to adopt mobile money payments on a large scale after resisting change for so long (Xinhua, 2019). Safaricom has developed a range of services through their M-Pesa platform to present their clients with avenues to save, plan and manage their finances, making it easier for them to meet costs for educating their children. Safaricom provides business or pay bill numbers to institutions through which they can receive payments (Safaricom, 2019). Schools provide pay bill numbers (see Figure 1) to the students and their sponsors through which they pay the fees. They then receive a confirmation message via SMS, which serves as the receipt and confirmation for payment.

*Figure 1. Example of a school pay bill number*
*(Source: Safaricom 2019)*

Other major service providers like Airtel, Orange Money and Mobile Telephone Network (MTN) employ different models in providing mobile money payment services to institutions and government departments. For example, in Cote d'Ivore, the government entered into partnership with four service providers to launch a platform for secondary school student registration and fee payment (Jennifer Frydrych, 2015). Similar partnerships between service providers and Universities or the governments through Ministry of education have been introduced in Cameroon, Guinea, Ghana and Liberia for payment of examination, counseling and registration fees (Bustinza, 2018; Biztech Africa, 2018 ;Dusza, 2016). The impact of implementing MMT for education related transactions has contributed strongly to the improvements in education attainment, enrollment rates and management of funds by governments and learning institutions. Along with the successes, there are some bottlenecks retarding vast adoption of mobile money payment systems in some places.

A review by a leading international money transfer company World Remit reported that remittances by families and friends in diaspora helped keep up to 3.5 million children in school worldwide in 2018 (Antoninis & Corcoran, 2019). Remittances to SSA were projected to grow by 9.8% to reach $45 billion in 2018 while in 2019 they are expected to increase by 4.2% (World Bank: Press Release, 2018). Some families in SSA depend on relatives in diaspora and donors to mitigate the deficit in meeting education costs for their children. Because it is relatively cheaper and faster to transfer money internationally via mobile money that online transfer – e.g World Remit transfers take less than five minutes for some countries – people in diaspora prefer to send money for school fees to their family members back home or make direct payments to the school's account via MMT. Widespread adoption of MMT options has made international remittance faster and more convenient to many families, thus promoting education and keeping more children in school.

Besides payment of fees by students to their learning institutions, MMT has been used by the learning institutions to provide parents flexible payment options where low-income households can access savings and credit services and pay fees in instalments instead of lumpsum. Payment of salaries to teachers and other school staffs, as well as paying suppliers of stationary and other school bills is being done via mobile money platforms to maintain efficient financial management.

## Payment Models Adopted In Kenya

The implementation of school fees payment via mobile money in Kenya has been very slow despite pioneering the innovation over a decade ago. Public schools have been the last government institutions to accept mobile money as the main avenue for fee payments due to resistance to change. In 2019, most learning institutions in Kenya acquired mobile money pay bill numbers from telecommunication and banking service providers for payment of fees after succumbing to pressure from the public (Xinhua, 2019).

In Kenya almost any service ranging from buying groceries, fuel, public transport, utility bills to government services among others can be paid for via mobile money. Resistance to change by sticking to the cumbersome conventional method where students queue at banks to make deposits or buy cheques for fee payment has slowed down digitalization of financial services in learning institutions (Braniff, 2017).

Mobile adoption in Kenya has surpassed 100% compared to 80% penetration in Africa with internet connectivity above 84% penetration rate (Tonui, 2018). There were 47.6 million active mobile money users and over 200,000 agents in 2018 across the country. This provides banks with a large customer base who prefer mobile transactions that has resulted in over 300 local loan apps (Makena, 2019). The banks have partnered with mobile money providers to provide credit and savings services to the unbanked through their mobile money accounts without having to visit any bank. This has raised financial inclusion rate and given low income families avenues to learn financial management skills by saving and making payments over a period enabling them to provide better education and living conditions for their children.

Since the inception of MMT in Kenya by Safaricom through the brand name M-Pesa, the telecommunication company has developed a whole range of services to meet different customer needs both at individual and cooperate level. They have provisions that fit government departments like the e-citizen, tax collection, health and many other P2G services. They have created products for the corporate market to be able to pay salaries, taxes, fines and utilities via mobile money. By providing a pay bill number, any business, institution or vendor can receive payments for their

*Figure 2. How the pay bill option is accessed from the M-pesa menu on a phone*
*(Source: Safaricom 2019).*

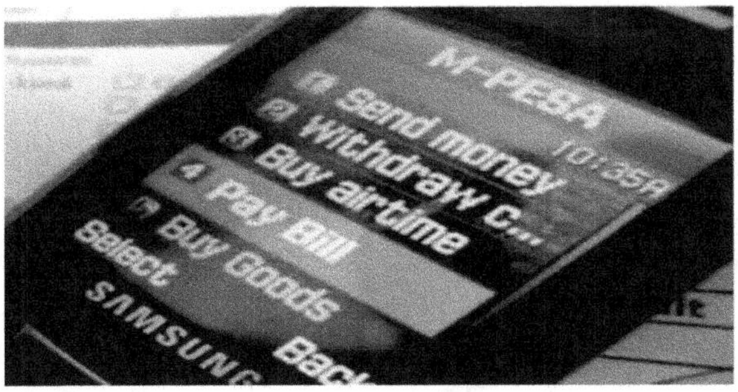


*Figure 3. Instructions on how to pay for school fees using the Lipa na M-Pesa service on M-Pesa menu*
*(Source: Safaricom 2019)*

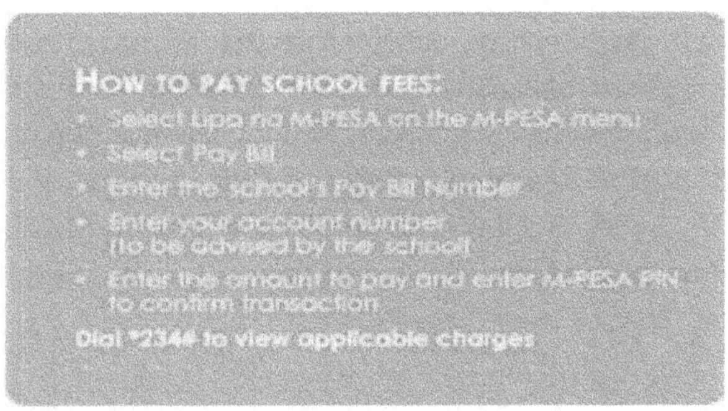


services from the clients (Safaricom, 2019). Figure 2 shows an example of how to access the pay bill from M-pesa menu using a simple phone. Most schools have acquired their unique pay bill numbers, which they give to parents and students for payment of all fees.

As an example, through Lipa na M-Pesa, Safaricom has provided its customers with avenues to pay for rent (Lipa Kodi), electricity bills, school fees (Lipa Karo), fuel, as well as majority of government services (Safaricom, 2019). Figure 3 shows instructions on how to pay school fees using Lipa na m-Pesa service. Other mobile money services by other providers on the market include Airtel, Equitel Money, T-Kash and Mobile Pay. Combined mobile money transactions by all providers in 2018 rose by 10% to $38.5 billion, which was equivalent to 44% of the country's GDP. This is attributed to increased popularity and easy access to loans, sport betting

(Rolfe, 2019), more affordable smartphones with features that meet customers' needs and an increase in mobile phone penetration surpassing 100% by end of 2018 (Tonui, 2018).

Service providers in partnership with banks have given low-income earners savings and credit services to allow them to save incrementally and plan for their financial responsibilities. For example, M-Shwari is a Safaricom product that allows the customer to open a mobile money account like a normal bank account with their M-Pesa account and save money according to their ability, access micro-credit loans and move the money to other accounts and transact with a lot of ease (Safaricom, 2019). Because income for most families is not regular and do not align with school terms, clients can save money and make several payments over the year to cover school fees, allowing for flexibility and increased access to education for children.

In 2011, Pesapal introduced an alternative online platform in Kenya called Schoolpay for paying school fees using visa, Mastercard, American Express or via mobile phones (Okuttah, 2011). Parents were enabled also to send bus fare, pocket money or any other transactions to their children conveniently. Pesapal has partnered with several local banks and Safaricom to provide an online service to enable schools to receive and track payments for various activities like sports, trips, exams, fees etc (Pesapal, 2019; Safaricom, 2019). After a payment has been completed, the parent receives a receipt, which they take to school as proof of payment. The money is first held in Pesapal's trust funds or that of the mobile provider from where it is transferred to the school's bank account. The school can track payments made from all possible avenues including remittances from abroad through credit card providers (Pesapal, 2019).

The mobile money model adopted in Kenya for education related payments has gained confidence between the clientele, government and service providers because of the success in other sectors. However, the model does not provide direct access to the school databases by government departments involved with education and service delivery to learning institutions. The current model creates a potential route for better management of data required to monitor progress in the education sector, which can be accessed through the service providers or school financial management systems. Having a national database for schools and students can help with planning and budgeting by the government to ensure equitable funding and support to the needy institutions.

## Bridge International Academies Case Study

One of the success stories of mobile money payment systems in Kenya is the Bridge International academies. The entire financial operations in collecting fees, paying salaries and all other transactions is digitalized and operated by smartphones or tablets. The school is managed through a custom-made cloud-based centralized system that can track all fee payments, expenses and salaries, thus minimizing administrative expenses and saving time. Parents can pay fees in advance for a full school year, term, or month. Families having trouble with paying for school fees over a limited time can be entered into the Bridge Financial Hardship Program where payments are put on hold until the end of the term when families are requested to pay the term amount (Leznicki, 2014). This allows households time to save and plan while their children continue studying.

Bridge International Academies was among the first corporate clients to have an M-Pesa account in 2009, making it also one of the first companies in the world to integrate mobile money in their operations. The institution prides itself of efficiency, accountability and transparency in their financial management and administration using their customized cloud-based digital system. They cite specific benefits of their system as (Leznicki, 2014);

### *Financial Transparency*

The school provides every parent personalized SMS reminders, bills and receipts so that parents always know what to pay and when. This ensures transparency between the school and parents and eliminates the possibility of students or school staff misusing the money. This also builds confidence and trust between the stakeholders.

### *Operational Sustainability*

School fees sustainability assures parents that the funds are used for what is intended. The payments and ensuing transactions can be traced in real time and financial statements can be obtained with ease.

### *Physical Security*

The danger of harm to managers, teachers and students is eliminated by removing cash payment/handling. Cases of robbery targeting school funds cannot arise because the entire system is cashless.

### *Education Accountability*

Financial transactions are automated using a custom app and mobile money freeing up time for academic managers to focus on other duties. This has improved operational efficiency and reduced on the number of administrative staffs required to run a school. There is more focus on the core business of the school – education of the students.

## School Registration Model In Cote D'ivore

A case study on digitalization of school fees payment in Cote d'Ivore was done in 2015 by GSMA which outlined in detail how the private-public partnership can be a great approach for streamlining fee payment infrastructure and improve service delivery by all players (Frydrych, 2015). The Cote d'Ivore model initiated in 2011 started by gathering all stakeholders to define clarity of roles, responsibilities and timelines. Secondly, a digitalized unique identifier system which identifies each student and school in the country was established to track which student makes payment to which school and how the funds would be remitted to the relevant school (The Glossary of Education Reform, 2015) This infrastructure made it possible for the government to enter into partnership with service providers to establish a real-time monitoring system (Scharwatt, 2016).

In 2014, the government invested in an in-house built application programming interface (API) which allowed the mobile money providers to access student databases in real time, creating a simplified customer experience with minimal complaints. The four service providers also provided over-the-counter mobile money services through local agents especially for the technically disadvantaged clients (Frydrych, 2015). The schools can access the database to see which students have paid their fees, thereby improving transparency, traceability and time saving. In 2016, 99.3% of 1.7 million secondary school students paid their annual registration fees through mobile money by eliminating cash payments (Scharwatt, 2016).

The Ministry of education works with all mobile money providers to ensure all areas of the country and customer bases are covered. The service providers have a central pool of funds for public awareness using posters across the country where students and parents can see them (Scharwatt, 2016). Every year campaigns are done to inform the public that payment of fees via the mobile money providers is open and provide details on how the payments can be made. The service providers also use billboards, SMS push messages and media advertisements to educate their customers on how to make the payments(Frydrych, 2015).

To ensure efficiency and continuity, a taskforce meets regularly throughout the year to discuss the planning, launch and management of the initiative to ensure its success. Each year, the ministry of education reviews the campaign process to draw lessons and identify improvements for the following year (Frydrych, 2015). This has ensured continued efficiency in service delivery, transparency in fee payment and improved funding of schools over the years. The continued involvement by the government in monitoring and managing the implementation of the system promotes the confidence of the public in the system.

## Benefits Reported in Cote d'Ivore

The report by GSMA highlighted the benefits accrued due to the implementation of mobile money payment system for registration and payment of school fees and grouped them into four (Frydrych, 2015);

### *Benefits to the Government*

Lost payments, fraud and theft of public funds reduced drastically as well as the costs and burden of managing cash and the risks associated with it. It allowed the Ministry of education to consolidate and update a national student database, which improved the quality of information and eliminated cases of double registration.

### Benefits to the Parents and Students

The convenience of mobile money payments allowed them to pay anytime and from anywhere, saving them time spent queuing at banks for hours waiting to make deposits and travel back to school to submit the cheque or payment slip. There was increased transparency and confidence in the system.

### Benefits to the Schools

Every school in the country can now access the national student database from the Ministry of education in real time and track registration and payments by their students. The schools now receive funding earlier in the year, which helps them with budgeting and planning. Minimal thefts and leakage of funds has resulted in schools getting larger budget allocations.

### Benefits to the Service Providers

Operators receive a commission for every payment made, making it an added revenue source for their business. The service also encouraged customers to reactivate their accounts to use for other transactions after paying for school fees. They also recruited new clients and expanded their customer base.

It is the author's opinion that this model, unlike that adopted predominantly in Kenya, offers additional benefit to the government and general public. This model allows central management of student and school databases, monitoring of school enrolments across the country, eliminating double or multiple registrations, provide evidence and data-based planning and budgeting and hence better service delivery and control by the government. Progression rates from primary to secondary to tertiary levels are easier to assess and provide information that can trigger intervention by concerned authorities. The government regulatory bodies can also protect parents from extreme charges that can be imposed by service providers by establishing relevant legislation and policies. Using the statistics obtained from the database, the government can also ensure equitable distribution of the national budget according to the need of each school.

## Payment Models In Other Countries

In 2016, the Liberian government launched a pilot program funded by the United States Agency for International Development (USAID) to pay Ministry of education and Ministry of health workers through mobile money. Lonestar Cell MTN and Orange Money partnered with the government to disburse the salaries. Mobile money salary payments received over 90% satisfaction rate from the customers, who saved an average of 33 hours and 1500 Liberian Dollar ($ 7.5) per month on picking up their salaries (Bustinza, 2018). This has seen an increase in private-public partnerships with government, banks, mobile money operators and other stakeholders to integrate digital finance to lower teacher absenteeism, increase children attendance in schools and ensure enough funding for schools. In addition, Lonestar Cell MTN has recently launched University fees payment product in collaboration with University of Liberia (The New Dawn, 2019).

The ministry of education in Liberia has embraced digitalization of fees payment where in 2018 they instructed that all public high schools collect their fees via Lonestar Cell MTN mobile money platform with the view to enhance registration and collection of data. The Ministry provided schools with unique Short-code identifier to be used for making payments. Through the process, the Ministry can capture students and school details such as school name, district, county, student names, grade level, gender, and section which are important for decision making. The schools are also allowed to access all legal tenders and display payments in those currencies (Spread the Love, 2018). This model allows the government more control on the fees being charged to students by schools and service providers as well as easy access to comprehensive data on the entire education sector.

In Cameroon, the Ministries in charge of secondary and higher education established partnerships with local mobile money providers for payments of fees. For example, in 2014 MTN Cameroon and University of Yaounde became the fourth university after Buea, Bamenda and Dschang to sign a partnership agreement for the use of MTN Mobile money ("MoMo" as it is known) services for payment of University fees by students (Bongben, 2014). Since MTN mobile money introduced such partnership with Universities in 2012, all public universities and secondary schools have adopted the services to improve transparency, consolidate student databases and streamline financial accounting processes.

In 2018, a partnership between the Ministry of secondary education and MTN Cameroon introduced payment of secondary school fees and related charges via mobile money (Biztech Africa, 2018). This was done to enhance transparency and traceability of fees collection and save parents the time spent in making payments at the bank. The involvement by the Ministry of education at both levels will boost the adoption of mobile money payment in all learning institutions and enhance the confidence of the public in the system (Digital Economy Blueprint, 2019.

There are several platforms that support mobile money payments for school fees in Uganda, although the infrastructure is still developing. People living in remote places still travel some distance to reach an agent although most people in those villages are not familiar with how the technology works. As an alternative, Fenix, an organization that provides a flagship product called ReadyPay power enabling off-grid households to access clean power by pay-as-you-go model, has introduced add-ons to support their customers meet the costs of educating their children. The solar power unit they provide their clients serves as collateral for the loans they provide (Braniff, Waldron, Foye, & Emmott, 2017).

In 2018, a new mobile payment platform called Kupaa was launched in Uganda by Mastercard, the United Nations Children's Fund (UNICEF) and the Ministry of education reaching 130,000 students up from 270 students in a year. The students register with an app on their phones using a unique identifier that is linked to their parent or caregivers enabling them to pay for fees and other expenses easily, securely and conveniently. The schools can then monitor and manage the funds in real-time and direct them where they are needed efficiently. This app also helps the school to track teachers' attendance and other performance indicators and enable the government to track grants and funding given to schools for efficient delivery and utilization (Staff Reporter, 2018).

It is evident from this review that every market presents different needs for mobile money services. Some models work well in some countries but not in others depending on various factors including regulatory frameworks, nature and level of involvement by the government, level of mobile phone penetration and network coverage as well as technological advancement of the economies. There is no single model that can be applied across all SSA countries. This gives service providers the challenge of understanding their customers' needs and creating products that will attend to them while remaining open for expansion and new innovations. The market is large and the impact in the education sector is significant.

## Benefits of Using MMT for Fee Payments

Digital transactions are more transparent and traceable than cash-based ones, and as such they are less susceptible to clerical errors and fraud. They are also faster and relatively cheap (Chiampo, 2018). One of the most successful countries in digitalizing registration and fee payment processes is Cote d'Ivore, where over 99% of their students paid their fees digitally resulting in enhanced cost efficiencies, increased operational efficiency, and transparency for all the beneficiaries - students and their parents, secondary schools, and the government (Jennifer Frydrych, 2015). Table 1 summarizes the benefits enjoyed by stakeholders in implementing MMT for education related payments (Nyakwawa, 2015; Frydrych, 2015; Leznicki, 2014; Braniff, 2016)

## Challenges Faced in Implementing Mobile Money Payments for Schools

The use of MMT is not without challenges. When payments are sent to school head's or bursar's mobile account, they must call the sender to verify who made the payment and for which student. Some parents do not include withdrawal fees, an additional cost that the school must incur. Some head teachers or bursars are tempted to use the money for personal expenses (Ndahiro, 2017). These challenges can be resolved by employing a comprehensive system that tracks and updates payments linked to a student database in real time. This way the school does not need to contact anyone to confirm payments.

In some cases, digitization initiatives run into resistance because they increase transparency and reduce the ability of middlemen to benefit from loop holes in administering cash-based programs (Chaimpo, 2018). On the other hand Braniff (2017) observes that the process of paying school fees requires a customer to first register for a mobile money account and then figure out how to use it, which can create some resistance towards embracing the innovation. Lack of familiarity with mobile money technology among rural customers has also slowed down the adoption of this technology but after learning the benefits, convenience and ease of mobile money transactions, the uptake by technologically challenged individuals eventually improves.

*Table 1. Benefits of implementing mobile money options for payment of education related expenses*

| Beneficiary | Outcomes |
|---|---|
| Government | • The payment of school registration fees via mobile money reduces lost payments, fraud, and theft of government funds.<br>• The cost and administrative burden of managing cash, and the risks associated with it are greatly reduced.<br>• Ministry of education can consolidate students' and schools' databases for effective management and monitoring of education quality.<br>• Easier disbursement and accountability of government funds to learning institutions. |
| Students & families | • Increased convenience because payments can happen at any time and from any location.<br>• Reduced risk of students misusing money due to transparency.<br>• Saves the time spent to travel and queue at banks to make payments.<br>• Low financial hurdle of paying school fees and other services by increasing payment options.<br>• Parents with irregular income can make regular payments over the course of the year with reduced stress.<br>• Increased opportunities for children to complete school.<br>• Opportunities to learn financial management skills by saving and accessing credit services. |
| Schools | • Access to real-time information from the government's student database for easier traceability and budgeting.<br>• Can closely track student registration and fee payments to improve management processes.<br>• Can receive government funding earlier on in the school year, which helps them to manage their budgets more effectively.<br>• Less theft and leakage of funds, thus schools can receive larger budget allocations.<br>• Increased opportunity for financial support from other organizations due to transparency.<br>• Saves staff's time spent traveling to banks to make deposit or collect salaries, providing extra time to focus on academic matters.<br>• Funds can be used automatically to pay for services, salaries, stationaries etc with proper record keeping.<br>• Reduces teacher absenteeism from school which translates to more teacher-student hours. |
| Service providers | • Operators can receive a commission from the government for each school fee payment they process, making this service a new revenue stream for them.<br>• Inactive customers activate their accounts to make other mobile money transactions after paying the school fees.<br>• Helps operators to recruit new customers to expand their market.<br>• They create complementary products like savings and credit accounts to support clients in planning their finances.<br>• New opportunities to innovate and invent new products and partnerships. |

Furthermore, low penetration in some places means that only few clients could be enrolled in a mobile money service to support a switch to digital delivery. In addition, rolling out digital payments for education institutions requires the support of mobile money agents and teachers to set up operations in expectation of transaction volume increases. A lack of mobile money agents may make it too difficult for recipients to convert digital payments into cash, rendering the payments useless. The government departments involved in a payments program may also be unwilling or lack the skills and structures to support a transition away from cash (Chiampo, 2018)

Lack of well-developed regulatory frameworks to control the market and protect customers from exploitation by service provides has limited the adoption of mobile money in learning institutions. In countries that enjoy a wide range of service providers and more than one official currency, extra services may be required to reconcile records from different suppliers and convert currencies especially in institutions without a comprehensive database that can allow real-time tracking (Braniff, 2017).

## Recommendations to Address Challenges

Some of these challenges can be resolved by having well-structured and clear regulatory frameworks in place. It is the responsibility of governments to create and provide conducive environments for businesses to be established and grow while protecting the customers from exploitation and exorbitant prices by the service providers. There is need also for increased awareness especially in remote areas where majority of the people are technologically illiterate. Diversification of transaction platforms and partnerships such as the collaboration between Safaricom and both local and international financial institutions have proved to be an effective way of extending inclusion to a wider customer base (Safaricom, 2019).

Deliberate initiatives by government institutions and ministries to implement more transparent ways of handling fee payment and transactions have been successful in several west African countries like Cameroon, Cote d'Ivore, Liberia among others (Biztech Africa, 2018; Bongben, 2014; Dusza, 2016; Scharwatt, 2016), and this can be adopted by other countries. A comprehensive accounting system linked to a database that contains details of all schools in the country and students in each school can bare increased benefits in managing distribution of resources by the government, obtaining and using statistical data for planning as well as enhanced financial monitoring at a national level.

## CONCLUSION

Mobile money has played a significant role towards achieving the fourth SDG on education for all children. Increased mobile phone penetration in SSA, partly due to access to affordable smartphones and enhanced connectivity to remote places, has been a major catalysis for the adoption and implementation of mobile money payment services in many countries. Although East Africa has been leading in terms of penetration and diversification of mobile money services, other regions like South Africa and West Africa are growing fast due to reforms in regulatory frameworks in telecommunication industry, which has allowed for partnerships between service providers, government departments and learning institutions to boost education for the disadvantaged masses.

The mobile money payment model adopted in Kenya provides a platform where the service providers establish business partnerships with their customers to avail customized products that meet their specific needs. The service provider gives an agent or pay bill numbers to business customers, institutions or government departments through which they can receive payments from their clients, but they cannot make payments for other services through the same pay bill number. In such a model, the service providers have more control on the payment platform and data. On the contrary, other countries like Cote d'Ivore have used public-private partnerships between the government department and service providers to launch a registration system for secondary schools by creating a national database for students and schools through with they can provide real-time access and monitoring of payments and student records for planning and budgeting. This model provides a large-scale platform for centralized information management by the government and stakeholders.

The impact of mobile money services on education has been felt by all stakeholders including governments, service providers, schools, students and their families. There has been increased safety, transparency, accountability, regulation and traceability in managing financial transactions in the sector. More children have got opportunities to complete school and teachers have saved on their income and time while reducing absenteeism, leading to more teaching hours. By extension, it is now easier for migrant relatives to send money to their families in the rural places with ease and at lower costs, which has enhanced the general living standards of many households. With continued investment in new technologies, products, partnerships and wider adoption of these services, SSA will continue to experience sustained economic growth and financial inclusion, which will eventually eliminate the persistent gender bias in the sector.

## REFERENCES

Antoninis, M., & Corcoran, B. (2019). *This one small change could transform education for millions*. Retrieved from: https://www.weforum.org

Antoninis, M., & Montoya, S. (2019). *The world is off track to deliver on its education commitments by 2030.* Retrieved from: https://gemreportunesco.wordpress.com

Batista, C., & Vicente, P. C. (2013). Introducing Mobile Money in Rural Mozambique: Evidence from a Randomized Field Experiment. *NOVAFRICA Working Paper Series No. 1301*, 1-46.

Biztech Africa. (2018). *Cameroon Ministry adopts MTN Mobile Money for the payment of school fees.* Retrieved from: https://www.biztechafrica.com

Bongben, L. (2014). *Yaounde I Pays Fees Through Mobile Money*. Retrieved from: https://cameroonpostline.com

Braniff, L. (2017). *Schools in Africa Aren't Taking Advantage of Mobile Money – Why?* Retrieved from: https://www.cgap.org/blog/

Braniff, L., Waldron, D., Foye, J., & Emmott, C. (2017). *Meeting Education Finance Needs in Rural Uganda.* Retrieved from: https://www.cgap.org/blog/

Bustinza, E. (2018). *Revolutionizing Payday: Mobile Money's Transformative Impact on Liberia's Public Workers.* Retrieved from: https://nextbillion.net

Clark, N. (2015). *World Education News + Reviews*. Retrieved from: https://wenr.wes.org/2015/06/education-kenya

Collins, D., Cojocaru, L., & Zollmann, J. (2015). *Getting an education in rural Kenya: Findings based on the Kenya Financial Diaries*. Zurich: Jacobs Foundation.

Du, L. (2019). *Can Mobile Money boost financial inclusion in Southern Africa?* Retrieved from: https://insights.som.yale.edu/insights/

Dusza, B. (2016, December 1). *Liberian Teacher ePayments: Stepping Stones to Inclusion.* Retrieved from: https://www.cgap.org/blog/

GSMA. (2017). Person-to-government (P2G) payment digitisation: Lessons from Kenya. London: GSMA Association.

GSMA. (2018). *The Mobile Economy Sub-Saharan Africa 2018*. London: GSMA Association.

Jennifer Frydrych, C. S. (2015). *Paying school fees with mobile money in Côte d'Ivoire: A public-private partnership to achieve greater efficiency*. Abidjan: GSMA.

Kaffenberger, M., & Braniff, L. (2016). *Paying for School: 6 Insights for Better Financial Services.* Retrieved from: https://www.cgap.org/blog/

Lauren Braniff, S. (2016). *Delivering on Education for All: The Role of Mobile Money.* Retrieved from: https://www.cgap.org/blog/

Leznicki, M. (2014). *Cashless Education: How mobile money helps Bridge International Academies deliver quality for-profit education for $6 a month – Part 5 in our Digital Finance Plus series.* Retrieved from: https://nextbillion.net/cashless-education/

Makena, P. M. (2019). *Kenya Mobile report.* Retrieved from: https://www.jumia.co.ke/mobile-report/

Matteo Chiampo, J. (2018). *How Bangladesh Digitized Education Aid for 10 Million Families.* Retrieved from: https://www.cgap.org/blog/

Ndahiro, R. (2017). *Digital Financial Services can reduce worries on how to pay school fees.* Retrieved from: https://www.uncdf.org/article/

Njeri, W. (2018). *Digital Payments in Zimbabwe Removing the Hassle from School Fees Payments.* Retrieved from: https://cellulant.com/blog/

Okuttah, M. (2011). *PesaPal launches school fees payment platform.* Retrieved from: https://www.businessdailyafrica.com/magazines/

Pasti, F. (2018). *2018 State of the Industry report on Mobile money.* London: GSMA.

Pesapal. (2019). Retrieved from: https://www.pesapal.com

Rolfe, A. (2019). *Mobile money transactions equivalent of half of Kenya's GDP.* Retrieved from: https://www.paymentscardsandmobile.com/

Safaricom. (2019). *Safaricom.* Retrieved from: https://www.safaricom.co.ke/

Scharwatt, J. F. (2016). *Mobile money facilitates 1.7 million school fee payments in Côte d'Ivoire.* Retrieved from: https://www.gsma.com/mobilefordevelopment/english/

Spread the Love. (2018). *School fees to be paid through mobile.* Retrieved from: https://newspublictrust.com

Staff Reporter. (2018). *Digitizing Uganda's Education Sector with Mobile Payment Platform.* Retrieved from: https://paymentsafrika.com/payment-news/

Suri, T. (2017). Mobile Money. *Annual Review of Economics*, *9*(1), 497–520. doi:10.1146/annurev-economics-063016-103638

The Glossary of Education Reform. (2015). *Unique Student Identifier*. Available at https://www.edglossary.org/unique-student-identifier/

The International Telecommunication Union (ITU). (2016) *Regulatory & Market Environment Digital financial services: Regulating For Financial Inclusion— An Ict Perspective*. Available at https://www.itu.int/dms_pub/itu-d/opb/pref/D-PREF-BB.REG_OUT02-2016-PDF-E.pdf

The New Dawn. (2019). *Lonestar Cell MTN launches University fees payment via Mobile Money*. Retrieved from: https://thenewdawnliberia.com/

Tonui, C. (2018). *Kenya's Mobile Phone Penetration Surpasses 100% Mark*. Retrieved from: https://kenyanwallstreet.com

UNDP. (2015). *United Nations Development Program*. Retrieved from: https://www.undp.org/content/undp/en/home.html

UNESCO. (2016). *Leaving no one behind: How far on the way to universal primary and secondary education?* Montreal: UNESCO.

UNESCO. (2019). *Education in Africa*. Retrieved from: http://tcg.uis.unesco.org/country-profile/

UNESCO. (2019). *Meeting Commitments: Are countries on track to achieve SDG 4?* Montreal, Paris: UNESCO.

UNESCO Institute for Statistics. (2011). *Financing Education in Sub-Saharan Africa Meeting the Challenges of Expansion, Equity and Quality*. UNESCO Institute for Statistics. Available at http://uis.unesco.org/sites/default/files/documents/financing-education-in-sub-saharan-africameeting-the-challenges-of-expansion-equity-and-quality-en_0.pdf

Vital Wave. (2014). *Digital Payments for Education in Uganda*. Uganda: Vital Wave.

World Bank Press Release. (2018). *Accelerated remittances growth to low- and middle-income countries in 2018*. Retrieved from: https://www.worldbank.org/en/

Xinhua. (2019). *Kenyan schools embrace mobile money fee payment*. Retrieved from: https://www.khmertimeskh.com

## KEY TERMS AND DEFINITIONS

**Digital Finance:** All products, services, technology and/or infrastructure that enable individuals and businesses to access payments, savings, and credit facilities via the internet without visiting a bank or dealing directly with the financial service provider.

**Enrolment Rate:** The quotient of the number of students of a particular age group enrolled in education by the total population of people of that age group.

**Financial Inclusion:** Availability and equality of opportunities to access financial products and services.

**M-Pesa:** A mobile phone-based services for money transfer, financing and microfinancing.

**Mobile Money:** Transfer of money between banks or accounts, deposit, withdrawal or payments done using a mobile phone.

**Pay Bill:** Cash collection service that allows an organization to collect regular funds from customers through M-Pesa.

**Transactions:** Agreement between a buyer and seller to exchange goods, services or financial instruments.

# Chapter 5
# Mobile Financial Services:
## Design and Development – An Unexplored Pathway to Financial Inclusion

**Alexander Maina Kimari**
*University of Johannesburg, South Africa*

**Eric Blanco Niyitunga**
*University of Johannesburg, South Africa*

## ABSTRACT

*The chapter explores financial exclusion, its causes, and consequences in society. The chapter found that the existing discrepancy in financial inclusion between the developed and developing world is driven by financial exclusion that makes it difficult for financial service providers to expand outreach to the poor at affordable prices. The chapter aims to investigate the role of mobile financial service design and development in dealing with financial exclusion. It was found that mobile financial services are promoting financial inclusion in various markets. However, few studies have been undertaken on the benefits of mobile financial services in dealing with the high rates of financial exclusion. The chapter recommended that to achieve financial inclusion, there is need for mobile financial services providers to take into account customer experience through the ease of using the phone interface. The chapter concluded that there is need for scholars in the fields of finance and economics to conduct research in the areas of mobile financial services and their role in society.*

DOI: 10.4018/978-1-7998-2398-8.ch005

## INTRODUCTION

Financial exclusion has become a major challenge around the globe more especially in the developing countries. The term has drastically attracted the interest of the world. For example, the World Bank Group effectively introduced several programs with the enthusiastic efforts to tackle the key barriers of financial exclusion by 2020. The literature has shown that, the barriers of financial exclusion are numerous, such as poverty, financial literacy, poor services, not trust, distance and safety (Dauda and Mamman 2018). Kunt and Klapper argue that the theoretical debate focus on a reason bear financial exclusion, which is not a recent phenomenon rather than a situation whereby people are having difficulties in accessing the mainstream of financial services over the last few decades (Demirguc-Kunt and Klapper 2012). According to Kempson and Whyley (1999), financial exclusion appears to be first to have been utilised as more broad sense to elude individuals who have compelled access to the financial institution. Since from then, various authors have respectfully contributed on how financial exclusion should be pursued (Anderloni and Carluccio 2006; Carbo, Gardener and Mol yneux 2007:21-27).

Financial exclusion is widespread in developing countries, as is evident from a recent report by the World Bank indicating that while bank account ownership is almost universal in high-income OECD countries, only 54 percent of adults in developing countries have a bank account (Demirguc-Kunt, Klapper, Singer and Oudheusden, 2015). This vital discrepancy in financial inclusion between the developed and developing world is driven financial exclusion that makes it difficult for financial service providers to expand outreach to the poor at an affordable price due to the high cost of establishing and running "brick and mortar" branches (Demirguc-Kunt et al. 2015). However, the growing use of mobile technology is altering access to financial services. It is changing and transforming the way people send/receive money, save, borrow and manage risk associated with the money. This means that the advent of mobile technology in financial services is a pathway that if used properly has the potential to bridge the gaps that have led to financial exclusion hence, lead to financial inclusion in our society. The global nature of mobile phones and the lower cost of data use have made mobile phones ideal in expanding financial services to large number of financially excluded population in developing countries where the growth in mobile phone subscription is phenomenal (Fanta, Mutsonziwa, Goosen, Emanueland Kettles 2016).

Literature depicts that Sub-Saharan Africa have seen rapid growth in mobile phone subscription since the onset of the millennium. World Bank report indicates that mobile phone subscriptions grew at an average annual rate of 954 percent in South Asia and 208 percent in sub-Saharan Africa (World Bank and InfoDev 2012). Fanta et al. further say that mobile subscription is extremely high compared to the annual growth of 46 percent in East Asia and Pacific, 23 percent in Central Europe and 15 percent in Europe and Central Asia and 12 percent in North America (Fanta et al. 2016). One can argue that the fact rapid growth of mobile phone subscriptions in Africa and in other developing countries makes the third world countries a "more mobile place" than the developed countries. The World Bank report says that in developing world, more people have access to a mobile phone than to clean water, a bank account or even electricity (World Bank, 2016). James (2014) highlights that the developing countries have experienced a high growth rate in mobile phones subscriptions. The developing world followed the "mobile first" development approach while mobile communications have added value to legacy communication systems and have supplemented and expanded existing information flows in the developed countries (World Bank and InfoDev 2012). Innovations in the mobile phone sector such as multi-SIM card phones, low value recharges and mobile payments have originated in developing countries (World Bank and InfoDev 2012).

It is important to note that before the arrival of mobile technologies, financial institutions depended on fixed lines or satellites to connect branches, ATMs, point of sale machines and other devices for providing services and products. However today, mobile data channels provide reliable and cheaper forms of data connectivity. This means that the probability of mobile financial services are promoting financial inclusion in our society. Andrianaivo and Kpodar say that one area through which mobile phone penetration affects economic growth is through its effect on financial inclusion by expanding mobile financial services to the financially excluded (Andrianaivo and Kpodar 2012). Furthermore, mobile money enables a reduction in the need for location-specific distribution channels such as ATMs and branches by helping to reduce costs of providing new services (Andersén, Hyytinenand Snellman 2000). The significance of mobile technology in enhancing financial services to the poor at affordable costs is driven by the fact that its major cost relates to initial development and other fixed costs, with very low marginal costs per transaction or per new customer (Honohan 2008). This mobile technology growth therefore have led to the rapid expansion of mobile financial services in developing countries leading to the promotion of financial inclusion in society.

The aim of this paper is to explain possible factors that make mobile financial services design and development to promote and enhance financial inclusion. The research question the paper sets to answer is: to what extent are mobile financial services design and development bridging the existing gaps that have led to financial exclusion, hence leading to an increased financial inclusion. The paper is therefore, divided into four main sections. The first section defines the concepts: MFS, financial inclusion and financial exclusion. This section also explains financial exclusion and its impact in the community. The second section explains factors that make financial exclusion a source of insecurity and instability in contemporary society. The third section investigates the role and effects of mobile financial services design and development in enhancing and promoting an increased financial inclusion. This section includes an investigation of the financial institutions and highlights their role in mobile financial services. The fourth section involves concluding remarks and proffers practical recommendations for policy-makers, as well as future research.

## DEFINITION OF MAIN CONCEPTS

### Mobile Financial Services

Jenkins argues that in the discipline of financial banking, there is no official or internationally accepted definition of mobile financial services (Jenkins 2008). However, mobile financial services can be understood as an umbrella term used to describe any financial service that is provided via a mobile device. Mobile financial service can be seen as any product or service a bank offers to its customers that the customer accesses via a mobile phone. This is what Chatain et al argue that the use of a mobile phone to access financial services and execute financial transactions (Chatain, Zerzan, Noor, Dannaoui and Koker 2011). It is transactional as well as non-transactional services, which for instance includes viewing financial information on a user's mobile phone. It also includes a mobile-based transactional service that can be electronically wired via the use of mobile networks.

Scholars have argued that a mobile money issuer may depend on local law and the business model and/or a third party such as a bank (Chatain et al. 2011). It is vital to note that mobile financial services is synonymously used with "mobile money" or mobile banking. Mobile banking is the application of a mobile device as a primary channel to conduct transactions from one or more bank accounts. These transactions may include payments from one bank account to other bank accounts. Mobile banking also offer a range of informational functions such as balance enquiries, simplified statements, transaction notifications and account alerts. Mobile banking is a subset of electronic banking (e-banking), which includes Internet banking and the use of non-mobile channels such as ATMs and Point of Sale devices (Fanta et al. 2016). The use of mobile money enables people to send or receive money easily and at affordable cost.

## Financial Inclusion

Broadly, financial inclusion is defined as the "access to and usage of appropriate, affordable and accessible financial services" (Klapper and Singer 2014:6). It is about development of financial policies that bring on board new talent from the disadvantaged communities (Beck and de la Torre, 2006). Financial inclusion helps "people manage their resources in a better way and building financial capabilities" (Arun and Kamath 2015:267). Scholars have argued that financial inclusion boosts the global economy by an additional $157 billion a year from unbanked adults (Allan, Massu and Svarer 2013). It taps on the estimated $380 billion fintech market opportunity to serve the unbanked and under-banked (Cheston and Rhyne 2016). Chauhan and Joshi (2018:25) refers to the inability to access financial services as the "financial untouchability phenomenon". They define financial untouchability as the "results from certain situations that prevents people to get financial services from formal financial system...and people are forced to go to local money lender who charges much interest rates" (Chauhan and Joshi 2018:25).

Accion International (2011:1) defines financial inclusion as a "state in which everyone who can use them has access to a full suite of quality financial services, provided at affordable prices, in a convenient manner, with respect and dignity". EIU (2014:6) further expounds on financial inclusion aims of providing "universal access to and use of, innovative financial products and services to traditionally underserved or excluded populations, so as to encourage economic growth and development in emerging economies and equip individuals with the tools necessary to improve their lives". Financial inclusion is therefore a redefinition of the global development agenda with a focus to individuals and communities operating at the periphery of the formal economic system also referred to as the unbanked, under-banked, poor or financially excluded. (Sarma and Pais 2011) argue that levels of human development and financial inclusion move in close correlation with each other at a country level . Financial inclusion efforts primarily seek to ensure that all households and businesses, regardless of income level, have access to and can effectively use the appropriate financial services they need to improve their lives (Mugo and Kilonzo 2017). Scholars like (Hulme and Mosley, 1996; Yunus and Alan 2003) have suggested that provisioning of financial services is among the most potent tools to reduce poverty and empower the poor.

## Financial Exclusion

Gloukoviezoff (1999) defines financial exclusion as "the process by which a person encounters such difficulties in accessing and/or using banking facilities that he is no longer able to have a normal social life in his society". This definition implies that a section of the population is discriminated against by the Government and private sector's ignorance of basic socio-economic needs. Kempson et al. further broadened the definition to include "exclusion by risk assessment and product design; exclusion through the cost of service relative to income; exclusion by ignorance; self-exclusion by people who believe they will be refused financial services, or may not wish to engage with financial institutions" (Caskey, Collard, Kempson and Claire Whyley 2000). From this definition, one can argue that financial exclusion is neither merely a geographic issue, nor is it related to closure of bank branches and the continued concentration of people on low incomes in specific communities. Financial exclusion refers to an "inability of less privileged to participate in a financial system of a country or developing process of building the country's economy" (Obaidullah and Latif 2007). Carbo, Gardener and Molyneux (2007) argues that financial exclusion refers to "lack of access to the mainstream of financial services". However, Martin (2002) financial exclusion is a process that prevents a particular group of people gaining access to financial services.

Scholars have said that financial exclusion is "the inability of some societal groups to access the formal financial system" (Carbo et al. 2007). Conroy (2005) on the other hand sees financial exclusion as a "process that prevents poor and disadvantaged social groups from gaining access to the formal financial systems of their countries". Mohan (2006) holds that financial exclusion signifies the "lack of access by certain segments of the society to appropriate, low-cost, fair and safe financial products and services from main-stream providers". It is significant to note that being financially excluded means households and micro and small enterprises, deal entirely in cash and are susceptible to irregular cash flows. For this reason, it is obvious that financial exclusion increases the risk of loss through theft and leaves people at the mercy of predatory practices from unregulated credit providers (Mohan 2006).

Finscope says that the most basic form of formal financial inclusion is access to a bank account (Finmark Trust, 2011). It is important to note that every person who does not have a basic bank account is hence, understood as being financially excluded. However, these people may make use of informal financial services. Banerjee and Newman (1993) have argued that a distinction therefore, needs to be drawn between being financially excluded and formal financial exclusion. They argue that at a macroeconomic level, financial exclusion can retard economic growth and increase poverty and inequality and that lack of broad access can generate persistent income inequality or poverty traps at a country level (Banerjee and Newman 1993). Majority of the poor people are locked out of the formal financial system; with little or no access to formal financial services that can help them increase their incomes and improve their lives.

On a number of occasions, banks have increased the sum needed to open an account and have become more selective in their provision of credit. Furthermore, many people can be excluded from financial services because of changes in family circumstances, such as illness or divorce, (Caskey, et al., 2000). They may also simply not having the required identity to open an account, such as a passport or a driving licence. They may also lack financial income to make the bank account functional. This therefore may lead to the financial predictable risk. Leyshon and Thrift describe a "predictable risk avoidance strategy whereby banks and insurance companies are more inclined to lend and give additional services to "low risk" customers, thereby often excluding those in most need (Leyshon and Thrift 1996:151). In addition, there has been a withdrawal of the financial infrastructure from poorer and rural areas within the past two decades (Goodwin, Adelman, Middleton and Ashworth 1999). Banks and building societies have closed branches in rural areas and in the less wealthy areas of towns and cities. Access to local branches is inevitably an important factor in participation in financial services and such closures have been linked to increasing financial exclusion (Goodwin et al. 1999). Despite the introduction of Internet services and telephone banking, those people who have been excluded by bank closures are often those who are least likely to have access to such facilities.

## CAUSES OF FINANCIAL EXCLUSION

Literature presents several reasons and evidences for financial exclusion. They include access to bank, higher charges, unsuitable products and biased market strategy (Sinclair 2001:21-41), low-income earning unworthy services (Kempson, 2001). Howell argues that low income, remote geographical areas, lack of financial literacy and unemployment constitute the main causes of financial exclusion (Howell 2008:2). However, for a person to identify a single problem or cause of financial exclusion is seems to be difficult. According to Demirguc-Kunt et al. (2015) the total number of financial exclusion approximately 2.3 billion people are financially excluded and the majority are from developing countries. However, low income and other denominators across the board are the causes (Anderloni and Carluccio 2006).

Scholars have argued that other causes of financial exclusion involves a lone parent cannot work due to family pressure; illiterates without educational qualifications; immigrant community and ethnic minority influence; and long-term unemployed (Farook 2008:27-29). Farooq further argued that crime or history of bad debt account that supersede with overdraft as a result of unable to settle overdraft which led to restriction to reopen another account, lastly cultural and religious reason (Farook 2008:29-30). The World Bank report says that almost 24% percent of people in sub-Sahara Africa are banked penetrators in 2011 (World Bank and InfoDev 2012). It also shows that the most recent notable findings displayed that the West African countries are less financial inclusion (World Bank and InfoDev 2012). This means that lower access to financial institutions than the sub-Sahara Africa average, moreover, disparities feature of the region suffer are Mali, Guinea and Senegal, are in lower ground of financial services (Muhammad et al 2018). For example, in Senegal, the recent CGAP survey 2013, indicated that the primary reason for their financial exclusion is religious issue and the others countries concern about mistrust or difficulties in an opening account (Demirgüç-Kunt et al. 2013).

## FINANCIAL EXCLUSION: A THREAT TO STABILITY IN SOCIETY

Fifty-six per cent of the world population is financially excluded because they do not have access to financial services (Ardic, Heimann and Mylenko 2011; CGAP 2010). In Africa, "less than quarter of adults have access to an account at a formal financial institution ...often due to the absence of business strategies developed by financial institutions that target low-income people as potential clients" (Demirgüç-Kunt et al. 2013:139). Chauhan and Joshi (2018) posit that when a person or community is financially excluded, it means that they lack capacity or exhibit inability to consume or use some or all of the financial services on offer by their country's mainstream financial institutions. A number of factors may contribute to a person's or community's inability to access financial services. Godinho and Singh (2013) bring to light an Australian example of physical exclusion of remote indigenous communities that have no access to the financial infrastructure within easy reach. Physical access here refers to ease of reach to finance institutions like banks, cooperative societies, microfinance institutions, Post Office savings accounts and automated teller machines (ATMs) and mobile payment systems.

### Social Exclusion

Financial exclusion may occur in an environment where the financial infrastructure is available but inaccessible because of the cost barrier (Accion International 2011). The user in this case finds it difficult to access the financial system because of high access costs, real or imagined. Ardic, Heimann and Mylenko (2011) argue that since poor people transactions are small but many, financial institutions find it difficult to provide such services. Imposing of a financial system on a community may create conflict between the culture of the financial system and that of the community. The conflict may be so high that members may experience indignity every time they attempt to access such services. Though Australia is a developed country, Godinho and Singh (2013) throws a spotlight on a major cultural clash between the government and the indigenous community that resulted to the financial exclusion of the entire community for most part of the 20th century. Only in the recent past has the government carried out a study to inform creation of a policy that would take into account the indigenous community cultural needs against the need to have the community financially included.

Finally, one can argue that the lack of skills in using bank services effectively may lead to law self-esteem and as well as self-isolation. This feeling may on the hand lead to depravation of social connections and alienation from with friends and even families. However, this deprivation or isolation depend on several factors such as history, status and life experience of people. It is further good to note that the severity of the consequences of financial exclusion will depend to a large extent on the prevailing level of financial exclusion in a country. Individuals who do not have access to mainstream banking facilities are at a disadvantage in paying bills, handling cheques and gaining access to credit and are often forced to resort to expensive alternatives (Goodwin et al. 1999). Access to short-term credit is also problematic without a bank account, leaving individuals at the mercy of 'loan sharks' charging excessive rates of interest on private loans, sometimes as high as 100 per cent (Goodwin et al. 1999).

Lack of access to a bank account also increases the cost of meeting some bills, particularly for utilities such as gas and electricity (Goodwin et al. 1999). Discounts are commonly offered to customers who pay these bills using the direct debit system (Molloy and Snape 1999). Anderloni et al. (2008) argue that financial inclusion may impact social inclusion in various ways:

- because some type of credit (e.g. overdraft facilities / credit cards) are already so much used in some EU region, lack may stigmatize;
- because lack of access to some goods impact access to the minimum national standard of living, lack of appropriate credit may stigmatize and reduce welfare level and self-esteem;
- because lack of access to appropriate credit may lead to reimbursement difficulties, it may increase household budget disequilibrium for long period of time and, finally, it may lead to over-indebtedness.

*Figure 1. Distribution of accounts*

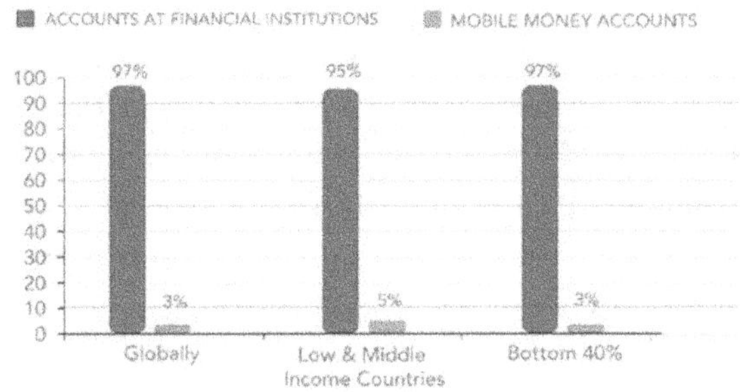


Hence, one can argue that over-indebtedness may lead to financial and social exclusion, which in turn leads to instability that leads to rise of crimes and insecurity in the society.

## Economic Consequences

Without savings, people have no means of coping with even small financial shocks or unexpected expenses (Kempson, et al., 2005). Moreover, those who keep savings in cash do not benefit from interest payments (Kempson et al. 2005). Those who keep savings in cash at home are vulnerable to theft (Kempson and Whyley 1999; Caskey, et al., 2000). European Union report shows that it difficult and mostly expensive for people who can only pay in cash, lack increases risk of being stolen and risk of poverty (Anderloni et al., 2008). This leads to time consuming and somehow annoying procedures, lack reinforce exclusion (Anderloni et al. 2008). It also leads to theft, which in turn leads to the increase of crimes in the society. It is good to note that if people are not financially excluded meaning that they have a bank account, Anderloni et al. (2008) highlight the following diverse types of transactions that can be linked to an account:

- Receiving regular (electronic) payment of funds such as wages, pensions or social assistance
- Converting cheques or vouchers into cash
- Storing money safely until it needs to be withdrawn
- Paying for goods and services other than in cash
- Paying bills electronically
- Making remittances

## FINANCIAL INSTITUTIONS

Cheston and Rhyne (2016) are of the opinion that the role of MFS on financial inclusion is overstated. These scholars have argued that though MFS small base shows striking growth rates, financial institutions still carry the heaviest load of the financial system (Cheston and Rhyne 2016). Chauhan and Joshi (2018) aver that banks are a great beneficiary of the electronic and mobile systems. Figure 1 shows the distribution of accounts between mobile financial systems and the traditional financial institutions.

Arun and Kamath (2015:268) are supportive of the policy of opening of "universal zero-balance, no-frills bank accounts" to increase financial inclusivity. A national financial inclusion programme named Radhan Mantri Jan Dhan Yojana initiative loaded with a debit card, overdraw facility, accident and life cover insurance policy per account was implemented in 2014 and 2015 by India's Government by funding the opening of accounts. This initiative was a great success towards financial inclusion in most of India but there are regions in the South where uptake was slower because of poor digital infrastructure and low levels of education in the population (Chauhan and Joshi 2018).

Rao (2008) identified that high interest rates and lack of transparency in microfinance institutions (MFIs) in India had a negative impact on financial inclusion. In South Africa, lack of demand for financial services was traced to behavioural lethargy due to the "perceived high cost nature of financial services" (Kostov, Arun and Annim 2014:268). In the case of Australia, the indigenous communities prefer face to face transactions and say "that money has been imposed on them from outside their culture and does not connect with traditional Indigenous knowledge systems" (Arun and Kamath 2015:284). Ulwodi (2017) study on financial inclusion and welfare: evidence from the Global Findex and Financial Access identified lack of regular income, low education, cost and distance of financial access as barriers to financial inclusion. These studies from Australia, India, South Africa and Kenya attest to the fact that literacy, culture, attitudes and behaviour are key factors on the financial inclusion success.

Scott, Reenen and Zachariadis (2017) posit that the banking sector in one of the largest consumer of Information and Communications Technology to achieve lower operational costs. On the other hand, mobile network operators (MNOs) are using their versatile networks to offer Fintech services to their customers (Muriu, 2016). This has transformed the way people bank, purchase, demand for service timeliness and mode of delivery factors that are unsettling banks. CapGemini, Linked In and Afma (2017) explain that although the banking sector still has an edge over non-traditional service providers in the areas of trust, quality and security, 50.2% of bank

*Figure 2. Kenya payment system throughput for 2018*

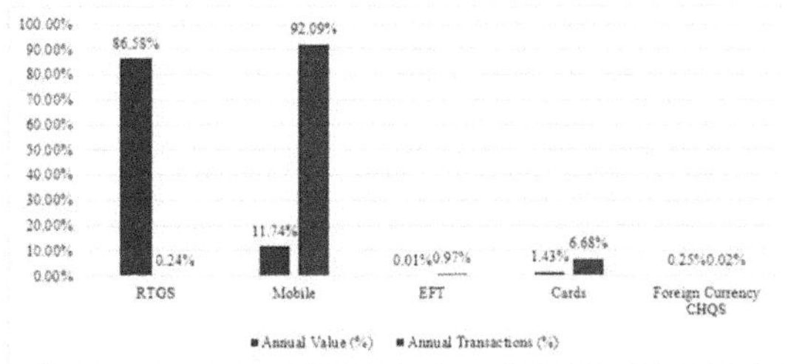


customers globally have already transacted at least once with Fintech providers because of their efficient service and better value for money.

Central Bank of Kenya (2014) has observed that banks are losing the monopoly as the only payment systems providers to innovative payment systems by non-banks. While banks are gradually enhancing the MFS adoption process, Says (2018) reveals new fintech entrants are daily bringing to the financial market innovative products that meet the ever increasing customer demands. Unless banks act fast, Fine (2000) argues that the hyper fast clock-speeds in MFS can according to Abadi (2009) obliterate the competitive edge that banks have. The objective of setting up the electronic Kenya Payment and Settlement System was to enhance the speed of the service delivery at a lower transaction cost so as to increase the financial depth of the domestic households and small and medium enterprises for financial inclusivity (CBK 2005; CBK, KNBS and FSD Kenya 2016). Britain, India and South Africa concerned with large excluded populations are mooting the plan to link their payment systems with their mobile networks (Guo et al. 2015).

Figure 2 shows the national average daily volume and value throughput of KEPSS shows that RTGS is indeed a Kenya Systemic Important System because although the transaction volume is a paltry 0.2 per cent of all payments, the value carried is 86.6 per cent of the total value (CBK 2019). To further simplify these statistics, low value systems carry a value of 13.4 per cent to serve 99.8 per cent of the transaction volume while large value systems carry a value of 86.6 per cent to serve 0.2 per cent of the transaction volume.

Mobile financial services on the other hand only entered the foray of payment remittance only 10 years ago and has acquired a market share of 11.7 per cent of value but 92.1 per cent of transaction volume (CBK, 2014). Nonetheless, both SIPS and low value systems carry equal significance in turning the wheel cogs of Kenya's economy. BIS (2017) quarterly review on international banking and financial market developments data reveals that while Mpesa daily trading value in 2017 was about 30% that of Bitcoin, Mpesa daily transactions were almost 30 times more than those

*Figure 3. Kenya income inequality*

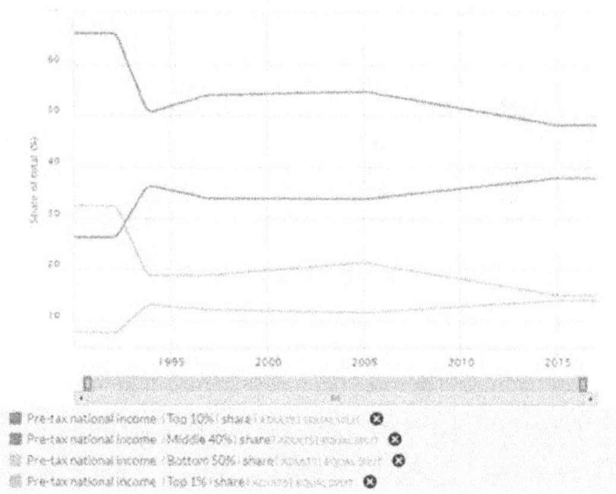


of the Bitcoin's global network. The Mpesa success is a pointer that Africa can leapfrog and use technology for develop innovative products for the world.

Mellor (2010) and, Orrell and Chlupatý (2016) posit that the utility of money is derived from its use to solve daily problems faced by human kind. Bendell, Slatera nd Ruddick (2015) however elucidated on the need to critically examine the societal and environmental outcomes arising from the way money is created and issued. Faure adds that non-bank private sector bank deposits (NBPS BD) make up between 96% and 98% of money supply the balance going for notes and coins. Bendell, et al., (2015) posit that notes and coins account for only 5% volume of monetary transactions in most countries worldwide. These studies show that the fiat financial systems in the form they exist today have created oligopolies that run the economic systems in every country making the rich even richer and the poor even poorer (Bernanke, Blinder and McCallum, 2005). Figure 3 shows Kenya income inequality and shows that in the early nineties, there was a policy that attempted to reduce the gap between the rich and the poor whose magic faded after 1995 (World Inequality Report, 2018).

CBK, KNBS and FSD Kenya (2016) reveals that 17.4 per cent of the Kenya population is excluded from the financial system. Though it is encouraging to note that the excluded Kenyan population had reduced to 11 per cent, the shopkeeper credit had a massive increase from 9.9 per cent in 2016 to 29.7 per cent in 2019 (CBK, KNBS and FSD Kenya 2019). The revelation that the poorer Kenyans sell assets to repay their loans while wealthier Kenyans refinance loans by borrowing more is evidence of the widening gap between the wealthy and poor. These studies give an irrefutable proof that fiat economic systems have shut out significant populations from financial inclusivity. Financial exclusion is an antecedent to long exposure to poverty that sooner than later yields social exclusion (Hanna 1991; Böhnke 2001; WHO 2016).

## MOBILE FINANCIAL SERVICES: A MAJOR SOURCE OF FINANCIAL INCLUSION

### Mobile Financial Services and Social Inclusion

Financial inclusion is delivery of banking services at an affordable cost to the vast sections of disadvantaged and low-income groups. (GSMA 2018:8) posits that "mobile money has done more to extend the reach of financial services in the last decade than traditional "bricks and mortar" banking has in the last century". For instance, GSMA reported that at least 19 countries in the world have more mobile money accounts than bank accounts and 37 countries have 10 times more registered agents than bank branches. A recent Global Findex report showed that "the growth in mobile money accounts which is particularly noticeable in sub-Saharan Africa, is a major driver of increased financial inclusion in the region" (Demirgüç-Kunt 2017). Mobile money was the principal driver of the increase in account ownership to 34 percent in 2014 from 24 percent in 2011 (Demirguc-Kunt et al. 2015). For example, the region of SADC account more than 20 million adults having mobile money accounts, mobile financial services are already proving important in the region (Fanta et al. 2016).

For instance, the widespread use of mobile technologies has created new channels, new instruments and new business models for providing financial services to people who have traditionally been excluded from the formal financial system. In 2009, it was estimated that more than one billion people in developing countries had mobile phones but did not yet have access to formal financial services (Wold Bank ,2018). To date, about 100 million people worldwide use mobile services, most of them in Asia and Africa and this group is growing fast (Data Report , 2019.). The potential to reach even more people with mobile financial services is considerable. While the scale of mobile financial service deployments remains modest in most places outside of a few pioneering markets, there are signs of accelerating uptake in several countries. In the region of SADC, for example, the number of people using mobile financial services has increased by 54 percent (Fanta et al. 2016). A large number of

*Figure 4. Hierarchy of consumer financial needs*
*Source: MasterCard Advisors Analysis 2014.*

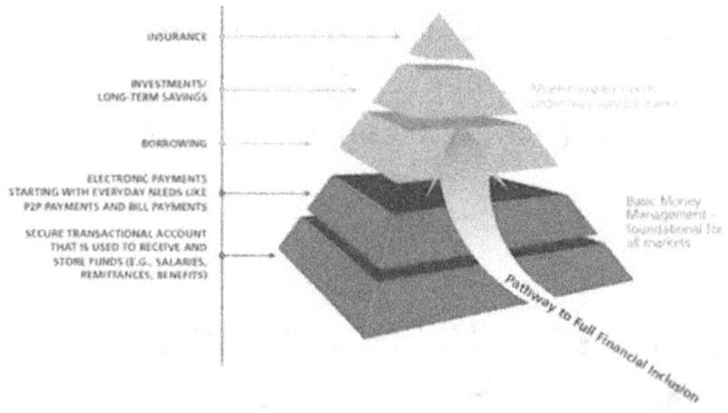


*Figure 5. Adoption progression stages*

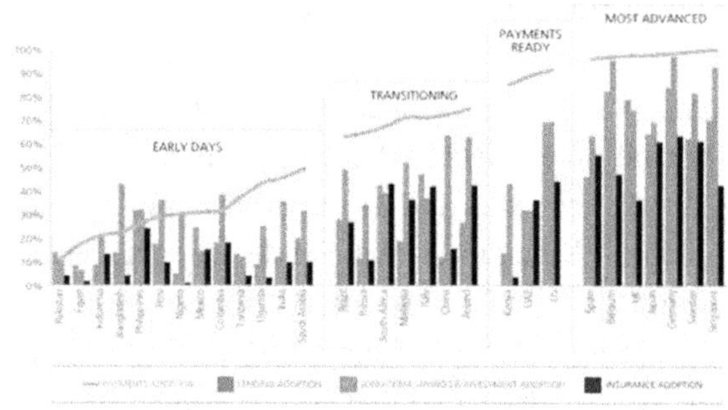


new deployments are also being reported and tracked by the mobile industry body, GSM Association (GSMA) (GSMA Intelligence, 2014).

The potential of mobile phones to promote financial inclusion is widely recognized, but some questions and uncertainties remain regarding the regulatory and policy environment required to develop its potential and the implications if it succeeds. Mobile phones have enabled mobile operators to participate in the provision of certain financial services in various markets, simultaneously increasing competition and raising issues of regulatory scope. It can be argued that the emergence of mobile financial services has achieved financial inclusivity or full integration into the nation's economic activity. Cheston and Rhyne (2016) argue that though possession of a mobile banking account is important, just possessing one is not guarantee to the achievement of financial inclusion. The utility of the mobile account is transforming lives of many people by solving the day to day problems of paying for services, borrowing, managing savings and investments with the account (Accion International, 2011).

*Figure 6. Overlaps in the use of financial services 2006-2019 (%)*

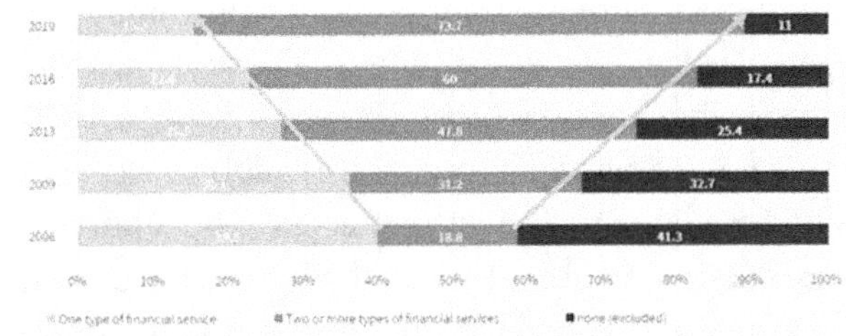


Jain, Zubenkoand Carotenuto (2012:7) have argue that mobile financial services has brought inclusion in a 4-stage progressive model. This model comprises of "payments, lending, long-term savings/investments and insurance" elements. Payment needs at the bottom of the pyramid are first met and once satisfied, the user develops an appetite for higher levels of services like borrowing, investment and insurance as illustrated by Figure 4.

Cheston and Rhyne (2016) approach the subject from a perspective of adoption from payments (inflows and outflows) as the first service then to other services like savings, investments and insurance. A country is considered to be at the low adoption stage if most of the population uses payment products. Jain, Zubenko and Carotenuto (2014) show that mobile financial services has brought progression in 4 stages. These stages include: early days, transitioning, payment ready and most advanced as illustrated by figure 5. It is worth noting that thanks to MPESA, Kenya is in the third stage - payment ready stage together with UAE and US.

## Mobile Financial Services and Advanced Technology

Mobile telephony has transformed the world economy in more ways than was predicted 2 decades ago. This power is dramatically demonstrated by Godinho and Singh (2013) findings that although mobile banking is yet to significantly pick up in the community because of cultural considerations, the mobile phone has reduced geographical exclusion because families are able to keep in touch, communities are able to record community events and handle emergencies better. The governments in third world countries have taken cognizance of the community's financial, geographical, social and cultural exclusion to make significant in-roads in creating a policy framework that will address all the community issues including indigenous money.

EIU (2014) Global Microscope 2014 study on 55 countries showed that the top ten performers among them Peru, Colombia and the Philippines had in common an independent, competent financial sector regulator. Those at the bottom like the Middle East do not have strong, independent financial sector regulators. Kenya merited the top score in electronic payments and its operability mobile virtual network operators (MVNO) policies had enviably been a great success. The report only marked Kenya low on consumer protection. Mobile financial services have been a major catalyst towards financial inclusion. Figure 6 clearly illustrates that Kenyans are embracing mobile money and digital platforms at a very fast rate, a clear illustration of inter-linkages between the traditional financial services providers, digital platforms and mobile money (CBK, KNBS, & FSD Kenya 2019).

Commercial Bank of Africa in partnership with Cannon Assurance Kenya are offering a mobile health product while Davivienda is offering a mobile micro-insurance product (Cheston and Rhyne 2016). Goland, Bays and Chaia (2010) have observed that because of the proliferation of mobile financial services in emerging markets, new banking services like Smart Money and G-Cash in the Phillipines and Mshwari and KCB Mpesa in Kenya and useful data on the previously unbanked are spreading like wildfire. Mobile banking has reduced need for banks to add many branches while achieving lowered cost of service by between 30% and 75% (Goland et al. 2010). In this regard, 96% of all Equity Bank transactions are executed outside the Branch (CryptoDavid 2019).

## CONCLUSION

The studies have shown that mobile financial services have made a major impact towards the achievement of financial inclusion for the marginalized communities of the world. Kenya's contribution to the global MFS is an excellent success story hailed mainly because of a competent friendly regulatory regime. While mobile accounts are a good starting point, they by themselves are not sufficient to achieve financial inclusion. Governments need to enact friendly regulation that will spur the private sector to develop cost effective easy to use solutions that speak to the culture of the communities they serve to build on top of payment platforms savings, investment and insurance products. Infrastructure on which these products are rolled out need to reach even the remotest communities of every country.

Though the growth of MFS has been rapid and its impact has been felt, the traditional financial institutions are still the pivot on which the global financial system operates. Though MFS transaction share is 92% in Kenya, its value share is just about 12%. Fintech growth based on mobile and internet technologies the world over is impressive. Banks have taken note of the Fintech threat and are rapidly embracing it by adopting internet and mobile technologies or buying off Fintech companies in order to offer greater convenience to new markets. Bank's adoption of fintech will certainly further enhance financial inclusion as long as the competitive environment is competitive enough to force them to keep lowering the cost of financial services.

Friendly regulation, vibrant banks, internet and MFS are certainly not the panacea of financial inclusion. There is a growing need to recognize the role of culture, attitudes, behaviour and community literacy as key ingredients to the financial inclusion design and development for a better world. To holistically achieve financial inclusion, it is therefore necessary for MFS providers to take into account customer experience through the ease of using the phone interface. This needs to include creation of customized menus to meet various demographic factors, ensuring the cost of accessing the services is affordable for the poorest and factoring in timeliness and a beautiful experience in the process of accessing these services.

## REFERENCES

Abadi, F. D. B. (2009). *Supply Chain Evolution and key elements of progress.* University College of Borås, School of Engineering.

Accion International. (2011). Financial Inclusion: What's the Vision? Center for Financial Inclusion, 3.

Allan, A., Massu, M., & Svarer, C. (2013). *Banking on Change: Breaking Barriers to Financial Inclusion. Barclays*. Plan, UK: CARE International.

Anderloni, L., Bayot, B., Błędowski, P., Iwanicz-Drozdowska, M., & Kempson, E. (2008). *Financial Services Provision and Prevention of Financial Exclusion*. Retrieved from European Commission website: http://Ec.europa.eu/employment_social/spsi

Anderloni, L., & Carluccio, E. M. (2006). *Access to Bank Accounts and Payment Services*. ResearchGate. doi:10.1007/978-3-540-46498-3_2

Andersén, A., Hyytinen, A., & Snellman, J. (2000). *Recent Developments in the Finnish Banking Sector* (No. 15/2000; p. 39). Retrieved from Bank of Finland website: https://ideas.repec.org/p/bof/bofrdp/2000_015.html

Andrianaivo, M., & Kpodar, K. (2012). Mobile Phones, Financial Inclusion, and Growth. *Review of Economics and Institutions*, *3*(2), 30. doi:10.5202/rei.v3i2.75

Ardic, O. P., Heimann, M. and Mylenko, N. (2011). *Access to financial services and the financial inclusion agenda around the world: A cross-country analysis with a new data set*. doi:10.1596/1813-9450-5537

Arun, T., & Kamath, R. (2015). Financial Inclusion: Policies and Practices. *IIMB Management Review*, *27*(4), 267–287. doi:10.1016/j.iimb.2015.09.004

Banerjee, A., & Newman, A. (1993). Occupational Choice and the Process of Development. *Journal of Political Economy*, *101*(2), 274–298. doi:10.1086/261876

Beck, T., & de la Torre, A. (2006). *The Basic Analytics of Access to Financial Services.* Policy Research Working Paper Series 4026, the World Bank.

Bendell, J., Slater, M., & Ruddick, W. (2015). *Re-imagining Money to Broaden the Future of Development Finance*. Academic Press.

Bernanke, B. S., Blinder, A. S., & McCallum, B. T. (2005). Panel Discussion I: What Have We Learned Since October 1979? *Federal Reserve Bank of St. Louis Review*, 228.

BIS. (2017). International banking and financial market developments. Bank for International Settlements Quarterly Review, 174.

Böhnke, P. (2001). *Nothing left to lose? Poverty and social exclusion in comparison. Empirical evidence on Germany.* Academic Press.

CapGemini, LinkedIn, & Afma. (2017). *World Fintech Report*. Academic Press.

Carbo, S., Gardener, E. P. M., & Molyneux, P. (2007). Financial Exclusion in Europe. *Public Money & Management*, *27*(1), 21–27. doi:10.1111/j.1467-9302.2007.00551.x

Caskey, J., Collard, S., & Kempson, E., & Whyley, C. (2000). In or Out? Financial Exclusion: A Literature and Research Review. *Financial Services Authority*, *3*, 5–100.

CBK. (2005). *Kenya Electronic Payments and Settlement System*. KEPSS.

CBK. (2014, March). *Effective and Efficient Payment Systems for Financial Stability and Transformative Development in Africa*. Caucus Meeting of the African Central Bank Governors, Abuja, Nigeria.

CBK. KNBS, & FSD Kenya. (2016). FinAccess Household Survey. Nairobi, Kenya: Author.

CBK. (2019). *National Payments System*. Retrieved October 11, 2019, from Central Bank of Kenya website: https://www.centralbank.go.ke/national-payments-system/# CBK

CBK, KNBS, & FSD Kenya. (2019). FinAccess Household Survey. Nairobi, Kenya: Author.

CGAP. (2010). *Financial Access 2010: The State of Financial Inclusion through the Crisis*. Retrieved from Consultative Group to Assist the Poor/The World Bank Group website: https://www.cgap.org/sites/default/files/CGAP-Financial-Access-2010.pdf

Chatain, P.-L., Zerzan, A., Noor, W., Dannaoui, N., & de Koker, L. (2011). *Protecting Mobile Money against Financial Crimes: Global Policy Challenges and Solutions*. World Bank Publications. doi:10.1596/978-0-8213-8669-9

Chauhan, J. & Joshi, D. Y. C. (2018). *Pradhan Mantri Jan Dhan Yojana (PMJDY): An Initiative towards Including the Excluded People*. Academic Press.

Cheston, S., & Rhyne, E. (2016, July 2). *The Business of Financial Inclusion: Insights from Banks in Emerging Markets*. Retrieved September 29, 2019, from Center for Financial Inclusion website: https://www.centerforfinancialinclusion.org/the-business-of-financial-inclusion-insights-from-banks-in-emerging-markets

Conroy, J. (2005). APEC and financial exclusion: Missed opportunities for collective action? *Asia-Pacific Development Journal*, *12*(1), 53–79. doi:10.18356/339ee7fc-en

CryptoDavid. (2019, March 28). *96% of All Transactions Are Happening Outside the Branch, Says Equity Bank*. Retrieved August 31, 2019, from Bitcoin KE website: https://bitcoinke.io/2019/03/96-percent-of-all-transactions-happening-outside-branch-says-equity-bank/

Dauda, S. A., & Mamman, D. (2018). The Contemporary Islamic Banking System (Jaiz Bank) in Tackling Financial Exclusion in Nigeria. *International Journal of Islamic Economics and Finance Studies*, *4*(1), 16.

Demirgüç-Kunt, A. (2017). *The Global Findex Database 2017*.

Demirguc-Kunt, A. & Klapper, L. (2012). *Measuring Financial Inclusion: The Global Findex Database*. doi:10.1596/1813-9450-6025

Demirguc-Kunt, A., Klapper, L., Singer, D. & Van Oudheusden, P. (2015). *The Global Findex Database 2014: Measuring Financial Inclusion around the World*. doi:10.1596/1813-9450-7255

Demirgüç-Kunt, A., Klapper, L., Stein, P., Bilandzic, N., Hommes, M., Taylor, S., … Sile, E. (2013). Financial Inclusion in Africa. *African Development Bank (AfDB)*, 74.

EIU. (2014). *Global Microscope 2014: The Enabling Environment for Financial Inclusion*. The Economist Intelligence Unit.

Fanta, A. B., Mutsonziwa, K., Goosen, R., Emanuel, M., & Kettles, N. (2016). *Policy Research Paper No. 03/2016*. Academic Press.

Farook, S. (2008). Social Responsibility for Islamic Financial Institutions: Laying Down A Framework. *ResearchGate*. Retrieved from https://www.researchgate.net/publication/238073328_Social_Responsibility_for_Islamic_Financial_Institutions_Laying_Down_A_Framework

Fine, C. H. (2000). Clockspeed-based strategies for supply chain design. *Production and Operations Management*, *9*(3), 213–221. doi:10.1111/j.1937-5956.2000.tb00134.x

Gloukoviezoff, G. (1999). *The Casse D'epargne and Households Financial Exclusion – Which Actions Should Be Taken and What Are the Prospects*. Retrieved from www.ishlyon.cnrs.fr

Godinho, V. & Singh, S. (2013). Technology Enabled Financial Inclusion and Evidence-Based Policy for the Underbanked: A study of Remote Indigenous Australia. *Social Science Research Network*, 15.

Goland, T., Bays, J. & Chaia, A. (2010). Global Financial Inclusion. *McKinsey & Company's Social Sector*, 44.

Goodwin, D., Adelman, L., Middleton, S. & Ashworth, K. (1999). *Debt, Money Management and Access to Financial Services: Evidence from the 1999 PSE Survey of Britain*. Academic Press.

GSMA. (2015). *GSMA Mobile Economy 2015*. Retrieved from GSMA Organisation website: http://www.gsma.com/mobileeconomy/global/2015/

Guo, Z., Kauffman, R. J., Lin, M. & Ma, D. (2015). *Near Real-Time Retail Payment and Settlement Systems Mechanism Design*. Academic Press.

HannaK. E. (1991). *Biomedical Politics*. doi:10.17226/1793

Honohan, P. (2008). Cross-Country Variation in Household Access to Financial Services. *Journal of Banking & Finance*, *32*(1), 2493–2500. doi:10.1016/j.jbankfin.2008.05.004

Howell, N. (2005). Financial Exclusion and Microfinance: An Overview of the Issues, Opportunity Knocks. *Microfinance as Pathway to Financial and Social Exclusion.*, *27*, 2.

Hulme, D., & Mosley, P. (1996). Finance Against Poverty: Volume 2: Country Case Studies. Taylor & Francis.

Jain, A., Zubenko, O. & Carotenuto, G. (2012). A Progressive Approach to Financial Inclusion. *MasterCard, Global Insights*, 87.

Jain, A., Zubenko, O. & Carotenuto, G. (2014). A Progressive Approach to Financial Inclusion. *Global Insights, Mastercard*, 17.

James. (2014). *The Risk Sharing Benefits of Mobile Money.* Working Paper, January 2011.

Jenkins, B. (2008). Developing Mobile Money Ecosystems. International Finance Corporation and Harvard Kennedy School, 36.

Kempson, E. (2001). Bank Exclusion in the United Kingdom. *Jon Carpenter Publishing*.

Kempson, E., McKay, S., & Collard, S. (2005). Incentives to Save: Encouraging Saving Among Low-Income Households. University of Bristol.

Kempson, E., & Whyley, C. (1999). *Kept Out or Opted Out? Understanding and Combating Financial Exclusion*. Bristol, UK: Policy Press.

Klapper, L., & Singer, D. (2014). *The Opportunities of Digitizing Payments* (Working Paper). Washington, DC: The World Bank.

Kostov, P., Arun, T. G. & Annim, S. K. (2014). *Financial Services to the Unbanked: The case of the Mzansi intervention in South Africa*. doi:10.5709/ce.1897-9254.140

Leyshon, A., & Thrift, N. (1996). Financial Exclusion and the Shifting Boundaries of the Financial System. *Environment & Planning*, *28*(7), 1150–1156. doi:10.1068/a281150

Martin, D. (2002). *Pentecostalism: The World Their Parish*. Oxford, UK: Blackwell.

Mellor, M. (2010). *The Future of Money*. Retrieved from www.plutobooks.com

Mohan, R. (2006). Economic Growth, Financial Deepening and Financial Inclusion. *Inclusive Growth – A New Challenge, 113*, 18. Retrieved from https://www.bis.org/review/r061121e.pdf

Molloy, D., & Snape, D. (1999). *Financial Arrangements of Couples on Benefit: A Review of the Literature*. London, UK: Department of Social Security, Social Research Branch.

Mugo, M. & Kilonzo, E. (2017). *Community – Level Impacts of Financial Inclusion in Kenya with Particular Focus on Poverty Eradication and Employment Creation*. Academic Press.

Muhammad, T., Dauda, S. A., & Mamman, D. (2018). The Contemporary Islamic Banking System (Jaiz Bank) in Tackling Financial Exclusion in Nigeria. *Uluslararası İslam Ekonomisi ve Finansı Araştırmaları Dergisi*, *4*(1), 24–40. doi:10.25272/j.2149-8407.2018.4.1.02

Muriu, M. D. (2016). Strategy Implementation and Performance of Mobile-Commerce in Kenya's Commercial Banks. United States International University - Africa.

Obaidullah, M., & Latif, A. (2007). Enhancing Islamic Financial Services for Micro and Medium sized Enterprises. *Conference Proceedings*. Presented at the First International Conference on Inclusive Islamic Financial Sector Development, Negara, Brunei.

Orrell, D., & Chlupatý, R. (2016). *The Evolution of Money*. Columbia University Press. doi:10.7312/orre17372

Rao, C. H. H. (2008). Achieving Inclusive Growth; Recent Experience and Challenges Ahead. *Chandra Shekar Memorial Lecture, I*(3), 16. Retrieved from http://isid.org.in/pdf/NLv01i3.pdf

*World Inequality Report*. (2018). Academic Press.

Sarma, M., & Pais, J. (2011). Financial Inclusion and Development. *Journal of International Development*, *23*(5), 613–628. doi:10.1002/jid.1698

Says, O. H. (2018, March 2). *Banking + Fintech Collaboration: More Important Than Ever*. Retrieved November 12, 2018, from The Financial Brand website: https://thefinancialbrand.com/71050/banking-fintech-collaboration-bigtech-trends/

Scott, S. V., Reenen, J. V., & Zachariadis, M. (2017). The Long-Term Effect of Digital Innovation on Bank Performance: An Empirical Study of SWIFT Adoption in Financial Services. The Centre for Economic Performance.

Sinclair, P. S. (2001). Financial Exclusion: An Introductory Survey. *Economic Journal (London)*, *95*, 21–41.

Trust, F. (2011). *Finscope, 2010. FinScope South Africa 2010. Finscope, 2011. FinScope South Africa 2011.* Retrieved from Finmark Trust website: www.finscopeafrica.com

Ulwodi, D. W. (2017). *Financial Inclusion and Welfare: Evidence from the Global Findex and Financial Access Surveys*. Nairobi, Kenya: University of Nairobi.

WHO. (2016, July 21). *One Health and the Sustainable Development Goals*. Asunción, Paraguay: World Health Organization.

World Bank. (2016). *Digital Dividends* (World Development Report No. 102725). Retrieved from The World Bank website: www.worldbank.org

World Bank and InfoDev. (Ed.). (2012). Maximizing Mobile: 2012 Information and Communications for Development. Washington, DC: World Bank : InfoDev.

Yunus, M., & Alan, J. (2003). Banker to the Poor: Micro-Lending and the Battle Against World Poverty (Rev. ed.). New York: Public Affairs.

# Chapter 6
# The Why and the Wherefores:
## A Case for Consumerism in the Marketing of Digital Loans

**Thaisaiyi Zephania Opati**
https://orcid.org/0000-0001-5470-8600
*Riara University, Kenya*

## ABSTRACT

*Though the digital loan industry is still in its diapers, the unprecedented growth of it is a concern to many stakeholders within the financial industry. In fact, the emerging apprehensions arising out of the process of lending, distribution, and use of the digital loans have become a cause for consumerism and consumer advocacy within this new emerging product category. Of great apprehension are issues relating to regulation, consumer privacy, and loan processing among others. With this regard, a survey was carried out in Nairobi County, Kenya with over 500 questionnaires being sent through email to respondents who fall within the middle-class category. A convenience sampling method was adopted for the study, and 243 were answered and returned. A further analysis was done given the objective of the study was to examine consumer and ethical concerns arising out of sale and marketing of digital loans. This chapter examines consumer issues arising out of the digital loan applications and addresses what the industry needs to do. It recommends the way forward in dealing with these issues.*

DOI: 10.4018/978-1-7998-2398-8.ch006

*Figure 1. Middle class pay as you earn (PAYE) to the Kenyan economy*
*Source; The Author ,2019*

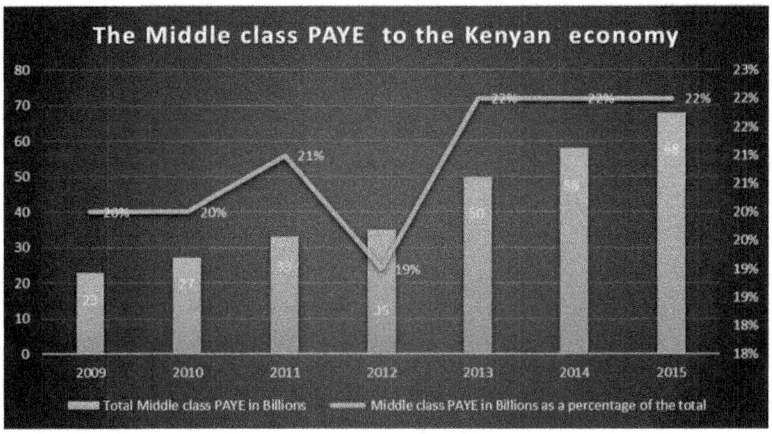


## INTRODUCTION

Africa is seen as the continent with the fastest growing middle class in the world (Deloitte and Touche, 2012) and a place to invest in with such phrases such as "African rising" becoming a clarion call to woo investors within the precincts of the continent. With over a billion people most of them within the dynamic youth bracket and an ever surging middle class, Africa is no longer "the dark continent" but a land filled with opportunities for all and sundry to come in. The Africa Development Bank in its bid to demystify the "middle class" within the continent has then classified the segment of the market as anybody with an annual income exceeding \$3,900 per year or who spends between \$2 and \$20 a day (AfDB, 2011; Banerjee and Duflo, 2008). In relative terms, the middle class can be defined as those individuals or households that fall between the 20th and 80th percentile of the consumption distribution (Birdsall, 2010) and the population earning \$2-\$13 a day threshold (World Bank, 2008). In Kenya the middle class is then construed as anyone among the population spending between Ksh. 23,670 (\$236.7 dollars and Ksh. 199,999 per month (\$1999) (KNBS, 2011).

It is in line with borrowing that Scott III and Pressman (2011) are concerned that that no group is more affected by rising consumer debt levels than the middle class. This segment of the population has become a darling to the financial world. This is because to the banking sector, the middle class is perceived as a cash cow and the nascent digital loan products are keen to create new products for them. Generally the middle class have access to high levels of consumer credit because banks have

*Figure 2. Percentage of the middle class residing in major towns in Kenya*
*Source; The Author ,2019*

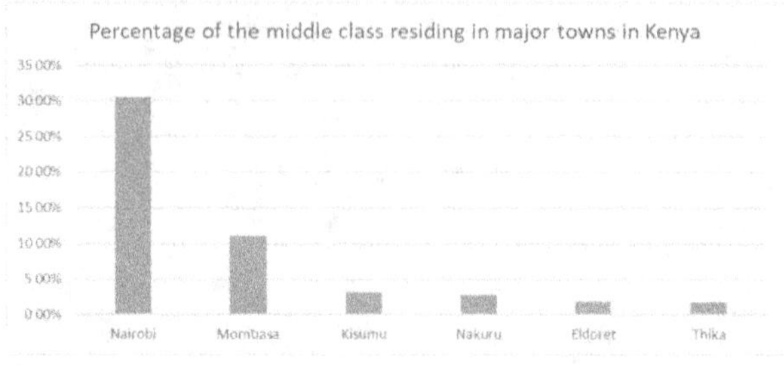


faith they will pay their debts and target these households with pre-approved lines of credit (Scott III & Pressman 2011).

Nairobi's population is estimated to have grown to 4,556,381 people from 3,138,369 at the last official population taken in 2009 (World Population Review, 2019). Out of this population Institute of Economic Affairs (2015) estimates that 30.1% of those who live in Nairobi, fall within the middle income group. Its appetite for the easy loans to fund their lifestyle has forced financial institutions to come with products to fill this void especially within the digital financial apps segment.

Banks are fond of the middle income group because in difficult times (job loss, illness, divorce), they can easily resort to consumer debt to fill the gap between the lost income and necessary household expenses (Scott III & Pressman 2011), a profitable catch to those in financial sector. Their contribution to the to the Kenyan GDP is estimated to be at 20% (IEA 2015) and about 44.9% of the Kenyan population, or around 17.3 million Kenyans, are in the middle class, up from 24% in 2011 (AfDB 2013; Business Today, 2015; Horn Affairs, 2015; KNBS, 2011).

Commercially, banks have to turn to the middle class because the wealthy apparently rarely accumulate significant consumer debt and they normally have savings to weather difficult economic times (Scott III & Pressman, 2011). Hurwitz and Luiz (2007) subsequently admits the rapidly emerging African elite and urban middle class, have altered the economic landscape and left companies fighting for a piece of this new market. It is this segment of the market that is being perceived to be a fertile ground for loans given their craving for easy and quick loans. Scott III and Pressman (2011) conclude that since the poor have less access to consumer credit, banks do not consider them as the debt becomes problematic to them when it is accumulated to large amounts.

*Figure 3. Middle class differentiation in Africa source*
*Source; The Author ,2019*

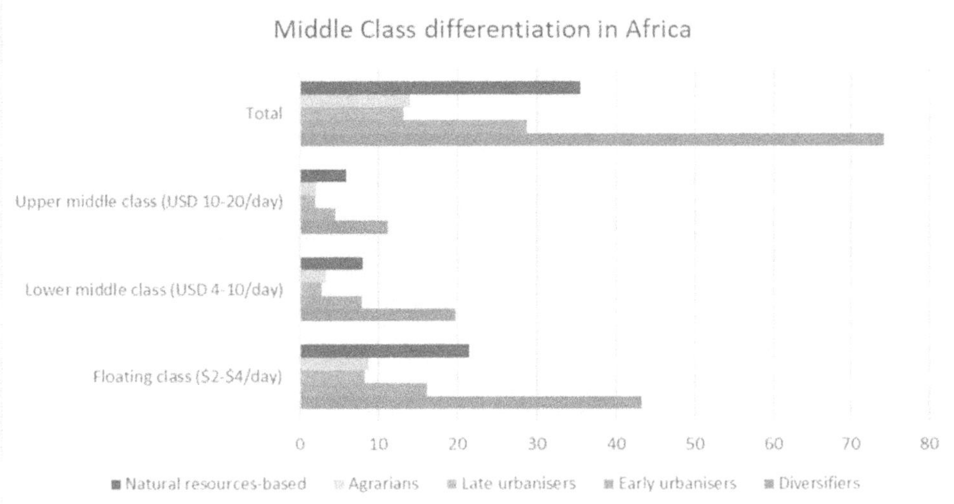


The easy access to mobile smart phones among the middle class has aided the uptake of digital loans. As such the innovation of new products such as digital loans within the financial sector has ushered in new ways of conducting financial transactions but mainly the development of new smart phones has supported the onslaught. This means that banks and other service providers have been forced to embrace mobile money technology (MMT) as a tactic of maintaining customer loyalty and increasing their market share (Oromo, 2015). The maturity of Information Technology (I.T) within the country has then led to development of Financial Apps that have redefined how the financial institutions attract, deal, and retain their customers. In the last quarter of 2016, world MMT inclusive of cash transfers, bill payment, and bulk disbursements, totaled over $22 billion, compared to $96.5 million a decade before (GSMA 2017b), indicating a whopping growth of 227.98%.

Namunwa (2019) explains that Kenya has been on the lead continent-wise in terms of smartphone penetration and internet usage utilizing the phone as the key to most transactions and activities. Kenya also boasts of having a 91% penetration of mobile subscriptions compared to Africa's 80% (Namunwa, 2019). The Communication Commission of Kenya Survey indicates a Mobile penetration rate at 76.2% in Nairobi the highest in the country depicted by the table 1.

Merritt (2010), acknowledges that the explosion MMT providers, including telecom firms, money transmitters, and technology developers and service providers, is motivation behind the development of innovative payment schemes for conducting mobile financial transactions. The advent of these digital loans has renovated the

*Table 1. Mobile phone, computer and internet penetration in Kenya*

| Town | Mobile Phone | Computer | Internet | Total Population |
|---|---|---|---|---|
| Nairobi | 76.20% | 32.70% | 28.30% | 3,024,059 |
| Central | 74% | 9.30% | 7.10% | 4,111,046 |
| Coast | 50.70% | 10.30% | 8.40% | 3,293,639 |
| Eastern | 64.20% | 6.60% | 4.90% | 4,017,958 |
| North Eastern | 41.10% | 3.80% | 3.60% | 1,228,945 |
| Nyanza | 57.30% | 7.80% | 5.80% | 4,629,954 |
| Rift Valley | 58.00% | 6.10% | 4.70% | 10,217,921 |
| Western | 49.50% | 3% | 1.50% | 4,045,792 |
| **Place of Residence** | | | | |
| Rural | 55.00% | 4.30% | 3.40% | 24,730,955 |
| Urban | 71.90% | 21.10% | 16.60% | 9,838,358 |
| **Sex** | | | | |
| Male | 60.80% | 10% | 8.40% | 17,082,230 |
| Female | 58.90% | 8.20% | 6.00% | 17,487,083 |

Source ; Kenya National Bureau of Statistics, 2019

market for credit and loans in Kenya, given the new product offerings within the market with that appeal. The growth in network coverage especially the 3G network coverage, for instance, has increased from 67% in 2014 to 85% in 2017, with a bigger proliferation of 4G, now reaching more than a third of the population has been a key driver of mobile related transactions (Namunwa, 2019).

Growth in network coverage has also been driven by accessibility, through mobile providers and new internet services providers which have provided more affordable internet solutions than is currently offered by Kenyan telcos. There are currently 47.6 million active mobile money accounts which accounted for a transaction value of $3.6 billion in 2018 alone; accessed through more than 200,000 agents (Namunwa, 2019). As such banks in Kenya have quickly adopted and provided digital offerings to the market in parallel to the consumer some of whom are not members or customer of the respective banks. Telecom firms, on the other hand, have contrasting inducements for engaging in financial services, explicitly, the ability to increase revenue from voice services by the addition of data transmissions, particularly in developed countries where mobile markets are reaching permeation levels (Bourreau & Verdier 2010).

This highlights the impact of the 11 year old innovation pioneered by *M-pesa* in driving financial inclusion and the race to turn mobile phones into banks for the unbanked. Actually according to an online survey done by this research between done 243 respondents were able to respond to the questionnaire. To cement the idea that digital loans were gaining preference, 12.3% percent indicated they strongly preferred digital loans to bank loans while 37.9 & agreed with the notion. On the

*Figure 4. Preference of mobile loan to bank loans (Field Study, 2019)*

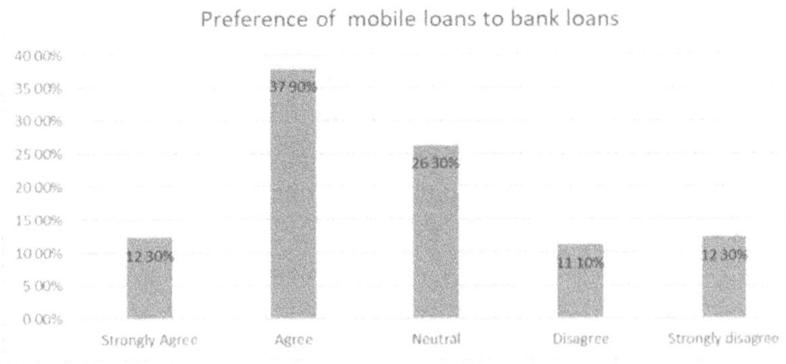


other hand 12.3% strongly disagreed as 11.1% disagreed preferring to get a loan from the bank, only 12.1per cent took a non-committal position.

Consequently Merritt (2010) insists that the growing ubiquity of MMT has the potential to extend even more financial services to unbanked people throughout the world. In reality few countries such as Philippines, Afghanistan and Uganda have tip toed towards that direction and many are still fidgeting with the idea. In some cases these gray areas in "regulation" have become a proxy for a growing business conflict between Mobile network operators (MNO) and banks which should take the lead (and thus the profits) in mobile money deployments (Rea and Nelms 2017). Consequently, as discussed early the adoption of Mobile Money Transfer (MMT) services created new products with a semblance of traditional banking albeit with online genes. These include opted loans services and overdrafts as part of their portfolio with customers phone serving as an active bank account.

Original mobile banking was specifically wired to target the unbanked population in rural and hard to reach areas (James, Odiek & Douglas, 2014) and undeniably these customers have embraced the use of their phones for different transactions such as making loan repayment and paying bills (Kirui, Okello, Nyikal and Njiraini 2013). However even for the banked among the wider population the MMT has become quite a critical tool in transaction in the financial sector. In fact *Safaricom*, a pioneer company in Kenya mobile transactions has created a platform that uses MMT to assist payments for enterprise in Kenyan business. This has brought on board enterprises and corporates who find the services useful in achieving their strategic goals including safety and traceable verifiable accounts. But core of the onslaught - the purview of this chapter- has to deal with mobile loans and the consumer issues arising due to the deployment of the service. These developments have led to a dash for banks to comply with the intermittent tech desired loans products from the market.

As a result James, Odiek and Douglas, (2014) found out that the stiff competition in Kenya's financial sector is forcing institutions into adopting new forms of technology to reduce the costs of doing business and widen customer outreach for enhanced profitability. Digital lending is particularly prevalent in low income countries and emerging markets, where the expansion of digital channels has enabled entire segments of the population to access credit and other financial services which they previously could not (International Financial Consumer Protection Organisation [FinCoNet], 2017).

## HISTORY OF DIGITAL LOANS IN KENYA

Accordingly Gubbins & Totolo (2016) intimated that mobile phones have an identity-linked digital footprints, automated credit scoring, agent networks and credit information sharing - the building blocks of digital credit - have enabled providers to deliver loans quickly and at a large scale. Kirui, et al (2013) are quick to concur that MMT has a clear edge over banks especially because it is fast and cost-effective. Putting this in perspective, only 700,000 people in Kenya had a personal bank loan when M-Shwari was launched in November 2012, and less than half this number (310,000) had loans from micro-finance institutions (FinAcess 2013).

Evidently, Bourreau and Verdier (2010) attest that currently Telecom firms take on the opportune and have dissimilar incentives for engaging in MMT, explicitly, to spike revenue from diminishing voice returns by complimenting it with MMT transmissions, predominantly in developed countries where mobile markets are reaching saturation levels. Mshwari was the first digital loan and saving product in the Kenyan Market, thus it made it easier for the larger unbanked population to access loans through their mobile phones, ideally M-Shwari seems to have benefitted from a first-mover advantage (Totolo, 2018) and established its foot prints in the market.

M-Shwari (meaning 'calm' or "everything is alright" in Kiswahili) is a combined savings and loans product launched through a collaboration between the Commercial Bank of Africa (CBA) and Safaricom (Cook, Tamara McKay &Claudia 2015). The M-Shwari account is issued by CBA but must be linked to an *M-Pesa* mobile money account provided by Safaricom. The only way to deposit into, or withdraw from, M-Shwari is via the *M-* wallet. Today, it has more than twice as many unique borrowers as its closest competitor, KCB *M-Pesa.* Both services are offered through Safaricom's *M-Pesa* platform — Kenya's largest telecommunication and mobile solution provider — and reach a network of customers that is far higher than any individual bank or FinTech can reach. Nevertheless, customers today can choose between plethoras of solutions.

*Figure 5. Kenyan Banks Adoption of Digital Lending by Gubbins, P. & Totolo, E. (2018) Digital credit in Kenya: Evidence from demand-side surveys. Nairobi, Kenya: FSD Kenya.*

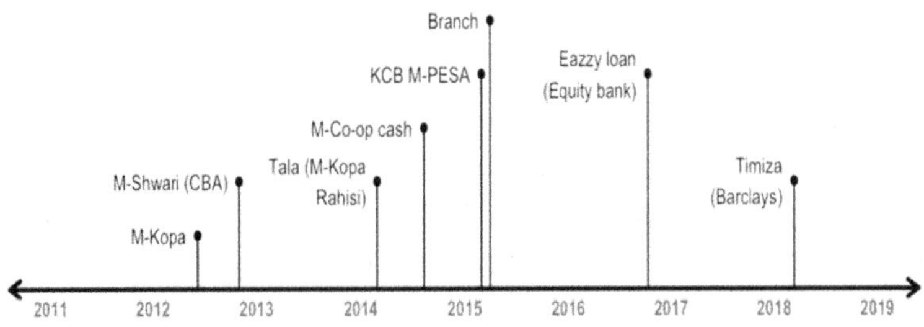


While M-Shwari is the most well-known among these types of lenders, there are several digital loans platform available to the Kenyan consumers. Many FinTechs have entered the market too, they include Tala, Saida Branch, Okash and Timiza among others. Inspired by its success in Kenya, in 2016, CBA took the M-Shwari product to three other African countries within its network, and through its partners on the continent (Totolo, 2018). In May 2014, CBA launched a variant of its M-Shwari product through a partnership with Vodacom in Tanzania (FSD Kenya & FSD Africa).

Most of these apps are downloaded from the Google play store, link the app to their social media accounts (e.g., Facebook) on their phone, and grant permission for the app to use social media data, GPS data, SMS and call logs, contact lists, and handset details from their phone (Kaffenberger & Chege 2016). Though the sensitive information is often used wrongly, the analysis of this data becomes the critical component of lending to customer who have no collateral except the information on the handset. It is with ease that these analytics use digital providers like Branch employ the use algorithms to analyze these data and determine a credit score and loan size (Kaffenberger & Chege 2016). Totolo (2018) is quick to point out that Kenya's three largest banks (Kenya Commercial Bank, Equity Bank, and Co-operative Bank) have since launched their own digital credit solutions since 2016, either by partnering with Safaricom (e.g., KCB), establishing an independent virtual mobile network operator (e.g., Equity's Equitel) or developing a standalone smartphone app (e.g., Cooperative Bank's M-Coop Cash).

Digital loans are instant since loan-eligibility decisions are automated based on a set of rules applied to available data, and not on human judgment applied on a case by case basis (Gubbins & Totolo 2016). The Mjiajiri (self-employed) model, for example, has elements that are similar to those of a pyramid scheme. It requires users to pay a KES 200 (an equivalent of two dollars with the current exchange rate) initial registration fee, after which users earn commissions of KES 40 for recruiting others to register for loan access; the user's available loan size increases as he or she recruits more members (Kaffenberger & Chege 2016). Micromobile on the other hand links lending to future payrolls and lends up to 50% of a borrower's monthly salary. This model is similar to payday lending in the United States, which often results in a debt cycle where the high-fee, short-term nature of the loans means customers must continue borrowing to pay off previous loans and associated fees (Gubbins & Totolo, 2016). Lal and Sachdev (2015) found out that *M-Pesa* service was poorly communicated and marketed to consumers in South Africa and as a result there was poor understanding and lack of trust in the service. In addition the systems for processing registrations were sluggish and undependable creating the need for a lengthy registration process eventually contributing to a weak adoption (Lal and Sachdev, 2015)

Consumer related issues have arisen as the digital loans pick, the concern for a framework to control and regulate this emergent trend is far from being complete. In essence while these providers seems to be offering an essential service, the ethical and consumer concerns are now towering. With the enactment of controlled interest rate bill, the reduced interest rate margins are forcing lenders to exploit other sources of income so as to maintain the required returns while at the same time cover the other operational costs (Ochenge & Tiriongo 2018), the challenge remains maintaining consumer –oriented focus. Given that another distinguishing factor of digital credit is that information, loan disbursements and repayments are managed remotely, without the need for customers to visit bank branches (Gubbins and Totolo 2016), the consumer privacy is of primary concern to regulators such as the Central Bank of Kenya. Ideally in most cases the interest regime is higher than the normal loans offered by the bank, the perception from the organized financial sector is that of a parasite.

## CONSUMER ADOPTION OF MMT

Chang, (2003) indicates that the rational decision approach can be useful for analyzing early adopters of new technology as they are usually tech-savvy users. As a result Sachdev and Lal (2015) believe that MMT are being deployed rapidly across emerging markets as a key tool to further the goal of financial inclusion. Chang, (2003) advocates for rational decision approach to be more in scrutinizing early adopters of new technology as they are usually tech-savvy users. Though the work of Robertson and Myers (2004) publicized that customers subliminally go through five stages in the process of new product adoption or service. Wan et al. (2005) research condensed psychological factors influencing customers' adoption of banking channels in Hong Kong as the ease of use, transaction security, transaction accuracy,

*Figure 6. KCB M-Pesa Adoption (KCB Bank Financial Reports 2014-2018)*

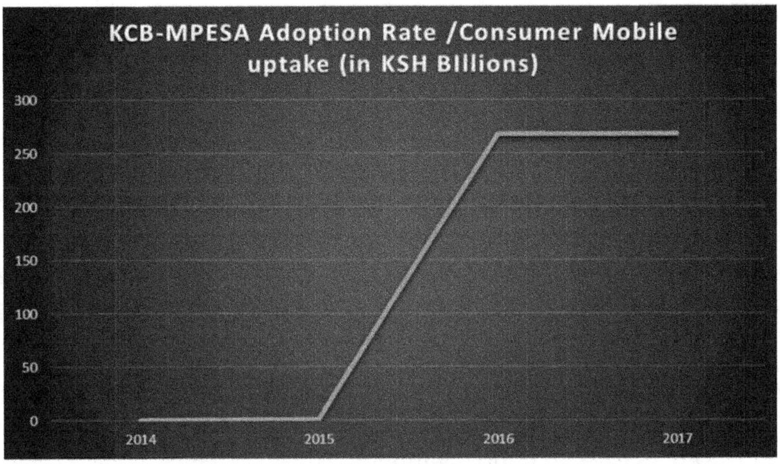


*Figure 7. Mshwari Growth and adoption (Safaricom Financial Reports)*

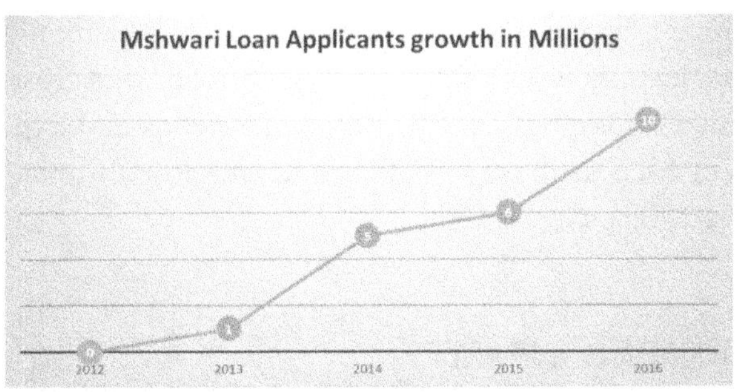


speediness, convenience, time utility, provision of different personal services, social desirability, usefulness, economic benefits, and user involvement. Robertson and Myers (2004), work indicated awareness, interest or information search, evaluation and trial and then the actual purchase decision on the product adoption and whether to make full and/or regular use of the new product.

Oromo (2015), highlights that in Kenya mobile money service introduced in 2007 with approximately 1.3m users and 1,582 agents moved 3.8b (an equivalent of $38 million at an exchange rate of 100ksh =$ 1) on its unveiling year compared with 1.9 Trillion shillings in 2013 and 2.3 Trillion shillings in 2014. Mobile money accounts stood at 25.2M in 2014 having increased from 1.3M in its unveiling year. Ram and Sheth (1989) revealed that consumer resistance to innovation adoption may be because of functional obstructions in the form of usage, value, risk and psychological barriers in the form of tradition and image.

Oromo (2015) indicated more than half of the banks in the country have partnered with M-Pesa to perform a number of transactions since evidence reveals that mobile money is instrumental in increasing customer deposits which in return enables (Commercial Banks) CBs to issue more loans and advances which translates into higher profits. In March 2015 KCB Group entered into a deal with Safaricom to enable subscribers of the telecom's mobile money platform access loans of between Sh50 and Sh1M repayable between one and six months. A month after launching its KCB *M-Pesa* account, Sh1 billion was lent out with 1.5M users depositing Sh100M (lender's 2015 first quarter financial report).

*M-Pesa* mobile money savings and credit appendage, M-shwari was propelled in 2012 in collaboration with CBA Bank and expanded in February 2014 as a product that permits users to save and borrow money. Today, M-shwari has over 18 million customers, processes to the tune of 50,000 loans everyday an uptake which has grown its savings and loans accounts to Sh153 billion and loan amounts to KSh 29 billion correspondingly. The gigantic uptake of M-shwari in Kenya has seen the loan amount distributed rise from 7 billion in February 2014 to 29 billion in March 2015. CBA has since grown its deposits making it the largest retail bank in Kenya by customer numbers, leading with 10M customers and followed closely by equity bank with 9.2M customers (Okuttah, 2015). Consumer needs and experience represent key components of each of these variables and were the ultimate determinants of adoption (GSMA, 2008).

## BUSINESS MODELS IN MMT

Ideally there are three business models in MMT. The most basic sense, a business model may adopt a bank-centric, mobile-operator led, or partnership led (Boer and de Boer 2010), with technology service firms often included to enable the application or platform for payment service delivery.

### Bank-Led Models

In the bank-led model, the financial institution controls the customer relationship and provides mobile services primarily as a new channel to existing services. The mobile operator provides the channel for the domestic transfers and international remittances conducted by the financial institution. Using a short-range wireless technology that stores account information in a chip embedded in a card, mobile handset, or some other device for the purpose of enabling proximity payments. One example is Rabobank in the Netherlands, which in 2006 launched its own mobile virtual network operator service (Boer & de Boer 2010).

## Mobile Network Operator-Led Models

For this arrangement to work a mobile network operator eliminates the involvement of the financial institution in the payment delivery, clearing, and settlement. This platform has been a source of linkage to establish partnerships with world remittance service providers such as Western Union and MasterCard, to expand their subscription and payment system networks. In most cases the mobile network operators governs the MMT market, fostering the customer relationship aspect and providing the service distribution channel, with clearing and settlement functions often agnostic to the participation of mainstream financial institutions or central banks. Examples of such include *Safaricom's M-Pesa* and Austria's *Mobilkorn* (Boer & de Boer 2010). They rely on short message service (SMS)-based low-value payments. A number of the evolving payment schemes with the wireless carriers that were able to charge the mobile-enabled payment sent via text message to the consumer's mobile phone bill, were used as an example of the Haiti earthquake relief efforts (Merritt 2010).

## Partnership Models

This model accommodates the financial institutions, mobile network operators and third-party service providers that make up the ecosystem partner and collaborate to provide payment services (Merritt 2010). As with the case of Afghanistan, when the prevalence of illiteracy rate become a hindrance, this model was embraced. A challenge arose in that the *M-Paisa* menu that could not be provided in the local languages partly due to irreconcilabilities between the platform and the Dari character set, consequently Roshan (the company providing MMT services) invested in the development of an interactive voice response (IVR) feature for *M-Paisa* (IFC-WB, 2011).

This model is conceivable to capitalize on each organization's respective strengths in terms of providing customer service, introducing innovation, and ensuring an environment of sound regulatory compliance. IFC-WB, (2011) reveals that Vodafone does not have any stake in Roshan but the two operators were able to establish a partnership agreement based on a profit share model for *M-Paisa* in Afghanistan. This model has its strengths and weaknesses. Since Roshan does not pay license fees to Vodafone they are able to register customers even if they are not generating large transactions volumes (IFC-WB, 2011). This is done to overcome limited barriers to market entry the new payments solution providers face with less stringent regulatory oversight and lower capital requirements than traditional bank counterparts.

They include *PayPal*, *Obopay*, and *Cashedge*, to Visa and MasterCard, have announced numerous money transfer initiatives in 2010 in partnership with financial institutions and money service businesses like Moneygram and Western Union (Merritt, 2010). However, the model can also slow down growth of the business since the operators sometimes have different motivations and may not immediately agree on strategic decisions IFC-WB, (2011).This model has its pros and cons; since Roshan does not pay license fees to Vodafone they are in a position to register customers even if they are not generating large transaction volumes (IFC-WB, 2011). Nonetheless, the model is known to slow down business prospects as operators tend to have diverse motivations that may not instantaneously agree on strategic decisions IFC-WB, (2011).

## CUSTOMER CONCERNS WITH DIGITAL LOANS

The digital loans offerings has flagged some issues particularly consumer protection and possible customer risks. While the development of the MMT in particular digital loans is something to appreciate, the consumer protection against prevailing circumstances should be a priority to the regulators, government and industry players. The MMT landscapes in Kenya without the strict regulation has bred digital "shylocks" who prey on unsuspecting customers who end up being hoodwinked and in some cases swindled. Rea and Nelms (2017) believe that as Mobile Network Operators (MNOs) financial institutions, governments, and development agencies similarly have endeavored to duplicate *M-Pesa* outside of Kenya—with varying degrees of success—their conclusion is that one size does not fit all within the sociocultural, regulatory, and economic specificity time and again leaving an important insight from the first decade of mobile money research. Due to the uniqueness of MMT, it is not surprising that many are quick to raise issues around consumer protection; the emphasis on the data digitization component of mobile money especially contributes to concerns regarding consumers.

### Interest Regime

Miller (2013) has reasoned that the theoretical enlightenments on the role of interest rate boundaries on credit market outcomes starts with the proper understanding of the composition of interest rates (price of credit) charged by lenders. The high Annual Percentage Rates (APRs) on many of the loans is a source of concern to the many consumers of MMT, to the regulators such as Central Bank of Kenya, given the capping rate of banks in 2016. In Kenya the amended law capping interest rates came into force in September 2016, thus setting limits on lending and deposit rates for financial institutions (Central Bank of Kenya, 2018). Nonetheless due to their ambiguity and lack of framework policy and laws governing them, the digital loans do not follow laws laid out for conventional registered banking industry players. In essence the digital loans are perceived to be too expensive for consumers and are generally associated with high interest rates (FinCoNet, 2017).

Despite its attractiveness the MMT interest rates can't be comparable to commercial banks at the moment. The interest rates act according to CBK, (2018) sets the maximum lending rate at no more than four per cent above the Central Bank base rate; and the minimum interest rate granted on a deposit held in interest earning account to at least seventy per cent of the same rate. Kaffenberger and Chege (2016) disclose that while most of these loans are short term, and the customer will not be paying on it for a full year, the time is short but the repay is humongous. Financial analysts envision APR as the most effective way to standardize costs and compare loans to alternative options. While the cost of these loans is high relative to alternate sources of finance, in an emergency or extraordinary situation, the benefits of having access to credit can outweigh the relatively high cost (FinCoNet, 2017); fundamentally this is the reason why most of the digital loans are embraced. The interest rates of the digital loans is the most undoing of digital loans in Kenya. Izaguirre and Mazer (2018) highlight that this regime is shrouded in poor transparency and as such this is correlated with high delinquency and default rates. As such transaction data further suggest that borrowers would benefit from more transparency

Ochenge and Tiriongo (2018), laments that putting a ceiling of interest rates has precipitated illegal lending and a significant change in loan portfolio. It is a wonder why the effective APR is higher if the borrower repays early – borrowers still must pay the full fee despite borrowing for a shorter period of time. As a reference point, Kaffenberger and Chege (2016) examined APRs in South Asia and found that it averaged about 23% in 2011, around the time of both the crisis in Andhra Pradesh and the Bangladeshi government's investigation of Grameen Bank, while in sub-Saharan Africa the rates were about 32% at that time. Many of the digital loans in the table 2 charge 5 to 10 times that rate. Ultimately, if the borrower doesn't pay a loan off on time, the loan is usually "rolled over," and the nominal interest rate is applied to the full balance, again increasing the effective APR (Kaffenberger & Chege 2016). Ellison and Forster (2008b) mourned that interest rate ceiling does not necessarily reduce the cost of credit, but it leads to credit exclusion especially of segments such as households that cannot borrow to meet cash emergencies or spread their major purchases.

*Table 2. Comparative analysis of Mobile Loans Providers Key Performance Indicators*

| | | *10,000Kshs = $100 USD | | period (days unless specified) | |
|---|---|---|---|---|---|
| **Branch** | App | 250–50,000 | 1%-14% (as monthly rates) | 14-365 | 12%–170% |
| **Equitel Eazzy Loan** | SIM toolkit | 50–200,000 | 14.5% annual rate + 1% of loan amount as appraisal fee | 30 | 27% |
| **Equitel Eazzy Plus Loan** | SIM toolkit | 1,000–3,000,000 | 14.5% annual rate + 2%–3% of loan amount as appraisal | 2–6 months | 21%–27% |
| **Jumo/ Kopa Cash** | USSD | 500–13,000 | 0.5% daily | 7–28 | 183% |
| **KCB-M-Pesa** | SIM toolkit | 50–1,000,000 | 14% annual rate + 2.5% of loan amount as negotiation | 30 | 73% |
| | | | | 90 | 61% |
| | | | | 180 | 49% |
| **Kopa Chapaa** | SIM toolkit | 500–10,000 | 8.5%–17% | 10 | 310%–621% |
| **Micromobile** | App-based payroll lending–repaid through employer | Lesser of 50% of monthly salary or 100,000 | Unspecified | 30–60 | |
| **Mjiajiri** | USSD | Varies; increases as user recruits members | 200 Ksh registration fee, earn commission to recruit new members | Varies | Similar to pyramid scheme |
| **M-pawa-Sacco** | USSD | 100–20,000 | Set by SACCO; interest deducted from loan before disbursement | Set by SACCO | Varies, as set by SACCO |
| **M-Shwari** | SIM toolkit | 100–20,000 | 7.50% | 30 | 91% |
| **Okoa Stima** | SIM toolkit; loans for electricity pay- | 100–1,000 | 10% | 7 | 521% |
| **Pesa na Pesa** | App | 500–100,000 | 10% | 7 | 521% |
| **Pesa Pata** | App | 2,000–20,000 | 30% | 30 | 365% |
| **Pesa Zetu** | Website | Varies | 6%–10% | 28 | 85%–130% |
| **Saida** | App | Up to 25,000 | 7.5% and up | 30 | 91% and up |
| **Tala** | App | 500–50,000 | 5%–20% | 30 | 61%–243% |
| **Zindisha** | Website | 100–1,000,000 | Initial membership fee of 5% of loan request, then 5% per loan | Varies | Varies according to repayment period |

Adapted from Kaffenberger M. & Chege P. (2016). Digital Credit in Kenya: Time for Celebration or Concern? Available at https://www.cgap.org/blog/digital-credit-kenya-time-celebration-or-concern. Blog 03 October 2016 Accessed on 8th April 2019)

*Figure 8. The use of facilitated loans (Field Survey, 2019)*

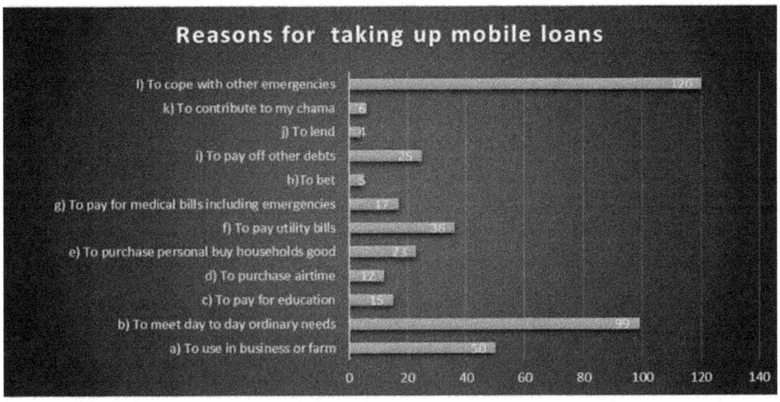


While some jurisdictions tend to implement caps on interest rates for consumer credit to address the risks posed by high-cost credit (FinCoNet, 2017), Merritt (2010) expounds that the telecom industry in most countries lacks experience in financial services and the business risks associated with this expanded role. Indeed Mbiti and Weil (2011) found the introduction of *M-Pesa* in Kenya led to a significant decrease in the prices of money transfer competitors but whether the control of interest rate have brought down the cost of borrowing in Kenya is a discussion that needs to be pursued.

## MARKETING

There is also the temptation and push loans through the throat of both willing and unwilling customers. Ideally, customer may not be inviting to such gimmicks and may resist at first but not eventually. Research and evidence from behavioral economics show that borrowing through a mobile phone feels different than borrowing through more traditional, in-person avenues, and is more tempting (Kaffenberger & Chege 2016). The "push" loans" promoted by some lenders include blasting unsolicited messages to potential borrowers saying things like "you have qualified for XX Shillings! To accept your loan call or SMS 07123456789." In this situation, both temptation and loss aversion – the feeling that you have been given something and that turning it down would be a loss – can drive borrowers to take loans they do not need (Kaffenberger & Chege, 2016). Given the emergencies they face, customers may give in to these loans. Though customers use the loans for various reasons majority of them tend to deal with emergencies and paying up for the daily ordinary needs, quite a few borrow digital loans to bet and to purchase as exemplified in *figure 8*.

*Figure 9. Why people prefer Mobile loans (Field Survey 2019)*

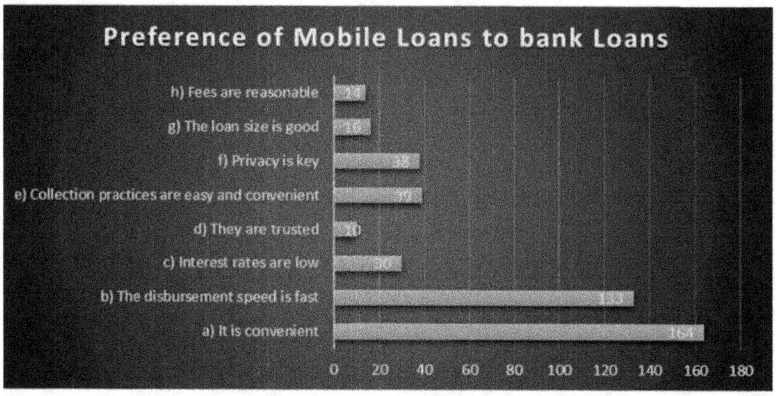


Undeniably the understanding of what is being pushed or sold may not be in the purview of the consumer understanding. While marketing, the unclear disclosure of interest rates, fees and other terms are also used and it means that customers often may not understand what they are agreeing to. Some of the offerings customers are supposed to read and understand are not available on basic phones as such mobile loan providers only provide terms only through a weblink, and therefore are inaccessible without an internet connection (Kaffenberger & Chege 2016). Fundamentally this is linked to issue and by large the marketing techniques by MMTs is the issue of poor disclosure.

In many some instances, loans are sold bundled with other products, and their associated fees not clearly disclosed to customers. The popularity of these loans stem from convenience and faster disbursement as depicted in the diagram rather than the size of the loan, and trust which seems to be ranking low to consumers of digital loan according to the survey.

A perfect case scenario is the bundling of a loan with credit life insurance, which covers the balance of the loan upon the death of the borrower. For a $10, 30-day loan, this makes little sense and provides little value. With the customer (and next of kin) poorly informed, these policies may never be redeemed even in the unlikely event that the borrower dies (Kaffenberger & Chege 2016).

Still on arising issues related to digital loans is the both implicit and explicit use of customers' personal data. While artificial intelligence can be employed to protect the company credit exposure, Kaffenberger and Chege (2016) believe that borrowers generally "consent" to the use of their data for calculating loans, and it is unlikely they read the full terms and conditions and understand exactly what data or how the data is going to be used by the lender. This infringes on customers privacy and in future may be a fertile ground for court cases. Other data-related policies such as how much data providers retain after calculating the loan amount, how long they hold it, how safely they store it and who would be liable if the data were accessed by an unauthorized party and could affect customers as well, or used in a way that harmed the customer (Kaffenberger & Chege 2016).

## REGULATIONS

The emergence of mobile commerce and Person-to-person (P2P) transactions in lightly controlled jurisdictions is inspiring the Central Banks of some countries to begin to scrutinize consumer issues such as security, consumer protection, fraud, and money laundering (Merritt 2010). Maurer (2012a) and Muthiora (2015) alluded that during the advent of *M-pesa* development in Kenya financial institutions pushed back against telcos, irritable that the latter were essentially taking deposits without conforming to the prudential norms and regulations of banks and essentially eating into their core business. A Report by Central Bank of Nigeria, specified that, the foremost challenge affecting mobile money in Nigeria was the regulatory framework (Central Bank of Nigeria, 2011).

In Ireland strides were taken and the Consumer Credit Act 1995 become a facilitator of MMT transactions. The act requires moneylenders to renew their licences annually, and enables the Central Bank of Ireland to refuse a licence application if it considers the cost of credit to be charged to be excessive (FinCoNet, 2017). Going forward Merrit (2010), opines that Telecom-specific consumer protections in most countries is lacking since the emerging industry was not created with the need for financial services regulation in mind. As such there has been a growing concern for most governments and Central Banks (as regulators) in different legal jurisdictions raising questions about regulation and the role of government in stimulating or inhibiting technological and economic innovation (Rea & Nelms 2017)

In Afghanistan, The Central Bank of Afghanistan commandeered MMT services as payment service providers. Adequately the during *M-Paisa* pilot phase in Afghanistan, the Central Bank enacted legislation to adjust the novel payment service providers' regulation to accommodate MMT (International Finance Corporation –World Bank IFC-WB,2011). It is prudent that the convergence of banking and telecom industries in a cross-border context in the MMT is posing bringing a challenge to regulators on how to establish effective regulatory infrastructures to provide oversight for this convergence (Merritt 2010). As an example within the Irish jurisdiction, payday lending models have not been authorised in licensed moneylender market (FinCoNet, 2017).

The case of Roshan is interesting, being a communication company, it has upheld close ties with the Central Bank of Afghanistan going a long way to facilitating regulatory support IFC-WB, (2011). In this case, the Central Bank was very enthusiastic to revise its legislation to house the distinctive facets of electronic funds transfer and this was a significant factor that enabled Roshan to launch the service. It's prudent to note that regulators need not to subjugate their critical role within the MMT ecosystem, there is need to strike an equilibrium between providing prudential, risk-based oversight and encouraging innovation, efficiency, and financial inclusion (Merritt, 2010). The Canadian government on the other hand allows the maximum allowable charge for a payday loan to vary across provincial jurisdictions but generally falls within the range of CAD$15 per $100 borrowed to $25 per $100 borrowed (FinCoNet, 2017).

For the Sri Lanka case, the Central Bank of Sri Lanka (CBSL) insisted that mobile money services be bank-led (Sachdev and Lal, 2015). CBSL permitted the National Development Bank, to launch a MMT service, CBSL furthermore obligated that all customers have a traditional bank account with the National Development Bank to satisfy standard commercial banking customer requirements. eZ Pay was launched and in conjunction with Dialog, the largest MNO in Sri Lanka, as its mobile partner. Nevertheless, eZ Pay failed to gain significant traction, netting only thirteen thousand customers (Sachdev and Lal, 2015). These limitations create a lacuna from the traditional financial regulation perspective for emerging MMT resulting in gaps in legal governance and ambiguity with respect to the responsibilities and liability among parties involved in the payment service (Merrit, 2010). As result CBSL successively brought in Dialog and another commercial bank, Hatton National Bank, to work with them to ensure that both eZ Pay were successfully launched (Sachdev & Lal, 2015).

While in the case of Afghanistan, the CBA has taken a positive step by regulating the service, they have also provided strict compliance guidelines and at times this serves as a constraint to further growth of the system service (IFC-WB, 2011). Preferably there should be need to manage the consumer protection efforts of both the telecom and financial services industry (Merrit, 2010). New regulatory regime should factor the emerging risk that accompany mobile transactions such as identity theft, lost payments over faulty transmissions, fraudulent transactions or criminal activities meted on part by mobile operators, agents, or other involved parties as service provider (Merrit,2010). In Afghanistan once a license was issued to Roshan (the MMT Company) to the operation of *M-Paisa*, the Central Bank policies were frequently reviewed to keep up with developments to the MMT within the jurisdiction and financial sector (IFC-WB, 2011). This means that as Merritt (2010) enlightens, the telecommunication industry in most countries is regulated on the basis of a public utility, whereas the banking sector is regulated on the basis of safety and soundness and capital adequacy.

Lal and Sachdev (2015) reports that in Philippines, the Filipino Central Bank, the Bangko Sentral ng Pilipinas (BSP), endeavors to facilitate the mobile industry with MMT services. The BSP played a critical role in the growth of the two main mobile money services, SMART Communications SMART Money and Globe Telecom GCASH. Initially BPS enabled non-banks (e.g. MNOs) to offer mobile money services since the bank viewed MMT services as a unique venture distinct from deposit-taking services, and consequently did not necessitate provident regulation of MMT thus, eradicating the need for mobile money operators to be banks.

Lal and Sachdev (2015) reveal that BSP also took time to test and learn about regulation while creating legal certainty, eventually, after both had been in the market for a number of years, more formal regulations were developed. Ideally BSP allowed non-bank agents to perform cash-in & cash-out to enable MMT operators to scale their agent networks by utilizing the country's existing retail infrastructure including pawn shops, airtime resellers, and money changers. It is interesting to note that BSP does require agents to apply to be agents, and to provide relevant business documentation as part of their application, in addition to receiving training on anti-money laundering (Lal &Sachdev 2015). Undecked the BSP has evolved these regulations over time to remove friction from the process. This is much different from the Peruvian regulatory framework which does not implement caps on interest rates for consumer credit provided through digital channels or for consumer credit provided through more traditional channels. The main reason for this is that freedom to set interest rates is considered to benefit the poorest population of the country by allowing them to access and use financial services.

Merritt (2010) fronts the argument that regulators need to keep up with the pace of innovation in MMT and should seek to shred opaqueness being witnessed in these payment transactions. The case of Econet and EcoCash, exemplifies this, when the first mobile money service was launched in Zimbabwe, the country had no specific mobile money regulation (Lal & Sachdev 2015). By providing an alternative to the formal financial system, Zimbabwe's Central Bank, the Reserve Bank of Zimbabwe (RBZ) was particularly interested in financial inclusion to help reduce poverty in the country.

This arrangement enabled Econet to establish a good rapport with the RBZ, and led to the RBZ developing a test-and-learn approach to regulation. EcoCash has been very successful, reaching 2.3million customer registrations within 18 months of its launch (equivalent to 31% of Zimbabwe's adult population), with one million of those active, and annualized transaction volume equivalent to 22% of the country's GDP (Lal & Sachdev 2015). Preferably one has to look at the fees being charged to facilitate transactions, this is because the amount the consumer has to repay is higher, reducing the consumer's income surplus and increasing the need for a subsequent loan to meet the consequent shortfall in income (Department of the Treasury, 2015).

Lal and Sachdev (2015) opined that the Brazilian government chose not to establish specific mobile money regulations, which created significant uncertainty among potential mobile money participants. The regulators were not sure if they had the authority to regulate mobile money services as such this created a situation where banks were comfortable operating a mobile money service, as they had pre-existing relationships with regulators which they could leverage, and which gave them comfort that regulators would be comfortable with what they chose to do.

Lal and Sachdev (2015) report indicates that technically deposit-taking institutions do have to register with the Central Bank, but regulators did not imply whether "cash-in" for a mobile money service would constitute deposit-taking, leaving this as a grey area. The report exemplifies Brazil finance sector constituting a very large correspondent banking system that enables retailers and merchants to act as agents of banks (the "correspondent banks"). It continues to indicate that one operator, *Oi Paggo*, has attempted to launch a MMT service under these conditions, it is the smallest of the major MNOs, and consequently due to the regulatory uncertainty, it did not offer P2P or cash-in / cash-out as part of its product set. Oi Paggo saw very limited growth and adoption, reaching only 250,000 users, and Oi therefore decided to try to partner with a bank and effectively re-launch the service with a different model (Lal and Sachdev 2015).

Di Castri (2013) intimates that the government should come in to regulate and to address certain risks posed to customers and the wider financial system, to fight fraud and money laundering and to guarantee best practices regarding liquidity management, customer identification, combating the financing of terrorism, and regulating interoperability across MMT actors. Lal and Sachdev (2015) highlights the South African story. For South Africa, the unsatisfactory quest for Vodacom to have the Kenyan *M-pesa* success replicated there did not work out. Pundits have it that the South Africa case failed because of the prevailing financial and payments infrastructure within the country was well developed and swarmed more with credit cards. The factor is other lack of identification of a particular target market or an analysis of the financial flows / potential use cases of such a market was the bone of contention. The distinction between South Africa and the Kenyan one is that the population of consumers and merchants in South Africa has a closed-loop system deployed there, not due to its robust banking environment (Lal & Sachdev 2015).

*Figure 10. Number of loans (Field Survey, 2019)*

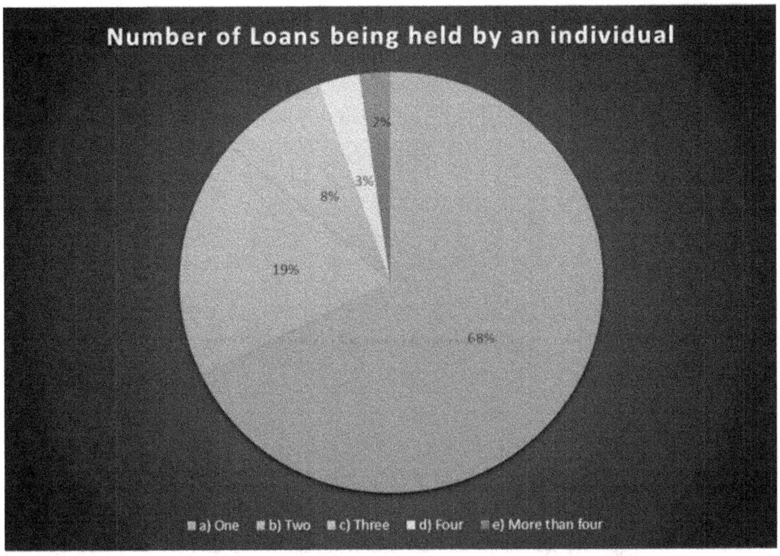


This has partly led to absence of digital money in South Africa and consequently no mobile loans. After a dismal performance, Vodacom discontinued the service at the end of 2013 and re-launched with a new banking partner and new model in the summer of 2014. The new service had a focus on serving the unbanked and lower-income segments of the population, and was geographically structured to support the pre-existing financial corridors of that population (Lal & Sachdev 2015).

## MULTIPLE LOANS

The issues of multiple borrowing is a concern to the stability of the Marco- environment of the economy. Kaffenberger & Chege (2016) observes that while some lenders report information to the Kenyan Credit Bureau, the information is often incomplete, and most digital lenders are nonbanks who are not required to report data at all. Across the sea, research into the Irish moneylending industry in 2013, found that 15% of moneylender customers surveyed were repaying two or more loans with their moneylender, with 1% having four or more loans outstanding. Over 1 in 5 customers (22%) were making repayments to at least two separate moneylenders while 2% reported having one or more loan with at least four different moneylenders(Central Bank of Ireland, 2013). Certainly this can lead to situations where borrowers take on more credit than they can manage, or borrowers take out one loan to pay off another loan, creating a debt cycle with potentially negative repercussions for the consumer.

*Figure 11. Source of Loan Repayment (Field Survey, 2019)*

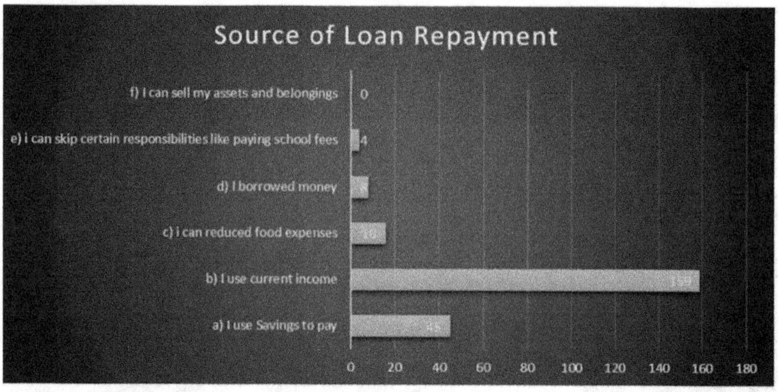


Similarly, in Australia quite a number the proportion of consumers with multiple payday loans has increased in recent years. Research by Digital Finance Analytics showed that the number of payday loan borrowers taking out more than one payday loan in the preceding 12 months had grown from 17.2% in 2005 to 38% in 2015. Undeniably such may lead to a microfinance crisis, there is no way for lenders to know how many (and what type of) other loans borrowers have. From the filed survey, over 68% of the respondents having one loan. Around 19% had two loans while 8 per cent had three loans and 5.5 percent had four loans while a paltry 1.1 percent had more than four loans.

This phenomena is not just limited to Kenya but a report by the Competition and Markets Authority in the UK found that around 75% of payday loan consumers take out more than one payday loan in a year and that, on average, a payday loan consumer takes out around six payday loans per year. The rise of the digital credit market has raised concerns about the risk of excessive borrowing and over-indebtedness among lower-income households. Digital loans are easy to obtain, short-term, carry a high interest rate and are available from numerous bank and nonbank institutions. The survey Carried out by researchers in Nairobi found that 14 percent of digital borrowers were repaying multiple loans from more than one provider at the time of the survey. This means that over 800,000 Kenyans were juggling multiple digital loans. Although having multiple loans is not necessarily an indicator of debt distress, it is important to closely monitor the market going forward and detect possible risks. Indeed, some customer go an extra mile in repaying of the loans as depicted in

The report also found that repeat borrowing typically accounts for a large proportion of lenders' business: 80% of all STHCCC contracts in 2012 were made to consumers who had previously borrowed from the same lender. When a consumer takes out more than one loan at a time, the repayment can consume a greater portion

*Figure 12. Reasons for not taking up loans Source; Field Survey (2019)*

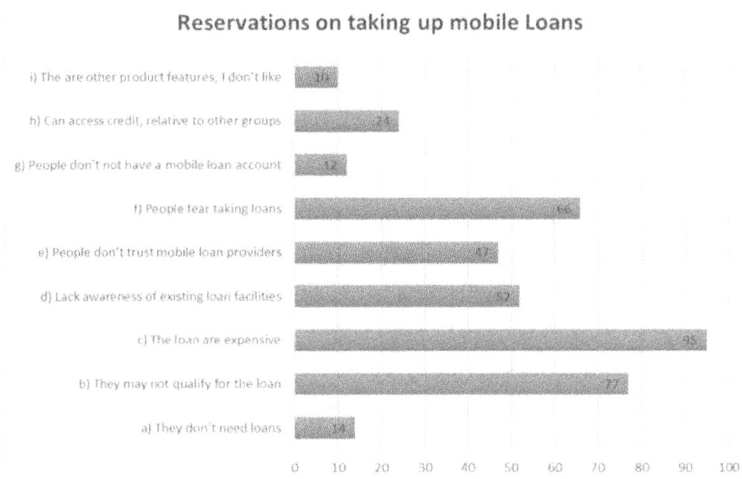


of their income for a longer period and become increasingly unaffordable. With a large portion of income being used to cover repayments, more credit may be needed to cover living expenses (or even to meet repayments on existing loans), limiting the consumer's capacity to improve their financial situation over time.

## FEES AND TRANSPARENCY

Several countries noted that consumers may be subject to additional fees if they extend the term of the loan or if they default on a loan, which further contributes to the high-cost nature of these loans and may increase a consumer's debt burden (FinCoNet, 2017). While this may be legal the morality of it is still in question. In Australia payday lenders have been charging numerous default fees such as a dishonor payment fee of AUS$38.50 (for each default), a missed payment fee of $38.50 (once-off fee), a default notice/letter of $10.00 (for each default, applied at 7, 14, 21 and 30 days) and a debt management fee of $50 (once off fee).

Lenders cannot however, collect more than 200% of the amount loaned, even in circumstances where the consumer defaults under the loan. They are also obliged to report users' complaints and their handling progress to the Financial Services Authority (OJK) monthly. Lack of transparency creating a perception that digital loan are expensive is one of the reason why people fear taking up mobile loans as depicted by figure 12. Other compelling reasons include the aspect trust and lack of awareness of existing loan facilities according to most respondents.

In their review of digital credit products, the Evans School Policy Analysis and Research (EPAR) identified 68 products on offer digitally in India, Kenya, Nigeria, Tanzania and Uganda. Although their study was not limited to STHCCC specifically, many of the products identified were short-term (30 days or less) and could be considered high-cost as they had relatively high interest rates and multiple fees. This study therefore is aware of the fact that new borrowers often begin by taking a string of short-term loans and shifted to longer-term loans with lower APRs over time. This suggests that customers had to learn the hard way that longer-term loans are cheaper. However these loans may be prove beneficial for consumers if it is used as an emergency or occasional source of funding for extraordinary or non-recurring expenses (FinCoNet, 2017). CGAP's analysis of Tanzanian transaction data depicted that granular data on repayment rates and loan costs can help regulators uncover troubling or unfair digital credit business models that may be relying on nontransparent fees and less on interest payments (Izaguirre & Mazer, 2018).

## LENDING LIMIT AND USE OF LOAN

The lending limit for consumer varies from one service provider to another. The limit factor may also vary from customer to customer in the same institution depending on credit worthiness. In some countries the limit has been placed by the state machinery. FinCoNet, (2017) clarifies that in some Canadian provinces there is a ceiling to the lending amount in that it is slated at the maximum of 50% of the borrower's pay check or net income to be received during the term of the loan. In Kenya, an employer is permitted to make further deductions from an employee salary if the employee will take home less than one third of their salary (Employment Act, 2007.) In Australian the credit law allows for SACCs up to AUS$2,480 (if the establishment fee and first monthly fee are also financed) while Canada limits the maximum amount for a payday loan toCAD$1,500 (FinCoNet, 2017).

Personal Finance Research Centre, University of Bristol (2013) and Momentum, (2014) studies in both the UK and Canada respectively found that large proportions of consumers use these loans to cover ordinary everyday expenses. In Ireland studies reveal that customers of licensed moneylenders are most likely to borrow for personal items (goods/clothes) and family-related occasions. As such using digital loans can be used to cover recurring everyday expenses is not top notch, consequently this may be difficult for the consumer to repay the loan while also being able to afford his or her everyday expenses in the future (FinCoNet, 2017).

*Figure 13. Lenders response to a delayed payment (Field Survey, 2019)*

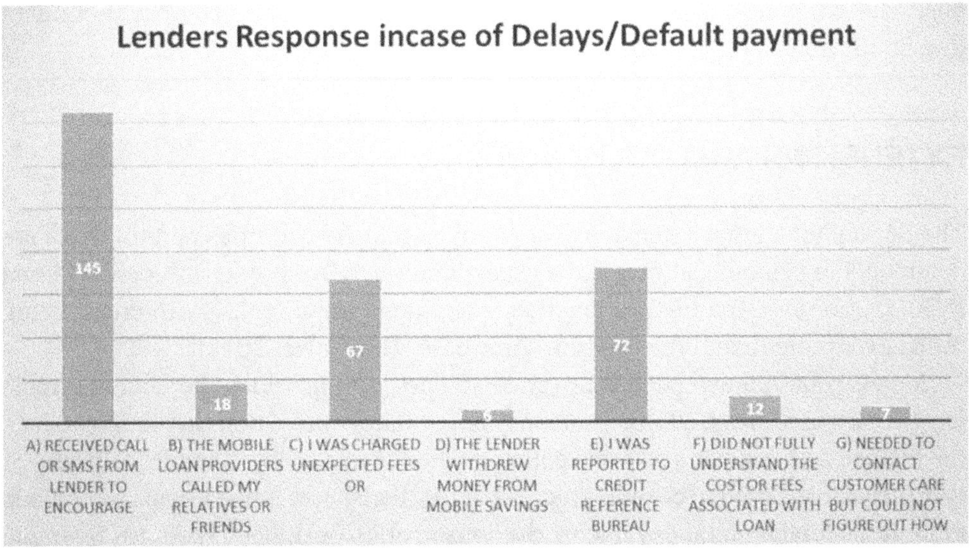


## CREDIT RISK AND REPAYMENT

Izaguirre and Mazer (2018) concluded that most first-time borrowers paid either too early or late and that they ended up paying much higher APRs than borrowers who paid on the official due date. From the field study most of the respondents used their income to settle the loans. GSMA (2009) acknowledges that in many countries, nonbank payment service providers are barred from accepting consumer deposits or using funds in financing payment activities, which serves to protect the consumer and limits financial system risk. Safaricom's *M-Pesa* for instance softens credit risk by collecting prepaid funds from agents. In managing Credit risk the lenders according to survey tend to institute several ways to mitigating it. Most of the respondents revealed that they tend to receive short message text or calls reminded them to honor their obligation to pay the risk. The respondents indicated that they also were charged roll over fees while some were reported to the CRB. There are ethical concerns of loan providers accessing constants of loan applicants and calling relatives and friends of the loan applicant through the artificial intelligence software's to demand for loans repayment in case of delays. Those who's relative or friends were called were to prompt repayment of loans were not amused.

Merrit (2010) tells of how Safaricom deposits into a trust account managed by a leading Commercial Bank of Africa (CBA) bank, which provides the legal protection for consumers. Merrit, (2010) invokes United States new P2P services as classically involving an established payment vehicle such as a depository account at a financial institution or a credit card to fund the mobile payment. In Haiti where the carrier posts charges to the consumer's phone bill to be postpaid has been largely limited to micropayments for charitable donations.

## EXTENSIONS AND ROLLOVERS

The Survey found that extensions are possible in many countries and rollovers are common. For example, although the usual duration for a 'short term' loan in Latvia is 30 days or less, the regular practice is to extend these loans, with credit being rolled over more than three times in some cases (FinCoNet 2017).

Mshwari has an extended rollover of 30 days, within which the defaulter must pay (Cook and McKay, 2015). There may be regulatory provisions in place to reduce the likeliness of rollovers in some countries. For example, in Lithuania rollovers of short-term loans used to be quite frequent before legislative amendments were made to limit the total amount payable by the consumer. (Consumer Credit 2015). In the UK, firms are prohibited from refinancing or rolling over a loan more than twice (Office of Fair Trading 2013). Most provinces in Canada prohibit payday lenders from issuing more than one loan to a borrower at the same time or rolling over one loan into another loan with new charges (Ben-Ishai, 2008). Additional protections and obligations were introduced in Australia (Consumer Credit 2015).

These protections include a presumption of unsuitability, postulates that a SACC will be unsuitable if either the consumer is in default under another SACC or the consumer has had two or more SACCs in the last 90 days (Consumer Credit 2015). The same report explains a prohibition on charging an establishment fee if any of the credit is to refinance another SACC was also introduced. Requiring mechanisms for customers to complain and even a redress mechanism is common sense and thus generating and processing and/or storing electronic data require some level of protection on behalf of the consumer (Consumer Credit 2015).

## IMPLICATION TO MANAGERS

While the development of the MMT in particular digital loans is something to appreciate there is need for managers' within the MMT to ensure that they recognize consumer rights with regard to MMT. Given the prevailing circumstances that loop in the regulators, government and industry players, the mangers and players need to understand the MMT landscapes should not be used to breed in digital "shylocks" who may end up preying on unsuspecting customers. The high APRs is an indication of a failure on regulatory bodies and scavenging on customers by MMT providers.

This is a concern to many an as such it needs to be regulated. The regulators such as Central Banks should be proactive in protecting consumers and educate the masses on how to identify these digital shylocks. Indeed the digital loans are perceived too expensive for consumers and are generally associated with high interest rates as such a call for general regulation that deals with MMT landscape should be enacted.

While marketing is a temptation to push loans through the throat of customers, these may be viewed as legal marketing activities but in the end the believability and legality of such practices comes into question and eventually into naught. Ideally this chapter and consumer behavioral patterns show that borrowing through a mobile phone feels different from borrowing through more traditional, in-person avenues. However, the so called push loans need to be controlled to avoid customer apathy towards the same.

There needs to be a way in which managers disclose interest rates, fees and clearly state other terms used for customers to understand what they are purchasing. Some of the defaults may be linked to poor disclosure which is related to poor marketing techniques used by MMTs. Of equal importance is the bundling of some loans which are sold with other products, and their associated fees, both of which may not be clearly disclosed to customers. This scenario takes an advantage of a customer only to charge him later with other hidden fees, as result it makes MMT loose appeal and eventually a de-marketing tool.

There is need to have Central Banks in full control to scrutinize consumer issues such as security, consumer protection, fraud, and money laundering. The dual regulation of Telcos and also rafting in Central Banks only serves to complicate the matter further. Though this operators serve the telecommunication industry, they are now deeply embedded in financial matter whose key regulator is the Central Bank. It is better to have such in the purview of Central Banks which are more experienced and have the legal backing of control of transfer of money and interest rates a statutory framework that needs to be adopted to deal with rogue MMTs providers. The rise of the digital credit market has raised concerns about the risk of excessive borrowing and over-indebtedness among lower-income households. These needs to be curtailed by sharing information through CRB and central banks and perceived a legal framework to handle this issue.

## CONCLUSION

The development of the regulatory environment facing marketplace lenders is just one development that will likely occur in coming years. However focusing on these types of regulatory requirements before having addressed the basic enabling regulatory framework is shortsighted and can impede the initial stages of development. Unquestionably, providers must also support the implementation of education activities which aim to increase financial literacy and inclusion. The challenge remains on how to balance amongst simplifying the operation of mobile money services and dealing with risk.

Regulators need to fill this critical role within the ecosystem, as they endeavor to strike a balance between providing prudential, risk-based oversight and encouraging innovation, efficiency, and financial inclusion. It is important for MMT providers to establish channels for customers to complain. Ideally it will be profitable for these companies to put a redress mechanism to sort out issues arising out of these transactions.

There is need to protect consumer data against abuse and manipulation. Data integrity, should be the utmost sacred thing in transaction of MMT, ideally generating and processing and/or storing electronic data should be accompanied with high level of protection on behalf of the consumer. However, sequencing of these regulations is critical to the development of sound MMT.

Regulators are then being challenged by the rate and turn of innovation in MMT and the increasing opaqueness in payment transactions from a regulatory oversight perspective. It becomes a rat race to keep up with these innovations in terms of regulations and if MMT services do not with the trend to protect the consumer or data subject, this undermines the whole process. So while not undermining the importance of having the right regulation on the demand side, the priority of any regulator today should be to create an enabling environment for mobile money and to address the supply-side barriers. Mobile transfer systems are giving rise to new challenges in how to establish effective regulatory infrastructures to provide oversight for converged banking and telecom industries in a cross-border context.

## REFERENCES

Ben-Ishai, S. (2008). Regulating Payday Lenders in Canada: Drawing on American Lessons. *Comparative Research in Law & Political Economy Research Papers, Working Papers, Conference Papers Research Report No. 16/2008*. Osgoode Hall Law School of York University Comparative Research in Law & Political Economy Research Papers, Working Papers, Conference Papers Research Report No. 16/2008.

Boer, R., & de Boer, T. (2010). *Mobile Payments 2010: Market Analysis and Overview, version 1.01. Innopay*. Retrieved from https://www.ebaportal.eu/_Download/Research%20and%20Analysis/2010/Mobile_paymen ts_2010_Innopay.pdf (accessed on 1st July ,2019)

Bourreau, M., & Marianne, V. (2010). *Cooperation for Innovation in Payment Systems: The Case of Mobile Payments*. Economix Working Paper 2010-05. Université de Paris Ouest Nanterre La Défense, Nanterre, France. Retrieved from http://economix.u-paris10.fr/pdf/dt/2010/WP_EcoX_2010-05.pdf (accessed on 21st June ,2019)

Central Bank of Ireland. (2013). *Report on the Licensed Moneylending Industry*. Available at https://www.centralbank.ie/docs/default-source/publications/consumer- protection-research/gns4-2-1-1-rep-on-licensed-moneyldg-ind-112013.pdf?sfvrsn=6 (accessed on 21st June ,2019)

Central Bank of Kenya. (2018). *The Impact of Interest Rate Capping on the Kenyan Economy*. Author.

Central Bank of Nigeria (CBN). (2011). *Annual Report 2011*. Available at https://www.cbn.gov.ng/Out/2012/publications/reports/rsd/arp2011/2011%20Annual%20 Report_C omplete%20Report.pdf (accessed on 1st July ,2019)

Chang, Y. T. (2003). *Dynamics of Banking Technology Adoption: An Application to Internet Banking*. Department of Economics, University of Warwick.

Communication Commission of Kenya (CCK) & Kenya National Bureau of Statics (KNBS). (2018). *National ICT Survey Report*. Available at https://ca.go.ke/wpcontent/uploads/2018/02/National-ICT-Survey.pdf (accessed on 1st June ,2019)

Ellison, A., & Forster, R. (2011). *The impact of interest rate ceilings*. London: Policis.

Employment Act Chapter 226 revised Edition. (2007). Available at http://kenyalaw.org/kl/fileadmin/pdfdownloads/Acts/EmploymentAct_Cap226- No11of2007_01.pdf (accessed on 29th June, 2019)

FATF. (2013). *Guidance for a Risk-Based Approach: Prepaid Cards, Mobile Payments and Internet-Based Payment Services*. Paris: FATF/OECD.

GSM Association (GSMA). (2007). *Regulatory Framework for Mobile Money Transfers.* Retrieved from http://www.mobilemoneyexchange.org/Files/8e31752b (accessed on 1st July ,2019)

GSM Association (GSMA). (2008b). *Outlook for Mobile Wallets and Mobile Financial Services: Results of EDC–GSMA Mobil Financial Services Survey 2007.* Retrieved from http://www.gsmworld.com/mmu/mmu_quarterly_update.pdf

GSMA. (2009). *Mitigating the Risks that Accompany Mobile Money.* Mobile money for the unbanked: Quarterly update 1. GSMA.

Gubbins, P., & Totolo, E. (2018). *Digital credit in Kenya: Evidence from demand-side surveys.* Nairobi, Kenya: FSD Kenya. Available at https://s3-eu-central-1.amazonaws.com/fsd- circle/wp-content/uploads/2018/10/18162055/Digital-Credit-in-Kenya.pdf (accessed on 1st July ,2019)

Hurwitz, I., & Luiz, J. (2007, March). Urban Working Class Credit Usage and over-Indebtedness in South Africa. *Journal of Southern African Studies, 33*(1), 107–131. (accessed on 1st July ,2019) doi:10.1080/03057070601136616

IFC-WB. (2011). *M-Money Channel Distribution Case – Afghanistan Roshan M-Paisa.* Available at http://documents.worldbank.org/curated/en/123191500276218363/M-money-channel-distribution-case-Afghanistan-Roshan-m-paisa (accessed on 3rd July ,2019)

International Financial Consumer Protection Organisation (FinCoNet). (2017). *Report on the Digitalisation of Short-term, High-Cost Consumer Credit.* Author.

Izaguirre, J. C., & Mazer, R. (2018). *How Regulators Can Foster More Responsible Digital Credit.* Available at https://www.cgap.org/blog/how-regulators-can-foster-more-responsible-digital-credit

Kaffenberger, M., & Chege, P. (2016). *Digital Credit in Kenya: Time for Celebration or Concern?* Available at https://www.cgap.org/blog/digital-credit-kenya-time-celebration-or-concern (accessed on 1st July ,2019)

Kirui, O. K., Okello, J., Nyikal, R. A., & Njiraini, G. W. (2013). Impact of Mobile Phone-Based Money Transfer Services in Agriculture: Evidence from Kenya. *Quarterly Journal of International Agriculture, 52*(2), 141-162.

Maurer, B. (2012a). Mobile Money: Communication, Consumption and Change in the Payments Space. *The Journal of Development Studies, 48*(5), 589–604. doi:10.1080/00220388.2011.621944

Maurer, B. (2012b). Regulation as Retrospective Ethnography: Mobile Money and the Arts of Cash. *Banking and Finance Law Review*, *27*(2), 299–313.

Mbiti, I., & Weil, D. N. (2011). *Mobile banking: The impact of M-Pesa in Kenya (No. w17129)*. National Bureau of Economic Research. doi:10.3386/w17129

Merritt, C. (2010). *Mobile Money Transfer Services: The Next Phase in the Evolution in Person-to-Person Payments.* Retail Payments Risk Forum White Paper. Federal Reserve Bank of Atlanta.

Miller, H. (2013). *Interest rate caps and their impact on financial inclusion. Economic and Private Sector*. Professional Evidence and Applied Knowledge Services.

Muthiora, B. (2015). *Enabling Mobile Money Policies in Kenya: Fostering a Digital Financial Revolution*. GSMA Mobile Money for the Unbanked. Available.

Ochenge, R., & Tiriongo, S. (2018). Gapss from the Cap: Implications for Financial Inclusion in Kenya. *KBA Centre for Research on Financial Markets and Policy Working Paper Series 23.*

Office of Fair Trading. (2013). *Payday Lending Consultation on a market investigation reference*. Available at https://assets.publishing.service.gov.uk/media/532ad541e5274a226800039f/oft1482.pdf

Oromo, M. A. (2015). *The Relationship Between Mobile Money And Loans Issued By Commercial Banks In Kenya* (Master's dissertation). University of Nairobi.

Ram, S., & Seath, J. N. (1989). Consumer resistance to innovation: The Marketing problem and its solutions. *Journal of Consumer Marketing*, *6*(2), 5–14. (accessed on 9th July, 2019) doi:10.1108/EUM0000000002542

Rea, S. C., & Nelms, T. C. (2017). *Mobile Money: The First Decade. Institute for money, technology and financial inclusion*. Working Paper 2017-1.

Robertson, T. S., & Myers, J. H. (2004). Personality correlates of opinions leadership and innovative buying behavior. *JMR, Journal of Marketing Research*, *6*(2), 164–168. (accessed on 9th July, 2019) doi:10.1177/002224376900600204

Scott, R. III., & Steven, P. (2011). A Double Squeeze on the Middle Class. *Journal of Economic Issues*, 45(2), 333-341.

Tamara, C., & Claudia, M. (2015). *How M-Shwari Works: The Story So Far. Access to Finance Forum Reports by CGAP and Its Partners.* Academic Press.

USAID. (2010). *Mobile Financial Services Risk Matrix.* Available https://www.gsma.com/mobilefordevelopment/wp-content /uploads /2012 /06/ (accessed on 1st July ,2019)

Wan, W. N., Luk, C. L., & Chow, C. W. C. (2005). Consumers' adoption of banking channels in Hong Kong. *International Journal of Bank Marketing*, *23*(3), 255–272. (accessed on 12th October ,2019) doi:10.1108/02652320510591711

World Population Review. (2019). *Nairobi Population 2019.* Available at http://worldpopulationreview.com/world-cities/nairobi-population (accessed on 12th October ,2019)/

# Chapter 7
# Using Electronic Payment Programs as an Anti-Corruption Strategy in Africa

**Olayemi Abdullateef Aliyu**
*Toi Ohomai Institute of Technology, New Zealand*

**Chris Niyi Arasanmi**
*Toi Ohomai Institute of Technology, New Zealand*

**Samuel M. Ekundayo**
*Eastern Institute of Technology, New Zealand*

## ABSTRACT

*The theft of public revenues is a daily ethical failing associated with corruption in African countries. Yet many government sectors and agencies in Africa have failed to use ICTs to create the required culture of transparency. What do recent literature and empirical research findings reveal about solutions to these problems? Thus, the primary focus of this chapter is to conduct an extensive literature review on how electronic payment programs can be used as an anti-corruption strategy in Africa. Given the complex nature of corruption, the focus in this proposed chapter is to understand how other developing countries like Malaysia have successfully used electronic payment programs to reduce corruption and improve national accountability. A critical review of the observed ambiguity in the contemporary definition of corruption from different cultures in Africa will be reviewed. The ambiguity of the true commitment of African power elites in fighting corruption will also be examined with alternative solutions from existing literature.*

DOI: 10.4018/978-1-7998-2398-8.ch007

## INTRODUCTION

Public revenue is at the heart of every government, both in first and third world nations. Public revenue collection is also a vital aspect of fiscal policy and administration. Gideon and Alouis (2013, p. 49) refer to it as "the fuel of every government" as it is often the primary instrument through which many government administrations are funded. Many developed countries have mastered the art of public revenue collection (mainly taxes) and have become efficient with systems and programs that curb corruption and appraise their investments. However, in Africa, this is still a challenge. Therefore, there is a need to strengthen the national revenue collection in Africa.

For most countries, tax revenues form the largest share of government revenue. This is especially the case for countries in Sub-Saharan Africa with the difference being countries with natural resources thereby making non-tax revenue more prevalent (Agbeyegbe, Stotsky, & WoldeMariam, 2006; Worlu & Nkoro, 2012). Tax revenue is from three primary sources – tax from income and profits, tax from goods and services, and tax from international trade. Revenue collection in African countries is a significant issue.

Many countries are faced with problems of fiscal deficit, and evidence suggests a lack of or limited forms of efficient systems with which to collect public revenue as a factor. For instance, Baharumshah, Jibrilla, Sirag, Ali, and Muhammad (2016) argue that South Africa, as well as many African countries, are on the list of countries that consistently suffer from the issue of fiscal deficit year in, year out. While other factors play a role, corruption in relation to public revenue collection is high on the list. Corruption, tax evasion, avoidance and non-compliance are strongly linked to the shortage of public revenue in Africa (Ojong, Anthony, & Arikpo, 2016; Worlu & Nkoro, 2012).

In the current dispensation, the internet has been identified as a significant contributor to public revenue. For instance, Gnangnon and Brun's (2018) study reveal that the quality of access to the internet can affect the level of public revenue either directly or indirectly. Electronic payment via the internet can check tax evasion and reduce double or multiple taxations (Jatau & Dung, 2014). Electronic payments have been assessed as a more effective method of blocking leakages or channels of leakages for revenue generation, salary payment, contract payment and an end to end transactions involving the government (Jatau & Dung, 2014). The World Bank (2014) identified some significant advantages the wide spread adoption of electronic payment has including the ability to overcome costs and physical barriers to payments including governmental revenue collection; and opportunity to rapidly scale up financial services using various technologies such as smartphones, retail points of sale, etc. Electronic payment can help reduce corruption in Africa and most developing countries as it promotes transparency and integrity of transactions on which international and domestic remittances can build on.

In this article, we review the literature on the use of electronic payment programs as an anti-corruption strategy in African countries.

## CAUSES OF CORRUPTION IN AFRICA

A critical review of the literature on corruption in African countries shows that the root causes of corruption may vary from country to country depending on their political situations, social and economic development and how materialistic the cultures are in that country. Below are five leading causes of corruption in Africa:

1. Pre-colonial greed and weak ethical values
2. of certain cultures,
3. foreign influence and the negative colonial mentality,
4. poor and incompetent leadership,
5. weak institutions of governance,
6. lack of accountability and transparency (Elizabeth & John, 2014).

### Definitions of Corruption Across Different Cultures in Africa

Key common terminologies in the definition of corruption include deception, fraud, deceit, dishonesty, lawbreaking etc. Historian and African literature have estimated a total of 3000 tribes in Africa, which varies in term of their languages and culture. Despite significant development in Africa as a continent over the past two millennia, tribal influences have continued to dominate the governmental systems (Hope, 1999). Below are the ten most popular tribes/culture in Africa:

1. Chaga – Tanzania.
2. Hausa – Nigeria, Chad, Togo, Sudan, Cote d'Ivoire and Ghana.
3. Himba – Namibia.
4. Kalenjin – Kenya.
5. Maasai – East Africa, Kenya etc.
6. Oromo – Ethiopia, Kenya & Somalia.
7. San Bushman – Botswana.
8. Xhosa – South Africa.
9. Yoruba – Nigeria, South Benin & Brazil.
10. Zulu – South Africa.

In Nigeria, the Hausas refer to corruption as rashawa, the Yorubas call it ibajẹ, and the Ibos refer to corruption as ire ure. However, a detailed review of the extant literature on the meaning of corruption in Africa can be summarised as "fraudulent conduct by those entrusted with power mainly involving looting money and collecting bribes" (Leo & Patrick, 2010). In Africa, these exploitations by people in power involve both government and private sectors for private gains. Researchers and political activist have argued that corruption is entrenched in Africa's culture, moral preferences and educational system.

Svensson (2005) argued that theft and misappropriation of public funds meant for public utilities and infrastructures are the most destructive forms of corruption in Africa, including the misappropriation and of public programs are very common. These prevailing corruptions in Africa were mainly occurring at the highest levels of local, state and federal governments. It usually is usually done in a way where the political elites through the country's president, state governors and local government chairman to significantly subvert the political, economic and legal systems for private gains (Leo & Patrick, 2010). A good example is Nigeria where the elite who supposed to protect the interest of the masses have formed groups of God Fathers to share the license for the exploration of national resources (Leo & Patrick, 2010). Their decisions are mainly for the interest of their families and associates who enjoys the national wealth to the detriment of the populace (Leo & Patrick, 2010).

For instance, Svensson, (2005) estimated the amount that the former President Mobutu Sese Seko looted from Zaire to the tune of $5billion. This fraud was proportionally estimated to be equal to Zaire's external debt as at the year he ouster from office. Similar grand corruption to that of Mobutu is in Nigeria, Congo, Angola, South Africa etc. During General Sani Abacha's regime in Nigeria, he was accused of stealing a total of £5 billion from Nigeria public fund. In 2004, General Sani Abacha was listed by transparency international as one of the most corrupt leaders in history. Further investigations of his corruptions showed that more than 20 private companies had paid him and his associates bribes to obtain many inflated government contracts (Adusei, 2009). Companies owned by his immediate family members had also been granted inflated contracts for personal interests. Although the current government of president Muhammed Buhari have extensively cut off corruption loopholes, issues of corruptions are still going on in Nigerian states and local government (Adusei, 2009).

Other significant issues of grand corruption in Africa is Angola, where the government was unable to account for $1 billion oil revenues to corrupt government officials in 2001. This was at a time when many Angola citizens were living below poverty lines with less than $1 a day and continuously seeking international aids (Isaksson, 2013).

## Issues and Challenges of Corruptions

African countries have been defined as the most impoverished region in the world and home to many of the world's ethnically fragmented corrupt countries (Peiffer & Rose, 2018). Despite the available evidence, existing literature has over-focused on the macro variation of corruption across countries with little attention to possible micro variation along with cultures and ethnic lines. This section provides relevant theoretical understanding of the correlation between corruption and the maturity of the economic and political systems of specific cultures and countries in Africa. Key questions include should culture be an excuse for involving in corruption? What is the causal relationship between corruption and poverty? What impact do our beliefs, principles and cultural values have on good governance in Africa?

Until the early 1990s, scholarly publications on corruptions in Africa were most primarily confined to reports on criminal law. However, the trend of writings on corruptions between different cultures in Africa has continued unabated. A detailed review of the extant literature has challenged us to better understand the cultural phenomenon as one of the major causes of corruption. Local and international reports like UNO have extensively established a stronger relationship between corruption and poverty (Nduku & Tenamwenye, 2014).

A good example is an argument from Agbaje (2004) that researchers should consider the cultural dimension when evaluating the extent of damage corruption has caused in Africa. Issues of gift taking as a culture of social solidarity and honorable gesture are often referred to as a corrupt practice from a western perspective (Vorster, 2012). Modern African literature has argued that due to different social systems, the traditional African societies draws its wisdom from peaceful coexistence (Peiffer & Rose, 2018). Hence, giving a gift as a request to maintain peace or for services rendered is a cultural norm and routine practices in African. However, over focusing on culture as antecedent of corruption may lessen the correlation between poverty and corruption in African. To empirically establish individual corruption experiences, Isaksson (2013) analyzed data from 23,000 respondents in 17 African countries. The result indicated that individual experiences of corruption systematically vary along different ethnic lines in Africa. Below is Figure 1 that classify these 17 countries shares of corruption experience with obtaining official document/permit for that year:

To evaluate corruption from an alternative continental perspective, UNO through the Economic Commission for Africa conducted a research in 2016 titled "*Measuring corruption in Africa: The international dimension matters*". Below is Figure 2, which indicated that the performance of Africa as a region was below South and Central America but better than South Asia. From these selected regions, it was only Central America that significantly exhibits a degree of improvement from 2009.

*Figure 1. Country shares with document/permit corruption experience*

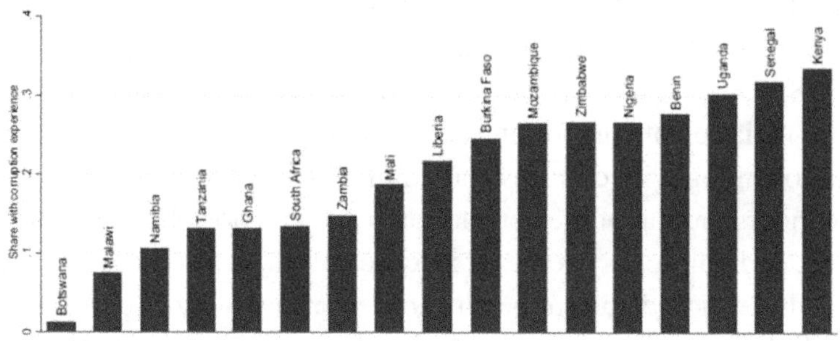


*Figure 2. Transparency international's coprruption perceptions index: comparable relative rankiongs of Africa and other regions*

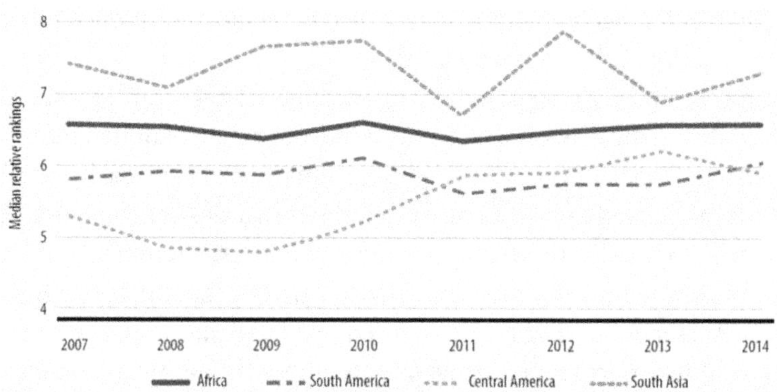


In addition to the above international perspective, Peiffer and Rose (2018) in "*why are the poor more vulnerable to bribery in Africa?*" show through the analyses of Afrobarometer data that poor Africans are not likely to offer bribes for state controlled monopoly services. This is because the inability of poor Africans to afford services provided by private, hence increased vulnerability to depend on the state. They conclude that this disproportionate vulnerability by poor Africans to offer bribery in order to utilise government provided services is more of institutional problems than the culture of the people.

Other researchers have also argued that corporate corruptions have been used to negatively explore the vulnerable African culture due to the high level of poverty (Peiffer & Rose, 2018). Particularly foreign multinational companies have consistently capitalised on poverty and weak government systems to bribe the State officials (Adusei, 2009). The critical area of exploitations by the multinational corporations include contracts, licensing, paying little or no taxes, etc. These issues have created unfair competitions for the local entrepreneurial who are in return forced to give a bribe in order to access state resources. It is important to note that corruption by these multinational corporations costs African countries billions of dollars that are much more than the cost of corruptions by the local firms (UNECA, 2016). The character of corruption as practiced by many of the multinational corporations extends to getting involved in the political affairs of African countries by financing political parties etc. For their local partners, these type of behavior depicts self-hate for the locals rather than showing any love for their people and country.

A politician like Julius Nyerere consistently argued that it is a pure misconception for poor countries to believe that money is the solution to their poverty. And in reality this is the actual situation in Africa where state and national governments are borrowing money from international organization to embark on local projects. A unique example is Singapore and Malaysia during the Asia financial crisis. These countries refused to externally borrow; instead, they cut their local expenditure and invest in capital projects. Available evidence indicated that those countries like Thailand, Indonesia and the Philippines that borrowed money from IMF etc. are economically struggling to meet the needs of their people. However, for Africa a region that is naturally endowed borrowing money should not be our priority.

## Unethical Leadership in Africa

Following independence, many African governments at federal and state levels shamelessly transformed their governmental institutions from bureaucratic systems of good governance to political systems that argue on the sovereignty of political power (UNECA, 2016; Hope, 1999). This shift has resulted in the emergence of economic and political monopolies with a severe lack of transparency and accountability to the rules and regulations of the society (Peiffer & Rose, 2018). As a result, these post-independence systems are the primary cause of corruption in Africa where personal and political loyalty is more rewarded than performance and merit. With inadequate experience of post-independence Africa leaders, the above causes of corruption became the norm, and foreign/local influence take advantage of the weak institutions of governance to engage in corruption (UNECA, 2016). Below are the findings from a recent survey titled "Citizens speak out about corruption in Africa". This research was conducted in July 2019 by the Global Corruption Barometer

*Figure 3. Corruption by institution*

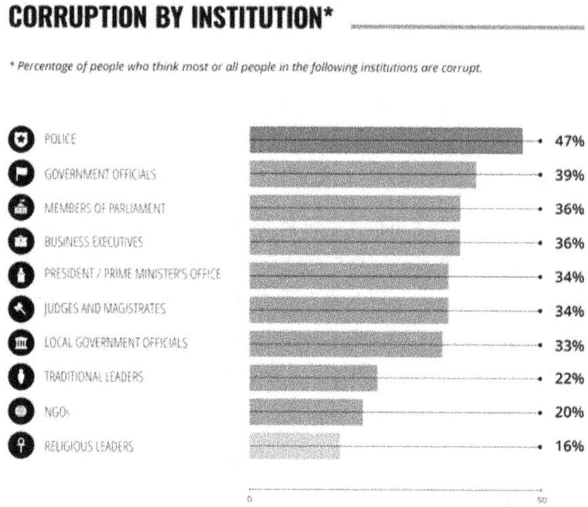


(GCB) – across 35 countries in Africa (Transparency International – GCB, 2019). Based on more than 47,000 citizens surveyed, the result reveals the percentage of employees perceived to be corrupt by institutions and public services:

As indicated in Figure 3 above, unsurprisingly African police force has consistently establish itself as the highest government institution collecting bribes across Africa. Key political office holders including the office of the presidents/prime ministers, parliaments, judiciaries etc. also have significant high bribery rates across Africa. The poor citizens are vulnerable to these civil servants who constantly demands bribe before providing public utilities like water, electricity, passports, licenses etc (Transparency International – GCB, 2019). The development of internet and intercontinental banking have made corruption to thrives in African countries. Western banks have now colluded with African leaders and civil servants to hide their stolen wealth in Europe and America. The silence of Western media on the unethical activities of Western banks, estate and property developments firms, oil and mining companies etc. with the looted funds in Africa calls for concern (Adusei, 2009). These companies are unethically promoting corruptions in Africa, and our people have failed to explore the opportunity of the internet to globally condemn these frauds.

## Commitment of African Power Elites in Fighting Corruption

Corruption is one of the most complex issues facing a large number of countries around the world (Ades & Tella, 1997). Corruption is a crime which goes unnoticed by its victims (Graeff 2005). Corruption is a response to either beneficial or harmful regulation which has a link to a country's legal, economic, cultural and political institutions (Svensson, 2005). This assertion seems to suggest that corrupt activities are a product of the benevolent regulations which rewards and permits individuals to avoid penalties for their harmful and dastardly acts. Corruption thrives in Africa, chiefly because the legal system is porous and openly manipulated, insufficient for monitoring and punishing offenders who constitute the ruling-elite class.

Elites in African countries lack a commitment to the fight against corruption. This is demonstrated by their flagrant abuse of court processes and open manipulation of the legal systems. One of the most potent weapons the elite class has used in undermining the fight against corruption is the legislative and court apparatuses. Elites within the political arena in Nigeria used their contacts, networks and political positions to weaken relevant sections and sub-sections of the legislative rules when promulgating laws that would assist the fight against corruption — thereby creating administrative bottlenecks vis-à-vis administrative corruption which further helps their corrupt practices. Secondly, the elite ruling class have emboldened legislative, legal and court corruption in Africa. Elites have deployed their ungodly wealth and proceeds from their criminal activities to get justice from law courts.

Corruption has been systematically weakened by elite networks which are everywhere and in all sectors of the economy. Recently, the president of the supreme court of Nigeria was removed from office for receiving bribes from the agents of a political party to subvert justice. In so many instances, corrupt politicians and administrators have gone unpunished or given soft landing judgements via plea bargaining even when there is compelling evidence against such individuals. Though, fewer cases have been determined against only opposition politicians and those ardent critics and those who diametrically opposed to the ruling party. Overall, elites have failed in the fight against corruption. The fight against corruption is cosmetic to a considerable extent or/and a tool used for tormenting critics of the ruling political party.

## ICT as a Solution to Corrupt Practices

Information and Communications Technologies, particularly the internet, has brought about significant technological innovations and sophistication in electronic networks which had consequently paved the way for new electronic payment methods and platforms. In both developed and developing countries, electronic payments have gained penetration. For instance, Gnangnon & Brun (2018) studied the economic impact of the internet on public revenue mobilisation in both developed and developing countries. They found that the 'internet gap', which is, the gap between the amount of internet usage in a country and the average internet usage of the world at large, affects its public mobilisation. In other words, countries with high use of the internet are more likely to be able to effectively utilize electronic payments for public revenue collection.

E-payment has become a major tool in achieving transparency in transactions and the fight against corrupt practices in the public sectors in Nigeria. It has also been assessed that electronic payments, when used well, have the potential to significantly reduce the cost of cash management and transactions, and curb corruption such as bribery by 47% (Dos Santos & Kvangraven, 2017). A report by the world bank in 2012 argues that developing countries would realise annual savings of about 1% in GDP by adopting electronic payment systems. Krolikowski (2014) examined the effect of Mobile-enabled payment methods in curbing corruption in Water service delivery in Dar es Salaam, Tanzania. He found that electronic payment reduces information asymmetry and promotes transparency in the billng and payment process. Electronic payment dimishes the 'discretionary powers' ofgovernment staff from perpetrating corrupt practices with Government funds and also discourages bribery in cash from government customers. This,, in turn, improves collection ratios, efficient and effective use of staff resources and financial management.

The Central Bank of Nigeria also introduced electronic payment, a part of the bank's cashless policy in Nigeria to help curb corrupt practices in the country. Jatau and Dung (2014) evaluated the effect of electronic payment in Plateau State of Nigeria. They found that since the adoption of electronic payment for the collection of Government revenue, there was a 50% increase in internally generated revenue. That's a staggering increase and a pointer to the value of electronic payments in curbing corruption in Nigeria. Electronic payment is capable of "blocking leakages or channels of leakages and as well provide audit trail of transaction" (p. 204). Mugambi and Wanjohi (2018) investigated the factors affecting implementation of revenue collection systems for the Kenyan government. Through a questionnaire administered to government workers in a county, they found electronic payment systems have made the government's revenue collection system more available and accessible to taxpayers. As a result, taxpayers compliance has surged. Within three months of implementing electronic payment, tax payment surged by a significant 60%. There was a significant reduction in the bottlenecks and errors that exist in the previous system.

Electronic payment systems have the capacity to curb corruption in Africa. Several studies have shown empirically the value it brings to government revenue collection in terms of reducing bottlenecks, reducing operational costs, providing an audit trail of transactions and blocking leakages in payment systems.

The result of the use of e-payment system has brought about efficiency, fraud reduction and innovativeness in the payment system (Oladeji, 2014). Public sector agencies are unnecessarily bureaucratic in their operations. Especially the payment for executed projects which often results in some corrupt collaborations and gratification culture between officials and contractors. This unwholesome relationships and interaction between the contractor and officials led to horrendous and criminal corrupt system entrenched in the in Nigeria's public sectors. However, the adoption of e-payment has reduced these tendencies because e-payment facilitates remote and swift payments and tracking of payments to beneficiaries account to assist in audit trail (Ogedebe and Jacob, 2012). Finally, the tremendous efficacy of e-payment has aided and escalated the fight against corrupt practices. Agencies against financial and corrupt practices like Economic Financial Crime Commission (EFCC) and Independent Corrupt Practices Commission (ICPC) in Nigeria have recorded sound legal victories in several cases in Nigeria. It can be concluded that e-payment adoption in African countries has restored some sanity and integrity in government transactions, resulting in the effective use of public funds. There exists plenty of opportunities for Africa where electronic payment systems are concerned.

## Electronic Payment Opportunities in Africa

The use of ICT for electronic payment in Africa is not without challenges. Maisiba & Atambo (2016) studied the effect of an electronic tax system on revenue collection efficiency in Kenya. They found that while the system is effective and efficient, the lack of computer knowledge by government staff, poor internet and epileptic power supply amongst many others did not let the country reap the full benefits of the system. Arora, Ujakpa, Jonathan, Appiah-Annin and Mwanza (2016) studied the challenges of E-Zwich, an electronic payment system in Ghana and found significant challenges to include people's resistance to change from the old cash system. The difficulty in accepting change appears to stem from the fear of technology and the lure for corruption which cash transaction tends to favour more.

In South Africa, Killian and Kabanda's (2017) study on the adoption of mobile payments by middle-income earners of the country found that habits and social influence affect the propensity to adopt mobile payments. People are finding it hard to adopt new technologies because the old habits (of cash transactions) die hard. Bultum (2014) examined the factors that affected the adoption of Electronic banking in Ethiopia and found that the limited ICT infrastructure and a lack of a legal framework to support electronic payments as a significant challenge. Security risks and lack of trust in E banking products and services are also some of the challenges the country is facing.

Frank and Binaebi (2019) also examined the effect of electronic payment systems on the performance of commercial banks in Nigeria. They found that electronic payment systems have led to the improvement of the performance of commercial banks. They recommended that banks increase their investments into electronic payment systems and most importantly for the government to boost the country's internet infrastructure in order to allow electronic payment systems penetrate the nooks and crany of the country's business landscape.

There is a plethora of gains and wins for African countries when it comes to the adoption of electronic payments. Economically, they are able to boost their revenue collection and improve the efficiencies of their systems. However, several challenges exist. Electronic payments systems are not yet fully embraced, and the level of infrastructure in many of these countries needs a lot of improvement if electronic payment systems being regarded as an effective tool in combating corruption. The concept of acceptance of electronic payment systems in these countries is worth investigating.

## Acceptance of Electronic Payments in Africa

Advances in internet technology have revolutionised modern society in multi-dimensional ways. Advancement in internet technology has increased the embrace and use of mobile devices for multiple and diverse internet-based activities. This trend has also changed the way businesses are conducted around the world and across international boundaries. In fact, the internet technology has influenced organisational and business strategies and business venturing. One of such new trends is online sales and purchasing, and payments for products and services using e-payment systems. Electronic or mobile payment is popular in e-commerce and business environments; this trend has not been fully embraced in G2C environments. The adoption of mobile and electronic payment has taken a global space. However, mobile and e-payment acceptance in Africa took too long to gain acceptance, especially in the public sectors among African countries; that is notorious for economic sabotage and corrupt practices.

Acceptance of e-payment systems has the potential to reduce these behemoths confronting African countries. Gradually, most of the countries are embracing the use of mobile and e-payments; for instance, Nigeria rolled out a model of mobile payment and e-payment systems which was termed "cashless economy''. e-payment payments can be classified into POS-point of sale (POS, ATMs, SMS, WAP—Wireless Application Protocol, NFC— Near Field Communication and USSD—Unstructured Supplementary Service Data), and others such as mobile order, mobile banking, mobile delivery, and mobile contract (Innopay (2013), while mobile payment systems as an e-payment involves the use of mobile devices, such as smartphones and tablets.

## Commercial Drivers of e-Payment Systems

It may be interesting to ask what is behind the positive attitude towards e-payment acceptance in Africa? Generally, several factors have been confirmed to influence payment systems, such includes; perceived ease-of-use, perceived usefulness, perceived cost, mobility, perceived trust, relative advantages, compatibility, complexity, network externalities.

In terms of the commercial importance of e-payments, the use of payment systems for e-commerce and mobile commerce transactions appears to be dominant. Businesses see e-payment systems as a source of competitive advantage. The internet has empowered users to share and exchange information, including commercial/ business information within their networks. As a result of this, marketplace or click business environment has encouraged more users to complete their purchases and transactions online. This shows that organisations can convert the attractiveness of the internet into a competitive advantage (Mastercard and Prime Research, 2014) by marshalling sound customer engagement and relationship policies for their customers.

E-payment systems as a purchasing mechanism facilitate fast, secure, and convenient, increased transaction volumes, reduced transaction costs, and increased customer loyalty (Slade, Williams, & Dwivedi, 2013). Closely related to this is the interaction between the perceived ease-of-use and perceived usefulness of e-payment systems. The 'cashless' nature of e-payment systems is perceived to be easy-to-use for any forms of transactions. It is also useful in a different transaction where cash payment is unacceptable. Several studies have confirmed that perceived ease of use and usefulness as essential predictors of user's acceptance of e-payment systems (Liebana-Cabanillas et al. 2018; Lee et al. 2012).

Research has explained the impact of digitalisation of payments on the payment ecosystem and concluded that digitalisation of payments creates a new arena for a competition that requires new collaboration among stakeholders (Hedman & Henningsson, 2012). The strategic resource-based view sees e-payment as a competitive asset for the financial institutions. e-payment system is a non-repudiation platform, and players can find it difficult to deny completed transactions. Overall, payment systems have several advantages, including convenience, interactivity, customisability and quick responses (Dastan & Gurler, 2016).

## Inhibitors of E-Payment Systems Adoption

There are several reasons why users hesitate to adopt e-payment systems. One of the protuberant reasons is lack of trust. Trust is the belief that a feature of an object faces a risky situation from achieving the intended purpose. E-payment faces environmental risk and uncertainties due to several nodes in the transaction process and ecosystem, and this negatively affects the trust of customers adoption attitude.

E-payments does not guarantee personal information privacy or the protection of its identifying features. Information privacy refers to the ability of individuals to maintain control of their personal information (Westin, 1967). People are concerned about the fact that their personal information can be made open and compromised. Uncertainties around personal information and privacy have heightened the fear of e-payment users. Customers are conscious of the presence and threat from online hackers who are involved in identity theft in the e-payment space. Risk perceptions of customers are inversely related to e-payment acceptance (Pavlou, 2003).

## Comparison With Other Developing Countries

A critical analysis of the barriers to adoption in Africa and other developing economies reveal numerous barriers in Africa that are quite different from the barriers in other developing economies. One of such is the infrastructural deficits noticeable in Africa. E-payment requires complex infrastructures from different stakeholders involved in e-payment delivery (Johnson et al. 2018). E-payments stakeholders like the financial institutions, government regulators, mobile network operators, device manufacturers, mobile content providers, and consumers all require adequate and alignment of the infrastructure for smooth and effective deployment and implementation of e-payment system.

The challenge of African economies stems from considerable deficits in infrastructural investment and upgrade that could support e-payment implementation. Therefore, full implementation and adoption of e-payment require a number of information technology infrastructures such as excellent and affordable internet connectivity, global payment systems software and connectivity. The cost internet connection and rates are high due to the free fall of the local currency and high exchange rates. In Nigeria, for instance, the subscription fee charged by the various internet service providers(ISPs) is quite high and unaffordable for many. Similarly, there are intermittent power supplies in most part of the continent. It is evident that power interruptions will affect the smooth usage of e-payment for transactions.

The high rate of illiteracy among the populace has also fuelled the resistance attitude towards e-payment systems (Okifo & Igbunu, 2015). Importantly, knowledge of ICT and the ability to read are required in e-payment optimisation. Lastly, e-payment service adoption is slow because there are a variety of available alternative payment systems. Alternatives to e-payment systems have an advantage over e-payment systems because consumers can make cash payments (Johnson et al., 2018), which are prevalent forms of payment in Africa.

## Curbing Corruption Using e-Payment Systems

Corrupt practices like fraud, mis-use of funds, mis-management, and embezzlement of public funds are prevalent in Africa. In fact, corruption has been entrenched in the system to the extent that it is accepted as a norm. Every year, public funds are distributed among public officials and contractors who are known partners.

Evidence from Nigeria shows that e-readiness and e-participation indices were inversely related to the levels of corruption, an that a country's e-readiness and e-participation may impact the levels of corruption. Recently, the Central Bank of Nigeria, implementated bank verification numbers(BVN) as part of the inter-bank settlement systems. BVN involves the collection and use of biometric data for identification purposes . The Nigerian model of BVN uses fingerprint component of the biometric to authentiticate customers' identity in the bank. This policy is unique because the BVN captures the biometric data of bank customers and allocates unique numbers for identification during bank transactions. This policy has reduced duplication or stolen of identities, thereby exposing frauds in the system. BVN is linked to all bank accounts, and this makes it possible to track and trace sources of all illicit deposits and transfer of funds within and outside of Nigeria. The use of this system made it possible for monitoring agency to track, trace, arrest, investigate and punish corrupt officials in Nigeria.

Similarly, government agencies,for instance, the taxation, and examination board etc have adopted the use of e-payment for services rendered to the public. Initially, most of the public agencies do embezzle proceeds from sales and services. BVN has been used to identify some illicit fund transfer and money laundering activities of some politicians in the past regime of Jonathan Goodluck. In other cases, owners of some slush fund were unidentifiable and such money was forfeited to the federal government. For thos who could not adequately the source of their bank deposit also forfeited such illicit money because most of them were linked to some disgraced policiticians. For instance, the wife of the fromer president, Goodluck Jonathan and the former minister of petroleum have forfeited millions of dollars to the federal government. To some extent, corrupt practices in the public sectors have reduced drastically due to the use of e-payment systems.

## Recommendations to African Governments

1. To achieve an efficiency of leadership in Africa, corruption must be eradicated. Below are essential points as alternative recommendations to African government on how the fight against corruption can be strengthened:
2. The governments of each country in Africa should have an obligation to protect their poor citizens who have little forums to raise their individual and collective concerns.
3. Regional unions like ECOWAS are expected to be very vocal. Their support in criticizing corrupt related activities that have consistently deny justice to Africans is significantly required.
4. African countries should create a hostile political environment for politicians who want to reap where they have not sowed.
5. African countries should make it a priority to recover and repatriate all stolen African resources and assets across the world.
6. To achieve good governance, African governments should develop sound social and economic and social policies that will ensure equitable distribution of wealth.
7. Discourage politics with little remuneration and strengthen the justice system with capital punishment for corruption.
8. Unnecessary materialism should be addressed from cultural norms in African societies.

# CONCLUSION

In this review, we have been able to discuss corruption as a complex issue facing African countries. Our review painted the frustrations of citizens over this evil plaquing African countries. Our review further shows the weaknesses in the legal and legislative instruments in fighting corrupt practices in Africa. Our conclusion is that the elites deliberately weakened relevant instititutional frameworks that are key to sustaining the fight against corruption., thereby making these institutions like the court and law to become benevolent apparatus for advancing their interest and pillaging the public funds. We concluded that the strong e-apyment system has been effective in curbing corruption and corrupt-tendencies in Africa, using the BVN cases and convictions in Nigeria. To sustain the fight, more administrative/policies and ICT innovations are required. Our review explained the effecticacy of BVN, biometric identification of customers has revolutionised e-payment system and has turned the heat on corrupt public officials and their accomplices.

## REFERENCES

Ades, A., & Di Tella, R. (1997). The new economics of corruption: A survey and some new results. *Political Studies*, *45*(3), 496–515. doi:10.1111/1467-9248.00093

Adusei, L. A. (2009). *Hiding Africa's Looted Funds: The Silence of Western Media*. Retrieved from https://wikileaks.org/wiki/Hiding_Africa%27s_Looted_Funds:_The_Silence_of_Western_Media

Agbaje, A. (2004). Corruption, Accountability and Good governance: Reflections on governance in the Nigeria Fourth Republic 1999-2003. *International Review of Politics and Development.*, *2*(2), 23–47.

Agbeyegbe, T. D., Stotsky, J., & WoldeMariam, A. (2006). Trade liberalization, exchange rate changes, and tax revenue in Sub-Saharan Africa. *Journal of Asian Economics*, *17*(2), 261–284. doi:10.1016/j.asieco.2005.09.003

Ann-Sofie Isaksson. (2013). *Corruption along ethnic lines: A study of individual corruption experiences in 17 African countries*. Working papers in economics, No 571. Retreived from: https://core.ac.uk/download/pdf/16337262.pdf

Arora, R., Ujakpa, M. M., Jonathan, F., Appiah-Annin, K., & Mwanza, P. T. (2016). Challenges Inhibiting E-Zwich Electronic Payment System. *Journal of Information Engineering and Applications*, *6*(10), 18–31.

Baharumshah, A. Z., Jibrilla, A. A., Sirag, A., Ali, H. S., & Muhammad, I. M. (2016). Public Revenue-Expenditure Nexus in South Africa: Are there Asymmetries? *The South African Journal of Economics*, *84*(4), 520–537. doi:10.1111aje.12130

Bultum, A. G. (2014). Factors affecting the adoption of the electronic banking system in Ethiopian banking industry. *Journal of Management Information System and E-commerce*, *1*(1), 1–17.

Daştan, I. & Gürler, C. (2016). Factors Affecting the Adoption of Mobile Payment Systems: An Empirical Analysis. *Emerging Markets Journal*. DOI doi:10.5195/emaj.2016.95

dos Santos, P. L., & Harvold Kvangraven, I. (2017). Better than Cash, but Beware the Costs: Electronic Payments Systems and Financial Inclusion in Developing Economies. *Development and Change*, *48*(2), 205–227. doi:10.1111/dech.12296

Frank, B. P., & Binaebi, B. (2019). Electronic Payment Systems Implementation and the Performance of Commercial Banks in Nigeria. *European Journal of Business and Management Research*, *4*(5). doi:10.24018/ejbmr.2019.4.5.112

Gaur, A., & Ondrus, J. (2012). The role of banks in the mobile payment ecosystem: a strategic asset perspective. In *Proceedings of the 14th Annual International Conference on Electronic Commerce*. ACM Press. 10.1145/2346536.2346570

Gideon, Z., & Alouis, M. (2013). Systems, processes and challenges of public revenue collection in Zimbabwe. *American International Journal of Contemporary Research*, *2*, 49–60.

Gnangnon, S. K., & Brun, J.-F. (2018). Impact of bridging the Internet gap on public revenue mobilization. *Information Economics and Policy*, *43*, 23–33. doi:10.1016/j.infoecopol.2018.04.001

Graeff, P. (2005). Why should one trust in corruption? The linkage between corruption, trust, norms, and social capital. In J. Graf Lambsdorff, M. Taube, & M. Schramm (Eds.), *The New Institutional Economics of Corruption* (pp. 21–42). London: Routledge.

Hope, K. R. (1999). Corruption in Africa: A crisis in ethical leadership. *Public Integrity*, 289-308. Retrieved from https://www.researchgate.net/publication/273944947_Corruption_in_Africa_A_Crisis_in_Ethical_Leadership

Jatau, V. S., & Dung, K. L. (2014). The Central Bank of Nigeria's cashless policy: A major panacea for eliminating corruption and enhancing sustainable development in Nigeria. *African Research Review*, *8*(4), 198–206. doi:10.4314/afrrev.v8i4.16

Johnson, V. L., Kiser, A., Washington, R., & Torres, R. (2018). Limitations to the rapid adoption of M-payment services: Understanding the impact of privacy risk on M- Payment services. *Computers in Human Behavior*, *79*, 111–122. doi:10.1016/j.chb.2017.10.035

Killian, D., Kabanda, S., & Kilian, D. (2017, July). Mobile Payments In South Africa: Middle Income Earners' Perspective. In PACIS (p. 53). Academic Press.

Krolikowski, A. (2014). Can mobile-enabled payment methods reduce petty corruption in urban water provision? *Water Alternatives*, *7*(1).

Lee, Y. K., Park, J. H., Chung, N., & Blakeney, A. (2012). A unified perspective on the factors influencing usage intention toward mobile financial services. *Journal of Business Research*, *65*(11), 1590–1599. doi:10.1016/j.jbusres.2011.02.044

Leo, O. C., & Patrick, B. E. (2010). Analysis of Corruption from the Ethical and Moral Perspectives. *European Journal of Scientific Research*, *44*(3), 466–476.

Liebana-Cabanillas, F., Munoz-Leiva, F., & Sanchez-Fernandez, J. (2018). A global approach to the analysis of user behaviour in mobile payment systems in the new electronic environment. *Service Business*, *12*(1), 25–64. doi:10.100711628-017-0336-7

Maisiba, G. J., & Atambo, W. (2016). Effects of the electronic-tax system on the revenue collection efficiency of Kenya Revenue Authority: A case of Uasin Gishu County. *Imperial Journal of Interdisciplinary Research*, *2*(4), 2454–1362.

Mastercard and Prime Research. (2014). *13 Million social media conversations show what consumers think about mobile payments*. Retrieved from http://newsroom.mastercard.com

Mugambi, F. K., & Wanjohi, J. M. (2018). Factors affecting the implementation of Revenue Collection Systems in county governments in Kenya, A case of Meru county. *International Journal For Research In Business, Management And Accounting*, *4*(8), 9-30.

Nduku, E., & Tenamwenye, J. (2014). *Corruption in Africa: A Threat to Justice and Sustainable Peace* (Vol. 14). Focus. Retrieved from https://www.amazon.com/Corruption-Africa-Threat-Justice-Sustainable/dp/2889310175

Ogedebe, P.M. & Jacob, B.P. (2012). E-Payment: Prospects and Challenges in Nigerian Public Sector. *International Journal of Modern Engineering Research*, *2*(5), 3104-3106.

Ojong, C. M., Anthony, O., & Arikpo, O. F. (2016). The impact of tax revenue on economic growth: Evidence from Nigeria. IOSR. *Journal of Economics and Finance*, *7*(1), 32–38.

Okifo, J., & Igbunu, R. (2015). Electronic Payment System in Nigeria: Its Economic Benefits and Challenges. *Journal of Education and Practice*, *6*(16).

Oladeji, K. (2014). *Integrated Personnel and Payroll Information Systems (IPPIS) for Universities and other Higher Institutions of Learning. A Paper Presentation at Northwest University*, Kano, Nigeria.

Pavlou, P. A. (2003). Consumer acceptance of electronic commerce: Integrating trust and risk with the technology acceptance model. *International Journal of Electronic Commerce*, *7*(3), 101–134. doi:10.1080/10864415.2003.11044275

Peiffer, C., & Rose, R. (2018). Why Are the Poor More Vulnerable to Bribery in Africa? The Institutional Effects of Services. *The Journal of Development Studies*, *54*(1), 18–29. doi:10.1080/00220388.2016.1257121

Svensson, J. (2005). Eight Questions about Corruption. *The Journal of Economic Perspectives*, *19*(3), 19–42. doi:10.1257/089533005774357860

Transparency International – GCB. (2019). *Citizens speak out about corruption in Africa*. Retrieved from https://www.transparency.org/news/feature/citizens_speak_out_about_corruption_in_africa

United Nations Economic Commission for Africa -UNECA. (2016). *Measuring corruption in Africa: The international dimension matters - African Governance Report IV*. Retrieved from https://www.uneca.org/sites/default/files/PublicationFiles/agr4_eng_fin_web.pdf

Vorster, J. M. (2012). Managing corruption in South Africa: The ethical responsibility of churches. *Scriptura*, *109*(1), 133–147.

Westin, A. F. (1967). *Privacy and freedom*. Athenaeum.

Worlu, C. N., & Nkoro, E. (2012). Tax revenue and economic development in Nigeria: A macroeconometric approach. *Academic Journal of Interdisciplinary Studies*, *1*(2), 211–223.

# Chapter 8
# Impact of Mobile Payment Applications and Transfers on Business:
## Financial Inclusion and Innovation – The Case of Mpesa in Kibera Slum, Kenya

**Gladys Wanjiku Thuita**
*Riara University, Kenya*

## ABSTRACT

*Despite Kenya having over 40 banks, only three banks are accessible to the residents of Kibera Slum. Kibera Slum is located on the outskirts of Nairobi and is home to approximately 0.75 million people. A majority of the population in Kibera Slum comprises of either unemployed or casually employed adults whose income levels are considerably low, making it impossible for many of them to operate formal bank accounts. However, the evolution of mobile money technologies has made financial inclusion and innovation possible for Kibera Slum residents. The mobile-banking facility known as M-Pesa enables mobile money remittances and has an outstanding record of financial inclusion and innovation. The objective of this research was therefore to examine financial inclusion and innovation in the Kibera Slum. The study used self-administered questionnaires to answer to two objectives. The study found out that M-Pesa services are accessible and widely used in Kibera Slum. The study also found that M-Pesa business is rated average as a source of income to M-Pesa agent. Ultimately, the study observed that financial inclusion and financial innovation are prevalent in Kibera Slum. These findings have significant implications: the study sheds light on the fact that the slum dwellers have embraced the use of M-Pesa services as a platform to access financial services, establishing more innovative financial services that will help the low income earners expand their businesses and training M-Pesa agents will enhance sustainable business growth and promote innovation.*

DOI: 10.4018/978-1-7998-2398-8.ch008

## INTRODUCTION

As a general economic and financial proposition, poor people are generally marginalized or quite often shut out of a country's economic and financial wealth. In this study, this is taken as a given truism. Accordingly, both the theme and rationale for this study is innovative financial inclusion for the low income population. Prior to the introduction of mobile money by Safaricom, financial inclusion for the poor was not only unthinkable but also impractical (Buku and Meredith, 2013). But because it is a desirable human trait for any country, sometimes efforts are made (publicly and/or privately) to establish ways and means for the poor to access ways and means of improving their lives. In Kenya, such an effort has been made by and through a private company's innovation in financial inclusion. Accordingly, this survey explores how innovative financing, and therefore financial inclusion, has indeed been technologically enhanced to include even those who live and work in the slums and, in particular, Kibera slum which is the subject of this inquiry. It is generally acknowledged that Kibera Slum is not only the largest slum in Kenya but also in Africa (Onyango and Tostensen, 2015).

Financial inclusion should target to give attention to a population that has been excluded from the financial sector due to their location, level of income, type of activity and financial literacy. Financial inclusion need to address the challenges of the unbanked by making finances available, accessible and affordable to all segments of the population. The majority of the unbanked uses phones that cannot access financial transactions and thus the need to address challenges such as reachability and affordability (Sangeetha & Koushik, 2018). The unbanked population in Africa is a sizeable market. Mobile banking has made it easy for the unbanked to receive, send and make payments. In the past ten years financial inclusion in Kenya has significant increased (Central Bank of Kenya, 2014).

## POVERTY AND DEMOGRAPHICS IN KENYA

According to the data released by Kenya National Bureau of Statistics and United Nations, (2018), the current population in Kenya is slightly above 50 million on an area of 580,370 km$^2$. Out of this population, about 70% are below the age of 30 years. The mean average age of the population is 19 years while life expectancy is 59.5 years. The ratio of male to female is almost 1:1. Out of the total population, about 36 million are in the rural areas and 14 million in the urban areas. As a result of harsh climatic conditions and land fragmentation, the urban areas are becoming over populated with young school leavers searching for formal employment. According to the United Nations Development Programme (2018), unemployment stood at

39.1% which is the highest in East Africa. In 2018, youth unemployment stood at 55% and this is ages between 15 years and 24 years (Ng'ethe, 2018). According to a joint report by World Bank and Peace Child International (2018), one of the major causes of youth unemployment is lack of access to capital.

According to a report released by United Nations Development Programme (2018), indicated that Kenya is still struggling with high poverty at 29.2% of the total population (16 million). A large portion of the population lives on less than $1.25 per day, and thus unable to meet most basic human needs (United Nations Development Programme, 2018). Further indication shows that the government of Kenya will not achieve the sustainable development goal number 1 (eradication of poverty) by the year 2030. Despite the fact that the country has shown progress in advanced economic activities meant to bring down the poverty levels, studies show that rural areas suffer from high poverty and uneducated population (World Bank, 2018).

A report by International Monetary Fund (2014) shows that wealth in Kenya is held by a few while majority live in either absolute or extreme poverty. Furthermore, men have higher income than women despite increased participation by women in social-economic development in the society (Society for International Development and Kenya bureau of Statistics, 2013). There is a big gap in earnings with a few Kenyan earning hefty income while the majority earning below $ 500 per month. Wealth is unequally distributed in Kenya which has led to majority of the population being financially excluded from the formal financial institutions (KNBS, 2018).

## Kibera Slum

Kibera Slum is home to about 750,000 (with some unofficial estimates being slightly over 1 million) residents from different ethnic groups. The total population comprises of 75% below the age of 18 years and 25% above the age of 18 years. The slum occupies an area of 2.38 $km^2$ Majority of Kibera dwellers take up informal jobs which are not recorded in official employment statistics (KNBS, 2018). According to World Bank (2018), a resident in Kibera lives on less than $ 1.25 per day. Kibera is home to different ethnical groups using 'Swahili' to communicate. Majority of the houses in Kibera are sub-standard and when it rains, the houses are swept away and sewerage system becomes unbearable. In recent years, the government of Kenya in collaboration with World Bank, has initiated housing projects to improve the decency of the houses in Kibera but still to date the larger population is yet to be relocated to the new houses.

## Challenges in Kibera

One of the key issues in a developing country has been and continues to be how to enable the poor and the marginalized citizens to access financial services in a sustainable manner. This study was designed and carried out in one of Kenya's poorest urban areas – the globally famous Kibera Slum. And as is generally acknowledged, Kibera Slum is not only one of the largest in Kenya but also probably the largest slum or ghetto in Africa. Majority of the residents in Kibera are either unemployed or temporary employed thus being unable to access formal banking. Lack of electricity (less than a third of the total population have power), lack of water (majority risk of typhoid) and poor sewerage (no toilets) are some of the major problems encountered by the residences of Kibera slums. Other challenges include unemployment, illicit brew, inadequate healthcare, poor schools, limited public utilities (schools), congestion, and crime and teenager pregnancy among others (Bandari, 2018).

## M-pesa

With the introduction of mobile banking (M-pesa), innovative financial inclusion among the residents of Kibera slum has been made possible. Over a decade ago, since its invention, M-pesa product has reached out to the poor and unbanked ghetto residents. According to Beck (2015), financial innovation is the development of new financial products and processes that enable fund transfer, borrowing and conducting business without involving physical monies. Financial innovation enhances sustainability of institutions and outreach to the poor.

M-Pesa was invented in March of 2007 in Kenya. According to the Communication Authority of Kenya the active M-pesa users were 24,206,341 by the end of September 2018. To be able to use M-pesa, one is required to buy and register a sim card with Safaricom. M-pesa is not only functional within Kenya and the Africa continent, but also across continents such as United States, Europe and Asia. Some of M-pesa products include sending money, withdrawing cash, buying airtime, borrowing loans and making savings, paying bills by lipa-na m-pesa. The lipa-na M-pesa product enables a customer to pay for bills, buy goods and services at their convenience time and place which reduces the risk of carrying cash. Loans and savings are paperless banking services offered through M-pesa and enables customers to save and access short term finances in commercial banks for a maximum period of one month.

M-pesa products do not work in isolation from the other mobile-money companies Airtel and Telkom. The other telecommunication companies are linked to Safaricom to enable customers buy airtime, send and receive money. M-pesa products are thus connected and enabled to use and facilitate financial transactions as per the needs of the customer. The most recent M-pesa innovation is 'FULIZA' which is a platform that enables M-pesa users to send money or pay for goods and services with insufficient balances (some kind of an overdraft) in their M-pesa user account to access up to Kshs. 50,000 ($ 500). The amount that the M-pesa user can access is based on the value of their M-pesa transactions. Safaricom rolled out the service to add to the other existing services (voice and data) that are widely used to grow revenue.

Although mobile banking has broaden financial inclusion, banks have lost revenue of 5% to 10% and as a result the banking sector has been destabilized (Moody's investor's service, 2019). According to Safaricom management, there has been significant increase M-pesa business by the second quarter of 2019, the total business contributed through M-pesa transactions amounted to 31.2% of the total revenue. In 2018, Safaricom revenue from M-pesa was Kshs. 55.1billion ($551million) (Safaricom, PLC, 2019). The company had proposed to split the business and have M-pesa have independent business but the move has been dropped (Communication Authority of Kenya, 2019).

## OBJECTIVES OF THE STUDY

This study had two main objectives, namely (a) to determine the extent of M-pesa services on financial inclusion in Kibera slum in Kenya and (b) to determine the effect of M-pesa services on financial innovation in Kibera slum in Kenya.

## THEORETICAL REVIEW

Diffusion of Innovation Theory, developed by Rogers in 1962, is one of the oldest social science theory. The theory prostates that a product/innovation diffuses in the social system over time. Although not everyone in the social system will accept the innovated product, the product will eventually be adopted and changes will manifest. Diffusion of the product entails awareness of the product, decision on whether to accept or reject the new idea, using the innovation for the first time, and the willingness to continue use of the innovation (Wayne, 2019). According to Dearing and Cox (2018), diffusion of innovation entails the processes of dissemination, implementation, sustainability and improvement. In view of this study, M-pesa products have diffused in Kibera Slum and continue to be used ten years after M-pesa services were launched. In addition the M-pesa service provider continues to innovate new products that are beneficial to both M-pesa users and M-pesa agents.

According to World Bank (2014), increasing financial inclusion is regarded as a challenge that hinders development. Although statistics vary, more than half of the world's population is financially excluded and cannot access formal banking services. More so, the population is categorized as low income earners with no bank accounts. Financial inclusion integrates political, economic and social pillars which are interwoven for purposes of economic growth. Where any group or a group of people are excluded from the financial system, the gains of economic development do not reach everyone and this leads to inequality. Financial inclusion theory of change states that participants within the inclusive financial systems will adapt to changing circumstance and transform their lives, if they are able to access, use, and afford a range of financial services. Further, the theory articulates that financial inclusion needs to bring changes such as poverty reduction, increased access to finances, new regulations, increase in capacity building on product innovation and technical assistance to facilitate strategy development process on production innovation (Burjorjee and Scola, 2015).

## EMPIRICAL LITERATURE REVIEW

Arnaboldi and Claeys (2010) contends that internet banking has brought an overhaul in the way business is being conducted. The study sought to investigate innovation and performance of European banks adopting internet. Furthermore, internet banking cuts down on labour costs and therefore considered to be profitable. Al-Jabri & Sohail (2012) conducted a study in Saudi Arabia using convenience sampling technique. The study found out that banks in Saudi Arabia offer mobile banking that are tailor-made towards the customer behavior/needs and those that fulfill their expectations. Mobile banking that support and provide a number of services are perceived to be better are easily adopted by the customers. The study recommends the banks to first, understand the customer needs and design mobile banking products that are useful and quality services.

In Rwanda, financial inclusion has been enabled through Umurenge Sacco, which is community based. About 90% of the population in Rwanda lives within 5km radius of Umurenge Sacco. In South Asia, millions of people live in poverty and are excluded from financial services. To address the challenge, International Finance Corporation has so far set a platform where the low-income entrepreneurs access finances (availability and affordability) and sustainable business advisory (technologies and transformed markets) to improve people's lives thus widening access to financial services, mobilizing savings for families, capital investment and business expansions (International Finance Corporation, 2017). Njeru (2018) conducted a descriptive study on 43 commercial banks on the relationship between bank innovations and financial inclusions among the commercial banks in Kenya. The study concluded that mobile banking has positive correlation with financial inclusion and that mobile banking products innovations have a strong correlations with innovations. The recommendation is to put strategies that encourage mobile banking and also for the government to reduce tax on mobile banking to encourage its uptake.

Nyathira (2012) conducted a study on financial innovation and its effect on financial performance of commercial banks in Kenya using a casual research design and secondary data from the published annual report by the Central Bank of Kenya. The population of the study was 43 commercial banks. The study found out that financial innovation is positively correlated to profitability in the banking sector. In conclusion, the banks should adopt more efficient payment platforms and which are adequately regulated. The recommendation on the financial institutions to embrace financial innovation and secure payments that spurs sustainable economic growth. According to the Africa Development Bank (2013), Africa have less than quarter of adults access to a formal financial institution due to lack of business strategies that aims to target the low income individuals. The study focused on the role of automated teller machine and point of sales for the promotion of financial inclusion. The study concluded that it is appropriate to put policies to foster financial inclusion.

Afandi and Mbugua (2015), conducted a descriptive study to establish the role of agent banking services in promotion of financial inclusion in Nyeri town. The study found out that customers prefer to pay extra charge to access banking services through agent banking outlets. In addition the geographical coverage had a positive relationship with financial inclusion. In conclusion, the study found out that when financial services are brought closer to the customers they save a lot of time which otherwise would have been used to queue in the banking halls. The study recommended the opening of more agent outlets to cover wider geographical areas and the same to be well monitored for liquidity flow and security issues. Muiruri and Ngari (2014), conducted a study on the effects of financial innovations on the financial performance of Commercial Banks in Kenya using descriptive research design. The objectives of the study was on the financial innovation platforms such as credit cards, mobile banking and internet banking. The target population was sixteen banks, both local and foreign, operating in Kenya. The study found out that banks have adopted financial innovation such as credit cards, mobile and internet banking. In conclusion, financial innovations was found to have great impact on financial performance of the commercial banks in Kenya. The study recommended the banks to be financially innovative and increase agent banking across the country to promote financial inclusion.

## DATA COLLECTION AND PRESENTATION METHODS

The target population for this study was drawn from M-pesa agents and M-pesa customers in Kibera slum. There are thirteen villages in Kibera namely; Soweto, Siranga, Lindi, Makina Kianda, Gatwekera, Kisumu Ndogo, Laini Saba, and Mashimoni. The study used purposive sampling, critical case sampling where the population chosen and studied revealed insights that apply to other like cases (Crossman, 2019). The research questionnaires were designed to target two (2) M-pesa agents and four (4) customers from each village. Both the M-pesa agents and M-pesa customers were above 18 years as the law stipulates that either of the two must have a national identification card (ID) or a passport. Therefore the total respondents were 26 M-pesa agents, two from each village and 52 M-pesa customers, four from each village which represented the total population in Kibera slum. The study results were summarized using descriptive statistics.

## RESULTS AND DISCUSSIONS

### Demographic Characteristics

From the demographics the study considered the gender and the age of the respondents. Among those who participated in the study, the majority (64%) were females while the remaining 36% were males. The disparity in gender distribution was as a result that it was easy to access female in the market place within Kibera slum, compared to men who mainly work outside the slum. All those who participated in the survey were aged above 18 years and registered M-pesa users. The majority of respondents were found to be aged between 30 years and 40 years old (50%).

### Descriptive Results From M-pesa Users

The following descriptive results were obtained from 52 M-pesa users based in Kibera slum. Table 1 below shows the results of the frequency of M-pesa usage. The respondents were expected to state how frequently they use M-pesa services.

From the results above, 98.1% of the respondents use M-pesa services every week while 1.9% will go beyond a week without using the M-pesa services. M-pesa services range from sending money, receiving money, paying bills, loans and savings, buying airtime and other services offered by Safaricom, the service provider. The usage frequency has been on the raise with majority of the M-pesa users embracing the paybill service to settle essential bills not limited to utility bills and statutory deductions such as National Insurance Hospital Fund. Unlike before where one

*Table 1. M-pesa Usage*

| | Frequency | Percentage |
|---|---|---|
| Every week | 51 | 98.1 |
| Not every week | 1 | 1.9 |
| | 52 | 100 |

Source ; Field Study, 2019

*Table 2. Uses of M-pesa services*

| Service | Frequency | Percentage |
|---|---|---|
| Pay your bills | 50 | 32.26 |
| Pay school fees | 26 | 16.77 |
| Buy food | 27 | 17.42 |
| Start a business | 16 | 10.32 |
| Help your family | 36 | 23.23 |
| | 155 | 100.00 |

Source ; Field Study, 2019

was expected to queue in the relevant offices and pay for the bills before or on the due date, M-pesa users pay bills at the comfort of their homes, social places and work place. The finding shows that M-pesa services are widely used. International Finance Corporation (2017), advocates for a financial platform that widens access to financial services to low-income entrepreneurs to improve their lives, save, borrow and expand business.

Table 2 below, shows the transactions that the respondents mainly use M-pesa services in Kibera slum.

The results above show that majority (32.26%) of the respondents use M-pesa services to pay their bills and that 23.23%% use the M-pesa services to send money to their family members. The fact that Kibera slum is in Nairobi and that majority of the residents migrated from the rural area thus explains that those in the village rely on those in the city to send them money, educate and pay for other basic needs. In addition, M-pesa has been a fast means of sending money in case of emergencies such as sickness. Paying school fees and buying food are averagely used at 16.77% and 17.42% respectively. From the findings, schools have also embraced the use of M-pesa to receive school fees from parents and guardians which is one way of reducing misappropriations of funds. Vendors, also encourage the customers to pay

*Table 3. Access to loan products*

| | Frequency | Percentage |
|---|---|---|
| M-Shwari | 11 | 18.64 |
| KCB M-pesa | 17 | 28.81 |
| M-Shwari and KCB M-pesa | 24 | 40.68 |
| M-Shwari, KCB M-pesa and Banks | 7 | 11.87 |
| | 59 | 100.00 |

Source ; Field Study, 2019

using M-pesa for purpose of security and other related issues. Only 16% have used M-pesa services to start a business, and therefore although M-Shwari and KCB M-pesa are available to M-pesa users there are conditions on how much one can borrow and the terms of repayment, and which might not be favorable to many M-pesa users in Kibera slum and so the findings concur with the findings of Al-Jabri,I. & Sohail, S. (2012), that found out that mobile banking systems that support and provide a number of services are perceived to be better and easily adopted by the customers.

To answer to the question concerning loans and where the respondents mainly access their loans, Table 3 below shows the results:

From the results above, 40.68% of the respondent accesses loans from M-Shwari and KCB M-pesa using M-pesa services. M-Shwari and KCB M-pesa platforms linked to Commercial Bank of Africa and Kenya Commercial Bank of Kenya respectively enable the M-pesa users to access short term loans. To access the loans, the applicant must be a registered M-pesa customer, and not a customer in the bank. The borrower must be an active M-pesa user and must have transacted used M-pesa services for not less than 6 months. The borrower must pay the principal amount and the interest on or before the agreed date and continue to send or receive money via M-pesa to increase his or her credit limit. Only 11.87% of the respondents confirmed that they have borrowed from the M-pesa platform as well as the bank. KCB M-pesa took the lead with 28.81% of the respondents having used the platform to borrow. From the findings, M-shwari is less popular as a borrowing platform compared to KCB M-pesa. Njeru (2018) found out that mobile banking has strong and significant correlations with financial inclusion and the study recommended that the government should put strategies that encourage mobile banking and also reduce tax on mobile banking to encourage its uptake.

M-Shwari took the lead as the most used platform for saving by the respondents (27.87%). Both M-shwari and KCB M-pesa are used to channel savings (32.79%) which is higher compared to those using the M-pesa platform and as well as the bank. Savings through the M-pesa platform to CBA and KCB increases the credibility of

*Table 4. Savings platforms*

| | Frequency | Percentage |
|---|---|---|
| M-Shwari | 17 | 27.87 |
| KCB M-pesa | 12 | 19.67 |
| M-Shwari and KCB M-pesa | 20 | 32.79 |
| M-Shwari, KCB M-pesa and Banks | 12 | 19.67 |
| | 61 | 100.00 |

Source ; Field Study, 2019

*Table 5. M-pesa services usage*

| | Frequency | Percentage |
|---|---|---|
| Send money | 52 | 100.00 |
| Withdraw money | 52 | 100.00 |
| Buy airtime | 48 | 92.31 |
| Loans and Savings | 52 | 100.00 |
| Lipa na M-pesa | 52 | 100.00 |
| My account | 48 | 92.31 |

Source ; Field Study, 2019

the borrowers. In addition the borrowers get a return on the savings which results to a desirable equilibrium between saving and borrowing. From the findings, M-shwari platform is desired mainly for saving while KCB M-pesa is popular to M-pesa users for borrowing. From the results, it is evident that the two platforms have different policies that are either favorable or unfavorable on savings and borrowing. Africa Development Bank (2013), contends that less than quarter of adults' have no access to formal financial institution due to lack of business strategies that aims to target the low income individuals and thus they need for appropriate policies to foster financial inclusion.

In Table 5 below, the results shows the usage of M-pesa services by the respondents. The respondents were required to state the M-pesa service that they rarely use and thus not important to them:

From the results above, it is only buy airtime (92.31%) and my account (92.31%) M-pesa services that are rarely used by the respondent. The other M-pesa services are frequently used and important to the respondent in terms of sending money, receiving money, applying for loans, savings and paying their bills. Generally the

*Table 6. Skills of M-pesa agents*

| Skills | Frequency | Percent |
|---|---|---|
| Financial Skills | 5 | 19.23 |
| Customer Care Skills | 8 | 30.77 |
| Do not have any Skills | 13 | 50.00 |
| Total | 26 | 100.00 |
| | | |

Source ; Field Study, 2019

*Table 7. Number of customers served per week*

| No. of Customers | Frequency | Percent |
|---|---|---|
| 11-20 | 7 | 26.92 |
| 21 and over | 19 | 73.08 |
| Total | 26 | 100.00 |

Source ; Field Study, 2019

M-pesa customers have rated M-pesa service has helpful. The findings concur with the financial report released by Safaricom in 2019 which showed that M-pesa contributes significant revenue to the company and the growth has been notable (Safaricom Financial Statements, 2018). Afandi and Mbugua (2015), found out that geographical coverage has a positive relationship with financial inclusion and thus save on time.

## Descriptive Results From M-pesa Agents

The following descriptive results were obtained from 26 M-pesa agents based in Kibera slum. Table 6: below indicates the skills of the M-pesa agents.

The results above indicated that 50% of the M-pesa agents do not possess any skills as they conduct the M-pesa business. Only 30.77% have customer care skills and 19.23% confirmed to have financial skills. From the results, it shows that to be an M-pesa agent, one is not required to produce their professional certificates and therefore other factors are considered. Arnaboldi and Claeys (2010) contends that internet banking has brought an overhaul in the way business is being conducted and notable is the reduction on labour costs which results to business profitability.

*Table 8. M-pesa business ratings*

| Rate M-pesa | Frequency | Percent |
|---|---|---|
| Good business | 4 | 15.38 |
| Average Business | 22 | 84.62 |
| Total | 26 | 100.00 |

Source ; Field Study, 2019

In the table below, the results shows the number of customers served by the M-pesa agent per week.

From the results in Table 7 above, majority of the agents (73.05%) serve above 21 customer in a week. In addition, 50% are new customers and 50% are returning customers. The customer repeat transactions are mainly deposit of money and withdraw of money. From the findings, M-pesa innovation has the capacity to handle numerous customers per day. Muiruri and Ngari (2014), found out that financial institutions have financial innovative platforms that serves the financial need of the customers and as such there is need to increase agent banking across the country to promote financial inclusion.

Table 8 below, shows the results of M-pesa ratings by the agent. The rating was based on viability of the business and the type of customers:

The results indicated that 84.62% of the agents confirmed that M-pesa business is an average rated business and only 15.38% confirmed that it is a good business. All the agents agreed that they want to continue being in M-pesa business, and that their customers live in the neighborhood. Majority of the agents (80%) earn more than Kshs.11, 000 ($110) per month from the M-pesa business. From the results, none of the M-pesa agents stated that the business results into losses. First, to conduct such a business, one need a small structure and secondly the commissions received from the Safaricom are based on the transaction executed. The study concurs with that conducted by Nyathira (2012), that financial innovation is positively correlated to profitability and that secure payments that spurs sustainable economic growth. Muiruri and Ngari (2014), concluded that financial innovations have great impact on financial performance.

## CONCLUSION

The study showed that both the male and the female have access to M-pesa services. The study also found out that M-pesa users access the M-pesa services on daily basis, which shows the importance of M-pesa services to the residence of Kibera slum. The availability of loan and savings products has positively contributed to the lives of the slum dweller; and as a result, they can access short term loans and repay back the loan and interest at the comfort of their seats. The study also found out that M-pesa services are of good quality and range from sending money, receiving money, paying bills, loan products and saving avenues. Conclusively, M-pesa services have been a solution to financial inclusion to the population of Kibera slum.

The study found out that the M-pesa agents are able to serve a number of customers and that the customers are in the neighborhood. The study also found out that no prerequisite skills are required to operate an M-pesa business. Further, the study showed that M-pesa agents are happy with the M-pesa business. There were also no reports of malfunction of the system that has caused them financial losses. The study also found out that the M-pesa business is profitable as the agents cited that they would like to continue in M-pesa business and that the earnings from the M-pesa services are average. Lastly the M-pesa service provider (Safaricom PLC) has set up platforms of access in case the agents encounter challenges while in the process of executing business transactions.

## RECOMMENDATIONS

The study indicates that M-pesa users do not primarily use the loan product to expand their business despite it being one of the facilities provided by the M-pesa services. For financial inclusion, the study recommends that the M-pesa service providers educate the Kibera slum residents on how to access loans and savings to expand their businesses. From the study, majority of the M-pesa agents have no requisite skills and they consider M-pesa business as average with average earnings per month. The study recommends that it would be worthwhile to train M-pesa agents, equipping them with the necessary skills that would enable them to exploit their businesses for full growth and innovation potential.

## SUGGESTIONS FOR FURTHER RESEARCH

It would be of value to interrogate the M-pesa services and seek to analyze why some services are more popular than others. Another suggested study would be to seek from the M-pesa agents whether lack of specific skills has affected their business performance negatively. Lastly, to conduct a comparative study between the M-pesa agents from Kibera Slum and M-pesa agents from other parts of the country.

## LIMITATIONS OF THE STUDY

Kibera slum is heavily congested, with some sections being rated as "high crime areas", thus making it almost impossible to access, more so during the rainy season. Another challenge was lack of cooperation by some of the respondents, who were apprehensive or suspicious about the purpose of the study and turned away the research assistant in spite of him having proper documentation from the University. To mitigate the drawbacks encountered with respondents, the researcher hired a research assistant, a resident of Kibera slum, who took four (4) months to distribute and collect the questionnaires.

## REFERENCES

Afandi, F., & Mbugua, S. (2015). Role of agent banking services in promotion of financial inclusion in Nyeri Town. *Research Journal of finance and accounting*, *6*(3), 148-173.

Africa Development Bank. (2013). *Financial inclusion in Africa*. Author.

Al-Jabri, I., & Sohail, S. (2012). Banking mobile adoption: Application diffusion of innovation theory. *Journal of Electronic Commerce Research*, *13*(4), 379–391.

Arnaboldi & Claeys. (2010). *Innovation and performance of European banking adopting Internet*. Working paper no. 04/10. Cass Business School.

Arunda, C. (2015). *The influence of innovation on competitive advantage: A case of M-pesa*. United States International University-Africa.

Bandari, A. (2018). *Evaluating access and use of community information Services by informal urban settlers in Nairobi County*. Moi University.

Beck, T. (2015). *Microfinance: A Critical Literature Survey*. Working paper no. 2015/4. World Bank Group.

Buku, M. & Meredith, M. (2018). Safaricom and M-pesa in Kenya. Financial inclusion and Financial integrity. *Washington Journal of Law, Technology and Arts, 8*(3).

Burjorjee, D., & Scola, B. (2015). *A Market Systems Approach to Financial Inclusion*. Washington, DC: Consultative Group to Assist the Poor.

Central Bank of Kenya. (2014). *Bank supervision annual reports*. Government Press.

Communication Authority of Kenya (2019). *Sector Statistics Report for 2018*. Author.

Crossman, A. (2019). *Understanding purposive sampling*. Retrieved from https://www.thoughtco.com/purposive-sampling-3026727

Dearing, J., & Jeffery, C. (2018). *Diffusion of Innovations Theory, Principles and Practice*. Retrieved from https://www.researchgate.net/publication/322941167_Diffusion_Of_Innovations_Theory_Principles_And_Practice

International Finance Corporation. (2017). *Financial inclusion. Creating opportunity through Financial services in South Asia*. Author.

International Monetary Fund. (2014). *Kenya at the Economic Frontier: Challenges and Opportunities*. Retrieved from https://www.imf.org/en/News/Articles/2015/09/28/04/53/sp010614 on 04/04/2019

Kenya Bureau of Statistics. (2018). *Economic Survey*. Retrieved from https://www.knbs.or.ke/download/economic-survey-2018/

Moody Investors Services. (2019). *Banks lose out on revenue to mobile money*. Retrieved from https://www.the-star.co.ke/business/kenya/2019-04-20-banks-lose-out-on-revenue-to-mobile-money/

Muiruri, J., & Ngugi, J. (2014). The effects of financial innovation on the financial performance of commercial banks in Kenya. *International Journal of Humanities and Social Science*, *4*(7), 51–57.

Ng'ethe, V. (2018). *How many young Kenyans are unemployed? A look at the numbers*. Retrieved from https://africacheck.org/2018/10/08/analysis-how-many-young-kenyans-are-unemployed-a-look-at-the-numbers/

Njeru, G. (2018). *Relationship between financial innovations and inclusion among the Commercial banks in Kenya*. University of Nairobi.

Nyathira, N. (2012). *Financial innovation and its effect on financial performance of commercial Banks in Kenya*. University of Nairobi.

Onyango, P., & Tostensen, A. (2016). *Situation of youth and children in Kibera*. Retrieved from https://www.cmi.no/publications/file/5527-the-situation-of-youth-and-children-in-kibera.pdf

Peace Child International. (2018). *Youth unemployment causes and solutions*. Retrieved from https://peacechild.org/youth-unemployment-causes-and-solutions/

Safaricom PLC (Kenya). (2019). *Financial Statements for the year 2018*. Author.

Sangeetha, C. & Kapul, K. (2018). *Catalyst for financial inclusion. Bank the unbanked with Digital channels*. Academic Press.

Society for International development and Kenya Bureau of Statistics. (2013). *Exploring Kenya's Inequality. Pulling apart or pooling together*. Author.

The Lunchbowl Network. (2011). *Facts and information about Kibera*. Retrieved from https://www.lunchbowl.org/

The World Bank. (2018). *Addressing the Youth Employment Crisis Needs Urgent Global Action*. Retrieved from http://www.worldbank.org/en/news/press-release/2015/10/13/addressing-the-youth-employment-crisis-needs-urgent-global-action on 31/03/2019

The World Bank. (2018). *Poverty incidence in Kenya declined significantly but unlikely to be eradicated by 2030*. Retrieved from https://www.worldbank.org/en/country/kenya/publication/kenya-economic-update-poverty-incidence-in-kenya-declined-significantly-but-unlikely-to-be-eradicated-by-2030 on 02/04/2019

United Nations Development Programme. (2018). Retrieved from http://www.ke.undp.org/content/kenya/en/home/countryinfo.html

Wayne, W. (2019). *Diffusion of Innovation theory*. Boston University.

# Chapter 9
# Ethics in Mobile Banking:
## A Case Study of Kenya's Mobile Money Platforms

**Rehema Kagendo Kiarie**
*Riara University, Kenya*

## ABSTRACT

*This chapter addresses the ethical issues relating to mobile money transfer in Kenya. The mobile money transfer industry has grown exponentially in Kenya. Both the formal and informal sectors have embraced the use of mobile money transfer as a convenient means of transacting. With a plethora of advantages, most notably financial inclusion of the informal sector, mobile money transfer also has its ethical demerits. Despite the ethical challenges being experienced, the use of regulation coupled with education of users on ethical issues and security of mobile money transactions will assist in reducing unethical conduct.*

## INTRODUCTION

The invention and embracement of money transfer commonly referred to as mobile banking has enabled consumers who would otherwise be locked out of access to financial services stand in a better position. Mobile Money Transfer (MMT) has pervasively cut across almost all economic sectors in the country paving way for a new way of substituting cash transactions that were seemingly tiresome.

In Africa, and particularly in Kenya, the industry has tremendously grown with numerous companies joining in to share the pie in the market space. Being the newest technological development in recent times, it has bridged a gap that existed

DOI: 10.4018/978-1-7998-2398-8.ch009

and people who were previously unable to access loans through the bank can do so now with ease, at the comfort of their phones. Financial services via the mobile phone is one principal way in which mobile telephony is transforming the life and business in developing countries (Gavin & Jesse, 2009).

With companies such as Tala, Zenku and Mshwari by Safaricom in Africa, the informal sector is now at a vantage point and they do not need to go through the bureaucracies associated with banks to access mobile cash and loans. Mobile money transfer has become an inordinate tool towards the achievement of Sustainable Development Goal (SDG) eight (United Nations, 2016). However, this might not be realized unless mobile industries integrate and implement the ethical and moral values and virtues in their business operations at this time when we are 'witnessing the disintegration of ethics or at least failure to apply it in business operations as argued by polo (2008) and (Gomez, 1999). However, the biggest question is 'what are the Ethical issues surrounding Mobile Money Transfer? '

Boatright (2009), indicates that this being a relatively, there are in-house plans by the regulators to establish a modern incubation laboratory in the region to advance their services in mobile money transfer and other mobile applications. However, the sector has not yet acted on the 'critical and moral issues' which if overlooked will contribute to unethical conduct in the industry (Every business has ethical codes and operating methods and industry principles, (Badi & Badi, 2009, p. 27).

Gichure (1997) defines ethics as "the systematic study of the actions of humans from the point of view of their rightfulness and wrongness as a means for the achievement of man's ultimate happiness. Weiss (2006) on the other hand posited that good business is equated to good ethics. As moral agents, our actions are a true reflection of our society.

Gichure (1997) explains that we are all guided by ethical values such as; accountability, honesty, integrity, reliability, loyalty, respect, truthfulness, diligence, fairness, self-restraint and citizenship. Undeniably, there are soft and hard ethical issues within the MMT industry that needs to be addressed. Legal frameworks applicable to mobile payments maybe insufficiently defined to clearly allocate rights and obligations between consumers and the network operators in the event of operational errors, incidences of theft or fraud or other unforeseen problems (Kenya Bankers Association [KBA] 2013).These issues are security threats from online hackers, fraudsters and money launderers which includes drug dealers and unethical conduct of some of the industry players. These security threats are actively contributing to emergence of 'economic bandits' in Kenya as inferred by Fisman and Miguel (2008) and Spinello (1997).

This review therefore outlines the ethical and moral issues witnessed in mobile payment applications specifically the Kenyan environment with an overview of how the ethical issues are affecting the mobile payment applications available. The background will highlight the pertinent issues growing day by day as well as the main ways that Mobile Network Operators (MNO) have adopted to counter them, The author will thereafter address the gaps that are glaring as witnessed by the current regulatory framework where consumer protection issues have not been sufficiently addressed.

## BACKGROUND

Mobile Money Transfer refers to the moving of money using mobile phone technology operated by either a mobile phone company or an independent operator (Gichuki, 2013). Cook (2015) explains that the M-PESA mobile money service was launched commercially in March 2007 by Safaricom. Safaricom, currently the leading mobile network company in Kenya embraced the idea and launched a new mobile phone based payment and money transfer service, known as M-Pesa (William,Tavnet & Mit, 2010). The innovation enabled users to have virtual accounts where they could deposit money on their mobile phones send balances using SMS technology to other users (including sellers of goods and services), and to redeem deposits for regular money. Usually, there are certain charges that are accompanied by such transactions. Subsequently, other mobile phone service providers in Kenya and around the world have since adopted this idea and launched similar services under their respective brands (Gichuki, 2013). For instance, Uganda has MTN and Airtel, while Tanzania has Tigo, Zantel, Vodaco, Zimbambwe Econet is doing well.

Minimum requirements have to be met to allow the users access the service, this includes owning a mobile phone which enables them to register and open accounts with the various providers if they meet the threshold specified. The most enviable aspect about MMT lies in the fact that their services are available round the clock not forgetting about their easy access to everyone even those living in remote regions. The use of mobile payment applications to execute transactions is gaining momentum progressively. Of grave concern is the protection of users as there are ethical and moral concerns largely witnessed that ought to be addressed. Though mobile money transfer is a new technology that has changed the lives of many Kenyans and other East African Countries, it has soft but hard ethical issues which ought to be addressed by the industry. Being ‘moral agents’ who are directed by ‘will and freedom’, mobile players need to pursue good motives which the society accepts and respect (Oruka 2007, p. 3).

In Kenya, the Communications Authority of Kenya (CA) formerly referred to as Communications Commission of Kenya (CCK) regulates the mobile network industry. Notably, CA is not at all sufficiently competent nor qualified to regulate the mobile money transfer services sector on its own (Gichuki, 2013). This could be attributed to the fact that Mobile Money Transfer services involve some finance aspect and information and technological aspects that may be beyond its proficiency. As much as MMT has its numerous pros, convenience being the most visible, there are many risks that are associated with its use, emphasis being on the nonexistence of a legal framework to control its actions. Consequently, there are no specific laws in Kenya explicitly regulating the MMT industry business despite the fact that it commands a wide consumer base and greatly impacts the economy in various sectors and ways (Museve, 2014).

Some of the glaring concerns include fraud, stemming from unprecedented and unregulated technology being used by consumers and service providers, unfair competition by new entrants looking forward to gain some market share by offering rates that are deleterious to other players in the market, money laundering, wooing clients by use of unfair means and others shall be explored under this study. It is also essential to determine which party is accountable whenever an error or fault occurs in the course of transactions. Additionally, proper guidelines to be followed when contracting agents for conducting transactions should be laid down clearly. In as much as MMT services have greatly impacted the economy in Kenya, there is a deficiency of laws that specifically seek to regulate the neophyte but transient industry. The present laws are touching on the areas of communication; electronic transactions, finances and banking are scattered but unfortunately do not address specific MMT services issues lurking by. Museve (2014) reveals that when one critically examines these scattered laws, it then dawns that there are many inconstancies and gray areas that need to be examined.

## LEGISLATION RELATED TO THE USE OF MOBILE MONEY TRANSFER IN KENYA

### The Kenya Communications (Amendment) Act 2009

In the definitions section of the Kenya Communications (Amendment) Act 2009, Mobile Money Transfer Services has not been given a definition. A definition of a computer been provided instead and the Act thereby goes on to limit itself to electronic materials in computers as opposed to those in mobile phones, quite operational in MMT. Njaramba (2013) reveals that this is why the MMT services remain unregulated by the Act. A closer examination of some sub-sections under section 83 will reveal that the mobile phones are not explicitly covered as they restrict themselves to computers only. The previous Kenya Communications Act 2 of 1998 that preceded this Act did not even provide for regulation of electronic transactions and neither did it provide for Mobile Money Transfer Services. It is through the amendment of this act that led to the 2009 Kenya Communications (amendment) Act that electronic transactions are provided for.

## The Kenya Information and Communications Act, Cap 411

This legislation recognizes electronic transactions by defining the terms electronic mail services, electronic mail services, electronic mail, electronic document interchange and electronic voice mail but it does not have provisions regulating the use of MMT (Mobile Money Transfer) services. The Act also does not define Mobile Money Transfer Services.

## The Banking Act Cap 488 of the Laws of Kenya

The Banking Act, Cap 488 of the Laws of Kenya regulates banking business and other connected services. The question that needs to be answered is whether MMT services may fall under "connected services" of banking businesses as envisaged by the Act. This Act falls short of defining mobile money transfer. When Safaricom approached the CBK in early 2007, there were no laws governing a mobile money service like M-Pesa, consequently the CBK issued a "Letter of No Objection," and M-Pesa was launched the following month. At the end of 2008, with the huge success of M-Pesa and the growing concern of the Kenyan Bankers Association (KBA), the Ministry of Finance asked that the CBK conduct a risk assessment of M-Pesa, which was done and published in the Kenya Gazette in early 2009, confirming that the CBK was satisfied with the risk situation and that they do not consider M-Pesa to be a banking business.

The CBK provides guidance to mobile money under Article 4 of the Banking Act, which covers Payment Systems, rather than banks. As such, it is the National Payment Systems Division (NPSD) of the CBK that provides oversight, not the Banking Supervision Department. As a safeguard, however, CBK exercises full supervisory oversight over the trust accounts for mobile financial services providers, which are held at commercial banks. This effectively sequesters the float and protects it against any eventual financial failure of M-Pesa. This also precludes M-Pesa from earning the interest on the float. Section 2(1) (a) defines banking business as accepting from members of the public of money on deposit repayable on demand or at the expiry of a fixed period or after notice. The act does not provide for a definition of mobile money transfer services.

MMT has adopted a similar process akin to the banking one given that there is the acceptance of deposits by the agents of the service providers, and the transfer of money from one's mobile account to another account as it happens in banking where there is transfer of funds from one's account to another. However, despite the similarity, mobile money transfer services cannot be said to fully and completely fall within the ambit of The Banking Act as seen under section 16(5) of the Act which clarifies that such a business should be one that lends money to others from the deposit or one that uses the deposit wholly or partly to finance its activities. This provision operates to exclude mobile money transfer service providers from the scope of The Banking Act.

### The Evidence Act, Cap 80

It does not expressly provide for admission of evidence from mobile phones. It only mentions a "computer". This limits the use of technology. Ideally this should be amended to include electronic gadgets like mobile phones.

### The National Information and Communications Technology (ICT) Policy Paper of March 2006

This policy paper does recognize the need for comprehensive policy, legal and regulatory framework on ICT. Further it acknowledges the lack of adequate infrastructure in ICT but does not provide for the solutions. It just states what the government intends to do. In as far as Mobile Transfer Services and Mobile payment services are concerned; this policy does not offer any assistance. These and other laws as shall be examined in detail are the existing laws that are supposed to contain provisions for regulating MMT services but unfortunately they are insufficient to do so and thus a lacuna exists in the regulation of MMT services.

## KEY PLAYERS IN MOBILE MONEY ECOSYSTEM

There are several players and stakeholders involved in a mobile money platform who all have different roles to execute. The following players and stakeholders exist in the MMT services in Kenya according to Ojijo (2014),

1. **Mobile Network Operator (MNO)**: Responsible in providing appropriate infrastructure as well as ensuring total compliance with the regulations and policies of telecommunications within the country.
2. **Financial Institutions**: They facilitate the exchange of money between parties through their infrastructure. They are also custodians of money.
3. **Regulatory Institutions**: These includes Central Banks (mandated for fiscal and monetary policy formulation and control) and the Telecommunications regulator such as Communication Authority of Kenya whose task is to control the communication infrastructure within a jurisdiction. These two regulate matters involving money laundering, anti-competition practices, data security etc.
4. **Agents**: They facilitate conversion of cash into mobile money and vice versa. They earn a commission in return of services rendered on behalf of MNO.
5. **Merchants and Retailers:** They offer a range of products and services and accept mobile money payments in return. By offering more avenues for users to spend their money, demand for mobile money is increased and the need to handle cash is reduced.
6. **Deposit Taking Business**: They use mobile money as a way to deliver their services i.e. financial institutions, bill users, insurance providers.
7. **Equipment Manufacturers and Platform Providers**: These include a wide array of stakeholders like mobile phone makers, network equipment vendors as well as application providers. These benefit from the increased sale of end-user devices like mobile phones, equipment to handle increased network capacity and fees or subscriptions respectively.
8. **Mobile Money Users**: These are the subscribers of a MNO who derive benefits of using its services. Users can also be non-subscribers, who send money to subscribers. (Ojijo, 2014).

On the other hand, Ojijo (2014), categorizes mobile money services categorized into three major categories:

1. **M-transfers:** Commonly referred as person to person transfer. Entails transfer of money from user to another which may be local or international.
2. **M-payments:** Which entails buying of goods or services and making payments via mobile money.it can range from paying utility bills, concerts, movie tickets etc.
3. **M-financial:** Services includes linking your bank account with your mobile money in order to transact away from your bank branch.
4. **Hybrid Services**: Involves transactions that use more than one service category.

*Figure 1.Improved Disclosure of Costs ; Person to Person Payments*
*Source: Mazer, 2018*

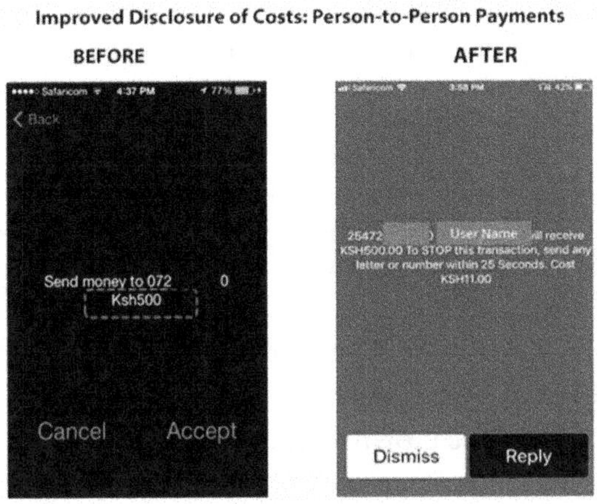


## ETHICAL ISSUES ARISING FROM THE USE OF MOBILE MONEY

### Transparency Issue

For years, Kenya's digital financial services (DFS) did not disclose to the consumers the amount they were charged for the mobile transactions. Due to the lack of transparency, the Competition Authority of Kenya (CA) in 2016 instructed mobile money providers to reveal the corresponding costs for all transactions undertaken by Clients. As such, disclosure has increased significantly in individual-to-individual payments, payment of bills and use of digital credit (Gubbins & Totolo 2018). The introduction of tariff charts assist consumers to check the transaction charges for each transaction and when the transaction goes through its accompanied by a text message stating clearly the charges incurred. Currently, there's enhanced transperency that was not evident before (Mazer 2018). The diagram below shows before and after scenarios.

The move is not unique to Kenya only but also the rest of Africa where we see various industry players imitating the same for instance in Uganda Ghana, Tanzania and Rwanda. As a result, consumers are now increasingly aware of the charges whether they are sending the money from one person to another or repaying the digital credits available. It is hard to put up a case against pricing disclosure, and it is quite easy to monitor on standardized modes of digital financial services. This makes lack of proper enforcement in several digital financial services markets stand out as a major issue. Rafe (2014) admits that if policies are crafted to ensure protection of consumers keep pace with innovation of products, they would assist in issuing minimum rules and monitoring service providers' transparency/disclosure of key terms as well as prices on the digital financial channels.

## Money Laundering Issue

Money laundering is a term often associated with ways in which illicitly acquired money is hidden, reclaimed and then reintroduced into the financial system (Francis 2017). The idea behind this process is to hamper the bid by authorities to trace the movement and earnings of this cash and connect them to the original illicit activity.

Until recently, Money laundering was frequently associated with financial and banking activities. It has since grown to be associated with mobile money due to the fact that mobile money is used as a way of money transfer and is linked to finance, banking and non-financial telecommunications sector, which is a huge risk that needs to be addressed by the AML regulator (Ojijo, 2014). Subsequently, since the launch of mpesa in March 2007, and the growth of its operations in ten different countries, different operators embrace the business model after seeing its impact within the unbaked and associated businesses. Masinde (2017) observes that Kenya is well known to be a transit point of international drug trafficking and global money laundering activities. As a result, The US state Department firmly points out that mobile money services are therefore susceptible to money laundering activities (Masinde, 2017). Worldwide other players also share in this concern, notably is the fact that mobile payments are commonly operated in countries with weak laws and enforcement of money laundering and financial fraud (Solin & Zerzan, 2010).

Usually, the identification needed from the customers end is very minimal and the entire process dodges the financial reporting system. This makes it futile for the authorities to screen mobile payments even with expertise as Cassara and Jorich (2010) reveal. Cassara and Jorich reveal that there is not much evidence of mobile payments facilitating crime and that is only because no one is monitoring the transactions for criminal activity.

Masinde (2017) reveals that other regional remittance channels like Hawala (a type of informal money transfer system popular in Kenya and Somalia) for international funds transfers make it harder to track transactions. Unlike M-Pesa which is closely regulated and has daily transfer limits of $1,400, the Hawala system allows transfer of large sums of money, is multi-currency and can be used without identification document requirements (Masinde, 2017),

*Figure 2.*
*Source; Singapore Stock Exchange (2019)*

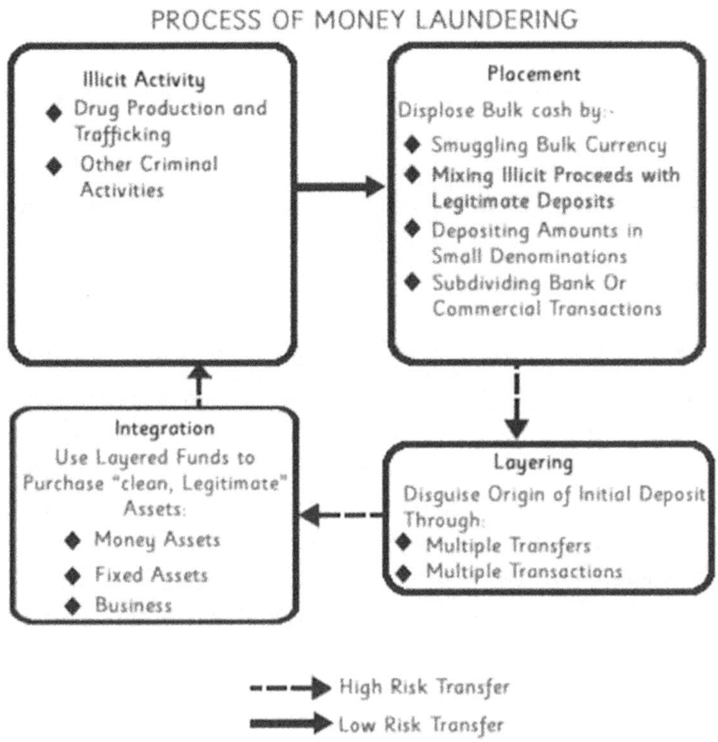


## Pestering Issue

Consumers are constantly being pestered repeatedly over the years and little has been done to curb it. According to the Cambridge dictionary, pestering means to behave in an annoying manner towards someone by carrying out an action repeatedly and against the will of the subject. Unknowingly consumers are fleeced off large amounts of cash when these fraudsters claim that a sum of money has been deposited erroneously into their account only for them to come to the realization that they have been swindled. On hindsight, it's usually a fraudulent claim but it comes a little too late for the consumer to realize it. The fraudsters may then keep pestering for a refund through numerous voice calls. Majority of them realize when it's a little too late. Others go to the extent of duping customers that someone close to then either a family member or friend has an emergency and urgent cash is required to get them out of the situation. It has now been revealed that hardcore criminals are usually the masterminds of these distressing messages and calls.

## Unfair Competition by New Entrants

Competition is inevitable in business and new entrants give consumers an option, in mobile money customers consider a variety of aspects when assessing them which include speed, convenience, security, ease of use and charges. Every customer is unique in their needs therefore they all have different preferences in reference to those features. MNO should to see it that they during the point of entry, they consider at least one or more of these dimensions in way that is grander than their opponents. Adopting all in the new offering in the name of competition is unethical and should not always be the case because what one customer values is different from another. The companies should adopt those features they can enhance and drop the redundant ones. Interestingly, in Kenya, MPESA has managed to consistently outshine the competition by adopting all the five dimensions mentioned by the author. There are three key things that they might consider before venturing into a new market: they must assess all the present options to the prospective service for instance the p2p payments, B2B payments they can provide through mobile money. Additionally, they need to decide whether they will provide a service that thumps the competitors along the five dimensions and lastly they need to be aware of the preferences of their target market (Neil & Yasmina, 2010).

## Fraud

Mudiri (n.d) indicates that a consumer using mobile money services is susceptible to incidences of fraud. Technology has always left an electronic trail that is good bait for fraudsters to access information and benefit from such (Sullins, 2019). The movement of money via these mobile apps happens instantaneously and detailed information on the users is usually stored virtually on the networks (Francis, 2017). Cash inflows and outflows between end users and other external entities such as merchants, subscribers, banks or retailers are evident. The typical mobile (easy access anywhere) nature of the product makes it an attractive proposition for the unscrupulous elements in the user base. OECD (2019) report reveals that transactions may have very small values and hence go undetected in traditional Suspicious Activity Reports or High Usage Reports. Given the built-in anonymity and easy access nature of the product, it has become a conduit for terrorism funding and money laundering activities OECD (2019).

## Categories of Fraud

Fraud can be categorized into: agent affecting fraud, consumer affecting fraud and fraud affecting the service providers.

### *Agent Affecting Fraud*

Occasionally, agents in various regions in Kenya encounter fraud in mobile money services. They may include but not limited to; float loss in the agent's account arising from unauthorized use, compromised PINs, and swindles relating impersonation by fraudsters who gain unauthorized access to the agent's float account. Notably, Customers can also commit fraud against agents for example, withdrawal reversal fraud or fake currency deposits (CGAP, 2017). The Helix Institute's 2015 surveys indicate that fraud is a primary concern for many agents.

### *Consumer Affecting Fraud*

Newman and McNall (2005) reveals that the most common type of fraud affecting the consumers is identity theft. Arising from fraudulent/offline SIM swaps that transfer the mobile wallet account from the customer's SIM to the fraudster's SIM, make it easy for the fraudster to intrude into the consumer's mobile wallet and bank account (Talla 2018). It's worth noting that a consumer's mobile number can be linked to almost everything including the subscribers' bank account and as such fraud can easily happen. Fraudsters can acquire a new SIM card issued to them against your registered mobile number (Mazer & Nitin, 2015). With basic information about you beforehand, they can easily access your online transactions, contact mobile operators to get your SIM card blocked then walk into the retailers shop and replace your SIM card using your personal details that were known to them easily accessing your assets. Moreover, employees are also involved in identity theft in the case where they access and ill-use customer's confidential information without consent (Mazer & Nitin, 2015). This has been witnessed as reported in the mainstream media. In Kenya, the extract below illustrates how this happens:

Source: Daily Nation, Kenya

## Example 1

Police recently unearthed a racket in Bomet district, where mobile phone subscribers lost cash through a popular money transfer service. According to the police, this seemed like a well-organized syndicate involving Safaricom officials, M-Pesa agents and fraudsters. The police said the man, who was in a prison warder's uniform, had copies of 10 identification cards and SIM cards of subscribers whose lines had been swapped. Two exercise books containing the names of people whose lines had been swapped were also found on the man. It is interesting to note that the man also had PIN details of subscribers whose lines were swapped (Kimutai, 2018).

Other consumer affecting fraud include: subscription fraud where a consumer is mistakenly subscribed to promotions at a fee. Research has revealed that they are usually ghost subscriptions. False promotions are also common where fraudsters impersonate the mobile money providers by letting them know that they won prizes in various promotions but they have to part with some amount in order for them to claim the prize. Fraudsters also go the extra mile of asking for PIN numbers from unsuspecting customers then later defraud them. Often, the fraudsters take advantage of the network downtime, and conduct offline SIM swaps and over the counter transactions that are detected much later when the network has been restored. Agents have not been left behind, sometimes they take advantage of the consumers commonly thought the over the counter transactions by charging the consumers above rates transaction fees or charging them for deposits that are meant to be absolutely free of charge (Mazer & Nitin, 2015).

Privacy issues in relation to customer data is yet another issue. Mobile money transfer companies sometimes find themselves exposed when customer's data falls in the wrong hands and that information is used to commit a crime. This can be achieved through the mobile malware and PC Malware. In mobile malware, malicious software that targets customer operating system on mobile phones, tablets, smart watches or wireless enabled personal digital assistants is used to get hold of customer data. Notable malicious software examples that are commonly used include gunpowder and shedun. Customer data is not always 100% safe in the hands of the employees and many times service providers encounter cases of customer data being exposed to unauthorized people by their own employees. The dark web which is a common platform used for fraudulent activities provides an avenue through which customer data is sold in these platforms. (Chertoff & Simon, 2015).

## Example 2: Impersonation of Company Officials

A lady and a gentleman visited an M-PESA outlet, claiming to be Safaricom supervisors. The two wore valid looking M-PESA badges and even carried M-PESA promotional material for the outlet. The two inspected the outlet's log books then left. About 20 minutes later, a man came to the same outlet requesting to withdraw Ksh 35,000. He was allowed to withdraw the desired Ksh 35,000 and proceeded to commence the withdrawal using his mobile phone. The outlet attendants immediately thereafter received an SMS appearing to authenticate and confirm the man's transaction. The SMS received by the attendant had a valid looking M-PESA transaction number and the old man's purported names which were verified against an original national ID which he presented. The M-PESA attendant, convinced about the validity of the transaction, paid out the Ksh 35,000. The M-PESA attendant proceeded to serve the next customer, expecting the amount of float to increase as a result of the withdrawal by Ksh. 35,000. The expected float was not reflected in the valid mpesa SMS after the next customer's transaction. The M-PESA attendant shortly thereafter called Safaricom's M-PESA service line for clarification and the service support person on the other end reported that the transaction withdrawing Ksh. 35,000 was not reflected in the M-PESA system.

Source, Telcom Africa

### *Fraud Affecting Mobile Money Providers*

Fraud within providers is also a concern. Several high profile instances of internal fraud have resulted in significant losses for MFS providers, while putting users' accounts at risk and raising financial integrity concerns for the system. For example, MTN, the largest mobile money provider in Uganda, lost an estimated US$3.4 million through internal fraud perpetrated by staff in 2011 (Morawczynski 2015), while a similar incident cost Tigo in Rwanda an estimated US$700,000 in 2014 (Mugisha 2014). Inadequate internal controls (facilitating internal data hacking), inadequate audit processes, poor corporate governance structures, lack of employee fraud education, and lack of whistle blowing mechanisms are among the key contributors to internal fraud

## ETHICAL THEORIES

### Virtue Ethics

This theory judges a person by the character they portray as opposed to the actions of his behavior. (Fisher & Lovell, 2008), infers that virtues are not the 'ends' rather they are the 'means'. These are personal qualities that present the basis for a person to exhibit a good, noble or happy/fulfilling life, (Debeljuh 2006). Aristotle was the proponent for virtue ethics in our daily ventures and undertakings. He had identified four virtues; wisdom, courage, self-control and justice (Kucukuysal & Beyhan, 2011). Virtue ethics as described by Aristotle has a central notion of improving oneself to be a better individual. If everyone endeavors to do this then the world would become a more productive and moral environment to live in.

The argument is that the rational side of the soul which revolves around intellectual values is the side which should be cared for by the individual. Aristotle states that virtue ethics is deemed to be at variance with the main feature of the current day economic order.' Aristotle felt that 'internal goods' were necessary for production, i.e. these are outstanding to a specific activity which uses 'analytical skills, use of strategic imagination and competitive intensity.' Money, fame and power would thus not come into and as such, they would be labelled as goals that are not virtuous. The virtue ethics creates a basis to understand and exemplify a life of moral character (Hursthouse, [2003). Through practice it posits that we are able to acquire virtues of generosity, wisdom, bravery, self-control and so on. As a result, it breeds an honorable and moral character (De Mol 2009). In other words, virtuous decisions are as a result of a virtuous character. Character is the path through which we can gladly derive meaning of what it means to be a virtuous being. It gives us a perfect guideline for living life without paying attention to explicit guidelines for resolving ethical dilemma.

## The Public Choice Theory

This theory posits that "man is a cogent being, acting or eager to act independently, and seeking to gratify his individual best interest. In relation to the study, this would mean that mobile money services have to be targeted or diverse (choice), therefore the mobile money provider would claim worth for money ('more for less') and liability," (Tolofari, 2005).

Accordingly Tolofari (2015), advocates for this notion in public administration terms, criticize the poor public service provision, incompetence and performance as well as surplus of resources and pursue to discourse this with the implementation of business-sector administration processes in the public platform. This study, on the flip side, is grounded on the model of mobile money adoption and the impact it has on people's lives in relation to what they regard as right and wrong practice. As a result, Tsilizani (2016) advocates for representatives of mobile money to see to it that they deliver superior service to the clients in line with the contractual terms binding them with the principal.

## The Principal Agent Theory

The principal agent theory originates from the transformation method within the government that is 'intended to create, within the public sector, independent or semi-autonomous organizations in which the enactment function is disjointed from the policy-making function' (Allen, et al 2015). It is the split-up of the supplier and user of public services. Fundamentally, the beneficiaries of public services are the government and the general public bindinded by an agreement. Notably is the contractual affiliation usually created between the principal and the agent. The principal is the party demanding a service or goods, and the representative is the party Providing the service or goods. Tolofari (2015) indicates that this arrangement is that the principal pays the representative and in return he/she is required to have expertise to deliver the service at a value lower than it would cost if the principal were to offer it personally.

In reference to this study, the mobile money provider is the principal and mobile money agents from different MNO are the agents since they are under pledged agreement to supply the mobile money service. Jensen and Maeckling (1976) define the Principal-Agency relationship as prescribed arrangement where the principal engages the agency to execute and deliver services on their behalf by giving the agent autonomy for decision making as they do the tasks agreed .It is a contractual relationship created between the principal and the agent, such that the principal pays the agent and the agent is expected (or is assumed) to have expertise and to be able, hopefully, to make available the service at a charge lower than it would cost if the principal were to provide it individually (Pratt & Zeckahuser, 1991).

It is this arrangement where the agent appears to possess more knowledge than the principal byvirtue of the task at hand that places the agent at a more advantaged position which sometimes brings about conflict of interest especially when the agent choses to abuse that authority to pursue his personal interest neglecting the interest of the principal as per contractual agreement. The challenge for the principal is usually to manage the agent in such a way that he adheres to contractual agreement terms (Tsilizani, 2016).

## HOW TO CIRCUMVENT ETHICAL ISSUES IN MOBILE MONEY BANKING (COUNTER MEASURES)

### General Counter Measures

The following counter measures can be applied:

- All-inclusive fraud management programs, including adoption of screening systems to facilitate early detection and prevention of fraudulent activity.
- ensuring that all MNO comply with the rules and regulations concerning agent recruitment, training, and management programs. This may entirely cope with internal and external risks associated with mobile money banking.

- applying the KYC requirements. Knowing your customer. Embrace Product risk assessments to certify all risks are identified and adequately lessened with appropriate controls
- Adoption of fraud awareness campaigns that offer to sensitize consumers, staff, and agents on fraud trends and prevention measures. For instance use of media campaigns, text messages, emails, that appear as periodic bulletins, working hand in hand with law enforcement agencies, trial and enquires of fraud related cases, safety measures that thwart efforts to compromise PINS
- Educating the consumers on novel fraud types and scams being used in the market. Weight should be given on the means the consumers can safeguard themselves, such as keeping their PINs secure and checking their balances before sending back money allegedly sent to them erroneously.
- Complete agent fraud deterrence measures that include training, compliance monitoring, sensitization programs, and general safeguards limiting the use of the till.
- Setting up of effective grievances resort channels with qualified staff acquainted in handling fraud and other complaints and devoted alternative channels for agents. Effective resort helps to reassure users of new financial services that their money is protected, and that they will be able to resolve the issue if they encounter a problem (Mazer & Nitin, Recourse in Digital Financial Services:, 2015)
- Effective staffing practices that include screening of staff before onboarding.
- Inculcation of an obedience culture, coupled with staff training, and enactment of corrective measures.
- Application of strict controls that limit user access privileges and implement double controls.

Apart from dealing fraud within their own networks, MFS providers need to take part in harmonized industry action directed at decreasing fraud. Regardless of the mobile money provider, similar strategies are used across the networks, therefore consumers correspondingly exposed to common susceptibilities. Market level business relations, for example, could monitor trends and encourage the conjoint sharing of information on scam fashions and sensible fraud management best practices. This has functioned well in most African countries where there are sturdy financiers. (Mazer & Nitin, Recourse in Digital Financial Services:, 2015)

## Regulatory Oversight

The lack of suitable regulatory regimes and supervisory oversight can create opportunities for rackets. The absence of permitting by-law can also stifle innovation, making it difficult for the providers to introduce new products without suitable regulatory frameworks. These regulatory gaps are further aggravated by poorly trained employees and incompetent law enforcement agencies who delay the time frame for fraud issues to investigated, prosecuted and resolved. Regulators in these markets should implement applicable regulatory reforms, for instance:

- Enactment of requisite legislation that makes mitigation controls compulsory and ensures application of the same by providers: notably, latest introduction of mobile money and electronic money guidelines in a number of leading mobile money markets, such as East and West Africa and South Asia, has assisted in sanctifying the sector and offering controllers with trappings to implement and direct tougher fraud monitoring and risk mitigation procedures.
- Constant meetings with regulators between consumer interest groups and financial inclusion agencies has seen the rise of support towards achieving statutory reforms, where applicable.
- Cross-border synchronization on fraud mitigation in countries that have several markets with widespread use of mobile money. (CGAP, 2017). Outstandingly, the East African community teamed up to develop a joint SIM card registration structure with a clear purpose of preventing mobile money fraud. (Business Daily, 2015)

Other ways include:

- Introduction of strict rules in relation to using mobile money platforms away from your residence country.
- Introduction of Customer risk analysis and assessments where you analyze the customer in the different transaction stages.
- M-wallet limit controls across providers that states the maximum amounts of transaction one can conduct in a day.
- Cross checking call transaction records for spamming customers.
- Cross checking peer to peer transactions for increase of cash into single accounts.
- Monitoring peer to peer transactions for cash dissemination into multiple accounts

## CONCLUSION

Kenya as a developing country has predicaments in ensuring that financial services are accessible to all citizens. However, this can be attributed to the limited infrastructure available, documentation requirements, costs involved in account opening, the proximity between the bank and individuals among other factors. Interestingly, majority of the population who cannot access the financial institutions own a mobile phone or have access to one. The advent of the mobile money banking services has seen the unbanked individuals catered for at a click of a button.

This accessibility has seen the rise of the mobile money banking industry, where even the numerous documents that conventional banking asks for have been eliminated. The advent of the mobile money banking has had numerous merits from easily paying for various utilities such as electricity bills, school fees, and bus fares, paying for goods and services in retail stores to purchase of airtime and provision of banking services. It is with no doubt that it is a good thing and has eased the day to day life in many aspects.

Notably, there are many aspects through which this technology has largely improved the lives of the netizens who use it as a social and economic device where relationships have been enhanced by sending money for the purpose of gifting or contributing to a particular course (contributions for events), airtime and vouchers to acquaintances and family members. At the same time, the relations and family bonds have drifted apart as a result of this platform. Home visits have become less regular since people working away from home can easily send money, save money, contribute to affiliated groups like chamas at a click of a button.

Secondly, lives have been transformed as a result of mobile banking. Particularly the rural men and women who had little knowledge about banking can now access the much hyped service similar to the urban population. This financial inclusion has in an immense way impacted on the social and family structures of this rural population. Although mobile money transfer has trendemendously grown in the recent past, the question of ethics still lingers on. The aim of this case study was to bring to light the need of incorporating and applying ethics to the letter in the mobile industry since it is susceptible to fraudulent activities, vulnerable to fraud, cybercrime and money laundering. It's just a matter of time and the government will come up with sound policies and guidelines that will see to it that the mobile money transfer services operate smoothly. This needs to be implemented expeditiously.

## REFERENCES

Allen, R. (2015). *IMF Working PaperFiscal Affairs Department The Evolving Functions and Organization of Finance Ministries Prepared by Authorized for distribution by 2015.* Available at https://www.imf.org/external/pubs/ft/wp/2015/wp15232.pdf

Anyanzwa, J. (2019, July 20). *How e-money is changing the face of banking. The East African.* Nairobi, Kenya: Nation Media Group.

Biasucci, C., Drumwright, M., Elliott, D., Gentile, M., Pierce, L., & Prentice, R. (2019). *Ethics Unwrapped.* Retrieved October 16, 2019, from University of Texas at Austin: https://www.utexas.edu/

Boatright, J. R., & Smith, J. D. (2009). *Ethics and the Conduct of Business.* New York: Pearson Education, Inc.

Buku, M. W., & Meredith, M. W. (2013). Safaricom and M-pesa in Kenya: Financial Inclusion and Financial Integrity. *Washington Journal of Law, Technology & Arts, 8*(3).

Buku, M. W., & Rafe, M. (2017, April). *Fraud in Mobile Financial Services.* Retrieved October 15, 2019, from Consultative Group to Assist the Poor (CGAP): https://www.cgap.org/sites/default/files/researches/documents/Brief-Fraud-in-Mobile-Financial-Services

Business Daily. (2015, October 24). EAC members move to tame mobile money fraud. *Business Daily.*

Cassara, J., & Jorisch, A. (2010). *On the Trail of Terror Finance: What Law Enforcement and Intelligence Officials Need to Know.* Arlington, VA: Red Cell IG.

CCK. (2012, April). *CCK releases 2nd quarter ICT sector statistics for 2011/2012.* Retrieved October 15, 2019, from Internet Archive Wayback Machine: https://web.archive.org/web/20121016002713/http://cck.go.ke/resc/downloads/SECTOR_STATISTICS_REPORT_Q2_2011-12.pdf

Chertoff, M., & Simon, T. (2015). *The Impact of the Dark Web.* Ontario: Centre for International Governance Innovation and Chatham House.

Cline, A. (2018, June 11). *3 Types of Ethical Systems.* Retrieved October 15, 2019, from Learn Religions: https://www.learnreligions.com/atheism-types-of-ethical-systems

Cook, T. (2015). *An overview of M-PESA*. FSD Kenya. Available at https://fsdkenya.org/an-overview-of-m-pesa/(Accesed on 28th September 2019)

De Mol, L. (2009). Turing Machines. In *Stanford Encyclopedia of Philosophy*. Retrieved from https://plato.stanford.edu/archives/win2018/entries/turing-machine/

Fisher, C., & Lovell, A. (2008). *Business Ethics and Values: Individual, Corporate and International Perspectives* (3rd ed.). Edinburgh, UK: Prentice Hall.

Fisman, R., & Miguel, E. (2008). *Economic Gangsters: Corruption, Violence, and the Poverty of Nations*. Princeton University Press.

Gichuki, E. N. (2013). *Law of financial institutions in Kenya* (2nd ed.). Nairobi: LawAfrica Publishers.

Gichure, W. C. (1997). *Basic concepts in ethics: with an outline of different methods in contemporary moral philosophy*. Nairobi: Focus Publications.

Gomez, R. (1999). *What's right and wrong in business? A primer on business ethics*. Manila: Sinag-tala Publishing.

Hursthouse, R. (1990). After Hume's Justice. *Proceedings of the Aristotelian Society*, *91*, 229–245.

Jack, W., & Suri, T. (2011, January). *Mobile Money: The Economics of M-pesa*. Retrieved October 15, 2019, from Georgetown University: http://faculty.georgetown.edu/wgj/papers/Jack_Suri-Economics-of-M-PESA.pdf

Jensen, M. C., & Meckling, W. H. (1976). Theory of the Firm: Managerial Behavior. *Journal of Financial Economics*, *3*(4), 305–360. doi:10.1016/0304-405X(76)90026-X

Kimutai, V. (2018, July 22). Mulot, the unlikely hotbed of rising mobile telephone fraud. *Daily Nation*.

Kucukuysal, B., & Beyhan, E. (2011). Virtue ethics in Aristotle's Nicomachean ethics. *International Journal of Human Sciences*, 44-51.

Luminzu. (n.d.). *Fraud in Mobile Financial Services*. Available at https://www.microsave.net/files/pdf/RP151_Fraud_in_Mobile_Financial_Services_JMud iri.pdf

Masinde, J. (2017, March 6). *US State Dept thinks Africa's leading mobile money platform is vulnerable to money laundering*. Retrieved October 16, 2019, from Quartz: https://qz.com/africa/924977/us-state-dept-thinks-africas-leading-mobile-money- platform-is-vulnerable-to-money-laundering/

Mazer, R. (2018, April 4). Retrieved October 2017, 2019, from Consultative Group to Assist the Poor: https://www.cgap.org/blog/kenyas-rules-mobile-money-price-transparency-are-paying

Mazer, R., & Nitin, G. (2015, December). *Recourse in Digital Financial Services.* Retrieved October 18, 2019, from Consultative Group to Assist the Poor: https://www.cgap.org/sites/default/files/researches/documents/Brief-Recourse-in-Digital-Financial-Services-Dec-2015

Meyer, J. (2013, June 17). *How mobile payments might be the global money-laundering machine criminals have dreamed about.* Retrieved October 17, 2019, from Quartz: https://qz.com/94570/how-mobile-payments-might-be-the-global-money-laundering- machine- criminals-have-dreamed-about/

Museve, R. K. (2014, April). *The Legal Implications of Mobile Money Transfer Services to the Economy in Kenya: The Need for Regulatory Reform.* Nairobi, Kenya: University of Nairobi.

Newman & McNally. (n.d.). *Identity Theft Literature Review.* U.S. Department of Justice Document No.: 210459. Available at https://www.ncjrs.gov/pdffiles1/nij/grants/210459.pdf

OECD. (2019). *Money Laundering and Terrorist Financing Awareness Handbook for Tax Examiners and Tax Auditors.* OECD. Retrieved from www.oecd.org/tax/crime/money-laundering- and-terrorist-financing-awareness-handbook-for-tax-examiners-and-tax-auditors.pdf

Ojijo, P. (2014). *26 Legal Issues in Mobile Money Transactions.* Kampala: LawPronto Limited. Paul Francis (06/05/17) Mobile App Development Process BHW Group. Available at https://thebhwgroup.com/blog/mobile-app-development-process

Paul, G., & Totolo, E. (2018). Digital Credit. In *Kenya:Evidence from demand-side surveys.* FSD Kenya.

Pratt, J. W., & Zeckahuser, R. (1991). *Principals and Agents: The Structure of Business.* Harvard Business School Press.

Rolfe, A. (2017, July 5). *Is mobile money a haven for money launderers?* Retrieved October 15, 2019, from PaymentsCM: https://www.paymentscardsandmobile.com/is-mobile-money- a-haven-for-money-launderers/

Senge, P. M. (1990). *The Fifth Discipline. The Art and Practice of the Learning Organization.* New York: Currency Doubleday.

Solin & Zerzan. (2010). Mobile Money Methodology for Assessing Money Laundering and Terrorist Financing Risk. In *Mobile Money: Methodology for Assessing Money Laundering and Terrorist Financing Risks*. GSMA Discussion Paper.

Spinello, R. A. (1997). *Case studies in information and computer ethics*. Prentice Hall.

Subex. (n.d.). *White Paper Preventing Mobile Money Frauds with Appropriate Countermeasures*. Retrieved October 18, 2019, from Subex: https://subex.com/pdf/Whitepapers/Mobile-Money-Whitepaper1

Tolofari, S. (2005). New Public Management and Education. *Policy Features in Education*, 75-89.

Tsilizani, E. N. (2016, November 2). *University of Bolton Institution Repository*. Retrieved October 19, 2019, from University of Bolton: http://ubir.bolton.ac.uk/id/eprint/960

United Nations. (2016, January 1). *Sustainable Development Goals*. Retrieved October 16, 2019, from United Nations: https://www.un.org/sustainabledevelopment/sustainable- development-goals/

# Chapter 10
# Impact of Mobile Money on Financial Crime, Money Laundering, and Terrorism Financing

**Gilbert Ouko Oyoo**
*Independent Researcher, Kenya*

## ABSTRACT

*Financial crime, money laundering, and terror financing have been perennial menaces that downplay the major headway made in the financial transaction space. Businesses and individuals have found it prudent to always try remaining ahead of the perpetrators behind the vices. The springing into life of the mobile money in the second half of the first decade of this century has revolutionized the manner with which risk management in this respect is handled. In this chapter, the author posits that although mobile money has led to greater financial inclusion, the rate with which the myriad financial crimes have been reported over the past decade in the face of this phenomenon raises the need to stay abreast of developments in this space.*

## OVERVIEW

Financial crime, money laundering and terror financing have been perennial menaces which have sort to downplay major headways made in the financial transaction space (Solin & Zerzan, 2010). Businesses and individuals have found it prudent to always try remaining ahead of the perpetrators behind the vices. The springing into life of the mobile money in the second half of the first decade of this century has

DOI: 10.4018/978-1-7998-2398-8.ch010

revolutionized the manner with which risk management in this respect is handled. However, though Castri (2013) noted that mobile money has reduced the risk of money laundering, the rate with which the myriad of financial crimes have been reported over the past decade in the face of this phenomenon raises the need to stay abreast of developments in this space.

In the emerging economies such as Ghana, Kenya, Tanzania, Nigeria, India, Uganda, Zambia and Argentina, mobile money has proved to be highly popular. This has been expedited by the huge unbanked population that, with an integral access to mobile gadgets, finds it easier and more convenient to make use of mobile money as an alternative to effecting financial transactions (Akomea-Frimpong et. al., 2018). As such, the traditional banking services provides have been left with a few reserve roles, less robust as they initially used to be. In Kenya, for instance, 44 per cent of the Gross Domestic Product (GDP) was represented by the value of the total mobile money transactions in 2018 (Munda, 2019). That implies that nearly half of the Kenya population is increasingly using the mobile platforms to initiate and complete corporate and retail transactions. In Ghana, with its largest Telco – Mobile Telecommunications Network (MTN) having over a 14 million subscriber base, mobile money can be seen to be the main platform that most of the unbanked in the West Africa nation get to join the formal banking system. As a matter of fact, PwC, 2015 asserts that over 80 per cent of the Ghanaian population has no access to the formal financial services.

Since it was embraced for wide use by commercial players and for person-to-person transfers, mobile money has been applauded for the efficiency it brought of facilitating fast and effective completion of payments between businesses, banks and consumers (Mirfin, 2019). Notably too, it mitigated the risk of carrying hard cash. As Castri (2013) confirms, individuals can now load their money into their mobile money transfer platforms and not feel the fear of being physically stolen from by sneak thieves and muggers. Further, the mobile money has not only expedited local funds transfers for the emerging economies but also international remittance, thanks to established players such as Apple Pay and PayPal joining the bandwagon (Mirfin, 2019). As such, customer experience has become very convenient with the use of mobile money, businesses have realized notable reduction in expenses and reduced paperwork and associated costs with regard to making and receiving payments, tremendously improved cash flows with swift payments, and enhanced the access to actionable data for clients that is stored in the applications (Castri, 2013).

Alongside this robust improvement in payment and money transfers has come one of the most covert yet pernicious manifestations of financial crime in our time. While the traditional criminal ways of fraud could not thrive with the mobile money tool, the criminals have equally adapted new tricks presented by changing technology and communications (Ghanaweb, 2019). GhanaWeb (2019) further observes that with the highly secured modes of mobile money transfers through the internet that has revolutionised business delivery processes, mobile money has created new avenues and opportunities for tech savvy criminals to defraud unsuspecting users. Identity theft, internet fraud and credit detail thefts all of which manifest as cybercrime, have stealthily crept into the mobile money platforms creating a huge risk of financial crime than what has been seen before. Money laundering, especially across countries has found a steady anchorage on this platform, calling for a deeper and a more intrinsically robust level of scrutiny to restrain (Kersop, 2016).

The pervasiveness of financial crimes done through the mobile money has often crippled the efforts put in place to reduce corruption in a number of countries using the payment system. Through illicit business activities such as drug dealing, illegal mining, wildlife crimes and human trafficking, funds have been injected into economies, oftentimes causing unprecedented macroeconomic distortions since the government banking systems are unable to track the points of the inflows into the economy. In countries like Kenya and Ghana where corruption perception index (CPI) is relatively high (Transparency International, 2018), government revenues have been swindled, tax evaded and questionable private businesses been erected all fuelled by the efficient mobile money payment systems that help unscrupulous officials transact without being caught easily. Individuals have gone further to open multiple accounts on the mobile money platforms, through which money laundering has efficiently been engineered to levels that have virtually almost thrown regulators to the dreadful realm of relenting (Solin & Zerzan, 2010).

In addition, the frequent terrorist attacks in countries like Somalia, Kenya and Uganda have not escaped linkage to mobile money. Terrorism is a heinous plot that is generally planned for months by the perpetrators and would often need huge sums of money to finance it (Mirfin, 2019). As such, since it is not as easy to effect the transfer of funds using the conventional banking systems, the use of mobile money has become a relatively safe channel as most of it is monitored post-the-fact. For instance in an attack done at a business complex in Kenya's capital in February 2019 by terrorists allied to the Somali Al-Shabab militia killing 21 people, the Anti-Terrorism Police Unit stated that one of the attackers had transacted at least 1 million US dollars (100 million Kenyan shillings) through mobile money, several months leading to the attack (Xinhua, 2019). It was also reported that one of the alleged terrorists had received 90,000 US dollars from South Africa using 47 Subscriber Identification Module (SIM) cards in the months leading to the attack (Xinhua, 2019).

Whereas the mobile money tool has been instrumental in bringing into place enhanced money transfers and instantaneous business payment modes, the various risks related to money laundering (ML) and terrorism financing (TF) across national and international jurisdictions is sure premise to deliberate upon the mitigations that can be set up in consequence.

## GENERAL MOBILE MONEY TRANSACTION FLOW

Before the advent of mobile money on a global scale, money transfer from one person to another was mainly via formal means or where possible it was expedited through agents or third persons, who characterized the informal means. For quite a while, in the developed economies, the electronic transfer of funds via the internet and using credit cards dominated the money transfer space. Also, organizations such as Western Union and MoneyGram played a great part in international money transfer. In most parts of Africa, the informal way of sending money applied so often, with people sending others going to the destination of the anticipated recipient of the money to help deliver the money.

Often, this was slow and unsecure due to the processes it had to go through. The invention of mobile money brought life of its kind in the money transfer realm, making it more convenient, safe and quick for the persons using the platform. For instance, in Ghana, as soon as the *MTN Mobile Money* was introduced into the market, person to person (p2p) money transfer totally transformed (Mattern, 2017). Settlement of debts, financial gifts and all person to person money transfers slowly moved to the use of mobile. This later set pace for the entrance into the same space by the *Airtel Money, TiGO Cash,* and *Vodafone MPESA*. The challenge that the baffled the users for a while are the credibility of the service that proved reliable with time.

P2P mobile money transfers and payments to other business transactions has now become part of people's lives and their financial engagements. In Kenya, two thirds of the adult population is using the mobile money transfer of funds and payments mainly *MPESA* and about 25% of the country's GDP flows through the platform (Munda, 2019). In China, the number of users using *Alipay* is more, standing at 800 million by the end of 2013, compared to those using the internet (600 million) (GSMA, 2014).

In the decades past, once the customer found their desired goods or product, there were not many modes through which they could make their payments to the business from which they were buying except by cash or bank in the case where amounts were huge. However, that is not the case since mobile money has made it easier, providing a number of ways to make payments beyond the conventional. In Kenya for instance, businesses have incorporated the mobile money account numbers in their advertisement in order to make it easy for the customers (Ignacio & Radcliffe n.d)Sometimes, the customers may make a purchase but they do not have cash, but find very convenient to clear the business using the mobile money in their accounts.

With this enhanced modes of payments and funds transfer, it will be unwise to turn a blind eye on the financial crimes that can take place in the process. One of the incredible risk measures that the Kenyan telco, *Safaricom,* has put in its mobile money transfer platform –*MPESA* is the 'reverse' option. It is a feature that helps an individual to retrieve their funds whenever they inadvertently send money to the wrong person or pay to the wrong business account in the case money transfer or making payments. Individuals and businesses alike are exposed to financial crime in this space, in terms of faked identity, money laundering especially in big businesses such as insurance, stock brokerage and investment firms.

## MOBILE MONEY LANDSCAPE: OVERVIEW OF CURRENT AND EMERGING TECHNOLOGIES

The Digital inclusion efforts put forth by governments in emerging economies and telecommunication firms, with the intention of connecting population and ignite the sprouting of business opportunities, have sparked a new paradigm of viewing the mobile technology space. Further, it has accelerated the creation of a good platform upon which a number of inventions have thrived and risen to full-fledged technology businesses. Mobile money (M-money) is one of those technologies that have enjoyed this enabling environment.

As 2003 was coming to an end, there were just slightly above one billion unique mobile subscribers globally, which implied that under one in six people had a subscription with a mobile service (GSMA, 2014). Exactly a decade later, by the end of 2013, this figure had dramatically increased to 3.4 billion unique subscriptions, with 6.9 billion SIM connections - slightly below half the world population at the time (GSMA, 2014). In 2019, with an estimated world population of 7.7 billion, there are 5.112 billion unique mobile subscribers –having a 67% penetration (DATAREPORTAL, 2019).

On the other hand, internet penetration is certainly one area that can be noted to be moving and growing in tandem with the mobile technology penetration and the advancement of the inventions emanating from efforts put into place to leverage the ease the way of doing business such as mobile money. In 2013, there was noted an accelerating growth of the high speed 3G and 4G network connections particularly in the developing countries and it was estimated that two thirds of the global mobile subscriber base utilizing internet would be connected- from the then one third coverage (GSMA, 2014). In 2019, Data Reportal (2019) confirmed that about 4.4 billion internet users globally, with a 57% penetration level. Startlingly, that was a 9% increase from 2018's figure, represented by 366 million new internet users (Data Reportal, 2019).

With this notable prolifereation of mobile internet and smartphone access particularly in the emerging markets, mobile money has found such a hub that has aided it manifest itself in multiple facets that have transformed the way economies are run. As a matter of fact, it has called for a reinvention of nearly all traditional financial markets' business models to suit the end users who are now inclined to the usage of the mobile services, which is characterized by quick, efficient and instant needs (Mirfin, 2019). One of this is the mobile-based banking, a feature that has proved to be crucial for a substantial number of banks to embrace to in constant touch with their customers.

The banking industry has come to an inevitable resolve that the banking space has tremendously evolved and majority of their customers are highly mobile with a connection with the internet. As such, most of the major retail banks globally have embraced the use of mobile apps to effect most of the traditional functions that required the customers to go to bank branches such as depositing, check account balances, withdrawing and applying for and servicing commercial loans (World Bank, 2014). Global Financial Inclusion Database released by the World Bank in 2014 indicated mobile banking had already started gaining tract and Botswana was leading in its popularity (44.5%), followed by Kenya(39.7%) (World Bank, 2014). South Korea, Sweden, the US and Australia are the other non-African countries that featured in that top ten list, implicitly showing that African countries had features in their mobile industry that accelerated the widespread use of mobile banking services amongst its population.

By the end of 2018, Juniper Research (2018) predicted that on a global scale, 2 billion people would be using their smartphone devices to access the digital banking services – an estimate of 40% of the world's adult population. The research also found out that with the increased adoption of the platform for banking especially in some of the key emerging economies in the globe such as China and India, it implied that the mobile banking users were a representative of 50% of the banked population around the world. Mobile banking has become an integral part of the banking financial services sector, with regions such as Eastern Europe increasing their market share to 47% in 2019 from 28% in 2018 of all the global mobile banking users(Eisenberg, 2019)

In countries such as Kenya, the mobile banking services which are facilitated in the form of applications have gone beyond the conventional banking services, to allowing customers to transfer funds from account to account, buy airtime, pay bills, account monitoring and even blocking their automated teller machine (ATM) cards whenever they may think they are at risk for whatever reason. In extension, the banks have also joined the now prevalent micro-loans space. Regional giant banks such as Barclays Bank, Housing Finance Group, Equity Bank, Cooperative Bank and Kenya Commercial Bank (KCB) have developed ingrained features on their mobile banking platforms to give out micro-credit services with short payment periods, often one month. One of the most effective loan platforms in the region has been KCB-MPESA, a loan facility provided by KCB in collaboration with the regions biggest mobile funds transfer platform, MPESA –having a systematic way of rewarding loans to its customers. In Nigeria, a similar scope of business with mobile banking with avenues such as the *Mainstream* loans wired and supported by the local banking players (Juniper Research, 2018).

Having come in handy in settling the headache that comes with lining up at the banking halls to wait for possibly hours in order to be served, the mobile banking technology, which has often been termed as an ideal solution, is plagued by a couple of risks. While the mobile use penetration especially in the developing economies has reached unprecedented levels, it is apparent that most of the current users are not necessarily computer literate nor are they educated in matters financial services. Individuals from all walks of life are compelled to use of the mobile banking services for their convenience, thanks to the easy nature of usability of most of the apps. They certainly lay their trust of their information in respect of the tool on the financial services providers. Notwithstanding, customers are often at risk since they would not be keen enough on verifying if the information they offer falls in the right or wrong hands, in which case if the latter occurs they stand to lose their financial resources by way of being swindled.

Individuals have not come to the realization that mobile devices can be hacked and attacked just as it happens for notepads and computers. In recent times, the mobile devices have become the soft targets for hackers. In this realm, the downloading of infected apps has become one of the most threats that mobile devices face. Once installed, knowingly or unknowingly, these already infected apps perform the malicious tasks for which they have been programmed, thus rendering the mobile banking user absolutely vulnerable and susceptible to being a victim of financial crimes (Castri, 2013). Checkpoint (2019) asserts that Wi-Fi, OS exploitations, SMS attacks, zero-day malware and device settings are some of the major threats that mobile devices are exposed to. Certainly, cybercrime and financial crime are stubborn confederates in this context. Penetration of the mobile devices' use and internet in developing countries like Kenya and Nigeria is praiseworthy, but it comes with a heavy price that calls for deep contemplation on setting in place watertight mitigation measures.

Checkpoint (2019) indicated that about 14 million devices were hit the *Copycat* mobile malware on a global scale in 2018, while those devices that were hit and injuriously affected another mobile malware –*Hummingbad* - summed to 10 million. Also, in respect of the fake apps that were installed totaled to 4.9 million, all resulting from the already infected devices. Further, Checkpoint (2019) noted that in 2018, hackers leveraged the use of dormant accounts to siphon huge chunks of money banks maliciously. Therefore, these malicious innovations put users of mobile banking at risk and stand to be a major stumbling block to the advancement of the use and trust of this useful technology (Checkpoint, 2019).

## Mobile Loan Apps

Mobile money has never been as active as it is currently with the rise of mobile applications that readily provide instant loans to the individuals in need of credit; to be repaid after specified times at an interest. Besides the mobile banking apps that offer loans, these mobile loan apps are solely meant to offer nothing else but loans. In order to show just how this space has mysteriously grown over the years, in a global scale, the mobile money providers in terms of loan services increased to 73 per cent in 2017 from 38 per cent in 2014 (GSMA, 2018). The improved smartphone access to a greater global adult population in regions such as Sub-Saharan Africa, South Asia, Latin America and Caribbean, can be attributed to the growth in the demand and yearn for the mobile loans.

Mobile loan apps business minds noted that what most of the population found out money to be relatively elusive, especially for the very time that they needed it to effect a transaction or make some sort of payments (Owuor, 2019). The fact that they are able to provide that facility at convenient times, with little or no requirement of a security as in the case of traditional banking service, makes the loan apps more attractive thus easily embraced. With this premise, the aspect of digital lending through the mobile loan apps has taken the microcredit space by a storm, inevitably changing the manner in which access to funds is viewed and treated especially in the developing economies.

In some countries, due to the high interest rates charged by the local banks when it comes to offering loans, the micro lending sector by banks has been stringent. As such, a time when people are desirous of easy and instantaneous solutions to most of their challenges with the wake of the digital age and access to the internet, including financial, the sprouting of alternative lending platforms has become compulsively necessitated. Nigeria is such an example, where the lending in the banking sector has been minimal due to various reasons, chief among them being the high defaulting levels of the customers who borrow in the economy for business, but more especially for consumption. In fact, due to this alarming phenomenon, the Central Bank of Nigeria compelled the banks to lend more, asserting that they should use 60% of their deposits to give out loans by the end of September 2019 (Brazil News.Net, 2019). It came in with a threat to have the cash reserve increased for the banks that do not lend more to the Nigerian public. The Nigerian banks are considered to be among the most reluctant lenders amongst the major emerging markets, having an average of below 60% loan-to-deposit ratio (Brazil News.Net, 2019).

Notably, the large population of Nigeria has been forced to gullibly rely on the services offered by the myriad mobile loan apps to their various financial needs. The *PayLater Loan App* has been the leading mobile loan app that has virtually found its way to becoming part and parcel of the lives of the most poor and middle-class population in Nigeria. It is preferred due to the high speed with which one can access a loan –in less than five minutes –and get to pay later, for a period spanning from 15 days to 6 months without collateral or any documentation. Whereas, on average, most Nigerian commercial banks charge between 18% and 36% on the personal loans they offer to the Nigerian public in addition to requiring collateral, the *PayLater loan App* charges only 15.5% rate per annum, making it more attractive (ValuePenguin, 2019). With this service, customers are able to recharge airtime, set up transactions that are to be effected in the future specified date, pay for utility bills -GoTV, DSTV, LCC, Bet9ja –send cash to family and friends etc. It is a feature that has equally been replicated in a number of other mobile loan apps in the country such as *Branch Loan App, Sokoloan App, Palmcredit Loan App, ALAT Loan App* and *FairMoney Loan App.*

In other jurisdictions like Kenya, the mobile loan apps have turned out to be quite extortive in their nature due to their relatively high interest rates in comparison to the mainstream bank loan rates. Kenyans pay very high interest rates to access the loan facilities, ranging on an average of between 10% and 14% per month (Nzayisenga, 2017). Global lending apps such as *Tala* and *Branch* have taken the local mobile loan business by storming to the extent of seeking more funding from financiers in the Silcon Valley in order to meet the high demand for loans by their customer base (Dahir 2019). The stringent economic times in the economy has compelled the majority of the adult population struggling with sustaining their livelihoods to result in depending on the mobile loan apps in order to meet their daily financial needs. On the other hand, a number of individuals have used the loans in order to start and scale up their business ventures, a feature that calls for applause since it effectively advanced their livelihoods without undergoing the shrewd lending terms in the mainstream banking sector. More mobile loans have thus sprouted in the region, including, *Shika LoanApp, Saida Loans, Okoa Stima, Zidisha Loan* and *Haraka.* Nearly all these apps have recorded a growing revenue base over the years.

In Kenya, the establishment of the Credit Reference Bureau (CRB), an entity that monitors and regulates the creditworthiness of an individual, has by far and wide fueled the thriving of the mobile loan apps (Xinhua, 2019). This is essentially because the customers taking the loans are cognizant of the fact that they shall be listed in the CRB and thus render unsuitable to take other loans in the future. This effort in regulation has to some great extent helped sanitize the borrowing craze, although it has in several occasions led to individuals contemplating suicide in the event when they did not manage to pay back their loans (Nzayisenga, 2017). Due to increasingly spiraling levels of poverty in the various regions in the developing economies, much of the borrowing done on the mobile loan apps is sadly used on personal consumption or put into uses that cannot be directly traced back to business gain. As a result, once consumption has been effected, there lacks means of making repayments when the loans fall, thus throwing individuals into deep debts. Either, it has also nearly become a norm in some countries like Kenya, whereby, borrowers on the mobile loan apps have found themselves in what can be termed as a debt trap as a result borrowing from multiple platforms for repayment purposes due to lack of a plausible repayment plan (Munda, 2019).

The major financial risk likely to hit hard the mobile loan apps is money laundering (ML). Essentially, the mobile loan apps are in the business of credit-only service provision. There are no clear regulations put in place across the emerging economies to be able to clearly carry out a thorough scrutiny on these firms to ascertain the source of the funds that they lend out to the public. This informational gap on the side of financial regulatory institutions and anti-money laundering entities is a huge doorway to the manifestations of financial crime. Monies illicitly acquired can easily be channeled into these apps for sanitized, and thus leading to an exposure of the economy to the evils that emanate from money laundering. The perpetrators of the illicit businesses and schemes will gain tract since they will find a safe haven through which they can enjoy their ill-acquired profits without being caught by authorities thus face no repercussions. For economies that are up to encouraging legit businesses among their people for fair and healthy competition, when money laundering finds its way to the mobile loan lending unnoticed in the emerging markets, there will more social evils will bluntly come out bare such as drugs in the streets; more fraud in the corporate space risking pensions for workers and collapsing of companies in the financial market space (Castri, 2013). Further, Juniper (2018) affirms to the fact that, losses in tax revenue will have to be made up for by the already impoverished persons in the emerging economies, ultimately yielding to a stiff financial strain that tremendously curtail any economic progress. The million dollar question now is why the regulatory entities are not yet able to tame this potentially deleterious phenomenon in the financial services space.

Calls for the financial regulators and the legislators for the various jurisdictions to come up with regulatory measures for the mobile loan apps must be heightened for the health of the financial space and safeguard of the users. One of the ways to effectively track the possibility of money laundering as being part of the drivers of the mobile loan apps is the establishment of concrete operational regulations (Castri, 2013). It is evident that with the evolution of the technology, the traditional financial regulatory provisions in the Banking Charters cannot be able to sustain the needs of this nascent digital space. It will be crucial to man and regulate issues such as the mobile loan apps' terms and conditions of their products, customer complaint processes, assert and disclose to the regulators their consumer data protection and privacy policy and any allowance period they give for purposes of cooling off in the instances of conflict. These regulations having the backdrop of possibility of money laundering in the mobile digital loan apps not only protect the customers but also the economy at large as an entity since the funds borrowed and lent are flowing within the economy (GSMA, 2014).

## Social Payments and Social Shopping

With the invention of social media sites and tools over the past nearly 15 years, connecting people through messaging, video calling, live streaming, photo sharing etc., the future of digital transformation is now inclined to social payments and social shopping. Undoubtedly, since majority of these tools are accessed and utilized through the mobile devices, mobile money will be a key integrating feature when it will come to closing deals and transaction on those sites. What is not clear though is whether the emerging markets and globe in general is equipped enough to manage any financial crimes that are likely to creep in through this technology.

Ideally, social payment involves the utilization of social media in the transfer of money from one person to another or from a person to a business. Features to effect payments from money transfer platforms are incorporated in the social media apps in order to assist in the transactions accordingly. *PayPal* can be noted to one of the pioneer platforms used to popularize this technology, but we have since seen similar features being hatched by other social media platforms such as *Snapcash, WeChat Pay, Venmo, Twitter Pay, Apple Pay* and *Google Wallet.* This robust growth of m-Commerce implies that we should expect to see improved merging between social networks and m-Commerce in the future.

In China, for instance, there were 31% of the users of *WeChat* already actively using its purchasing features by April 2019, when the company launched a new feature called "Good Product Circle" (Pan, 2019). This feature allows the users of the platform to be able to share various e-commerce Mini Program stores with their friends, effectively creating demand shopping more conveniently and seamlessly. The integration makes the users to share products of any kind from other platforms and then interact with their friends using the same feature (Pan, 2019). Arguably, Pan (2019) points out that the social shopping sites will leverage on the acquaintance recommendations thus assuring some credibility of the product at hand, as opposed to the sometimes supposed fake ads that are meant to influence a potential customer to buy, only to have a terrible experience with product when they receive –feeling less value for their money.

With the notable cybercrime scenes in the past few years, financial crime is an imminent tragedy yet to hit the social shopping space. It will have to take the regulators and the firms an extra effort to close loopholes that could give way for fraudulent persons from siphoning funds from unsuspecting users of these social apps. Either, the mobile money payments through these social apps is prone to fueling acts of money. This is more so because, anonymity is part of the process of 'cleaning dirty' money, and once the masterminds of money laundering manage to register fake accounts, they are likely to accomplish their heinous acts without the possibility of ever being caught. It is certainly not clear if these social sites have amicably managed to put in place the right Anti-Money Laundering (AML) measures such as keeping the records of transactions, setting limits of amounts of money that can be transferred on accounts with certain times and generally critical and keen monitoring of the transactions taking place on level of the system (Pan, 2019).

In addition, in light of the users of the social networking platforms using their acquaintances with individuals as a basic basis to accept recommendation for particular products on sale, there lays a risk of identity theft or account takeover. This will result in fraudulent dealings that will hurt the users, rip them of their finances and possibly render the platforms unpopular. FinTech companies working upon which the mobile money payments is based in the context of the social shopping and payments will have to develop proper terms and conditions to guide and govern the social payments (Datareportal, 2019).

## Mobile Money and Terrorism Financing (TF)

Whereas mobile money has tremendously transformed the way of doing business and transfer of funds from one individual to another, the rate at which it is being misused to harm the very people in various jurisdictions that it serves is indubitably alarming. One of the debasing roles that mobile money has come to play in making life difficult for nations is terrorism financing (TF). TF can be defined as the acts that support the flow of funds to terrorists or non-state actors (Castri, 2013). It is a global phenomenon that keeps raising the economic and political antennae of nations, often begging for a concerted effort in order to curb it. The technology of mobile money came at a time when the national financial intelligence units (FIUs) were not utterly prepared to tackle it and hit it by its very root.

High level criminals such as the terrorists possess some sense of sophistication and knowledge about their target victims to such an extent that it requires an equipped anti-terrorism team to be able to dismantle their tact. The International Convention for the Suppression of the Financing of Terrorism (1999) and the Security Council resolution 1373 (2001) urge states across the globe to be vigilant enough to "prevent and suppress the financing of terrorism, inter alia, by criminalizing the collection and provision of funds for terrorist purposes, and urges them to set up effective mechanisms to freeze funds and other financial assets of persons involved in or associated with terrorism, as well as to prevent those funds from being made available to terrorists" (UN, 1999). While this is an international resolution that is being acted upon by high level intelligence, when the sinister perpetrators and supporters of terrorism find out any loophole to this end, they tend to leverage it to undermine and water down any preparations put in place. Mobile money has proved to be an effective and insidious tool that terrorists have found lobby for funding in order to expedite their acts of cowardice.

Appearing more frequently on the world's map for the same reasons, Kenya has possibly seen the different facets of terrorism financing in its fight against the Somalia-based militia, Al-Shabaab than most nations in the emerging economies. It is certainly distressing that it has suffered the spread of this evil under the fuelling of its reputable mobile money innovation –MPESA. It is one of the most performing mobile money platforms in the continent, and now made its reputation known all over the world –users can send and receive funds from other countries in the world, over 200. As at December 2018, the mobile money platform had 30 million customers. On overall, with the total of about 48 million mobile money subscribers in Kenya, a record of Sh. 3.98 trillion was transacted in 2018 and Sh. 270 billion came into the country majorly from North America and Europe (CBK, 2019). It was noted that is within this period that huge chunks of money were transacted through the mobile money platforms to plan and execute the terrorist attack at a Nairobi based business complex, DusitD2 complex on 15$^{th}$ January 2019, leaving 21 people dead (Wechsler, 2019)

About four months leading to the attack, one of the suspects arraigned in court for financing it had received up to Sh. 100 million (US$ 1 million) that he later sent to the terrorism group based in Somalia (Ahmed, 2019) The amount was withdrawn from the bank in little chunks before distributed to other individuals via mobile money. Another suspect also received Sh. 9 million from South Africa, withdrawn to the *Mpesa* and then sent to individuals noted to be part of the Al-Shabaab outfit based in Somalia. CBK (2019) further indicates that prior to this act, the second suspect was found to have registered 47 SIM cards between the months of October and December in 2018 which were used to seamlessly carry out the mobile money transfer without being noticed nor suspected. This particular incident affirmed to the possibility that terrorist sympathizers have an easy way manoeuvring around the loose regulatory environment in respect of the mobile money business, which does not necessarily provide for a deep knowledge and understanding of the background of the users, to do plan and support the terrorist activities with little hindrance.

From a report released in October 2018 by the Central Bank of Kenya on the Financial Sector Stability, very few among the digital outfits such as the mobile money apps had comprehensive information about the nature and business of their customers. It possibly did not matter to them, in the sense that all that is crucial is that they lend and have the loans repaid in good time with interest –business in its simplest form with respect with their mandate. However, this gives a huge opportunity for terrorists to receive their services, thus implicitly financing a rogue cause. There stands to be a significant gap in the level of scrutiny conducted by the mobile money operators across the emerging economies to ascertain the sources of funds being moved, and whether the individuals receiving or sending cash are doing so with the right intentions. Consequently, some of the concerns that still beg for a more elaborate deliberation are that, expansion in the usage of mobile money payments and other digital credit is seemingly creating a predisposition to financial crime risks –money laundering, technology risks and terrorist financing on the developing economies (Isaac Akomea-Frimpong, 2018).

With respect to the financing of the Somali-based terrorist group, Al-Shabaab, a report by the US Bureau for International Narcotics and Law Enforcement Affairs published in 2015 established that the main financing for terror activities is by mobile money and Somali's hawalas. Hawalas in the Somali community are the agents who act as remittance banks (Thompson, 2007). Hawala featured prominently during the 9/11 attacks as having played a pivotal role in funding it, coming out in the eyes of the non-Muslim world as a "black" channel through which terrorists moved funds. Following the infamous attack in Kenya in 2015 at the Garissa University that left 148 students dead, thirteen firms associated with playing a role of hawalas in financing the attack were shut down over a State crackdown (Thompson, 2007).

In West Africa, besides the porous borders that allowed the terrorists to transfer material resources and funds across and support from charities and Non-profit organizations (NPOs) to finance terrorist activities, online and mobile based money payments have come in handy in the facilitation TF (Mirfin, 2019). ML has been part of the tools used to support terrorism without the knowledge of the state, particularly from rich business owners who are part and parcel of the sympathizers of the infamous *Boko Haram* terrorist group in the region. Further, with widespread use of mobile phones in the transfer of funds, according to one of the suspects brought to book in 2012 following the November 4 2011 attack by the *Boko Haram* that left 148 people dead including police officers, the militia group receives already registered Subscriber Identity Module (SIM) cards from members of the public that were sympathizers to the terrorist activities (FATF, 2013). These kinds of SIM cards can then be used in the transfer of funds from multi-agencies, local and abroad, to communicate and receive huge amounts of finances through the mobile money platforms and online payments, effectively equipping the terrorists with the resources they need to ignite fire on innocent lives in the West Africa region indiscriminately (FATF, 2013).

The future of the countries prone to attacks by terrorists is at stake if the advancements in the technology of mobile money grow at a faster speed than it can be regulated to arrest the unexpected criminal activities as soon as they pop up. The policy makers in the various states have a responsibility to create principles on responsible finance which may include regulations on consumer protection, development of the pragmatic codes of conducts to be followed by the financial services players especially those that are leveraging on the mobile money as part of their business models and instilling mechanisms in place to assure financial integrity. Part of the reason which has made ML/TF possible is the fact that state financial regulators such as central banks do not have elaborate regulatory policies that assist in the management of the nonbank financial services firms (UN, 1999).

## Mobile Money Regulation in Relation to ML and CFT

Essentially, the telecommunication firms are meant for facilitating communication and access to internet, but the invention of the mobile money to their platforms is not a space that had originally been in any regulation. Therefore, legislation on how these online financial platforms ought to be managed is crucial, so that financial providers of mobile money are able to provide their risk mitigation measures with respect to money laundering (ML) and assuring a firm policy on combating terrorism financing (CFT) (Ghanaweb, 2019). These platforms move huge volumes of money on a daily basis and therefore it the state agencies and regulators would want to be keen at following up to ensure that good business takes and not activities that will highly undermine the state security. Moreover, from the scenario in Kenya where the key player in financing the DusitD2 attack who happened to be an agent of the mobile money provider, a more smart and flexible oversight is needed to restrain the activities that these may do to effectively fund terrorism.

On the other hand, the Financial Action Task Force (FATF), being an intergovernmental body that recommends countries on CFT, there have been reactive nature to terrorism attacks around the global, in light of the manner of financing. It will be more prudent to have a collaborative engagement with the state parties such as the Financial Intelligence Units (FIUs) order to effectively influence the strengthening of policies that are engulfed with loopholes that terrorism financiers could leverage on. An informed government in matters terrorism planning and financing will be to act more proactively towards possibly freezing the accounts involved in the transfer and arraign the suspects to courts of law. It is clear from the precedents of terrorism in the emerging economies in the past decade has often caught the government and state security agencies by surprises, even when it is later confirmed that it took months and months of planning (Mirfin, 2019). FIUs should stay abreast of the developments in the digital payments, more so the mobile money, to gather intelligence that can guide in the establishment of the right tact to bring to book terrorist financiers.

Regtechs are certainly one of the latest technologies in the Fintech space that regulators in the financial services industry can use to mitigate any risks that mobile money may involve. With regtech tools, regulatory requirements for the nonbank financial services such as the mobile money firms, "nimble, configurable, easy to integrate, reliable, secure and cost-effective regulatory solutions" can be developed to grab financial crime perpetrators by their necks (Checkpoint, 2019). It would remain a continued crisis if such deliberate efforts are not taken to ensure that even people and business enjoy the mobile money technology, it does not turn out to be the tool that effectively wipes them out over terror attacks.

## CONCLUSION

Presently settled in most of developing economies, versatile money related administrations are entering another stage in their advancement. Portable cash, specifically, has turned into a key area of interest as nations continue to develop interests in portable frameworks and further adding to budgetary consideration and financial advancement.

On the same breath; it is more than apparent that more needs to be done to contain financial crimes such as money laundering and terrorism financing. P2P mobile money transfers are at an all-time fast speed, but there lies the tragedy too that with the same pace, terrorism activities can be financed and executed. Through the mobile money loan apps, due to the limited knowledge of the customers at the hands of the service providers, terrorists have a far from being elusive source of funding to help them plan their heinous acts. FIUs would want to dig deeper into the issue of money laundering and terrorism for these reasons so that the evils do not rob the emerging economies of good people and the opportunity to grow legitimate businesses that will compete in the world market.

## REFERENCES

BrazilNews.Net. (2019, July 5). Retrieved July 29, 2019, from brazilinews.net: https://www.brazilnews.net/news/261625727/nigeria-orders-banks-to-loan-more-money

Castri, S. D. (2013). *Mobile Money: Enabling Regulatory solutions*. GSMA.

CBK. (2019). *Mobile Payments*. Nairobi: Central Bank of Kenya.

Checkpoint. (2019). *Cyber Attack Trends: 2019 Mid-Year Report*. Tel Aviv-Yafo, Israel: Checkpoint.

DATAREPORTAL. (2019, January 31). Retrieved July 28, 2019, from datareportal.com: https://datareportal.com/reports/digital-2019-global-digital-overview

Eisenberg, A. (2019, March 21). *Ignite*. Retrieved July 28, 2019, from igniteoutsourcing.com: https://igniteoutsourcing.com/fintech/mobile-banking-application-development/

FATF. (2013). *Terrorist Financing in West Africa*. Paris, France: FATF.

Ghanaweb. (2019, April 1). Retrieved July 20, 2019, from ghanaweb.com: https://www.ghanaweb.com/GhanaHomePage/business/Fight-against-money-laundering-must-focus-on-mobile-money-GIABA-734744#

GSMA. (2014). *The Mobile Economy 2014*. London, UK: GSMA.

GSMA. (2018). *Beyond the basics: How Smartphones will drive future opportunities for the mobile money industry*. London, UK: GSMA Mobile Money. Retrieved from http://siteresources.worldbank.org/AFRICAEXT/Resources/258643-1271798012256/YAC_chpt_20.pdf

Isaac Akomea-Frimpong, C. A.-F.-O. (2018). Control of fraud on mobile moneyservices in Ghana: anexploratory study. *Journal of Money Laundering Control*, 20-39.

Juniper Research. (2018, February 28). Retrieved July 28, 2019, from juniperresearch.com: https://www.juniperresearch.com/press/press-releases/digital-banking-users-to-reach-2-billion

Kersop, M. (2016). Anti-money laundering regulations and the effective use of mobile money in South Africa - Part 1. *P.E.R.*, 205.

Marina Solin, A. Z. (2010). *Mobile Money: Methodology for Assessing Money Laundering and Terrorist Financing Risks*. Barcelona: GSMA.

Mattern Max. (2017). *How Ghana Became One of Africa's Top Mobile Money Markets*. Available at https://www.cgap.org/blog/how-ghana-became-one-africas-top-mobile-money-markets

Mirfin, J. (2019, February 11). *Refinitiv*. Retrieved July 20, 2019, from refinitiv.com: https://www.refinitiv.com/perspectives/financial-crime/combating-payments-related-financial-crime/

Mohamed Ahmed. (2019). *Star footballer who ditched it all for life as a Al- Shabaab agent*. Available at https://www.nation.co.ke/news/Star-footballer-who-ditched-it-all-for-life-as-a-Shabaab-agent/1056-5300146-kvvvqu/index.html

Munda, C. (2019, Jan 24). *Business Daily Africa*. Retrieved July 07, 2019, from businessdailyafrica.com: https://www.businessdailyafrica.com/economy/Sh4trn-mobile-phone-deals-move-half-Kenyas-GDP/3946234-4948816-tg94g1/index.html

Nzayisenga, A. (2017). *Effect of Mobile Lending on the Financial Performance of Commercial Banks in Kenya*. Nairobi: University of Nairobi.

Owuor. (2019). *Mobile-based lending is a double-edged sword in Kenya—helping but also spiking personal debt*. University of Colorado. Retrieved from https://qz.com/africa/1722613/mobile-money-lending-in-kenya-helps-but-also-spikes-debt/

Pan, Y. (2019, June 9). *Jing Daily*. Retrieved July 29, 2019, from jingdaily.com: https://jingdaily.com/wechat-social-commerce/

PWC. (2015, Dec. 12). *Bank of the Future: What bank customers want to experience by 2020*. 2015 Ghana Banking Survey.

Thompson, E. A. (2007). *Misplaced Blame: Islam, Terrorism and the Origins of Hawala*. The Hague: Koninklijke Brill N.V.

UN. (1999). *International Convention for the Suppression of the Financing of Terrorism*. New York: General Assembly of the United Nations.

ValuePenguin. (2019, April 14). Retrieved July 29, 2019, from Valuepenguin.com: https://www.valuepenguin.com/personal-loans/average-personal-loan-interest-rates

Wechsler. (2019). *Mobile Money Transfers Suspected of Financing Dusit D2 Terror Attack*. The DFS Observatory.

World Bank. (2014, January 13). Retrieved July 28, 2019, from databank.worldbank.org: https://databank.worldbank.org/reports.aspx?source=1228

Xinhua. (2019, January 30). Retrieved July 20, 2019, from xinhuanet.com: http://www.xinhuanet.com/english/2019-01/30/c_137787614.htm

# Chapter 11
# Financial Inclusivity:
## Women Riding on Wave of M-Pesa

**Joy Mueni**
*Riara University, Kenya*

## ABSTRACT

*M-Pesa is a mobile phone-based money transfer system in Kenya that was introduced in 2007 by Safaricom, a subsidiary of Vodafone. Since its inception, the mobile money industry has witnessed some unprecedented growth mainly due to the diverse products, key among them M-Pesa. Powered by the over 100% mobile phone penetration in Kenya, M-Pesa has revolutionized the social and economic lives of Kenyans. In this chapter, using case studies, the author explores the impact M-Pesa has had on women in Kenya. In reference to banking, the author looks at the regulations, polices, and restrictions of M-Pesa against the formal banking industry to understand which is more suited to women and hence its rate of adoption. Another parameter that the author explores is the convenience that M-Pesa guarantees the user and how this has impacted on the effectiveness and efficiency of transactions among women.*

## INTRODUCTION

Before the advent of mobile money transfer services such as M-Pesa, a mobile money service, life was marred with money transaction difficulties. One had to do face to face transactions or visit a banking hall to subscribe to a solution. As a solution to these challenges, Safaricom, the largest telecom company in Kenya, introduced M-Pesa in March 2007 to a resounding adoption almost overnight. Within one year, Rosenberg and Morawczynski (2008) confirm that there were over 2.3 million registered users of M-Pesa. As it was bound to happen, the early adopters of this

DOI: 10.4018/978-1-7998-2398-8.ch011

technology were largely men. Due to rural-urban migration, "it is the young, male, urban migrants who are driving the uptake of services – customer adoption", note Rosenberg and Morawczynski (2008). Whereas women eventually adopted this technology, it was not without hindrances.

For Kenya to achieve its vision 2030 and the United Nations Sustainable Development Goals (SDGS) as supported by four development pillars in Agriculture, Health, Manufacturing and affordable housing, there is need for an inclusive participation that also involves women who are a strong pillar to a healthy family and to the economy at large (White, 2012).

This chapter looks at how the M-Pesa mobile money transfer services have impacted on the social and economic life of both urban and rural women by contrasting various parameters of their lives. In reference to banking, the chapter examines the regulations, polices and restrictions of M-Pesa services against the formal banking industry to unravel the one that is more suited to women and hence its rate capitalize on its adoption. Additionally, the paper explores the convenience that M-Pesa guarantees the user and how this has impacted on the effectiveness and efficiency of transactions among women. Also in the midst of these benefits, the author elucidates how to mitigate the social evils that have come up with the M-Pesa mobile money transfer and how they can be mitigated.

## BACKGROUND

M-Pesa is a mobile phone based money transfer system originating from Kenya which was introduced in 2007 by Safaricom, a subsidiary of Vodafone. Since its inception, the mobile money industry has witnessed unprecedented growth mainly due to the diverse products key among them is M-Pesa. Powered by the over 100% mobile phone penetration in Kenya according to Communication Authority of Kenya (CAK), M-Pesa has revolutionised the social and economic lives of Kenyans and more so to the banking lives of women.

A unique factor of the M-Pesa system is that it empowers users to make electronic payments via ordinary mobile phones without the requirement to connect to online banking using the internet (Katz & Berry, 2014). Users merely need to register at M-PESA retail stores by carrying their national identification (henceforth ID) cards. Users create electronic accounts and link those accounts to their phone numbers and Subscriber Identity Module (henceforth SIM) cards. In addition, users create a private PIN for using when accessing the account. The M-PESA users deposit cash money in the retail stores or using online banking and, they in-turn receive equal float (henceforth e-float). Transactions are confirmed with a notification in the form of an SMS for both users and the retail agent. Through the confirmation and notification, users are able to see new account balance and the retail agent as well remains with the transaction records of the money sent and received (Bosire, 2012).

Katz and Berry, (2014 indicate that the launch of M-PESA was an enormous success as it brought instant benefits to the users, financial institutions and mobile providers. Within a short period of time, M-PESA outperformed Kenya's bank branches, at 17 million users by the end of 2013. Today, two-thirds of the population actively uses M-PESA, which handles 25% of the national gross domestic product (henceforth NGP). Rightfully so, Jack and Suri (2011), note that the adoption of mobile phones and M-PESA in Kenya occurred at the fastest pace of any consumer-level technology in the history of technology adoption.

Before M-Pesa was introduced, many women could not access banking services and hence remained unbanked. And even when they could access banks, according to the World Economic Forum, women in emerging markets such as Kenya are six to nine percentage points less likely to have a bank account than their male counterparts. The GSMA mobile gender gap report 2019 indicates that since 2014, women's mobile phone ownership has increased significantly in low and middle income countries. By 2009, the number of mobile money accounts in Kenya had indeed surpassed the number of traditional bank accounts (GSMA, 2019).

The GSMA 2017 report indicates that mobile subscribers and use of transfer services is on the rise and that by the end of 2016, there were 420 million unique mobile subscribers in Sub-Saharan Africa. The region accounts for nearly 10% of the global mobile subscriber base, a share set to rise given that the mobile penetration rate of 43% is significantly lower than the global average penetration rate of 66%. Although annual subscriber growth has now slowed to single digits, Sub-Saharan Africa is still growing faster than any other region and will record a compound annual growth rate of 2% over the five years to 2020, compared to a global average of 4.2% for the same period. By 2020, there will be just over 500 million unique mobile subscribers in the region and the penetration rate will have risen to 50% (GSMA, The Mobile Economy Sub-Saharan Africa, 2017).

However, with the benefits that has come with the increase of mobile subscribers and money transfer, Mobile Gender Gap report (2019) indicate that women are 10% less likely to own a mobile phone translating to 313 million fewer women than men who use mobile internet, and 23% less likely to use mobile internet while closing the gap would create a commercial opportunity of 140 Billion USD associated with equalizing male and female mobile ownership and use in low-and middle income countries by 2023 as per the GSMA Intelligent Estimates.

The report further indicates that Kenya is among the countries with a huge gender gap between men and women who own and regularly utilise mobile phones thereby indicating that M-Pesa mobile money transfer services may not benefit more women due to low penetration of the mobile use by women. The number of mobile use cases utilized at least weekly in Kenya stood at 61% for men compared 69% for women. On the other hand, the percentage difference in monthly expenditure on mobile services for men and women, not including devices, stood at 29%. In overall, the study reveals that 80% of women in low- and middle-income countries are now mobile owners. According to the report, mobile phones are the primary means of internet access in these markets, where 48% of women use mobile to get online.

Studies like Kimeli (2016) and Andiva (2013) show that ensuring digital and financial inclusion for women is critically important since when women thrive; societies, businesses and economies thrive. Therefore, the statistics of 432 million women in Sub-Saharan countries who are still unconnected will require concerted effort and coordination from the mobile industry, as well as policy makers and the international community. The findings of the Gender Gap Report indicate that some important factors leading to poor participation of women in mobile money transfer include mobile phone affordability; literacy and lack of digital skills acquisition; a perceived lack of relevance; and safety and security concerns as the top barriers needing to be addressed in order to further decrease the mobile gender gap. According to the report; 56% of men and 45% of women surveyed in Kenya cited affordability as the reason they do not own phones; while those who cited literacy and skills was lower for men at 23% compared to 31% for women. Additionally, 4% of men and 3% of women cited relevancy as a barrier to owning a mobile phone while those who attributed it to safety and security stood at 8% for men and 12% for women. The percentage of those who cited accessibility issues, such as mobile coverage, access to phone charging and family approval was marginal. Addressing the above challenges which involves empowering women to economic opportunities and literacy is critical in liberating them out of poverty by making them participate effectively in the use of M-Pesa services as supported by Ndiaye (2014).

An evaluation of the contribution of the M-Pesa on women is crucial to highlight and bring out the benefits it has brought to women in an effort to increase their participation to harness more opportunities created by the M-Pesa services since empowering a woman, empowers a family and the Nation.

## WOMEN AND MOBILE BANKING

M-Pesa mobile money is widely cited as the game-changer for financial inclusion and the growth driver for the African mobile industry. However, studies such as Omwansa (2009) and Kimeli (2016) have shown that in Kenya and across Africa, women are consistently less likely than men to use mobile financial services which is a loss to women, many of whom have yet to reap the benefits of mobile money such as M-Pesa and consequently a loss to mobile money providers who have yet to capture these women as subscribers. Some of the reasons cited for this is that most women live in rural areas where the literacy rate is high and also inadequate infrastructure and low incomes. M-Pesa has revolutionised the social and economic lives of Kenyans and the study investigates how it has empowered and changed the banking lives of women. Before M-Pesa was introduced, many women could not access banking facilities and hence remained unbanked and even when they could access banks, according to the World Economic Forum, women in emerging markets (like Kenya) are six to nine percentage points less likely to have a bank account than their male counterparts. The mobile gender gap report 2019 indicates that though women mobile phone ownership has increased significantly in low and middle income countries since the year 2014, the use of mobile services by women is still low compared to men. An investigation of the impact of M-Pesa services on women in Kenya brings a clear viewpoint to enhance women participation and use of the mobile money which in turn has a great potential of changing their social and economic lives.

## THE SOCIO-ECONOMIC IMPACT OF M-PESA SERVICES TO WOMEN

Most urban women are more exposed and are more likely to use M-Pesa services payment and platform than the rural women. The study investigates the impact of mobile money transfer services in Kenya by taking into account other new services built on the M-Pesa platform such as (*M-Shwari, Lipa na M-Pesa, Linda Jamii* and *M-Kopa* among others) in order to elucidate their effectiveness and use to spur business growth. To get a better understanding of the impact of M-Pesa on women, it is important that we understand the services offered under the M-Pesa umbrella.

1. **Lipa Na M-Pesa:** This service enables organisations to allow their customers to buy goods or pay bills via M-PESA. Launched in March 2015 the service has around 36,000 merchants. It's mainly used by urban customers who prefer to use it purchase of goods and services in supermarkets, petrol stations, and other outlet stores.
2. **M-Shwari:** This is a savings and loans product for M-Pesa users. Launched by Safaricom in partnership with the Commercial Bank of Africa (CBA), M -Shwari is a bank account issued by CBA and subject to all the regulatory requirements of a bank account in Kenya. CBA is responsible for maintaining a dedicated management information system, regulatory compliance, reporting to the credit bureau and providing capital to fund the loan portfolio. Critically, it is CBA that carries the risk and absorbs losses from non-performing loans.

The uptake and usage of M-Shwari in the recent past has been remarkable with over 10 million M-Shwari accounts some of which are owned by women and CBA disburses 50,000 loans every day. One-third of all active M-Pesa users are also active M-Shwari customers. M-Shwari leverages M-pesa's unparalleled mobile money reach (7 out of 10 Kenyans are active mobile money users) as M-Shwari accounts are the only financial service that customers can access directly via the M-Pesa menu on a mobile device. It is free to transfer funds between M-Pesa and M-Shwari unlimited number of times (CGAP 2015)

3. **Linda Jamii-:** *Linda Jamii* (a Kiswahili phrase meaning protect the family) was launched to provide an affordable health insurance option to Kenyans. It provides comprehensive coverage for inpatient and outpatient services, as well as some dental and optical services. Benefits coverage includes a hospitalization income replacement benefit as well as funeral costs, should a beneficiary pass away. Using M-Pesa and a robust e-health IT system, it delivers innovative administration and services to users. Clients use the mobile-based platform to register and to make incremental payments toward the annual premium (Ksh 12,000 - an equivalent 117.6 U.S. Dollars-per family).
4. **M-Kopa:** *Kopa* is a Kiswahili term meaning borrow. Pay-as-you-go products such as M-Kopa's solar kits allow users to purchase products at a low upfront cost and pay for them over time via M-Pesa. Established in 2012, M-Kopa set out to address the tremendous demand for affordable off-grid energy by offering a pay-as-you-go solar energy service. Currently it has over 250,000 customers who are mostly women have used this service. This growth has been achieved using solar home energy systems that are connected using cellular communications (GSM) technology. This allows for remote monitoring and real time control of each unit (Mkopa, 2015).

The above M-Pesa linked platform services are getting admiration from women across all divides. Consequently, some women are creating business empires in various sectors including agriculture, wholesale and retail, health, building and construction, infrastructure development and manufacturing among other sectors due to the ease of which money can be transacted.

In analysing the effect of the M-Pesa linked platforms, both the existing quantitative and qualitative data from the World Bank Global index survey data (2014), Intermedia Financial Inclusion Insights Datacentre, and Kenya Financial Diaries Shilingi Kwa Shilingi, and the financial lives of the poor were studies and analysed by the author. The study employed comprehensive interviews where eight in-depth interviews with rural male and female mobile money users were conducted to explore ecosystem barriers and drivers. Also, focus group discussions were used and four workshops were conducted with male and female farmer groups to explore opportunities and effect of current mobile transfer services in their lives. Value Chain interviews were also conducted where (10) interviews with actors along the agricultural value chain were carried out to explore barriers and drivers of M-Pesa.

## M-Pesa Impact on Urban Businesses

Kenya Women Holding (KWH), founded by Dr. Jennifer Riria, is one of Africa's leading women entrepreneurs through microfinance, banking and insurance group of businesses that works with over 900,000 women, employs 2,800 people and since inception it has disbursed $1.3bn of loans, each one averaging less than $600. It is Kenya's largest micro-finance provider working together with many leading civil rights organizations. Kenya Women Holding also coordinates the Tuvuke Initiative for a Peaceful and Fair Electoral Process, which works to prevent violence and create a safer, healthier environment for Kenyan democracy (The Lionesses of Africa, 2017).

Cofounded by Evylin Munyi, KOFAR Kenya offers the solution to many small-holder farmers, to work and repair their farm soil by using organic materials to boost crops and farm efficiency to improve yields and better their livelihoods. KOFAR supplies farmers, especially small-holder farmers, with Organic and Natural inputs to use on their farms so as to restore the soil back to health from overuse and abuse from conventional inputs. Some of the inputs are supplied on loan and women are embracing group contributions through M-Pesa which are made and repaid on agreed schedules. The farmers use the products and within one month to three months the results are clear that their soils needed to be applied with the Organic inputs. The inputs are applied for all crops but the application rates are different.

To make real social change happen in Africa, there is need for people with the vision and passion to make a difference, and to find practical solutions to challenges faced each day. Mariam Mpaata is one such social entrepreneur on a mission to empower youth and women through the power of soccer, through her Junior Stars Football Academy. She started the Junior Stars Youth Development Programme to make a huge impact on young people's lives in Kenya. Mariam's enterprise offers a Junior Stars Football Academy, a Soccer Divas Club for amateur women footballers, it organises the Watoto Africa Soccer Awards (WASA) and the Youth Mentorship Summit, and it holds its Women Series of talks and conversations. Mariam's plans for the future include setting up a modern sports centre for football that can be used to nurture more talent on a greater professional level; to have players in the international leagues; to take WASA to other African countries; and to turn the MMM's Women Series into a talk show in the near future.

Like many such programs, Kenya has been in the fore-front to champion grants and donations through their M-Changa platform that uses M-Pesa as one of the options for making donations and grants.

## M-Pesa Impact on Rural Businesses

A study looking into the social and economic impact of M-Pesa on the lives of women in the fishing industry on Lake Victoria was conducted by White (2012). The study targeted communities in Migori County, which is located on the Kenyan side of Lake Victoria with a population of over one million people who rely mostly on fishing for their livelihood.

The findings reveal that the uptake of M-Pesa services by women living in the rural areas is low compared to that of urban women. Most of the rural women are organised in various social groups where they embrace the power to do vested in groups. Women were also found to be much less likely to use their money when they saved it in M-Pesa rather than in their homes. Before M-pesa, women indicated that their husbands often used their money to buy alcohol or other personal items and left them with no money to be able to process fish the following day. With their money saved with M-Pesa, their husbands no longer have easy access to their money. Women now have the ability to save for more costly activities and purchases, helping their families or expanding their business and more importantly, sending their children to school (Ndiaye, 2014).

Another study titled, "Poor People Using Mobile Financial Services: Observations on Customer Usage and Impact from M-Pesa in Kibera in Nairobi County and Bukura, Vihiga County" was conducted within a fourteen month period was completed in 2008. Kibera is an informal settlement (a slum) on the outskirts of Nairobi with more than one million people living there. They are mostly migrants from rural villages who came to the city to find work. The money trail was thereafter followed to a second site, a farming village in western Kenya called Bukura. A segment of the urban migrants has rural homes in Bukura or surrounding villages. More than 350 people were interviewed, and 21 focus groups were organized during the fieldwork. Fourteen financial diaries were distributed, mostly to frequent M-Pesa users who recorded their daily financial transactions over one month in November and December 2008. These diaries provide insights into how M-pesa fits into and altered the financial practices of poor Kenyans. The study made two main observations.

The first was that there are two types of M-Pesa users: urban senders, who are mostly men, and rural recipients, who are mostly women. For Instance, in Kibera, a majority of customers are young men. Customers deposit money into M-Pesa and transfer money to their rural relatives. In Bukura, a majority of customers are women and retirees. They use M-Pesa to withdraw money sent to them by relatives in the city. Most transfers fall into two categories: one, recurrent transfers that function as income support for the recipient and second, transfers used to address lump sum needs, such as the purchase of farm inputs. Recurrent transfers are more frequent (once per month or more) and smaller in value than lump sum transfers. The most common reason for a lump sum transfer is to pay school fees (CGAP 2009).

The findings also indicate that urban users adopted M-Pesa because it is cheaper, easier to access, and safer than other money transfer options. Urban users usually persuade rural recipients to also register with the service. Most interviewees in Kibera say they chose M-Pesa because of cost. For example, sending 1,000 Ksh (US$13.06) through M-Pesa cost US$0.39, which is 27% cheaper than the post office's PostaPay (US$0.52), and 68% cheaper than sending it via a bus company (US$1.16). Urban users say they prefer M-Pesa because it is faster (the transfer occurs almost instantaneously), easier to access (there is a wide agent network), and safer (they don't have to travel with money). In Bukura, a majority of interviewees say their relatives in urban areas asked them to sign up and use M-Pesa. The price structure is designed so that it is cheaper to send money to a registered user. For example, it costs 30 Ksh (US$0.39) to transfer 1,000 Ksh (US$ 13.04) if the user is registered. The recipient pays 25 Ksh (US$ 0.33) to make the withdrawal. If the recipient is not registered, Safaricom charges a higher total fee of 75 Ksh (US$0.98), which the sender must pay.

M-Pesa empowers rural women by making it easier for them to solicit funds from their husbands and other contacts in the city. The mobile phone, in conjunction with M-Pesa, is a powerful tool for mobilizing remittances. Before these technologies were introduced, rural women had to travel to the city or post office by bus to get money. They then had to travel back to the village. This process could take over a week. Now they can use a mobile phone to request a remittance and receive it at a nearby agent, making it easier for rural women to solicit funds from their husbands in the city. It is also easier for them to solicit cash from other contacts when their husbands refuse to make the transfers. This has increased the financial autonomy of the women and has made them less dependent on their husbands for their livelihoods (CGAP 2009).

Users are integrating M-Pesa into their savings portfolio as a result, savings patterns are changing. The financial diaries reveal that M-Pesa is being used in conjunction with popular savings mechanisms, including having a bank savings account, using informal savings clubs, and keeping money at home. M-Pesa users spread out their savings across all of these mechanisms to decrease the risk of money being "wiped out" if one mechanism fails. When M-Pesa became available, users began to make frequent deposits of "small money" into their M-Pesa accounts. The financial diaries reveal that users make, on average, 15 of these deposits per month. Because most participants who kept financial diaries are frequent users, this high number of deposits cannot be generalized across the user base. This finding, however, reveals the intensity with which some are using M-Pesa. Some made frequent deposits to accumulate a larger amount of money, which they then invest in their rural home (e.g., to purchase a cow). Others put the accumulated amount into their bank account to gain some interest on the money stored (CGAP 2009).

Income of rural recipients increased up to 30% since the start of M-Pesa usage. Seventy respondents were asked whether household income had changed since they adopted M-Pesa. Fifty-four rural respondents (77%) note an income increase since adopting M-Pesa. For 38 respondents, this increase is 5–30% of household income. Such an increase is the result of money being sent more frequently. By breaking up their transfers, urban migrants end up remitting more money back home. Also, rural recipients save money when retrieving cash. They no longer need to pay for transport costs to urban centers, where most of the money transfer services are located. Instead, they make the withdrawal directly from Bukura. Such an increase is vitally important for the rural recipients, who depend heavily on remittances for their livelihoods. The financial diaries reveal that such remittances constitute as much as 70% of rural household income (CGAP 2019).

In another case study under review was the GSMA Connected Women, "Women and Mobile Money, Insights from Kenya" study. GSMA conducted a study in Kenya by combining existing quantitative datasets on male and female mobile money use with qualitative consumer insights research in two areas of rural Kenya in Nakuru and Baringo Counties. The study aimed at identifying where the gender gaps are on the journey to mobile money use and to understand the most common reasons behind these gaps. Focus groups and ethnographic interviews were then conducted with rural women at differing levels of mobile money use. The objective was to understand what separates a woman who uses mobile money very infrequently from a regular user of mobile money services.

The findings reveal that women who are well connected socially are likely to have higher confidence and awareness of how to use services. Women with higher income levels and greater liquidity were less likely to see M-Pesa transaction fees as a barrier, and women who were more integrated with the formal economy were more likely to see mobile financial services as relevant to them. However, it is important to note that even those rural women interviewed, those who were using mobile money on a daily basis were still making at least half of their transactions in cash. This indication shows that urban women are more likely to increase their uptake of M-Pesa services than those in the rural areas.

The study also notes that in managing transactions Ruth (infrequent M-Pesa user), a single mother with three school-aged daughters, living on her 1.5 acre farm where she is building a house with any extra income she gains grows and sells maize, carrots, onions, potatoes, spinach which she sells at the market, and also owns two cows, three sheep and five goats and a farmer living in a village outside of Naivasha perceives transaction with M-Pesa differently from her other counterpart.

The findings show that the infrequent M-Pesa user regularly uses M-Pesa on Savings and loans regularly to receive payments from family member, and rarely uses M-Pesa to remit government remittances such as school fees where she chooses to pay directly into the school bank account. In borrowing from the local community, the infrequent user would prefer to borrow small cash amounts needed and spend the money immediately. She doesn't use Lipa na M-Pesa services and prefers to pay cash rather than with M-Pesa transactions for fear of transaction costs.

On the contrary, Anne (a frequent M-PesaUser) from Kerio Valley, Baringo County, is a farmer, a school teacher and a mother of school-aged children who grows cotton and also grows small amounts of maize, millet and sorghum which she sells in the community with a well connection socially and is part of three formal and informal savings groups. She belongs to a farmer co-operative, a church group and a women's savings group.

For the frequent M-Pesa user, the findings indicate that she uses M-Pesa more frequently in meeting domestic remittances, savings on M-Shwari and social saving groups, making business payments, and receiving salary in an M-Pesa through teacher's salary account. She also does farm labourer payment in M-Pesa when the labourer has left village by time of payment.

The two scenarios indicates that some social, economic and environmental factors may create difference in the adoption of M-Pesa services and also the differences in harnessing full potential that has been created by M-Pesa services. The rural women should therefore be empowered to participate effectively in technological innovations.

The International Labour Organization (ILO), key observations on the differences of working in rural areas in the 21st Century. The study elucidates key differences between Rural and Urban women in Relation to their Socio-economic environment that impacts their choices for Mobile Financial Services.

ILO estimates that rural women comprise one-quarter of the world's population. Women also make up 41% of the world's agricultural labour force, a ratio that rises to 49% for low-income countries. In many South-East Asian and sub-Saharan African countries, more than 60% of working women are engaged in the agricultural sector (ILOSTAT, 2015). Significant number of women in the rural economy work as subsistence farmers, small-scale producers, own-account workers, and in plantations and agro-industries, but women in rural economy are also employed in other sectors, such as education, tourism and domestic work (2016)

Despite their crucial roles in the rural economy, women face inequalities and challenges that hinder their access to decent work opportunities and improvements to their productivity. About 68% of working women in extreme poverty operate in the agricultural sector, the other sectors being fisheries, forestry, handicrafts and livestock rearing. Women tend to be involved in more than one economic activity simultaneously, and take up informal and unprotected work in the absence of alternative means of generating income (ILO, Geneva 2016).

Compared to urban counterparts, and men, rural women spend more time on reproductive and household work, including time spent collecting water and fuel, husking, processing food and caring for children and the sick. Other challenges that women face in the rural economy include lack of information on job availability, as well as opportunities for training and education, limited access to property, land and financial and non-financial services much of this is linked to gender-based inequality and discrimination (Rome FAO, 2010). Social norms on the role of women in the family and preconceived ideas of what is "appropriate" work for women are among factors perpetuating sectoral and occupational segregation between women and men and further reinforcing inequality. Rural women workers are less likely to engage in wage employment compared to men and to women in urban areas, and when they do, they tend to earn less than their male counterparts (ILO, World Employment Social Outlook, 2016).

Women play important roles in the rural economy as farmers, wage earners and entrepreneurs. They also take responsibility for the well-being of the members of their families, including food provision and care for children and the elderly. Rural women's unpaid work, particularly in poor households, often includes collecting wood and water. Women from indigenous and grassroots communities are often also custodians of traditional knowledge, which is key for their communities' livelihoods, resilience and culture. However, with the advent of M-Pesa rural women are finding it easy to save some part of their earnings and thus are able to increase their savings overtime. However, women in rural areas compared to those in urban areas face constraints in engaging in economic activities that can give them meaningful employment earnings and therefore they save less compared to those in towns.

## LEGAL AND REGULATORY FRAMEWORK OF MOBILE MONEY TRANSACTIONS

The adoption of M-Pesa and other mobile money transfer services is also affected by the regulations, polices and restrictions against the formal banking industry that increases financial inclusion and deepening thereby giving opportunities for the participation of the rural poor at the base of the development ladder where majority of women are.

According to Competition Authority of Kenya, Mobile money transactions have presented regulatory challenges that could potentially hinder maximum development benefits. This is because firstly, mobile money blurs the traditionally distinct and independent sectors of regulation (most notably, the telecommunications and financial banking sectors). It often involves an overlap between multiple ministries and Government agencies, thus adding to the complexity of oversight needed. Secondly, due to the rapid growth in technological advancement, mobile network operator (MNOs) and other stakeholders are exploring emerging business opportunities like mobile banking. This in effect is changing the traditional business models and the financial landscape. Thirdly, there is limited legislative and regulatory experience in other countries and regions to draw lessons from when drafting relevant legislation and regulations. As is the case in most other developing regions, national regulations have not kept pace with developments in the field. It is therefore imperative that regulators identify and address the gaps and potential overlaps between their existing legislative and regulatory frameworks (CAK).

The pertinent legislations that influence the operations of Mobile Financial Services (MFS) within Kenya include:

Central Bank of Kenya Act (enacted 1966, amended through 2009), creating the Central Bank of Kenya and defining its mandate; Banking Act (enacted 1991, amended through 2010), regulating the activities of banking institutions within the financial sector in Kenya; Guideline on Agent Banking (2010), providing for the appointment of agents to extend banking services within Kenya; Draft Electronic Retail Transfers Regulation and Draft E-Money Regulation regulating electronic money issuance and exchange, as well as its transfer between different parties within Kenya; The Kenya Information and Communications Act (enacted 1998, amended in 2010 and 2013), providing the mandate of Communications Authority of Kenya (CA) and a framework to regulate the information, communications, media, and broadcasting subsectors; and a range of Kenyan information and communications regulations made by the Minister in charge of Information and Communications in tandem with the CA to regulate various aspects of the communications sector that include consumer protection, competition, tariffs, numbering, inter-connection, quality of service, among others.

Enabling mobile financial services brings new models of financial services like mobile payments requires that regulators balance openness to experimentation and innovation with sufficient certainty about the legal framework that protects users and clearly assigns liabilities. Without openness, a new mobile service can become bogged down by restrictions that are applied to more traditional channels and business models. Without certainty and clear regulatory frameworks, reputable providers are likely to be unwilling to commit the resources to launch and sustain deployments (Porteous, 2006). At the same time, clients might find offers from new entrants unreliable and therefore unattractive. Enablement must also provide adequate safeguards for consumers' interests, without which large-scale adoption is unlikely anyway (Lyman et al, 2008). The Principles for Innovative Financial Inclusion issued in June 2010 by the G20 Financial Inclusion Experts group recognizes this by advocating a 'test and learn' approach by regulators rather than regulating in advance of market conditions:

Mobile Payment Instruments-the growth of mobile financial services has raised foundational policy questions for regulators of how to distinguish a 'payment' (mobile or not) from a 'deposit, and what differentiates the business of providing payments from that of deposit taking. This boundary questions are not new, but the spread of the mobile phone is necessitating greater clarity because it has enabled the creation and distribution of electronic payment instruments on a widespread scale, which was neither easy nor even possible in many places until recently. There is a clear trend towards creating legal certainty through guidance or new legislation that regulates e-money issuance. In Kenya, where oversight of non-bank e-money has been under general regulatory powers, have announced their intention to publish guidelines that may become regulations once an enabling payment law is in place.

Mobile Channel- mobile channels are a subset of electronic channels available for financial services. The regulatory questions raised around the channel are therefore a subset of electronic banking transactions more generally. Many of the risks associated with using mobile channels are the same as Internet banking with a PC or using a card at an Automated Teller Machine, but there are other risks that are unique. One of the risks would be the relationship in the value chain for MNOs and financial institutions in that not only do MNOs compete with banks and other providers in the provision of mobile financial services (MFS) but also owns key communication infrastructure required to provide MFS. USSD has been identified as the channel of choice for MNOs. Unstructured Supplementary Service device (USSD)- this is a communication channel controlled by Mobile Network Operators (MNO) which is critical to securely provide MFS on nearly all phones at a low cost. It enables customers to securely send instructions to MFS providers along with personal identification number (PIN) for authentication while enabling the MFS provider to send responses to clients and confirmation of transactions. MNOs therefore provide a critical infrastructure to competitors, for this reason, there is need to identify the following special issues regarding the supply of financial services through the mobile channel.

Consumer Protection- a concern that touches on consumer protection is the transparency especially of the transaction costs. Section 56 (3) of the Competition Act No. 12 of 2010 requires that a consumer shall be entitled to be informed by a service provider of all the charges and fees intended to be imposed for the provision of a service. Lack of sufficient transparency in the terms and conditions of products and services impacts competition in a market in several ways (Rafe &Phillip, 2014). When customers face significant impediments or costs in their search for alternatives, sellers may be able to set prices with only limited regard to competition, enabling firms to enjoy market power. When consumers face difficulties in comparing the offers available from different providers this can hinder new entrants ability to compete with dominant firms on price and quality of service (Mazer & Rowan, 2014).

Transparency of mobile money transfer costs- in Kenya there is a degree of price transparency at the point of cashing in and cashing out, as agents display tariff boards. However MNOs do not disclose the transaction costs for person-to person payments either before or after the transaction is completed, either in the USSD session or in the confirmation SMS messages. In this instance consumers only seem to be able to figure these charges out by subtracting new balance from the balance in their previous confirmation SMS, then removing the amount transferred, to obtain the charge paid for the P2P transfer. This makes it difficult to compare the total cost of sending and receiving money across mobile financial services providers, both impeding effective competition and raising potential consumer protection concerns. It can also create situations where outdated price information is kept in consumers' mind as the market price (Rafe &Phillip, 2014).

Transparency of USSD costs- there is also poor disclosure of the cost of accessing Value Added Services, such as bill pay and bank to wallet/wallet to bank transfers, via USSD. This is due to the low disclosure of both the charges paid by the third-party aggregators and financial service providers to the MNOs for access to the MNO's USSD infrastructure, as well as the costs they subsequently pass on to consumers for these Value Added Services. Transparency of terms and conditions- as markets develop and move gradually from simple payments conducted via mobile, towards products like merchant payments, credit, savings and insurance, new issues around transparency will develop. For example Safaricom has launched M-Shwari, offering micro-loans and interest paying savings accounts via the M-Pesa mobile money platform.

Upon opening an M-Shwari account the consumer is not informed of the interest rates and rollover charges of the loan directly, but is instead directed to review the Terms and Conditions (T&Cs) on the Commercial Bank of Africa (CBA) and Safaricom websites. Aside from the obvious effort that must be made to view these terms and conditions, this information will not be accessible to consumers without internet/data access or a smartphone, resulting in many consumers failing to understand the terms of their savings or loan product. Consumers do receive an SMS with some basic information immediately after accepting a loan, however this is only after entering a binding loan agreement, and the loan amount is not separated from the charges to make clear the finance costs, the breakdown of how much of this is the loan principal and how much the interest owed, nor the interest rate applied. Customers may not understand the complexity of the contract signed, making it possible for them to face additional fees/services without being aware.

M-Pesa continues to have a significant impact on Kenya's society, banking sector and e-commerce. In the Kenyan case, M-Pesa remains unique in terms of rapid integration of new technology and its unprecedented effects on overall economy and transformation of financial service sector. The introduction of M-Pesa did not only make financial services accessible to unbanked members of society, but the service transformed the perception of financial service and money transfers in the country, affecting not only individuals, households and business units but also the entire economy of Kenya (Jack, Ray & Suri, 2013). M-Pesa has made it possible for employers to transfer wages in small amounts to employees' accounts. Consequently, the social side of M-Pesa influence is tremendous, because the system facilitates lives of many impoverished individuals and women in the Society. People with low incomes are able to receive remuneration, no matter how meagre, on time (Karugu, Mwendwa 2007).

The microfinance of wages has a potential to influence the economy (Buera et al. 2012). Since more payments are made through M-Pesa, service payments have become less complex leading to a decrease in transportation costs. Additionally, microfinance establishments experience a diminishment in costs concerning loan repayment and disbursement. Thus, M-PESAhas had a considerable effect on the economy of Kenya saving many funds on now redundant services (Buera et al. 2012). Since M-Pesa was integrated into the functioning of microfinance institution, entrepreneurial activities experienced an extensive rise at the low end of the market (Karugu, Mwendwa, 2007). It has become apparent that small and medium-sized businesses began to grow upon the introduction of the system into the society. Additionally, people whose business activities are executed by just one entrepreneur who does not receive more than one dollar per day now have access to an alternative to bank establishments. Such entrepreneurs include shoe shiners, grocers, barbers, and other similar professions (Mwobobia, 2012).

The contribution of M-Pesa to the SDGs) cannot be underestimated. In September 2015, the UN introduced the Sustainable Development Goals (SDGs) a seventeen (17) point plan to end poverty, combat climate change and fight injustice and inequality by 2030. Mobile connectivity will play a central role in the realization of the SDGs in Kenya, for the fact that the digital divide is narrowing faster than funding and infrastructure gaps. There are more than 700 million mobile connections in the Sub-Sahara region, enabling various services that directly impact the SDGs; for example, mobile money is helping reduce poverty and inequality, with more than 13 million connections in the region, is enabling smart city and off-grid utilities solutions. The GSMA and mobile operators in the region are working together to deploy mobile-enabled solutions that deliver greater inclusion in cities and remote communities, enable access to essential services such as health and education, create employment and income opportunities, and empower people with the tools to reduce poverty and inequality. Enabling high absorption of M-Pesa services by women would ensure that they harness the benefits of the Sustainable development Goals.

SDG1: End poverty in all its forms everywhere. The financial inclusion positively ends poverty. With more than 400 million registered users, mobile money facilitates access to financial services, many of which contribute to building the resilience of the poor by reducing their vulnerability to economic, social and environmental shocks and disasters.

A study taken in Kenya by GSMA indicate that by providing the poor with the financial services they need to make investments and manage unexpected expenses, the mobile money industry is helping to eliminate extreme poverty. Recent estimates found that access to M-Pesahas lifted 194,000 households in Kenya out of poverty since its inception in 2007.

SDG 2: Zero Hunger. The zero hunger SDG in Agriculture aims to end hunger, achieve food security and improved nutrition, and promote sustainable agriculture. Agriculture contributes 17% of GDP and employs more than half of the labour force in Sub-Saharan Africa. Mobile is uniquely positioned to deliver the critical information quickly that rural smallholder farmers need, enabling them to make better decisions and investments that boost their productivity and profit.

Innovation in Agriculture that provides farmers' Club - a package of agricultural farming advice, weather updates, market prices delivered via SMS is crucial towards achieving this goal. One Acre provides loans for inputs and training to farmers in Kenya, Burundi and Rwanda. One Acre Fund began piloting mobile repayment with about 1,000 farmers in one district in mid-2013 (roughly 1.5% of Kenya clients at the time). In the initial trial, group leaders collected loan repayment from individual farmers, and then submitted an aggregate payment through Mpesa. This trial went well, and One Acre Fund decided to expand it in 2014. The expanded trial included two configurations: group leader repayment (like the 2013 trial), and farmer repayment (new). The group leader repayment trial included 3,500 farmers (roughly 4% of Kenya clients), and the farmer repayment trial included 400 farmers (roughly 0.5% of Kenya clients). With funding from the Gates Foundation, One Acre will test over 40 potential technologies over the next three years, with the goal of rolling out at least 4 technologies to at least 200,000 One Acre families (FSD Kenya, 2015)

In Kenya, Agricultural sector is one of the first to fully devolve the function of service provision to the county governments underscoring the importance of County Governments' role in ensuring food security. Agriculture is key to Kenya's economy, contributing 26% of the Gross Domestic Product (GDP) and another 27% of GDP indirectly through linkages with other sectors. The sector employs more than 40% of the total population and more than 70% of Kenya's rural people. Agriculture in Kenya is large and complex, with a multitude of public, parastatals, non-governmental and private sectors.

The sector accounts for 65% of the export earnings, and provides the livelihood (employment, income and food security needs) for more than 80% of the Kenyan population and contributes to improving nutrition through production of safe, diverse and nutrient dense foods. The sector is also the min driver of the non-agricultural economy including manufacturing, providing inputs and markets for non-agricultural operations such as building/construction, transportation, tourism, education and other social services.

SDG 3: Good Health and Wellbeing. M-Pesa innovation and other platform has developed packages that are geared to ensuring healthy lives and promote well-being for all. For instance, Linda Jamii was launched to provide an affordable health insurance option to Kenyans. It provides comprehensive coverage for inpatient and outpatient services where women have been found to take more responsibility, as well as some dental and optical services. Benefits coverage includes a hospitalization income replacement benefit as well as funeral costs, should a beneficiary pass away. Using M-Pesa and a robust e-health IT system, it delivers innovative administration and services to users. Clients use the mobile-based platform to register and to make incremental payments toward the annual premium (KSh12, 000 -an equivalent of 117.6 U.S. Dollars-per family (FSD 2015).

SDG 4: Quality Education. M-Pesa services are raising revenues to businesses including those owned by women thus making them pay school fees and buy books. Consequently, Safaricom Limited through in supporting corporate social responsibility (CSR) started Safaricom Foundation that supports social and economic projects. Through the Safaricom foundation Academy, Safaricom has supported many bright and needy students thus making them participate effectively in the job market. This ensures inclusive and equitable quality education and promotes lifelong learning opportunities for all. Mobile operators are working to support students and teachers in integrating mobile technologies into the classroom, enabling access to greater learning opportunities in urban hubs and remote locations.

SDG 5: Women Empowerment. M-Pesa empowers rural women by making it easier for them to solicit funds from their husbands and other contacts in the city. The mobile phone, in conjunction with MPesa, is a powerful tool for mobilizing remittances. Before these technologies were introduced, rural women had to travel to the city or post office by bus to get money. They then had to travel back to the village. This process could take over a week. Now they can use a mobile phone to request a remittance and receive it at a nearby agent, making it easier for rural women to solicit funds from their husbands in the city. It is also easier for them to solicit cash from other contacts when their husbands refuse to make the transfers. This has increased the financial autonomy of the women and has made them less dependent on their husbands for their livelihoods.

SDG 7: Affordable and Clean Energy. On energy, the M-Kopa Solar a product on the M-Pesa platform, have already connected 90,000 Kenyan homes to clean energy and with this upcoming suite of Safaricom-branded devices we aim to reach at least 1 million homes within the next four years. The M-Kopa is more affordable compared to other lighting alternatives for people who do not have electricity. It also provides families with improved health, brighter light and reduces the risks associated with having a naked flame.

Following the removal of VAT on solar-powered devices, M-Kopa Solar has also announced a price reduction on the new units. Customers will now only pay an initial deposit of KES 2,999 (an equavalent of 29.4 U.S Dollars) followed by 365 daily payments of KES 40 (down from KES 50). The M-Kopa III is available on a risk-free basis to customers who want to test the benefits of solar power for themselves. The KES 2,999 deposit is fully refundable at any time during the payment period, and the M-Kopa III comes standard with a 2-year warranty. After 365 of KES 40 daily payments, the device is unlocked with no further payments required. M-Kopa businesses have also been dominated by women especially in rural areas where they use the product to generate incomes for their empowerment and that of their families.

## CONCLUSION

To ensure adoption of M-Pesa services by women, it's crucial to use clear contracts that fully disclose all fees to be charged, tailored for various customer situations, including different languages and illiteracy so that all women can understand the cost involved in the use of M-Pesa services.

There is need for monitoring and evaluation in ensuring that service charges are posted clearly at each agent's location. Disclosure that is reasonably comprehendible to all customer groups is necessary. Where some women don't understand the legal jargon due to literacy issues, it's important for the agents to explain to them in clear terms.

Mobile financial services can only be offered by already-regulated entities such as banks, then the supervision of the mobile channel involves extending existing procedures such as e-banking supervision practices to cover the features of mobile financial services.

Since technology is evolving fast in this area, understanding the operational risks arising from new channels, communication standards, and security protocols is an uphill task for regulators. Whatever the appropriate scope and location for supervision of new instruments and channels, it is clear that financial regulators need expanded resources to train and build the capacity to oversee fast-moving technology. Electronic reporting and oversight may reduce the need for physical inspection but increase the need for specialist skills in the regulator.

## REFERENCES

Andiva, B. (2014). *Mobile Financial Services and Regulation in Kenya*. Competition Authority of Kenya.

CGAP. (2009). *Poor People Using Mobile Financial Services: Observations on Customer Usage and Impact from M-PESA*. Available at: https://openknowledge.worldbank.org/bitstream/handle/10986/9492/503060BRI0Box31MPESA1Brief01PUBLIC1.pdf?sequence=1&isAllowed=y

CGAP. (2015). *Top 10 Things to Know About M-Shwari*. Available at: https://www.cgap.org/blog/top-10-things-know-about-m-shwari

Davis, F. D. (1989). Perceived Usefulness, Perceived Ease of Use, and User Acceptance of Information Technology. *MIS Quarterly, 13*(3), 319-339.

Davis, F. D., Bagozzi, P. R., & Warshaw, P. (1989). User acceptance of computer technology: A comparison of two theoretical models. *Management Science, 35*(8), 982–1003. doi:10.1287/mnsc.35.8.982

Fishbein, M., & Ajzen, I. (1975). *Belief, Attitude. Intentions and Behavior: An Introduction to Theory and Research*. Boston: Addison-Wesley.

FSD Kenya. (2015). *One Acre Fund*. Available at https://fsdkenya.org/retail-innovation/linda-jamii/

GSMA Connected Women, . (2017). *The mobile Economy. Sub-Saharan Africa.* GSMA.

GSMA Connected Women. (2019). *Women and Mobile Money; Insights from Kenya GSMA Intelligence modelled estimates as in GSMA Connected Women, Mobile Gender Gap Report 2019.* Retrieved from http://www.nber.org/papers/w16721.pdf

ILO. (2016). *Decent work for food security and resilient rural livelihoods, Portfolio of policy guidance notes on the promotion of decent work in the rural economy.* Geneva: Sectoral Policies Department.

ILO & ILOSTAT. (2015). 2 ILO: Working in the rural areas in the 21st century: Reality and prospects of rural employment in Latin America and the Caribbean, Regional Office for Latin America and the Caribbean (Geneva, Thematic Labour Overview No. 3, 2017). ILO.

ILO. (2016). World Employment Social Outlook 2016: Transforming jobs to end poverty. ILO.

Jack, W., & Suri, T. (2011). *Mobile money: The economics of M-PESA.* Cambridge, UK: National Bureau of Economic Research. doi:10.3386/w16721

Lyman, T., Porteous, D., & Pickens, M. (2008). Regulating Transformational Branchless Banking: Mobile Phones and Other Technology to Increase Access to Finance. In *Focus Note 43*. Washington, DC: CGAP.

Mazer, R., & Rowan, P. (2014). *Competition in Mobile Financial Services in Kenya.* Draft Brief Prepared by CGAP for Competition Authority of Kenya.

Meet 40 Inspiring Women Entrepreneurs Putting the Country on the Global Business Map. (n.d.). *The Lionesses of Africa.* Available at: http://www.lionessesofafrica.com/blog/2017/6/27/meet-40-kenyan-women-entrepreneurs-putting-the-country-on-the-global-business-map

MKOPA. (2015). *Affordable, clean energy: a pathway to new consumer choices; Lessons from M-KOPA's first three years of innovative energy service.* Retrieved from http://www.m-kopa.com/wp-content/uploads/2015/10/Lightbulb-series_Paper-1-2.pd

MKOPA. (2017). *MKOPA Solar and Safaricom Launch MKOPA III.* Available at: http://www.m-kopa.com/m-kopa-solar-and-safaricom-launch-m-kopa-iii/

Ndiaye, O. K. (2014). Is the success of M-Pesa empowering Kenyan rural women? *Feminist Africa, 18*, 156–161.

Porteous, D. (2006). *The Enabling Environment for Mobile Banking in Africa*. DFID.

Rome, F. A. O. (2010). *The average rate of female agricultural land ownership is less than 20% in developing countries*. Rome: FAO.

Rosenberg, J., & Morawczynski, O. (2008). *Why has M-Pesa become so popular in Kenya?* Retrieved from https://www.cgap.org/blog/why-has-m-pesa-become-so-popular-kenya

Sarker, S., & Wells, J. D. (2003). Understanding mobile handheld device use and adoption. *Communications of the ACM*, *46*(12).

WB. (2016). Feminization of agriculture in the context of rural transformations: What is the evidence? WB.

White, D. (2012). *The Social and Economic Impact of M-PESAon the Lives of Women in the Fishing Industry on Lake Victoria*. Independent Study Project (ISP) Collection. Paper 1246.

# Chapter 12
# Adoption of Mobile Payment Application and Its Impact on Business

**Ahmad Fayaz Sayed**
*Department of Engineering Management, Institute of Business Management, Pakistan*

**Muhammad Khalil Shahid**
*Higher Colleges of Technolgies, UAE*

**Sayed Fayaz Ahmad**
*Institute of Business Management, Pakistan*

## ABSTRACT

*Technology development has blessed the business environment with many tremendous opportunities and created several challenges. One of these developments is mobile payment applications, which are inevitable in the modern word. Companies, customers, etc. are adopting this modern mobile application to avail the service of mobile payment. Without any doubt it has many advantages, but it has also many challenges in adoption. This chapter discusses the adoption of mobile application and its impact on business. Security, ease of use, service availability, and risk are some of the main factors contributing to the adoption of mobile payment application. These factors not only affect the adoption of MPA but also have a strong link with business. As MPA changes the mood of business, again its pros and cons exist, and there is a need to be addressed. This chapter concludes a proposed model for the adoption of mobile payment application after thorough literature review.*

DOI: 10.4018/978-1-7998-2398-8.ch012

## INTRODUCTION

Developments and the digitalization of modern technology is changing the behavior of consumers and ways of doing business (Khan at el. 2014). With the advent of digitalization, there is a developing trend of companies keen on finding opportunities and benefits associated with it. In the digital era, mobile devices are one of the most prominent products (Venkatesh, 2003). Not only this device fulfills the need for communication but also captured space for its use in entertainment, business etc. and it itself became one of the necessities of the modern world (Sayed at el. 2014). Mobile devices not only incarcerate the above-mentioned dimensions but has also give users access to the internet and in some countries, it is preferable on other devices for accessing the internet (Venkatesh, 2012; Comscore, 2014). Internet users are checking their emails on mobile more than they do on other devices (Burdge, 2014).

With the advent of modern mobile phones and their operating system, their applications have further extended (Sayed at el. 2015) to the business platforms with the addition of the above areas; payments of any desired business activity or the business transaction can be done through them (Venkatesh, 2012). Business organizations around the world have developed software for online business and mobile payment (Wallace, 2014). Mobile payment has many advantages both for business organization and for customers, yet it is slightly burdened with a few challenges also (Lian, 2015). Gradually, its adoption has gone global (Yang, 2012). In some countries, its adoption rate is quite impressive though it faces the traditional laggard tendencies in some. However given time it is expected to be adopted more business organizations and countries. This chapter reviews the current literature on mobile payment adoption and proposes a conceptual framework.

## MOBILE PAYMENT

The impact of mobile technology development on society is now visible within the developing countries social fiber strata. As technology develops further, its sale increases exponentially (Gul at el. 2014). The use of the services associated with these devices has brought social revolution in humans (Pramis, 2013). Mobile phones not only act as a source of communication but also act as a spring and conduit of mobile payment through its advanced features and computing capabilities (Flatraaker, 2013). Although many researchers have discussed mobile payment, most of them do not agree on the definition and so have proposed different models. For example, Dahlberg et al. (2008) has defined as "payment for goods, services, and bills with a mobile device" via "wireless and other communication technologies". While Au et. al., (2008) sees it as "a payment in which a mobile phone is used to initiate, authorize, and confirm a transaction".

Studies opine MMT is not just the extension of mobile service but the result of highly developed infrastructure, business models, users, etc. (Kang & Park, 2014). Due to its recognition and impact worldwide, many organizations are now investing in mobile payment apps (Chen, et al, 2013) but some of the service providers are not getting the desired volumes (Schierz et al., 2010). Mobile payment is then seen as a business activity payment of business activity using a mobile phone (Arthur, 2014). It is one of the extended applications of mobile sets technology, world over.

Modern technology has changed the mood of the marketplace in many ways (Wallace, 2014). In particular the development of applications is hooked on modern technology such as a mobile application (Baptista, 2015) is encouraging. Initially, some companies gave such investments a wide berth but with the passage of time and the adoption rate of mobile payment application on its astronomical investment have been realized within the sector (Brigham Young University, 2013). As such merits of payments through mobile application are numerous relative to the conventional payment system and deserving customers accrue myriads of benefits from it (Pousttchi & Weidemann, 2005). Mobile payment is different from electronic payment and it is shockingly more vulnerable to security breaches, loss, theft, and damage (Chari, Smith & Tassiulas, 2000). Varied reasons are then alluded to this unexpected immoral behavior and the sale and usage of the smartphone (Ankar & D'Incau, 2002). This area has attracted a considerable amount of interest with researchers keen on finding out the variables having an associative impact on the usage of mobile payment services and applications (Wang and Li, 2012). Keeping this objective in perspective, many technology acceptance models have been developed (Schierz et al., 2010) and many variables were found associated with the goal (Lu et al., 2011).

## Security Concern of Mobile Payment Application

The dynamics of business today are strongly associated with the use of technology. Technology then creates both new ways of doing business and opens up new wave of opportunities for savvy business enterprise. It is a fact that technology is very beneficial in many aspects however, some challenges that have been linked to these technology influences (Chandra, 2010). Though the mobile payment application has been strongly linked to modern business and has made payments in the contemporary business easy, it has created a challenge in the context of security (Chiu, 2014). Although its benefits are not substantial, the bulk of its problems cannot ignored (Engau, 2011). One of these defined challenges is security i.e. any threat related to data or information theft, wrong use or re-use (Sayed & Khalil, 2015). A mobile device capable of Mobile payment applications can be used for payment operation

(Wan, 2004) and consequently consumer's information is stored in the application and the device. Ruefully if it is stolen a major risk occurs in terms of the misuse such information (Laurn, 2005).

The mobile payment application is employed via the use of an internet network. When a consumer sends data over an unencrypted network, there is a chance to spy on it (Heavey, 2013). Hackers can get into a consumer device and can eventually access the data stored there (Martins, 2014). Undeniably many hackers have developed neophyte varieties of viruses which can be used to retrieve precious data or misuse it. These hackers tend to attack consumers through scam applications which could access information easily. And if the system is compromised then financial transactions and data may be retrieved by the hackers. In addition, the data can also be retrieved from the stolen device (Mann, 2013). So it is clear that although there are tremendous benefits of MPA yet its security concern tends to overshadow and urgently needs to be addressed. It has minimized the risk associated with cash theft on one side yet created security concerns associated with data and information theft on the other side.

## Privacy Risks

Heavey, (2013) reveals that a mobile payment system has brought about new privacy risks. To catch a good glimpse of this situation, it is necessary to be familiar with information flows in a standard credit card transaction. All parties get an incomplete assessment of the sale in a typical credit card transaction (Martins, 2014). The dealer only collects information which is given by the customer, particularly the name (Sayed et al. 2015). This collecting of information is called the Stock Keeping Unit (SKU) information or "Level 3" data. Level 3 data, in most of the mobile payments cases, is not transferred to any other person involved in the transaction. The dealer then, cannot identify their customers because they are not supposed to misuse the information revealed by the customer (Yang, 2009). Names are not uniquely identified since they are not used for creating customer record, indeed the dealer cannot use credit card swipes only. Because of this issue, many dealers preferred to use loyalty cards, which allow the dealer to identify customers uniquely even if he or she is using various payment methods (Arthur, 2014). In a particular transaction, payment networks (Visa, MasterCard, and American Express) receive very little information. These networks also receive very little information itself i.e. account number, customer identity, and transaction charges.

In banks transactions, information like payment network, amount of transaction, place of transaction, and customer identity are received by the dealer and customer simultaneously. This limited information has a common exception in Airline and hotel reservations. In most cases, this information is moved back to the customer and it is reflected in his or her bill (Yang, 2009). These arrangements are being displaced by new mobile payment systems. In these systems, the dealer collects as much information from the customer such as their identity, contact number, level 3 data and their transformation characteristic to payment networks. All the participants within the payment ecosystem like banks i.e. dealers and payment networks can generate more valuable and detailed databases (as compared to the typical one they have today) about the costumer. This helps the dealer in building customer information without resorting to loyalty cards.

These partakers of technology have enormous very deep results for ensuring customer privacy and the relationship between the payment provider and dealer (Mann, 2013). The loyalty card need will be soon eliminated together with its handicap of failing to profile people. However many customers are uncomfortable with the information being collected during the transaction. In some cases such queries are inclined to cause embarrassments and as such customers tend to avoid to buy certain things and contribute to systems that common service and price discrimination. It is important to note that privacy is still a major concern in MPA. Data shared by the customer may stir the hornet nest and invite myriads of problems and worst tend to be misused. The adoption of MPA is strongly linked with this factor.

## Service Availability

Mobile payment is becoming widely accepted with the development of mobile payment applications. In such self-service technologies, there is only a human-technology interface that enables a business transaction (Meuter, 2000). Previous studies, have identified several technological and consumers related issues that hinder or amplify the adoption of self-service applications. One of them is service availability.

Services that are more and easily available tend to be more attractive to consumers for adoption and those that are not easily available and technically difficult to understand do not entice or influence consumers (Weijter, 2007). It is important to note that service availability is necessary for the adoption of MPA and it can improve the serviceability in alternative media such as LBS (location-based service) internet banking. The reason impeding the use of LBS is because most mobile users don not have LBS experience on the wire-line.

Sources keen streaming the concept of compatibility as used in new management. The first literature is related to technical component integration for proper functioning on a large scale (Sousa, 2006). The second is related to expectation compatibility. It is concerned with a new technology that satisfies the potential user expectations (Gefen, 2004). Karahanna and Agarwal, (2006) have advocated for four dimensions of compatibility to overcome non-comprehensive definitions of compatibility construct. Any suggestive definitions should be compatible with, existing work practice, preferred work style, values and prior experience. The foremost proposition is examine how technology limits the first user functionality at his or her current work process. The preferred working style enhances the maximization the possibility offered by technology through the desired work style. Compatibility with prior experience measures a balance between target technology and user. In short compatibility with values optimizes the balance between possibility offered by technology and user. It is expected from new mobile services determined by wire-line to maintain more compatibility when compared to new brand-mobile service.

Different kinds of media may provide equal service because of development in telecommunication technology. The potential of success in computing service media, has to do with the incentive to offer a service for new business and their advantages should similar be to the device via multiple media is necessary (Kim & Prabhakar, 2000). In the digital era, heterogeneous communication services devices have competed against each other to provide identical services to potential consumers. Mobile banking is internet banking through mobile wireless devices. It can be done via a telephone network, ATM network, mobile network, and internet access. These types of services have been here for more than 20 years and indeed most users are aware of their existence. Koening-Lewis et al., (2010) suggested that consumers weigh the compatibility of technology with their lifestyle. As such finding a new acquaintance in a well-positioned type of service on the mobile network that has unique features can be adopted within the mobile communications network. Sadly very few services are technologically available on most devices for users, partly because, the awareness of such is low and mobile industry has not spent a huge amount on advertising these innovative services.

In summary, service availability is very essential for the adoption of MPA. Service availability can be divided into two. The first one is the availability of MPA geographically, technically and organizationally and whether the same service is being provided for by competitors or other organizations or not. Both types are linked to the adoption of the service and therefore business organizations need to make service available to their customers in order to maximize the speed of adoption of the service.

## Ease of Use

One of the major characteristics influencing acceptance of modern technology and effect human behavior is its perceived ease of use (Adams, 1992). Many studies have then considered it as one of the largest influencer of technology adoption (Davis & Bagozzi, 1989). Many technology acceptance models, developed for mobile banking have this as one key component (Ibrahim &Fayaz, 2015). It is extent to which a human-made device or tool is learnable and usable. In mobile banking and mobile payment application, it is the learnability and usability of such applications or software that makes the difference in the totality of transactions. In the ideal, any technological development must be useable in an easy way. In other words, it is the parameter for the efficient and effective use of the application which should contribute to the satisfaction of its users. In today's banking market, there are many applications and service providers that prove useful within the industry. Nowadays almost all banks are furnishing their customers with online services and mobile accounts. Consumers can check their balance from their mobile phones and can transfer money through the mobile payment applications provided by their respective banks. If the system is seen from the EU for instance, then favorable perception which is more useful to consumers (Phonthanikitithaworn, 2015) evaluating it. It means systems and products from EU origin have not only playing its role in framing consumer's attitudes but also gives them the courage of the productive use of MPA (Oliveira, 2014).

Behavioral scientists believe that this characteristic (ease of use) tends to enhances firm performance by increasing its users and maintaining its customers. With more people having low education or lack exposure to the mobile devices, mobile payment applications can work through to get the benefits if it is indeed easy to use (Varnali, 2014). Ease of use then contributes to decrease financial and security risk and ultimately increase trust during payment when employing such applications (Zarmpou, 2014). Consumers tend to adopt technology that is easy to use. It is evident from the literature and TAM adoption models that this factor is one of the most important elements in providing value and shaping consumer's attitudes (Liebana et al, 2014). Literature shows that technology or any other development cannot make sense if consumers find it difficult to understand how to use it. Some people prefer the EU factor in the adoption of MPA and undeniably if the masses if it is easy, it will be adopted quickly and by more people.

## Proposed RESS (Risk, Ease of Use, Security and Service) Model for Mobile Payment Application

It is evident that the adoption of mobile phones has instigated a new routine and habits in our lives. Indeed after its development, the mobile phone has changed human behavior but also added a significant contribution to human development etc. (Liébana-Cabanillas, De Luna, & Montoro-Ríos, 2015). According to global statistics, the number of mobile users has risen to more than seven billion (ITU, 2016). Keeping in mind this development business sector organizations and mobile service operators are trying to increase the uptake mobile services to mobile phone users through different apps through different apps (Liébana-Cabanillas, De Luna, & Montoro-Ríos, 2015). One of the areas, an area researchers are keen on is mobile payment service. It has given consumers a platform to pay for goods and other services via the mobile phone (Lee, et al. 2012).

This service is now available in most of the developed and developing countries and it is forecasted that payments will reach unprecedented level in the near future (Slade, Williams, & Dwivedi, 2013). It is becoming necessary understand how and why people are quickly adopting the mobile money transfer technology. The most effective technology acceptance model was presented by Davis, (1989), which states that Perceived Ease of Use and Usefulness of the product are the two main factors of TAM. Other theoretical models for technology acceptance are Universal Technology Adoption and Use Theory (UTAUT) brought forth by Venkatesh & Davis, (2000), Theory of Planned Behavior (Ajzen, 1991), Theory of Reasoned Action (Ajzen, 1991), the Diffusion of an Innovation Theory (Rogers, 1995), Technology Readiness Index (Parasuraman, 2000) and TAM (Ibrahim et al. 2015).

Each model focuses on some specific variable and their interconnectivity, necessary for technology adoption. For example, Parasuraman, (2000) examined drivers and inhibitors, while Parasuraman & Colby, (2014) focused on an updated TRI model by explaining it in terms of structure, content, and psychometric characteristics needed for technology acceptance. Lu, Yu, Liu, & Yao, (2003) concluded that -in their model- that innovation implementation of technology largely depends upon consumers' differences. Accordingly Lin et al., (2007), mentions that innovativeness and optimism are the drivers of technology readiness while security issues and discomfort are inhibitors. Other drivers necessary for technology acceptance are convenience (Liébana-Cabanillas et al., 2015) and compatibility (Teo, Tan, Ooi, Hew, & Yew, 2015). Some inhibitors which have also a great impact on technology acceptance are perceived cost (Chong et al., 2012), perceived risk (Pham & Ho, 2015), etc. (Liébana-Cabanillas et al., 2018) studied technology acceptance under the umbrella of human behavior by adding social networks and some moderating variables like gender, age, and experience.

This chapter presents a novel theoretical model for the adoption of mobile payment applications. Some of the main variables involved were previously supported by the other studies with keen eye on technology are embraced by technological gurus. It gives a new structure and interlinks the variables of interest in a novel way. These variables include are security, risk (Liébana-Cabanillas et al., 2013), availability and ease of use. Previously researchers have not focused on the availability as compared to other factors. This chapter includes availability along with other variables to enrich the model. The proposed theoretical framework is given below.

*Figure 1. Adoption of mobile payment application system*

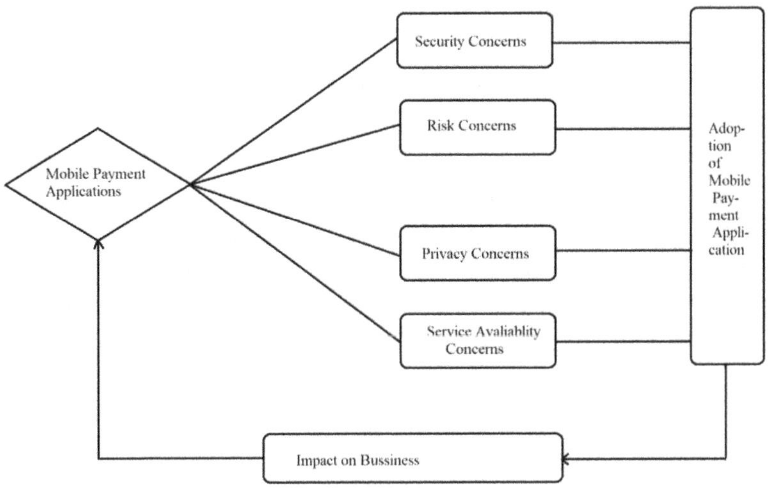


# PROPOSED THEORETICAL FRAMEWORK

## Connecting Mobile Payment Application to Business

Mankind started paying in business from barter, metal coins, paper and phones (Shatskikh, 2013). They have since been replaced by smartphones within the field communication technology after the dominance of cash and credit cards (Vodafone. 2013). Myriads of businesses have adopted mobile payment applications to make the exchange process easy and comfortable for their customers (Wu, 2005; Ibrahim at el. 2015). Mobile payments therefore are eliminating cash, checks writing and waiting for invoices. This reveals that technology is in a continuous development stratum and its improvement on regular basis to its best option for today's business.

Mobile transaction initially estimated to reach 1.3 Trillian in 2012 (Holden, 2012a) and according to Business insider, 75% of payments will be made through this technology by 2025. There are varied reasons which have inspired businesses to adopt to MMT technology. First of all, convenience is cited as a major reason, it is has become an easy way to pay as many people do not feel comfortable walking around with loads of cash (Gefen, 2003). Certainly the masses believe that it is more secure to have this technology than to walk around with cash or plastic money. There are many security concerns associated with cash and cards. It also reduces waiting time and improves the experience of customers (Pousttchi, 2008) as customers just need the account details for transactions. It is then considered a more secure to pay with this application than to pay in cash or through cards. Research also shows that using technology stimulates the customer's mind to purchase more (Ibrahim at el. 2015). This means that the businesses which use mobile payment application can capture more revenue and profits than those using conventional methods for payments. With the use of MPA, business organizations can increase their sales by reducing the long queues of the customer to pay in cash. Customers can get a good experience and they can pay from the comfort of their homes or offices. It can be summarized that MPA has a constructive and favorable impact on business. In today's market, it not only reduces payment time for customers but also provides a quick payment directly to a business account. It gives a positive experience and attracts customers to use modern technology. Therefore, MPA is linked with business and it is expected that its use will increase in the future.

## DISCUSSION

Every development comes along with several advantages and challenges. The same is the case of MPA and its adoption. Although it is the latest technology in use in today's business, it is yet to achieve intended purpose it was meant for since its inception.

It is in the human nature to resist change and technological changes are no exceptions. So the adoption of this service in business is a very big challenge not only for business but also for customers. Many factors having a significant impact on the adoption of MPA and its impact on business cannot be wished away (Ibrahim at el. 2015). It can consequently serve to add a huge value to business provided it is meant to serve the customer needs and demands. Currently many businesses are using these applications worldwide, therefore the need to adopt such business practices to make it more successful.

It is a fact that modern business practitioners are facing lots of challenges and problems. This means that many firms usually go an extra mile to eliminate their rivals from the market or make their appeal repugnant. While others may hesitate to adopt these applications due to perceived security and privacy issue, wise firms work on minimizing these associated risks and do their best to maximize service availability. Many researchers have developed TAM but unlike these models, this chapter has focused on the factors associated with this application's adoption and its impact on business. So it cannot be claimed these MPA are 100 percent effective, but even with challenges MPA are very inspiring and effective and businesses should be adopted. Though the MPA are perceived as partially beneficial for business they should be adopted and creases of privacy, security, and risks be ironed out. MPA creators and providers need to ensure privacy, security, availability and less risky environment for MMT enterprise to thrive. Organizations also need to provide

MPA service to their customers in a superior way than their competitors. Enhanced service with better availability will help the adoption of MMTs and will ultimately influence the business enterprises positively and profits northwards.

From MPA service provider's perspective, it is not only the latest mood of payment in business but also easy where payment can be made directly to account, etc. This should not only be easy but also be more secure- from a customer perspective, it should be secure, risk-free, keep privacy and available. The following model has been proposed for the adoption of MPA.

## CONCLUSION

With the development of modern technology and its application, the way organizations do business has to change. Not only is the technology has converged with business methods, it is impacting the environment in which business is done. Although it is a great development in technology and the business world it is yet to permeate into all consumers utility purview. The main reasons for not using these applications are factored as challenges accompany the availability and adoption of modern technologies. As humans are reluctant to change, so there should be enticing attributes in within the technology related industry to lure people to these apps not drive them away. This study summarizes them into risk-free, secure, ease of use and availability. These are the factors needed to be in the mobile payment application so that it is adopted by the people and help the business organization to play the infinite game of conquering financial excellence.

## REFERENCES

Ahmad. M (2014). Impact of Telecom Services Characteristics on Consumer for Use in Pakistan. *Advances in Economics and Business*, *2*(4), 172–179.

Ahmad. (2015a). Reengineering of Information and Communication Technology Services (A need of Society). *Industrial Engineering Letters, 5*(8).

Ahmadl. (2015b). Role of Knowledge Management in Achieving Customer Relationship and its Strategic Outcomes. *Information and Knowledge Management, 5*(1).

Ajzen, I. (1991). The theory of planned behavior. *Organizational Behavior and Human Decision Processes*, *50*(2), 179–211. doi:10.1016/0749-5978(91)90020-T

Ankar, B., & D'Incau, D. (2002). Value creation in mobile commerce: Findings from a consumer survey. *Journal of Information Technology Theory and Application*, *4*(1), 43–64.

Arthur, C. (2014). How many Google Wallet users are there? Google won't say—but us can. *The Guardian*. Retrieved from http://www.theguardian.com

Au, A. U., & Kauffman, R. J. (2008). The economics of mobile payments: Understanding stakeholder issues for an emerging financial technology application. *Electronic Commerce Research and Applications*, *7*(2), 141–164. doi:10.1016/j.elerap.2006.12.004

Baptista, G., & Oliveira, T. (2015). Understanding mobile banking: The unified theory of acceptance and use of technology combined with cultural moderators. *Computers in Human Behavior*, *50*, 418–430. doi:10.1016/j.chb.2015.04.024

Benbasat, I., & Barki, H. (2007). Quo vadis TAM? *Journal of the Association for Information Systems*, *8*(4), 211–218. doi:10.17705/1jais.00126

Brigham Young University. (2013). *Theories Used in IS Research Wiki*. Information Systems Preparation Program of the Marriott School of Management of Brigham Young University.

Chandra, S., Srivastava, S. C., & Theng, Y. (2010). Evaluating the role of trust in consumer adoption of mobile payment systems: An empirical analysis. *Communications of the Association for Information Systems*, *27*(10), 561–588.

Chiu, C., Wang, E. T. G., Fang, Y., & Huang, H. (2014). Understanding customers' repeat purchase intentions in B2C e-commerce: The roles of utilitarian value, hedonic value and perceived risk. *Information Systems Journal*, *24*(1), 85–114. doi:10.1111/j.1365-2575.2012.00407.x

Chong, A. Y. L., Chan, F. T. S., & Ooi, K. B. (2012). Predicting consumer decisions to adopt mobile commerce: Cross-country empirical examination between China and Malaysia. *Decision Support Systems*, *53*(1), 34–43. doi:10.1016/j.dss.2011.12.001

Dahlberg, T., Mallat, N., Ondrus, J., & Zmijewska, A. (2008). Past, present and future of mobile payments research: A literature review. *Electronic Commerce Research and Applications*, *7*(2), 165–181. doi:10.1016/j.elerap.2007.02.001

Davis, F. D. (1989). Perceived Usefulness, Perceived Ease of Use, and User Acceptance of Information Technology. *Management Information Systems Quarterly*, *13*(3), 319–340. doi:10.2307/249008

Davis, F. D. (1989). Perceived usefulness, perceived ease of use, and user acceptance of information technology. *Management Information Systems Quarterly*, *13*(3), 319–340. doi:10.2307/249008

Engau, C., & Hoffmann, V. H. (2011). Strategizing in an unpredictable climate: Exploring corporate strategies to cope with regulatory uncertainty. *Long Range Planning*, *44*(1), 42–63. doi:10.1016/j.lrp.2010.11.003

Flatraaker, D. I. (2013). Mobile payments changing the landscape of retail banking: Hype or reality? *Journal of Payments Strategy & Systems*, *7*(2), 150–158.

Gefen, D., Karahanna, E., & Straub, D. W. (2003). Trust and TAM in online Shopping: An Integrated Model. *Management Information Systems Quarterly*, *27*(1), 51. doi:10.2307/30036519

Gefen, D., & Straub, D. (2004). Consumer Trust in B2C E-Commerce and the Importance of Social Presence: Experiments in E-Products and E-Services. *Omega. International Journal of Management Sciences*, *32*, 407–424.

Heavey, C., & Simsek, Z. (2013). Top management compositional effects on corporate entrepreneurship: The moderating role of perceived technological uncertainty. *Journal of Product Innovation Management*, *30*(5), 837–855. doi:10.1111/jpim.12033

Holden, W. (2012a). *Press Release: Mobile Payments to Reach $1.3tn Annually by 2017, as NFC and Physical Goods Sales Accelerate*. Academic Press.

Ibrahim. (2015a). The Impact of Influencing factors on Adoption of Mobile Banking in Pakistan. *MAGNT Research Report, 3*(4), 97-109.

Ibrahim. (2015b). Determining the Effect of Innovations for Mobile Banking Adoption in Pakistan. *Journal of Information Engineering and Applications*, *5*(11), 16–23.

Ibrahim. (2015c). Impact of Risk and Ethics on Adoption of Mobile Banking in Pakistan. *Journal of Economics and Sustainable Development, 6*(7).

International Telecommunication Union. (2014). *The world telecommunication/ICT indicators database*. Retrieved from http://www.itu.int/en/ITU-D/Statistics/Pages/publications/wtid.aspx

Kang, D. & Park, Y. (2014). Review-based measurement of customer satisfaction in mobile service: Sentiment analysis and VIKOR approach. *Expert Systems with Applications*, *41*(4), 1041–1050.

Karahanna, E., Agarwal, R., & Angst, C. M. (2006). Reconceptualizing Compatibility Beliefs in Technology Acceptance Research. *Management Information Systems Quarterly, 30*(4), 781–804. doi:10.2307/25148754

Khan. (2012). Analysis of Consumer Perception towards Telecommunication Services. *Journal of Social and Development Sciences, 3*(3), 89-98.

Khan. (2014). Convergence of Broadcasting and Telecommunication Technology Regulatory Framework in Pakistan. *International Journal of Management and Commerce Innovations, 2*(1), 35-43.

Kim, K., & Prabhakar, B. (2000). Initial Trust, Perceived Risk, and the Adoption of Internet Banking. *Proceedings of the 21st International Conference on Information Systems.*

Koenig-Lewis, N., Palmer, A., & Moll, A. (2010). Predicting young consumers' take up of mobile banking Services. *International Journal of Bank Marketing, 28*(5), 410–432. doi:10.1108/02652321011064917

Lee, Y. K., Park, J. H., Chung, N., & Blakeney, A. (2012). A unified perspective on the factors influencing usage intention toward mobile financial services. *Journal of Business Research, 65*(11), 1590–1599. doi:10.1016/j.jbusres.2011.02.044

Lian, J. W. (2015). Critical factors for cloud-based e-invoice service adoption in Taiwan: An empirical study. *International Journal of Information Management, 35*(1), 98–109. doi:10.1016/j.ijinfomgt.2014.10.005

Lie ́bana-Cabanillas, F., Mun ̃oz-Leiva, F., & Sa ́nchez-Ferna ́ndez, J. (2013). The impact of risk on the technological acceptance of mobile payment services. *Global Business Perspectives, 1*(4), 309–328. doi:10.100740196-013-0020-9

Lie ́bana-Cabanillas, F., Ramos de Luna, I., & Montoro-Rı ́os, F. J. (2015). User behaviour in QR mobile payment system: The QR Payment acceptance model. *Technology Analysis and Strategic Management, 27*(9), 1031–1049. doi:10.1080/09537325.2015.1047757

Liébana-Cabanillas, Muñoz-Leiva, F., & Sánchez-Fernández, J. (2018). A global approach to the analysis of user behavior in mobile payment systems in the new electronic environment. *Service Business, 12*(1), 25–64. doi:10.100711628-017-0336-7

Liébana-Cabanillas, F., Sánchez-Fernández, J., & Muñoz-Leiva, F. (2014). Antecedents of the adoption of the new mobile payment systems: The moderating effect of age. *Computers in Human Behavior, 35*, 464–478. doi:10.1016/j.chb.2014.03.022

Lin, C.-H., Shih, H.-Y., & Sher, P. J. (2007). Integrating technology readiness into technology acceptance: The TRAM model. *Psychology and Marketing*, *24*(7), 641–657. doi:10.1002/mar.20177

Lu, J., Yu, C. S., Liu, C., & Yao, J. E. (2003). Technology acceptance model for wireless internet. *Electronic Networking Applications and Policy*, *13*(3), 206–222. doi:10.1108/10662240310478222

Lu, Y., Yang, S., Chau, P. Y., & Cao, Y. (2011). Dynamics between the trust transfer process and intention to use mobile payment services: A cross-environment perspective. *Information & Management*, *48*(8), 393–403. doi:10.1016/j.im.2011.09.006

Luarn, P., & Lin, H. H. (2005). Toward an understanding of the behavioral intention to use mobile banking. *Computers in Human Behavior*, *21*(6), 873–891. doi:10.1016/j.chb.2004.03.003

Mann, B. J. S., & Sahni, S. K. (2013). Role of trust and customer loyalty in reducing perceived security risk in internet banking. *International Journal of Electronic Business*, *10*(4), 331–354. doi:10.1504/IJEB.2013.056783

Martins, C., Oliveira, T., & Popovič, A. (2014). Understanding the Internet banking adoption: A unified theory of acceptance and use of technology and perceived risk application. *International Journal of Information Management*, *34*(1), 1–13. doi:10.1016/j.ijinfomgt.2013.06.002

Oliveira, T., Faria, M., Thomas, M. A., & Popovič, A. (2014). Extending the understanding of mobile banking adoption: When UTAUT meets TTF and ITM. *International Journal of Information Management*, *34*(5), 689–703. doi:10.1016/j.ijinfomgt.2014.06.004

Parasuraman, A. (2000). Technology readiness index (TRI): A multiple-item scale to measure readiness to embrace new technologies. *Journal of Service Research*, *2*(4), 307–320. doi:10.1177/109467050024001

Parasuraman, A., & Colby, C. L. (2014). An updated and streamlined technology readiness index: TR 2.0. *Journal of Service Research*, *18*(1), 59–74. doi:10.1177/1094670514539730

Pham, T. T. T., & Ho, J. C. (2015). The effects of product-related, personal-related factors and attractiveness of alternatives on consumer adoption of NFC-based mobile payments. *Technology in Society*, *43*, 1–16. doi:10.1016/j.techsoc.2015.05.004

Phonthanikitithaworn, C., Sellitto, C., & Fong, M. (2015). User Intentions to Adopt Mobile Payment Services: A Study of Early Adopters in Thailand. *Journal of Internet Banking and Commerce*, *20*(1), 1–29.

Pousttchi, K. (2008). A modeling approach and reference models for the analysis of mobile payment use cases. *Electronic Commerce Research and Applications*, *7*(2), 182–201. doi:10.1016/j.elerap.2007.07.001

Pramis, J. (2013). *Number of Mobile Phones to Exceed World Population by 2014*. Available online at: http://www.digitaltrends.com/mobile/mobile-phone-world-population-2014

Rogers, E. M. (1995). *Diffusion of innovations* (4th ed.). New York, NY: Free Press.

Schierz, P. G., Schilke, O., & Wirtz, B. W. (2010). Understanding consumer acceptance of mobile payment services: An empirical analysis. *Electronic Commerce Research and Applications*, *9*(3), 209–216. doi:10.1016/j.elerap.2009.07.005

Shatskikh, A. (2013). *Consumer acceptance of Mobile Payments in Restaurants* (Master Thesis). University of South Florida, Department of Hospitality Administration.

Slade, E. L., Williams, M. D., & Dwivedi, Y. K. (2013). Mobile payment adoption: Classification and review of the extant literature. *The Marketing Review*, *13*(2), 167–190. doi:10.1362/146934713X13699019904687

Sousa, R., & Voss, C. A. (2006). Service Quality in Multichannel Services Employing Virtual Channels. *Journal of Service Research*, *8*(4), 356–371. doi:10.1177/1094670506286324

Teo, A. C., Tan, G. W. H., Ooi, K. B., Hew, T. S., & Yew, K. T. (2015). The effects of convenience and speed in m-payment. *Industrial Management & Data Systems*, *115*(2), 311–331. doi:10.1108/IMDS-08-2014-0231

Varnali, K., Yilmaz, C., & Toker, A. (2012). Predictors of attitudinal and behavioral outcomes in mobile advertising: A field experiment. *Electronic Commerce Research and Applications*, *11*(6), 570–581. doi:10.1016/j.elerap.2012.08.002

Venkatesh, V., & Davis, F. (2000). A theoretical extension of the technology-acceptance model: Four longitudinal field studies. *Management Science*, *46*(2), 186–204. doi:10.1287/mnsc.46.2.186.11926

Venkatesh, V., Morris, M. G., Davis, G. B., & Davis, F. D. (2003). User acceptance of information technology: Toward a unified view. *Management Information Systems Quarterly*, *27*(3), 425–478. doi:10.2307/30036540

Venkatesh, V., Thong, J., & Xu, X. (2012). Consumer acceptance and use of information technology: Extending the unified theory of acceptance and use of technology. *Management Information Systems Quarterly*, *36*(1), 157–178. doi:10.2307/41410412

Vodafone. (2013). *Tokyo-drift-how-japan-leads-the-way-on-m-payments*. Retrieved from http://www.vodafone.com/business/globalenterprise/tokyo-drift-how-japan-leads-the-way-on-m-payments-2013-08-13

Wallace, L. G., & Sheetz, S. D. (2014). The adoption of software measures: A technology acceptance model (TAM) perspective. *Information & Management*, *51*(2), 249–258. doi:10.1016/j.im.2013.12.003

Wan, G., & Che, P. (2004). Chinese air travelers' acceptance towards electronic ticketing. *Proceedings of Engineering Management Conference*. 10.1109/IEMC.2004.1407118

Wang, W. T., & Li, H. M. (2012). Factors influencing mobile service adoption: A brand-equity perspective. *Internet Research*, *22*(2), 142–179. doi:10.1108/10662241211214548

Watkins, E. (2013). Mobile payment has hotel applications. *Hotel News Now*. Retrieved from http://www.hotelnewsnow.com/Article/12378/Mobilepayment-has-hotel-application

Wu, J. H., & Wang, S. C. (2005). What drives mobile commerce? An empirical evaluation of the revised technology acceptance model. *Information & Management*, *42*(5), 719–729. doi:10.1016/j.im.2004.07.001

Yang, A. S. (2009). Exploring adoption difficulties in mobile banking services. *Can. J. Admin. Sci.*, *149*(2), 136–149. doi:10.1002/cjas.102

Yang, S., Lu, Y., Gupta, S., Cao, Y., & Zhang, R. (2012). Mobile payment services adoption across time: An empirical study of the effects of behavioral beliefs, social influences, and personal traits. *Computers in Human Behavior*, *28*(1), 129–142. doi:10.1016/j.chb.2011.08.019

Zarmpou, T., Saprikis, V., Markos, A., & Vlachopoulou, M. (2012). Modeling users' acceptance of mobile services. *Electronic Commerce Research*, *12*(2), 225–248. doi:10.100710660-012-9092-x

# Compilation of References


Abadi, F. D. B. (2009). *Supply Chain Evolution and key elements of progress*. University College of Borås, School of Engineering.

Accion International. (2011). Financial Inclusion: What's the Vision? Center for Financial Inclusion, 3.

Ades, A., & Di Tella, R. (1997). The new economics of corruption: A survey and some new results. *Political Studies*, *45*(3), 496–515. doi:10.1111/1467-9248.00093

Adusei, L. A. (2009). *Hiding Africa's Looted Funds: The Silence of Western Media*. Retrieved from https://wikileaks.org/wiki/Hiding_Africa%27s_Looted_Funds:_The_Silence_of_Western_Media

Afandi, F., & Mbugua, S. (2015). Role of agent banking services in promotion of financial inclusion in Nyeri Town. *Research Journal of finance and accounting*, *6*(3), 148-173.

Africa Development Bank. (2013). *Financial inclusion in Africa*. Author.

Agbaje, A. (2004). Corruption, Accountability and Good governance: Reflections on governance in the Nigeria Fourth Republic 1999-2003. *International Review of Politics and Development.*, *2*(2), 23–47.

Agbeyegbe, T. D., Stotsky, J., & WoldeMariam, A. (2006). Trade liberalization, exchange rate changes, and tax revenue in Sub-Saharan Africa. *Journal of Asian Economics*, *17*(2), 261–284. doi:10.1016/j.asieco.2005.09.003

Ahmad & Amirmadhi. (2011). Application of Artificial Intelligence Techniques for Credit Risk Evaluation. *International Journal of Modeling and Optimization*, *1*(3).

Ahmad. (2015a). Reengineering of Information and Communication Technology Services (A need of Society). *Industrial Engineering Letters, 5*(8).

Ahmad. M (2014). Impact of Telecom Services Characteristics on Consumer for Use in Pakistan. *Advances in Economics and Business*, *2*(4), 172–179.

Ahmadl. (2015b). Role of Knowledge Management in Achieving Customer Relationship and its Strategic Outcomes. *Information and Knowledge Management, 5*(1).

Ajzen, I. (1991). The Theory of Planned Behavior. *Organizational Behavior and Human Decision Processes*, *50*(2), 179–211. doi:10.1016/0749-5978(91)90020-T

Ajzen, I., & Fishbein, M. (1977, September). Attitude-Behavior Relations: A Theoretical Analysis and Review of Empirical Research. *Psychological Bulletin*, *84*(5), 888–918. doi:10.1037/0033-2909.84.5.888

Alexandre Claire and Eisenhart Lynn Chang. (2013) Mobile Money as an Engine of Financial Inclusion and Lynchpin of Financial Integrity. *Washington Journal of Law, Technology & Arts*, *8*(3). Available at https://digitalcommons.law.uw.edu/cgi/viewcontent.cgi?article=1178&context=wjlta

Al-Jabri, I., & Sohail, S. (2012). Banking mobile adoption: Application diffusion of innovation theory. *Journal of Electronic Commerce Research*, *13*(4), 379–391.

Allan, A., Massu, M., & Svarer, C. (2013). *Banking on Change: Breaking Barriers to Financial Inclusion. Barclays*. Plan, UK: CARE International.

Allen, R. (2015). *IMF Working PaperFiscal Affairs Department The Evolving Functions and Organization of Finance Ministries Prepared by Authorized for distribution by 2015*. Available at https://www.imf.org/external/pubs/ft/wp/2015/wp15232.pdf

Al-Somali, S. A., Gholami, R., & Clegg, B. (2009). An investigation into the acceptance of online banking in Saudi Arabia. *Technovation*, *29*(29), 130–141. doi:10.1016/j.technovation.2008.07.004

Anderloni, L., Bayot, B., Błędowski, P., Iwanicz-Drozdowska, M., & Kempson, E. (2008). *Financial Services Provision and Prevention of Financial Exclusion*. Retrieved from European Commission website: http://Ec.europa.eu/employment_social/spsi

Anderloni, L., & Carluccio, E. M. (2006). *Access to Bank Accounts and Payment Services*. ResearchGate. doi:10.1007/978-3-540-46498-3_2

Andersén, A., Hyytinen, A., & Snellman, J. (2000). *Recent Developments in the Finnish Banking Sector* (No. 15/2000; p. 39). Retrieved from Bank of Finland website: https://ideas.repec.org/p/bof/bofrdp/2000_015.html

Andiva, B. (2014). *Mobile Financial Services and Regulation in Kenya*. Competition Authority of Kenya.

Andrianaivo, M., & Kpodar, K. (2012). Mobile Phones, Financial Inclusion, and Growth. *Review of Economics and Institutions*, *3*(2), 30. doi:10.5202/rei.v3i2.75

Ankar, B., & D'Incau, D. (2002). Value creation in mobile commerce: Findings from a consumer survey. *Journal of Information Technology Theory and Application*, *4*(1), 43–64.

Ann-Sofie Isaksson. (2013). *Corruption along ethnic lines: A study of individual corruption experiences in 17 African countries*. Working papers in economics, No 571. Retreived from: https://core.ac.uk/download/pdf/16337262.pdf

Antoninis, M., & Corcoran, B. (2019). *This one small change could transform education for millions*. Retrieved from: https://www.weforum.org

Antoninis, M., & Montoya, S. (2019). *The world is off track to deliver on its education commitments by 2030.* Retrieved from: https://gemreportunesco.wordpress.com

Anyanzwa, J. (2019, July 20). *How e-money is changing the face of banking. The East African.* Nairobi, Kenya: Nation Media Group.

Ardic, O. P., Heimann, M. and Mylenko, N. (2011). *Access to financial services and the financial inclusion agenda around the world: A cross-country analysis with a new data set.* doi:10.1596/1813-9450-5537

Arnaboldi & Claeys. (2010). *Innovation and performance of European banking adopting Internet.* Working paper no. 04/10. Cass Business School.

Arnold, D., Dobbie, W., & Yang, C. S. (2018). Racial bias in bail decisions. *Quarterly Journal of Economics.* Available at https://www.princeton.edu/~wdobbie/files/racialbias.pdf

Arora, R., Ujakpa, M. M., Jonathan, F., Appiah-Annin, K., & Mwanza, P. T. (2016). Challenges Inhibiting E-Zwich Electronic Payment System. *Journal of Information Engineering and Applications*, *6*(10), 18–31.

Arthur, C. (2014). How many Google Wallet users are there? Google won't say—but us can. *The Guardian.* Retrieved from http://www.theguardian.com

Arunda, C. (2015). *The influence of innovation on competitive advantage: A case of M-pesa.* United States International University-Africa.

Arun, T., & Kamath, R. (2015). Financial Inclusion: Policies and Practices. *IIMB Management Review*, *27*(4), 267–287. doi:10.1016/j.iimb.2015.09.004

Attaran, M. (2004). Exploring the relationship between information technology and business process reengineering. *Journal of International Management*, *41*(5), 585–596. doi:10.10160378-7206(03)00098- 3

Au, A. U., & Kauffman, R. J. (2008). The economics of mobile payments: Understanding stakeholder issues for an emerging financial technology application. *Electronic Commerce Research and Applications*, *7*(2), 141–164. doi:10.1016/j.elerap.2006.12.004

Baharumshah, A. Z., Jibrilla, A. A., Sirag, A., Ali, H. S., & Muhammad, I. M. (2016). Public Revenue-Expenditure Nexus in South Africa: Are there Asymmetries? *The South African Journal of Economics*, *84*(4), 520–537. doi:10.1111aje.12130

Balaji, R. P., & Vijayakumar, D. T. (2018). Diffusion of Digital Payment System in Rural India. *Global Journal of Management and Business Research: G*, *14*(4), 29-32.

Bandari, A. (2018). *Evaluating access and use of community information Services by informal urban settlers in Nairobi County.* Moi University.

Banerjee, A., & Newman, A. (1993). Occupational Choice and the Process of Development. *Journal of Political Economy*, *101*(2), 274–298. doi:10.1086/261876

Baptista, G., & Oliveira, T. (2015). Understanding mobile banking: The unified theory of acceptance and use of technology combined with cultural moderators. *Computers in Human Behavior*, *50*, 418–430. doi:10.1016/j.chb.2015.04.024

Barocas, S., & Selbst, A. (2016). Big Data's Disparate Impact. *California Law Review*, *104*, 671–732.

Bartlett. (2019). *Consumer-Lending Discrimination in the FinTech Era*. Available at https://faculty.haas.berkeley.edu/morse/research/papers/discrim.pdf

Batista, C., & Vicente, P. C. (2013). Introducing Mobile Money in Rural Mozambique: Evidence from a Randomized Field Experiment. *NOVAFRICA Working Paper Series No. 1301*, 1-46.

Beck, T. (2015). *Microfinance: A Critical Literature Survey*. Working paper no. 2015/4. World Bank Group.

Beck, T., & de la Torre, A. (2006). *The Basic Analytics of Access to Financial Services*. Policy Research Working Paper Series 4026, the World Bank.

Benbasat, I., & Barki, H. (2007). Quo vadis TAM? *Journal of the Association for Information Systems*, *8*(4), 211–218. doi:10.17705/1jais.00126

Bendell, J., Slater, M., & Ruddick, W. (2015). *Re-imagining Money to Broaden the Future of Development Finance*. Academic Press.

Ben-Ishai, S. (2008). Regulating Payday Lenders in Canada: Drawing on American Lessons. *Comparative Research in Law & Political Economy Research Papers, Working Papers, Conference Papers Research Report No. 16/2008*. Osgoode Hall Law School of York University Comparative Research in Law & Political Economy Research Papers, Working Papers, Conference Papers Research Report No. 16/2008.

Bernanke, B. S., Blinder, A. S., & McCallum, B. T. (2005). Panel Discussion I: What Have We Learned Since October 1979? *Federal Reserve Bank of St. Louis Review*, 228.

Bertram, I. G., & Watters, R. F. (1985). The MIRAB Economy in South Pacific Microstates. *Pacific Viewpoint*, *26*(3), 497–519. doi:10.1111/apv.263002

Bertrand, S., & Ahmad, K. (2014). *Mobile payments: Finally ready to take off?* Bain & Company.

Berutich, J. M., Francisco, L., & Quintana, D. (2016). Robust technical trading strategies using GP for algorithmic portfolio selection. *Expert Systems with Applications*, *46*, 307–315. doi:10.1016/j.eswa.2015.10.040

Bhattacharya, R., Devinney, T. M., & Pillutla, M. M. (1998, July). A Formal Model of Trust Based on Outcomes. *Academy of Management Review*, *23*(3), 459–472. doi:10.5465/amr.1998.926621

Biasucci, C., Drumwright, M., Elliott, D., Gentile, M., Pierce, L., & Prentice, R. (2019). *Ethics Unwrapped.* Retrieved October 16, 2019, from University of Texas at Austin: https://www.utexas.edu/

Bill & Melinda Gates Foundation. (2013, September). *Fighting Poverty Profitably: Transforming the economics of payments to build sustainable, inclusive financial systems.* The Gates Foundation's Financial Services for the Poor program. Bill & Melinda Gates Foundation. Retrieved from www.gatesfoundation.org: https://docs.gatesfoundation.org/Documents/Fighting%20Poverty%20Profitably%20Report%20Full%20Appendices.pdf

BIS. (2017). International banking and financial market developments. Bank for International Settlements Quarterly Review, 174.

Biztech Africa. (2018). *Cameroon Ministry adopts MTN Mobile Money for the payment of school fees.* Retrieved from: https://www.biztechafrica.com

Boatright, J. R., & Smith, J. D. (2009). *Ethics and the Conduct of Business.* New York: Pearson Education, Inc.

Boer, R., & de Boer, T. (2010). *Mobile Payments 2010: Market Analysis and Overview, version 1.01. Innopay.* Retrieved from https://www.ebaportal.eu/_Download/Research%20and%20Analysis/2010/Mobile_paymen ts_2010_Innopay.pdf (accessed on 1st July ,2019)

Böhnke, P. (2001). *Nothing left to lose? Poverty and social exclusion in comparison. Empirical evidence on Germany.* Academic Press.

Bongben, L. (2014). *Yaounde I Pays Fees Through Mobile Money.* Retrieved from: https://cameroonpostline.com

Borst, N., & Creehan, S. (2017, December 5). *Banking: How Technology Can Build Trust for the Newly Banked.* Retrieved from Federal Reserve Bank of Francisco Web Site: https://www.frbsf.org/banking/asia-program/pacific-exchanges-podcast/how-technology-can-build-trust-for-the-newly-banked/

Bourreau, M., & Hoernig, S. (2016). *Interoperability of mobile money: International experience and recommendations for Mozambique.* Retrieved from https://www.theigc.org/wp-content/uploads/2017/01/Hoernig-et-al-2016-Final-Report.pdf

Bourreau, M., & Marianne, V. (2010). *Cooperation for Innovation in Payment Systems: The Case of Mobile Payments.* Economix Working Paper 2010-05. Université de Paris Ouest Nanterre La Défense, Nanterre, France. Retrieved from http://economix.u-paris10.fr/pdf/dt/2010/WP_EcoX_2010-05.pdf (accessed on 21st June ,2019)

Braniff, L. (2017). *Schools in Africa Aren't Taking Advantage of Mobile Money – Why?* Retrieved from: https://www.cgap.org/blog/

Braniff, L., Waldron, D., Foye, J., & Emmott, C. (2017). *Meeting Education Finance Needs in Rural Uganda.* Retrieved from: https://www.cgap.org/blog/

BrazilNews.Net. (2019, July 5). Retrieved July 29, 2019, from brazilinews.net: https://www.brazilnews.net/news/261625727/nigeria-orders-banks-to-loan-more-money

Breiman, L. (1994). *Bagging predictors. Tech. rep. 421*. Department of Statistics, University of California.

Brigham Young University. (2013). *Theories Used in IS Research Wiki*. Information Systems Preparation Program of the Marriott School of Management of Brigham Young University.

Bruckner, A. M. (2018). The Promise and Perils of Algorithmic Lenders' Use of Big Data. *Chicago-Kent Law Review, 93*(1).

Brynjolfsson, E., & Hitt, L. M. (2000). Beyond Computation: Information Technology, Organizational Transformation and Business Performance. *The Journal of Economic Perspectives, 14*(4), 23–48. doi:10.1257/jep.14.4.23

Buku, M. & Meredith, M. (2018). Safaricom and M-pesa in Kenya. Financial inclusion and Financial integrity. *Washington Journal of Law, Technology and Arts, 8*(3).

Buku, M. W., & Meredith, M. W. (2013). Safaricom and M-pesa in Kenya: Financial Inclusion and Financial Integrity. *Washington Journal of Law, Technology & Arts, 8*(3).

Buku, M. W., & Rafe, M. (2017, April). *Fraud in Mobile Financial Services*. Retrieved October 15, 2019, from Consultative Group to Assist the Poor (CGAP): https://www.cgap.org/sites/default/files/researches/documents/Brief-Fraud-in-Mobile-Financial-Services

Bultum, A. G. (2014). Factors affecting the adoption of the electronic banking system in Ethiopian banking industry. *Journal of Management Information System and E-commerce, 1*(1), 1–17.

Burjorjee, D., & Scola, B. (2015). *A Market Systems Approach to Financial Inclusion*. Washington, DC: Consultative Group to Assist the Poor.

Business Daily. (2015, October 24). EAC members move to tame mobile money fraud. *Business Daily*.

Bustinza, E. (2018). *Revolutionizing Payday: Mobile Money's Transformative Impact on Liberia's Public Workers*. Retrieved from: https://nextbillion.net

CapGemini, LinkedIn, & Afma. (2017). *World Fintech Report*. Academic Press.

Carbo, S., Gardener, E. P. M., & Molyneux, P. (2007). Financial Exclusion in Europe. *Public Money & Management, 27*(1), 21–27. doi:10.1111/j.1467-9302.2007.00551.x

Caskey, J., Collard, S., & Kempson, E., & Whyley, C. (2000). In or Out? Financial Exclusion: A Literature and Research Review. *Financial Services Authority, 3*, 5–100.

Cassara, J., & Jorisch, A. (2010). *On the Trail of Terror Finance: What Law Enforcement and Intelligence Officials Need to Know*. Arlington, VA: Red Cell IG.

Castri, S. D. (2013). *Mobile Money: Enabling Regulatory solutions*. GSMA.

CBK, KNBS, & FSD Kenya. (2019). FinAccess Household Survey. Nairobi, Kenya: Author.

CBK. (2005). *Kenya Electronic Payments and Settlement System*. KEPSS.

CBK. (2014, March). *Effective and Efficient Payment Systems for Financial Stability and Transformative Development in Africa*. Caucus Meeting of the African Central Bank Governors, Abuja, Nigeria.

CBK. (2019). *Mobile Payments*. Nairobi: Central Bank of Kenya.

CBK. (2019). *National Payments System*. Retrieved October 11, 2019, from Central Bank of Kenya website: https://www.centralbank.go.ke/national-payments-system/# CBK

CBK. KNBS, & FSD Kenya. (2016). FinAccess Household Survey. Nairobi, Kenya: Author.

CCK. (2012, April). *CCK releases 2nd quarter ICT sector statistics for 2011/2012*. Retrieved October 15, 2019, from Internet Archive Wayback Machine: https://web.archive.org/web/20121016002713/http://cck.go.ke/resc/downloads/SECTOR _STATISTICS_REPORT_Q2_2011-12.pdf

Central Bank of Ireland. (2013). *Report on the Licensed Moneylending Industry*. Available at https://www.centralbank.ie/docs/default-source/publications/consumer- protection-research/gns4-2-1-1-rep-on-licensed-moneyldg-ind-112013.pdf?sfvrsn=6 (accessed on 21st June ,2019)

Central Bank of Kenya. (2014). *Bank supervision annual reports*. Government Press.

Central Bank of Kenya. (2018). *The Impact of Interest Rate Capping on the Kenyan Economy*. Author.

Central Bank of Nigeria (CBN). (2011). *Annual Report 2011*. Available at https://www.cbn.gov.ng/Out/2012/publications/reports/rsd/arp2011/2011%20Annual%20Report_C omplete%20Report.pdf (accessed on 1st July ,2019)

CGAP. (2009). *Poor People Using Mobile Financial Services: Observations on Customer Usage and Impact from M-PESA*. Available at: https://openknowledge.worldbank.org/bitstream/handle/10986/9492/503060BRI0Box31MPESA1Brief01PUBLIC1.pdf?sequence=1&isAllowed=y

CGAP. (2010). *Financial Access 2010: The State of Financial Inclusion through the Crisis*. Retrieved from Consultative Group to Assist the Poor/The World Bank Group website: https://www.cgap.org/sites/default/files/CGAP-Financial-Access-2010.pdf

CGAP. (2015). *Top 10 Things to Know About M-Shwari*. Available at: https://www.cgap.org/blog/top-10-things-know-about-m-shwari

Chandra, S., Srivastava, S. C., & Theng, Y. (2010). Evaluating the role of trust in consumer adoption of mobile payment systems: An empirical analysis. *Communications of the Association for Information Systems*, *27*(10), 561–588.

Chang, Y. T. (2003). *Dynamics of Banking Technology Adoption: An Application to Internet Banking*. Department of Economics, University of Warwick.

Charness, N., & Boot, W. R. (2009, October). Aging and Information Technology Use: Potential and Barriers. *Current Directions in Psychological Science*, *18*(5), 253–258. doi:10.1111/j.1467-8721.2009.01647.x

Chatain, P.-L., Zerzan, A., Noor, W., Dannaoui, N., & de Koker, L. (2011). *Protecting Mobile Money against Financial Crimes: Global Policy Challenges and Solutions*. World Bank Publications. doi:10.1596/978-0-8213-8669-9

Chauhan, J. & Joshi, D. Y. C. (2018). *Pradhan Mantri Jan Dhan Yojana (PMJDY): An Initiative towards Including the Excluded People*. Academic Press.

Checkpoint. (2019). *Cyber Attack Trends: 2019 Mid-Year Report*. Tel Aviv-Yafo, Israel: Checkpoint.

Cherowbrier, J. (2019, November 1). *Statistics: Global consumer fintech adoption rates 2015-2019, by category*. Retrieved from Statista Web Site: https://www.statista.com

Chertoff, M., & Simon, T. (2015). *The Impact of the Dark Web*. Ontario: Centre for International Governance Innovation and Chatham House.

Chester, A. N. (1994). Aligning Technology with Business Strategy. *Research Technology Management*, *37*(1), 25–32. doi:10.1080/08956308.1994.11670951

Cheston, S., & Rhyne, E. (2016, July 2). *The Business of Financial Inclusion: Insights from Banks in Emerging Markets*. Retrieved September 29, 2019, from Center for Financial Inclusion website: https://www.centerforfinancialinclusion.org/the-business-of-financial-inclusion-insights-from-banks-in-emerging-markets

Chiu, C., Wang, E. T. G., Fang, Y., & Huang, H. (2014). Understanding customers' repeat purchase intentions in B2C e-commerce: The roles of utilitarian value, hedonic value and perceived risk. *Information Systems Journal*, *24*(1), 85–114. doi:10.1111/j.1365-2575.2012.00407.x

Chong, A. Y. L., Chan, F. T. S., & Ooi, K. B. (2012). Predicting consumer decisions to adopt mobile commerce: Cross-country empirical examination between China and Malaysia. *Decision Support Systems*, *53*(1), 34–43. doi:10.1016/j.dss.2011.12.001

Chopde, K., Pratik, G., Paras, K., Niharika, M., & Pramila, M. C. (2012). A Study of Classification Based Credit Risk Analysis Algorithm. *International Journal of Engineering and Advanced Technology*, *1*(4).

Clark, N. (2015). *World Education News + Reviews*. Retrieved from: https://wenr.wes.org/2015/06/education-kenya

Cline, A. (2018, June 11). *3 Types of Ethical Systems*. Retrieved October 15, 2019, from Learn Religions: https://www.learnreligions.com/atheism-types-of-ethical-systems

Collins, D., Cojocaru, L., & Zollmann, J. (2015). *Getting an education in rural Kenya: Findings based on the Kenya Financial Diaries*. Zurich: Jacobs Foundation.

Communication Authority of Kenya (2019). *Sector Statistics Report for 2018*. Author.

Communication Commission of Kenya (CCK) & Kenya National Bureau of Statics (KNBS). (2018). *National ICT Survey Report*. Available at https://ca.go.ke/wpcontent/uploads/2018/02/National-ICT-Survey.pdf (accessed on 1st June ,2019)

Connell, J. (2015). Samoa and Tonga: Migration and Remittances in the Twenty-first Century. In W. H. Khonje (Ed.), *Migration and Development: Perspectives from Small States* (pp. 122–181). London: Commonwealth Secretariat. Retrieved from https://books.google.com.mx/books?id=CJhlsrSuIMUC&pg=PA3&vq=%22en+ella.+II.+Preparar+al+trabajador+para+ocupar+una+vacante+o+puesto+de+nueva%22&hl=es&source=gbs_selected_pages&cad=2#v=onepage&q=%22en

Conroy, J. (2005). APEC and financial exclusion: Missed opportunities for collective action? *Asia-Pacific Development Journal*, *12*(1), 53–79. doi:10.18356/339ee7fc-en

Cook, T. (2015). *An overview of M-PESA*. FSD Kenya. Available at https://fsdkenya.org/an-overview-of-m-pesa/(Accesed on 28th September 2019)

Creehan, S. (2018, February 28). *Pacific Exchange Blog: India's Digital Payments: Growing Consumer Trust, but Merchants Needed*. Retrieved from Federal Reserve Bank of San Francisco Web Site: https://www.frbsf.org/banking/asia-program/pacific-exchange-blog/indias-digital-payments-growing-consumer-trust-but-merchants-needed/

Crossman, A. (2019). *Understanding purposive sampling*. Retrieved from https://www.thoughtco.com/purposive-sampling-3026727

CryptoDavid. (2019, March 28). *96% of All Transactions Are Happening Outside the Branch, Says Equity Bank*. Retrieved August 31, 2019, from Bitcoin KE website: https://bitcoinke.io/2019/03/96-percent-of-all-transactions-happening-outside-branch-says-equity-bank/

Dahlberg, T., Mallat, N., Ondrus, J., & Zmijewska, A. (2008). Past, present and future of mobile payments research: A literature review. *Electronic Commerce Research and Applications*, *7*(2), 165–181. doi:10.1016/j.elerap.2007.02.001

Daştan, I. & Gürler, C. (2016). Factors Affecting the Adoption of Mobile Payment Systems: An Empirical Analysis. *Emerging Markets Journal*. DOI doi:10.5195/emaj.2016.95

DATAREPORTAL. (2019, January 31). Retrieved July 28, 2019, from datareportal.com: https://datareportal.com/reports/digital-2019-global-digital-overview

Dauda, S. A., & Mamman, D. (2018). The Contemporary Islamic Banking System (Jaiz Bank) in Tackling Financial Exclusion in Nigeria. *International Journal of Islamic Economics and Finance Studies*, *4*(1), 16.

Davis, F. D. (1989). Perceived Usefulness, Perceived Ease of Use, and User Acceptance of Information Technology. *MIS Quarterly, 13*(3), 319-339.

Davis, F. D. (1989, September). Perceived Usefulness, Perceived Ease of Use, and User Acceptance of Information Technology. *Management Information Systems Quarterly*, *13*(3), 319–340. doi:10.2307/249008

Davis, F. D., Bagozzi, P. R., & Warshaw, P. (1989). User acceptance of computer technology: A comparison of two theoretical models. *Management Science*, *35*(8), 982–1003. doi:10.1287/mnsc.35.8.982

De Mol, L. (2009). Turing Machines. In *Stanford Encyclopedia of Philosophy*. Retrieved from https://plato.stanford.edu/archives/win2018/entries/turing-machine/

Dearing, J., & Jeffery, C. (2018). *Diffusion of Innovations Theory, Principles and Practice*. Retrieved from https://www.researchgate.net/publication/322941167_Diffusion_Of_Innovations_Theory_Principles_And_Practice

Deloitte. (2019). *Chasing Cashless? The Rise of Mobile Wallets in the Nordics*. Retrieved from https://www2.deloitte.com/content/dam/Deloitte/dk/Documents/financial-services/Downloads/Chasing_Cashless-The_rise_of_Mobile_Wallets_in_the_Nordics.pdf

Demirguc-Kunt, A. & Klapper, L. (2012). *Measuring Financial Inclusion: The Global Findex Database*. doi:10.1596/1813-9450-6025

Demirguc-Kunt, A., Klapper, L., Singer, D. & Van Oudheusden, P. (2015). *The Global Findex Database 2014: Measuring Financial Inclusion around the World*. doi:10.1596/1813-9450-7255

Demirgüç-Kunt, A., Klapper, L., Stein, P., Bilandzic, N., Hommes, M., Taylor, S., … Sile, E. (2013). Financial Inclusion in Africa. *African Development Bank (AfDB)*, 74.

Demirgüç-Kunt, A. (2017). *The Global Findex Database 2017*.

Demirguc-Kunt, A., Klapper, L., Singer, D., Ansar, S., & Hess, J. (2018). *The Global Findex Database 2017: Measuring Financial Inclusion and the Fintech Revolution*. Washington, DC: World Bank. doi:10.1596/978-1-4648-1259-0

Dobbie, W., Liberman, A., Paravisini, D., & Pathania, V. (2018). *Measuring Bias in Consumer Lending*. doi:10.3386/w24953

Donner, J., & Tellez, C. A. (2008). Mobile banking and economic development: Linking adoption, impact, and use. *Asian Journal of Communication*, *18*(4), 318–332. doi:10.1080/01292980802344190

dos Santos, P. L., & Harvold Kvangraven, I. (2017). Better than Cash, but Beware the Costs: Electronic Payments Systems and Financial Inclusion in Developing Economies. *Development and Change*, *48*(2), 205–227. doi:10.1111/dech.12296

Du, L. (2019). *Can Mobile Money boost financial inclusion in Southern Africa?* Retrieved from: https://insights.som.yale.edu/insights/

Dusza, B. (2016, December 1). *Liberian Teacher ePayments: Stepping Stones to Inclusion*. Retrieved from: https://www.cgap.org/blog/

Dwoskin, E. (2015), Lending Startups Look at Borrowers' Phone Usage to Assess Creditworthiness. *Wall Street Journal*. Available at https://www.wsj.com/articles/lending-startups-look-at-borrowers-phone-usage-to-assess-creditworthiness-1448933308

Dzokoto, V. A., & Appiah, E. (2012). Making Sense of Mobile Money In *Urban Ghana: Personal, Business, Social And Financial Inclusion Prospects*. Available at https://www.imtfi.uci.edu/files/docs/2014/dzkoto_final_report_feb2014.pdf

Economist Intelligence Unit. (2012). *2011 Government E-Payments Adoption Ranking*. Economist Intelligence Unit Limited. Retrieved from http://graphics.eiu.com/upload/eb/Visapayments.pdf

Eisenberg, A. (2019, March 21). *Ignite*. Retrieved July 28, 2019, from igniteoutsourcing.com: https://igniteoutsourcing.com/fintech/mobile-banking-application-development/

EIU. (2014). *Global Microscope 2014: The Enabling Environment for Financial Inclusion*. The Economist Intelligence Unit.

Eletter, S., Yaseen, S., & Elrefae, G. (2010). Neuro-based artificial intelligence model for loan decisions. *American Journal of Economics and Business Administration*, *2*(1), 27–34. doi:10.3844/ajebasp.2010.27.34

Elhachlouf, M., Guennoun, Z., & Hamza, F. (2012). Stocks portfolio optimization using classification and genetic algorithms. *Applied Mathematical Sciences*, *6*(94), 4673–4684.

Ellison, A., & Forster, R. (2011). *The impact of interest rate ceilings*. London: Policis.

Employment Act Chapter 226 revised Edition. (2007). Available at http://kenyalaw.org/kl/fileadmin/pdfdownloads/Acts/EmploymentAct_Cap226-No11of2007_01.pdf (accessed on 29th June, 2019)

Engau, C., & Hoffmann, V. H. (2011). Strategizing in an unpredictable climate: Exploring corporate strategies to cope with regulatory uncertainty. *Long Range Planning*, *44*(1), 42–63. doi:10.1016/j.lrp.2010.11.003

Erdélyi, O. J., & Goldsmith, J. (2018). *Regulating Artificial Intelligence Proposal for a Global Solution*. Paper presented at the AAAI/ACM Conference on Artificial Intelligence, Ethics and Society.

European Union. (2019). *EU Cash Compendium 2019: Doing More Cash, Better*. Retrieved from https://ec.europa.eu/echo/sites/echo-site/files/eu_cash_compendium_2019.pdf

Fanta, A. B., Mutsonziwa, K., Goosen, R., Emanuel, M., & Kettles, N. (2016). *Policy Research Paper No. 03/2016*. Academic Press.

Farook, S. (2008). Social Responsibility for Islamic Financial Institutions: Laying Down A Framework. *ResearchGate*. Retrieved from https://www.researchgate.net/publication/238073328_Social_Responsibility_for_Islamic_Financial_Institutions_Laying_Down_A_Framework

FATF. (2013). *Guidance for a Risk-Based Approach: Prepaid Cards, Mobile Payments and Internet-Based Payment Services*. Paris: FATF/OECD.

FATF. (2013). *Terrorist Financing in West Africa*. Paris, France: FATF.

FinCo Net. (2017). *Report on the Digitalisation of Short-term, High-Cost Consumer Credit*. Available at http://www.finconet.org/Digtalisation-Short-term-High-cost-Consumer- Credit.pdf

Fine, C. H. (2000). Clockspeed-based strategies for supply chain design. *Production and Operations Management*, *9*(3), 213–221. doi:10.1111/j.1937-5956.2000.tb00134.x

Fishbein, M., & Ajzen, I. (1975). *Belief, Attitude. Intentions and Behavior: An Introduction to Theory and Research*. Boston: Addison-Wesley.

Fisher, C., & Lovell, A. (2008). *Business Ethics and Values: Individual, Corporate and International Perspectives* (3rd ed.). Edinburgh, UK: Prentice Hall.

Fisman, R., & Miguel, E. (2008). *Economic Gangsters: Corruption, Violence, and the Poverty of Nations*. Princeton University Press.

Flatraaker, D. I. (2013). Mobile payments changing the landscape of retail banking: Hype or reality? *Journal of Payments Strategy & Systems*, *7*(2), 150–158.

Frank, B. P., & Binaebi, B. (2019). Electronic Payment Systems Implementation and the Performance of Commercial Banks in Nigeria. *European Journal of Business and Management Research*, *4*(5). doi:10.24018/ejbmr.2019.4.5.112

FSD Kenya. (2015). *One Acre Fund*. Available at https://fsdkenya.org/retail-innovation/linda-jamii/

Gaur, A., & Ondrus, J. (2012). The role of banks in the mobile payment ecosystem: a strategic asset perspective. In *Proceedings of the 14th Annual International Conference on Electronic Commerce*. ACM Press. 10.1145/2346536.2346570

Gefen, D., Benbasat, I., & Pavlou, P. A. (2008, Spring). A Research Agenda for Trust in Online Environments. *Journal of Management Information Systems*, *24*(4), 275–286. doi:10.2753/MIS0742-1222240411

Gefen, D., Karahanna, E., & Straub, D. W. (2003). Trust and TAM in online Shopping: An Integrated Model. *Management Information Systems Quarterly*, *27*(1), 51. doi:10.2307/30036519

Gefen, D., & Straub, D. (2004). Consumer Trust in B2C E-Commerce and the Importance of Social Presence: Experiments in E-Products and E-Services. *Omega. International Journal of Management Sciences*, *32*, 407–424.

Ghanaweb. (2019, April 1). Retrieved July 20, 2019, from ghanaweb.com: https://www.ghanaweb.com/GhanaHomePage/business/Fight-against-money-laundering-must-focus-on-mobile-money-GIABA-734744#

Giang, H. (2005). Using neural network in predicting corporate failure. *Journals of Social Science*, *1*, 199–202.

Gichuki, E. N. (2013). *Law of financial institutions in Kenya* (2nd ed.). Nairobi: LawAfrica Publishers.

Gichure, W. C. (1997). *Basic concepts in ethics: with an outline of different methods in contemporary moral philosophy*. Nairobi: Focus Publications.

Gideon, Z., & Alouis, M. (2013). Systems, processes and challenges of public revenue collection in Zimbabwe. *American International Journal of Contemporary Research, 2*, 49–60.

Giffin, K. (1967). The Contribution of Studies of Source Credibility to a Theory of Interpersonal Trust in the Communication Process. *Psychological Bulletin, 68*(2), 104–120. doi:10.1037/h0024833 PMID:6065581

Gloukoviezoff, G. (1999). *The Casse D'epargne and Households Financial Exclusion – Which Actions Should Be Taken and What Are the Prospects*. Retrieved from www.ishlyon.cnrs.fr

Gnangnon, S. K., & Brun, J.-F. (2018). Impact of bridging the Internet gap on public revenue mobilization. *Information Economics and Policy, 43*, 23–33. doi:10.1016/j.infoecopol.2018.04.001

Godinho, V. & Singh, S. (2013). Technology Enabled Financial Inclusion and Evidence-Based Policy for the Underbanked: A study of Remote Indigenous Australia. *Social Science Research Network*, 15.

Goland, T., Bays, J. & Chaia, A. (2010). Global Financial Inclusion. *McKinsey & Company's Social Sector*, 44.

Gomez, R. (1999). *What's right and wrong in business? A primer on business ethics*. Manila: Sinag-tala Publishing.

Goodwin, D., Adelman, L., Middleton, S. & Ashworth, K. (1999). *Debt, Money Management and Access to Financial Services: Evidence from the 1999 PSE Survey of Britain*. Academic Press.

Graeff, P. (2005). Why should one trust in corruption? The linkage between corruption, trust, norms, and social capital. In J. Graf Lambsdorff, M. Taube, & M. Schramm (Eds.), *The New Institutional Economics of Corruption* (pp. 21–42). London: Routledge.

GSM Association (GSMA). (2007). *Regulatory Framework for Mobile Money Transfers*. Retrieved from http://www.mobilemoneyexchange.org/Files/8e31752b (accessed on 1st July ,2019)

GSM Association (GSMA). (2008b). *Outlook for Mobile Wallets and Mobile Financial Services: Results of EDC–GSMA Mobil Financial Services Survey 2007*. Retrieved from http://www.gsmworld.com/mmu/mmu_quarterly_update.pdf

GSMA Connected Women, . (2017). *The mobile Economy. Sub-Saharan Africa*. GSMA.

GSMA Connected Women. (2019). *Women and Mobile Money; Insights from Kenya GSMA Intelligence modelled estimates as in GSMA Connected Women, Mobile Gender Gap Report 2019*. Retrieved from http://www.nber.org/papers/w16721.pdf

GSMA. (2009). *Mitigating the Risks that Accompany Mobile Money*. Mobile money for the unbanked: Quarterly update 1. GSMA.

GSMA. (2014). *The Mobile Economy 2014*. London, UK: GSMA.

GSMA. (2015). *GSMA Mobile Economy 2015*. Retrieved from GSMA Organisation website: http://www.gsma.com/mobileeconomy/global/2015/

GSMA. (2016). *The Impact of Mobile Money Interoperability in Tanzania: Early data and market perspectives on account-to-account interoperability*. GSM Association.

GSMA. (2017). *Licensing Mobile Money Remittance Providers: Early Lessons*. GSM Association. Retrieved from https://www.gsma.com/mobilefordevelopment/wp-content/uploads/2017/02/GSMA_Licensing-mobile-money-remittance-providers_Early-lessons-1.pdf

GSMA. (2017). Person-to-government (P2G) payment digitisation: Lessons from Kenya. London: GSMA Association.

GSMA. (2018). *Beyond the basics: How Smartphones will drive future opportunities for the mobile money industry*. London, UK: GSMA Mobile Money. Retrieved from http://siteresources.worldbank.org/AFRICAEXT/Resources/258643-1271798012256/YAC_chpt_20.pdf

GSMA. (2018). *The Mobile Economy Sub-Saharan Africa 2018*. London: GSMA Association.

GSMA. (2018a). *Mobile Money Competing with Informal Channels to Accelerate the Digitisation of Remittances*. GSM Association. Retrieved from https://www.gsma.com/mobilefordevelopment/programme/mobile-money/competing-with-informal-channels-to-accelerate-the-digitisation-of-remittances

GSMA. (2018b). *Mobile Money Interoperability in Bolivia: A case study for Latin America*. GSM Association. Retrieved from https://www.gsma.com/mobilefordevelopment/programme/mobile-money/mobile-money-interoperability-in-bolivia-a-case-study-for-latin-america

GSMA. (2019a). *Mobile Money enabled Cash aid Delivery: Essential Considerations for Humanitarian Practitioners*. GSM Association. Retrieved from http://www.cashlearning.org/downloads/essentialconsiderationsforusingmobilemoney.pdf

GSMA. (2019b). *State of the Industry Report on Mobile Money 2018*. London: GSM Association. doi:10.1002/9781118290743.wbiedcs023

GSMA. (2019c). *The Mobile Economy 2019*. GSM Association. Retrieved from https://www.gsma.com/r/mobileeconomy/

Gubbins, P., & Totolo, E. (2018). *Digital credit in Kenya: Evidence from demand-side surveys*. Nairobi, Kenya: FSD Kenya. Available at https://s3-eu-central-1.amazonaws.com/fsd- circle/wp-content/uploads/2018/10/18162055/Digital-Credit-in-Kenya.pdf (accessed on 1st July ,2019)

Gu, J.-C., Lee, S.-C., & Suh, Y.-H. (2009). Determinants of behavioral intention to mobile banking. *Expert Systems with Applications*, *36*(9), 11605–11616. doi:10.1016/j.eswa.2009.03.024

Guo, Z., Kauffman, R. J., Lin, M. & Ma, D. (2015). *Near Real-Time Retail Payment and Settlement Systems Mechanism Design*. Academic Press.

Haggblade, S., Hazell, P., & Reardon, T. (2007). *Transforming the Rural Nonfarm Economy: Opportunities and Threats in the Developing World.* Baltimore, MD: Johns Hopkins University Press.

Hair, J. F., Black, W. C., Babin, B. J., & Anderson, R. E. (2015). *Multivariate Data Analysis* (7th ed.). Noida, India: Pearson Education Limited.

HannaK. E. (1991). *Biomedical Politics*. doi:10.17226/1793

Hansen, T., Jensen, J. M., & Solgaard, H. S. (2004). Predicting online grocery buying intention: A comparison of the theory of reasoned action and the theory of planned behavior. *International Journal of Information Management, 24*(6), 539–550. doi:10.1016/j.ijinfomgt.2004.08.004

Heavey, C., & Simsek, Z. (2013). Top management compositional effects on corporate entrepreneurship: The moderating role of perceived technological uncertainty. *Journal of Product Innovation Management, 30*(5), 837–855. doi:10.1111/jpim.12033

Holden, W. (2012a). *Press Release: Mobile Payments to Reach $1.3tn Annually by 2017, as NFC and Physical Goods Sales Accelerate*. Academic Press.

Honohan, P. (2008). Cross-Country Variation in Household Access to Financial Services. *Journal of Banking & Finance, 32*(1), 2493–2500. doi:10.1016/j.jbankfin.2008.05.004

Hope, K. R. (1999). Corruption in Africa: A crisis in ethical leadership. *Public Integrity*, 289-308. Retrieved from https://www.researchgate.net/publication/273944947_Corruption_in_Africa_A_Crisis_in_Ethical_Leadership

Howell, N. (2005). Financial Exclusion and Microfinance: An Overview of the Issues, Opportunity Knocks. *Microfinance as Pathway to Financial and Social Exclusion., 27*, 2.

Huang, W. (2004). Forecasting foreign exchange rates with artificial neural networks: A review. *International Journal of Information Technology, 3*, 145-165.

Hulme, D., & Mosley, P. (1996). Finance Against Poverty: Volume 2: Country Case Studies. Taylor & Francis.

Hung, S.-Y., Chang, C.-M., & Yu, T.-J. (2006). Determinants of user acceptance of the e-Government services: The case of online tax filing and payment system. *Government Information Quarterly, 23*(1), 97–122. doi:10.1016/j.giq.2005.11.005

Hursthouse, R. (1990). After Hume's Justice. *Proceedings of the Aristotelian Society, 91*, 229–245.

Hurwitz, I., & Luiz, J. (2007, March). Urban Working Class Credit Usage and over-Indebtedness in South Africa. *Journal of Southern African Studies, 33*(1), 107–131. (accessed on 1st July ,2019) doi:10.1080/03057070601136616

Ibrahim. (2015a). The Impact of Influencing factors on Adoption of Mobile Banking in Pakistan. *MAGNT Research Report, 3*(4), 97-109.

Ibrahim. (2015b). Determining the Effect of Innovations for Mobile Banking Adoption in Pakistan. *Journal of Information Engineering and Applications*, *5*(11), 16–23.

Ibrahim. (2015c). Impact of Risk and Ethics on Adoption of Mobile Banking in Pakistan. *Journal of Economics and Sustainable Development, 6*(7).

IFAD. (2017). Sending Money Home: Contributing to the SDGs, One Family at a Time. *International Development Fund for Agricultural*, 60. Retrieved from https://www.ifad.org/documents/38714170/39135645/Sending+Money+Home+-+Contributing+to+the+SDGs%2C+one+family+at+a+time.pdf/c207b5f1-9fef-4877-9315-75463fccfaa7

IFC-WB. (2011). *M-Money Channel Distribution Case – Afghanistan Roshan M-Paisa.* Available at http://documents.worldbank.org/curated/en/123191500276218363/M-money-channel-distribution-case-Afghanistan-Roshan-m-paisa (accessed on 3rd July ,2019)

ILO & ILOSTAT. (2015). 2 ILO: Working in the rural areas in the 21st century: Reality and prospects of rural employment in Latin America and the Caribbean, Regional Office for Latin America and the Caribbean (Geneva, Thematic Labour Overview No. 3, 2017). ILO.

ILO. (2016). *Decent work for food security and resilient rural livelihoods, Portfolio of policy guidance notes on the promotion of decent work in the rural economy*. Geneva: Sectoral Policies Department.

ILO. (2016). World Employment Social Outlook 2016: Transforming jobs to end poverty. ILO.

International Finance Corporation. (2017). *Financial inclusion. Creating opportunity through Financial services in South Asia*. Author.

International Financial Consumer Protection Organisation (FinCoNet). (2017). *Report on the Digitalisation of Short-term, High-Cost Consumer Credit*. Author.

International Monetary Fund. (2014). *Kenya at the Economic Frontier: Challenges and Opportunities*. Retrieved from https://www.imf.org/en/News/Articles/2015/09/28/04/53/sp010614 on 04/04/2019

International Telecommunication Union. (2014). *The world telecommunication/ICT indicators database*. Retrieved from http://www.itu.int/en/ITU-D/Statistics/Pages/publications/wtid.aspx

Isaac Akomea-Frimpong, C. A.-F.-O. (2018). Control of fraud on mobile moneyservices in Ghana: anexploratory study. *Journal of Money Laundering Control*, 20-39.

Izaguirre, J. C., & Mazer, R. (2018). *How Regulators Can Foster More Responsible Digital Credit*. Available at https://www.cgap.org/blog/how-regulators-can-foster-more-responsible-digital-credit

Jack, W., & Suri, T. (2011, January). *Mobile Money: The Economics of M-pesa*. Retrieved October 15, 2019, from Georgetown University: http://faculty.georgetown.edu/wgj/papers/Jack_Suri-Economics-of-M-PESA.pdf

Jack, W., & Suri, T. (2011). *Mobile money: The economics of M-PESA*. Cambridge, UK: National Bureau of Economic Research. doi:10.3386/w16721

Jain, A., Zubenko, O. & Carotenuto, G. (2012). A Progressive Approach to Financial Inclusion. *MasterCard, Global Insights*, 87.

Jain, A., Zubenko, O. & Carotenuto, G. (2014). A Progressive Approach to Financial Inclusion. *Global Insights, Mastercard*, 17.

James. (2014). *The Risk Sharing Benefits of Mobile Money*. Working Paper, January 2011.

Jatau, V. S., & Dung, K. L. (2014). The Central Bank of Nigeria's cashless policy: A major panacea for eliminating corruption and enhancing sustainable development in Nigeria. *African Research Review*, *8*(4), 198–206. doi:10.4314/afrrev.v8i4.16

Jenkins, B. (2008). Developing Mobile Money Ecosystems. International Finance Corporation and Harvard Kennedy School, 36.

Jennifer Frydrych, C. S. (2015). *Paying school fees with mobile money in Côte d'Ivoire: A public-private partnership to achieve greater efficiency*. Abidjan: GSMA.

Jensen, M. C., & Meckling, W. H. (1976). Theory of the Firm: Managerial Behavior. *Journal of Financial Economics*, *3*(4), 305–360. doi:10.1016/0304-405X(76)90026-X

Jeong, B.-K., & Yoon, T. E. (2013, January). An Empirical Investigation on Consumer Acceptance of Mobile Banking Services. *Business and Management Research*, *2*(1), 31–40. doi:10.5430/bmr.v2n1p31

Johnson, V. L., Kiser, A., Washington, R., & Torres, R. (2018). Limitations to the rapid adoption of M-payment services: Understanding the impact of privacy risk on M- Payment services. *Computers in Human Behavior*, *79*, 111–122. doi:10.1016/j.chb.2017.10.035

Juniper Research. (2018, February 28). Retrieved July 28, 2019, from juniperresearch.com: https://www.juniperresearch.com/press/press-releases/digital-banking-users-to-reach-2-billion

Kaffenberger & Chege. (2016). *Digital Credit in Kenya: Time for Celebration or Concern?* Available at https://www.cgap.org/blog/digital-credit-kenya-time-celebration-or-concern

Kaffenberger, M., & Braniff, L. (2016). *Paying for School: 6 Insights for Better Financial Services*. Retrieved from: https://www.cgap.org/blog/

Kaffenberger, M., & Chege, P. (2016). *Digital Credit in Kenya: Time for Celebration or Concern?* Available at https://www.cgap.org/blog/digital-credit-kenya-time-celebration-or-concern (accessed on 1st July ,2019)

Kang, D. & Park, Y. (2014). Review-based measurement of customer satisfaction in mobile service: Sentiment analysis and VIKOR approach. *Expert Systems with Applications*, *41*(4), 1041–1050.

Karahanna, E., Agarwal, R., & Angst, C. M. (2006). Reconceptualizing Compatibility Beliefs in Technology Acceptance Research. *Management Information Systems Quarterly*, *30*(4), 781–804. doi:10.2307/25148754

Kavitha, K. (2016). Clustering loan applicants based on risk percentage using K-means clustering techniques. *International Journal of Advanced Research in Computer Science and Software Engineering*, *6*(2), 162–166.

Kaya, O. (2019) Artificial intelligence in banking a lever for profitability with limited implementation to date. *EU Monitor Global financial markets.* Retrieved from https://www.dbresearch.com/PROD/RPS_EN-PROD/PROD0000000000495172/Artificial_intelligence_in_banking%3A_A_lever_for_pr.pdf

KCB Bank. (2015). *KCB Bank Financial Reports 2015*. Available at https://kcbgroup.com/wp-content/uploads/2019/05/KCB-Group-Integrated-Report-and-Financial-Statements- 2018.pdf

Kempson, E., McKay, S., & Collard, S. (2005). Incentives to Save: Encouraging Saving Among Low-Income Households. University of Bristol.

Kempson, E. (2001). Bank Exclusion in the United Kingdom. *Jon Carpenter Publishing*.

Kempson, E., & Whyley, C. (1999). *Kept Out or Opted Out? Understanding and Combating Financial Exclusion*. Bristol, UK: Policy Press.

Kenya Bureau of Statistics. (2018). *Economic Survey*. Retrieved from https://www.knbs.or.ke/download/economic-survey-2018/

Kersop, M. (2016). Anti-money laundering regulations and the effective use of mobile money in South Africa - Part 1. *P.E.R.*, 205.

Kesharwani, A., & Bisht, S. S. (2012). The impact of trust and perceived risk on internet banking adoption in India. *International Journal of Bank Marketing*, *30*(4), 303–322. doi:10.1108/02652321211236923

Khan. (2012). Analysis of Consumer Perception towards Telecommunication Services. *Journal of Social and Development Sciences, 3*(3), 89-98.

Khan. (2014). Convergence of Broadcasting and Telecommunication Technology Regulatory Framework in Pakistan. *International Journal of Management and Commerce Innovations, 2*(1), 35-43.

Khandani, A. E., Kim, A. J., & Lo, A. W. (2010). Consumer credit-risk models via machine-learning algorithms MIT Sloan School of Management and Laboratory for Financial Engineering, United States. *Journal of Banking & Finance*, *34*, 2767–2787. doi:10.1016/j.jbankfin.2010.06.001

Killian, D., Kabanda, S., & Kilian, D. (2017, July). Mobile Payments In South Africa: Middle Income Earners' Perspective. In PACIS (p. 53). Academic Press.

Kim, K., & Prabhakar, B. (2000). Initial Trust, Perceived Risk, and the Adoption of Internet Banking. *Proceedings of the 21st International Conference on Information Systems*.

Kimutai, V. (2018, July 22). Mulot, the unlikely hotbed of rising mobile telephone fraud. *Daily Nation*.

Kirui Oliver, K. (2013). Impact of Mobile Phone-Based Money Transfer Services in Agriculture: Evidence from Kenya. *Quarterly Journal of International Agriculture, 52*(2), 141-162.

Kirui, O. K., Okello, J., Nyikal, R. A., & Njiraini, G. W. (2013). Impact of Mobile Phone-Based Money Transfer Services in Agriculture: Evidence from Kenya. *Quarterly Journal of International Agriculture, 52*(2), 141-162.

Klapper, L., & Singer, D. (2014). *The Opportunities of Digitizing Payments* (Working Paper). Washington, DC: The World Bank.

Koenig-Lewis, N., Palmer, A., & Moll, A. (2010). Predicting young consumers' take up of mobile banking Services. *International Journal of Bank Marketing*, *28*(5), 410–432. doi:10.1108/02652321011064917

Kostov, P., Arun, T. G. & Annim, S. K. (2014). *Financial Services to the Unbanked: The case of the Mzansi intervention in South Africa*. doi:10.5709/ce.1897-9254.140

Kotha, S., Rajgopal, S., & Venkatachalam, M. (2004, April). The Role of Online Buying Experience as a Competitive Advantage: Evidence from Third-Party Ratings for E-Commerce Firms. *The Journal of Business*, *77*(S2), S109–S133. doi:10.1086/381639

Krishna, Krishna, & Vijay. (2012). Indian Banking Industry: Challenges and Opportunities. February 2012. *Global Business and Management Research: An International Journal*, *3*(1), 18–28.

Krolikowski, A. (2014). Can mobile-enabled payment methods reduce petty corruption in urban water provision? *Water Alternatives*, *7*(1).

Kucukuysal, B., & Beyhan, E. (2011). Virtue ethics in Aristotle's Nicomachean ethics. *International Journal of Human Sciences*, 44-51.

Laukkanen, T., & Pasanen, M. (2008). Mobile banking innovators and early adopters: How they differ from other online users? *Journal of Financial Services Marketing*, *13*(2), 86–94. doi:10.1057/palgrave.fsm.4760077

Lauren Braniff, S. (2016). *Delivering on Education for All: The Role of Mobile Money*. Retrieved from: https://www.cgap.org/blog/

Lee, B. C., Cho, J., & Hwang, D. (2013, July). An integration of social capital and tourism technology adoption—A case of convention and visitors bureaus. *Tourism and Hospitality Research, 13*(3), 149–165. doi:10.1177/1467358414522055

Lee, Y. K., Park, J. H., Chung, N., & Blakeney, A. (2012). A unified perspective on the factors influencing usage intention toward mobile financial services. *Journal of Business Research*, *65*(11), 1590–1599. doi:10.1016/j.jbusres.2011.02.044

Leo, O. C., & Patrick, B. E. (2010). Analysis of Corruption from the Ethical and Moral Perspectives. *European Journal of Scientific Research*, *44*(3), 466–476.

Leyshon, A., & Thrift, N. (1996). Financial Exclusion and the Shifting Boundaries of the Financial System. *Environment & Planning*, *28*(7), 1150–1156. doi:10.1068/a281150

Leznicki, M. (2014). *Cashless Education: How mobile money helps Bridge International Academies deliver quality for-profit education for $6 a month – Part 5 in our Digital Finance Plus series.* Retrieved from: https://nextbillion.net/cashless-education/

Lian, J. W. (2015). Critical factors for cloud-based e-invoice service adoption in Taiwan: An empirical study. *International Journal of Information Management*, *35*(1), 98–109. doi:10.1016/j.ijinfomgt.2014.10.005

Lie ́bana-Cabanillas, F., Mun ̃oz-Leiva, F., & Sa ́nchez-Ferna ́ndez, J. (2013). The impact of risk on the technological acceptance of mobile payment services. *Global Business Perspectives*, *1*(4), 309–328. doi:10.100740196-013-0020-9

Lie ́bana-Cabanillas, F., Ramos de Luna, I., & Montoro-Rı ́os, F. J. (2015). User behaviour in QR mobile payment system: The QR Payment acceptance model. *Technology Analysis and Strategic Management*, *27*(9), 1031–1049. doi:10.1080/09537325.2015.1047757

Liebana-Cabanillas, F., Munoz-Leiva, F., & Sanchez-Fernandez, J. (2018). A global approach to the analysis of user behaviour in mobile payment systems in the new electronic environment. *Service Business*, *12*(1), 25–64. doi:10.100711628-017-0336-7

Liébana-Cabanillas, F., Sánchez-Fernández, J., & Muñoz-Leiva, F. (2014). Antecedents of the adoption of the new mobile payment systems: The moderating effect of age. *Computers in Human Behavior*, *35*, 464–478. doi:10.1016/j.chb.2014.03.022

Liébana-Cabanillas, F., Sánchez-Fernández, J., & Munoz-Leiva, F. (2014). The moderating effect of experience in the adoption of mobilepayment tools in Virtual Social Networks: The m-Payment Acceptance Model in Virtual Social Networks (MPAM-VSN). *International Journal of Information Management*, *34*(2), 151–166. doi:10.1016/j.ijinfomgt.2013.12.006

Limsombunchai, V., Gan, C., & Lee, M. (2005). An analysis of credit scoring for agricultural loans in Thailand. *American Journal of Applied Sciences*, *2*(8), 1198–1205. doi:10.3844/ajassp.2005.1198.1205

Lin, C.-H., Shih, H.-Y., & Sher, P. J. (2007). Integrating technology readiness into technology acceptance: The TRAM model. *Psychology and Marketing*, *24*(7), 641–657. doi:10.1002/mar.20177

Lin, H.-F. (2011). An empirical investigation of mobile banking adoption: The effect of innovation attributes and knowledge-based trust. *International Journal of Information Management*, *31*(3), 252–260. doi:10.1016/j.ijinfomgt.2010.07.006

Luarn, P., & Lin, H.-H. (2005). Toward an understanding of the behavioral intention to use mobile banking. *Computers in Human Behavior*, *21*(6), 873–891. doi:10.1016/j.chb.2004.03.003

Lu, J., Yu, C. S., Liu, C., & Yao, J. E. (2003). Technology acceptance model for wireless internet. *Electronic Networking Applications and Policy*, *13*(3), 206–222. doi:10.1108/10662240310478222

Luminzu. (n.d.). *Fraud in Mobile Financial Services*. Available at https://www.microsave.net/files/pdf/RP151_Fraud_in_Mobile_Financial_Services_JMud iri.pdf

Lu, Y., Yang, S., Chau, P. Y., & Cao, Y. (2011). Dynamics between the trust transfer process and intention to use mobile payment services: A cross-environment perspective. *Information & Management*, *48*(8), 393–403. doi:10.1016/j.im.2011.09.006

Lwin, K. T., Qu, R., & MacCarthy, B. L. (2017). Mean-VaR portfolio optimization: A nonparametric approach. *European Journal of Operational Research*, *260*(2), 751–766. doi:10.1016/j.ejor.2017.01.005

Lyman, T., Porteous, D., & Pickens, M. (2008). Regulating Transformational Branchless Banking: Mobile Phones and Other Technology to Increase Access to Finance. In *Focus Note 43*. Washington, DC: CGAP.

Maisiba, G. J., & Atambo, W. (2016). Effects of the electronic-tax system on the revenue collection efficiency of Kenya Revenue Authority: A case of Uasin Gishu County. *Imperial Journal of Interdisciplinary Research*, *2*(4), 2454–1362.

Makena, P. M. (2019). *Kenya Mobile report.* Retrieved from: https://www.jumia.co.ke/mobile-report/

Malhotra, R., & Malhotra, D. K. (2003). Evaluating consumer loans using neural networks. *Omega*, *31*(2), 83–96. doi:10.1016/S0305-0483(03)00016-1

Mallat, N., & Tuunainen, V. K. (2008). Exploring Merchant Adoption of Mobile Payment Systems: An Empirical Study. *e-Service Journal*, *6*(2), 24–57. doi:10.2979/esj.2008.6.2.24

Mann, B. J. S., & Sahni, S. K. (2013). Role of trust and customer loyalty in reducing perceived security risk in internet banking. *International Journal of Electronic Business*, *10*(4), 331–354. doi:10.1504/IJEB.2013.056783

Marina Solin, A. Z. (2010). *Mobile Money: Methodology for Assessing Money Laundering and Terrorist Financing Risks*. Barcelona: GSMA.

Marque, A., Garci, V., & Nchez, J. (2013). A literature review on the application of evolutionary computing to credit scoring. *The Journal of the Operational Research Society*, *201364*(9), 1384–1399. doi:10.1057/jors.2012.145

Martin, D. (2002). *Pentecostalism: The World Their Parish.* Oxford, UK: Blackwell.

Martins, C., Oliveira, T., & Popovič, A. (2014). Understanding the Internet banking adoption: A unified theory of acceptance and use of technology and perceived risk application. *International Journal of Information Management*, *34*(1), 1–13. doi:10.1016/j.ijinfomgt.2013.06.002

Masinde, J. (2017, March 6). *US State Dept thinks Africa's leading mobile money platform is vulnerable to money laundering*. Retrieved October 16, 2019, from Quartz: https://qz.com/africa/924977/us-state-dept-thinks-africas-leading-mobile-money- platform-is-vulnerable-to-money-laundering/

Mastercard and Prime Research. (2014). *13 Million social media conversations show what consumers think about mobile payments*. Retrieved from http://newsroom.mastercard.com

Matteo Chiampo, J. (2018). *How Bangladesh Digitized Education Aid for 10 Million Families*. Retrieved from: https://www.cgap.org/blog/

Mattern Max. (2017). *How Ghana Became One of Africa's Top Mobile Money Markets*. Available at https://www.cgap.org/blog/how-ghana-became-one-africas-top-mobile-money-markets

Maurer, B. (2012a). Mobile Money: Communication, Consumption and Change in the Payments Space. *The Journal of Development Studies*, *48*(5), 589–604. doi:10.1080/00220388.2011.621944

Maurer, B. (2012b). Regulation as Retrospective Ethnography: Mobile Money and the Arts of Cash. *Banking and Finance Law Review*, *27*(2), 299–313.

Mazer, R. (2018, April 4). Retrieved October 2017, 2019, from Consultative Group to Assist the Poor: https://www.cgap.org/blog/kenyas-rules-mobile-money-price-transparency-are-paying

Mazer, R., & Nitin, G. (2015, December). *Recourse in Digital Financial Services*. Retrieved October 18, 2019, from Consultative Group to Assist the Poor: https://www.cgap.org/sites/default/files/researches/documents/Brief-Recourse-in-Digital-Financial-Services-Dec-2015

Mazer, R., & Rowan, P. (2014). *Competition in Mobile Financial Services in Kenya*. Draft Brief Prepared by CGAP for Competition Authority of Kenya.

Mbiti, I., & Weil, D. N. (2011). *Mobile banking: The impact of M-Pesa in Kenya (No. w17129)*. National Bureau of Economic Research. doi:10.3386/w17129

Meet 40 Inspiring Women Entrepreneurs Putting the Country on the Global Business Map. (n.d.). *The Lionesses of Africa*. Available at: http://www.lionessesofafrica.com/blog/2017/6/27/meet-40-kenyan-women-entrepreneurs-putting-the-country-on-the-global-business-map

Mellor, M. (2010). *The Future of Money*. Retrieved from www.plutobooks.com

Merritt, C. (2010). *Mobile Money Transfer Services: The Next Phase in the Evolution in Person-to-Person Payments*. Retail Payments Risk Forum White Paper. Federal Reserve Bank of Atlanta.

Metawa, N., Hassan, M. K., & Elhoseny, M. (2017). Hassan, Mohamed Elhoseny Genetic Algorithm Based Model for Optimizing Bank Lending Decisions. *Expert Systems with Applications*, *80*, 75–82. doi:10.1016/j.eswa.2017.03.021

Meyer, J. (2013, June 17). *How mobile payments might be the global money-laundering machine criminals have dreamed about*. Retrieved October 17, 2019, from Quartz: https://qz.com/94570/how-mobile-payments-might-be-the-global-money-laundering- machine- criminals-have-dreamed-about/

Miller, H. (2013). *Interest rate caps and their impact on financial inclusion. Economic and Private Sector*. Professional Evidence and Applied Knowledge Services.

Mirfin, J. (2019, February 11). *Refinitiv*. Retrieved July 20, 2019, from refinitiv.com: https://www.refinitiv.com/perspectives/financial-crime/combating-payments-related-financial-crime/

Mitchell & Pavur. (2002). Using modular neural networks for business decisions. *Manage., 40*, 58-63. Doi:10.1108/00251740210413361

MKOPA. (2015). *Affordable, clean energy: a pathway to new consumer choices; Lessons from M-KOPA's first three years of innovative energy service*. Retrieved from http://www.m-kopa.com/wp-content/uploads/2015/10/Lightbulb-series_Paper-1-2.pd

MKOPA. (2017). *MKOPA Solar and Safaricom Launch MKOPA III*. Available at: http://www.m-kopa.com/m-kopa-solar-and-safaricom-launch-m-kopa-iii/

Mohamed Ahmed. (2019). *Star footballer who ditched it all for life as a Al- Shabaab agent*. Available at https://www.nation.co.ke/news/Star-footballer-who-ditched-it-all-for-life-as-a-Shabaab-agent/1056-5300146-kvvvqu/index.html

Mohammed, H. A., & Tafti, E. N. (1993). Neural Networks and Expert Systems: New Horizons in Business Finance Applications. *Information Management & Computer Security*.

Mohan, R. (2006). Economic Growth, Financial Deepening and Financial Inclusion. *Inclusive Growth – A New Challenge, 113*, 18. Retrieved from https://www.bis.org/review/r061121e.pdf

Molloy, D., & Snape, D. (1999). *Financial Arrangements of Couples on Benefit: A Review of the Literature*. London, UK: Department of Social Security, Social Research Branch.

Moody Investors Services. (2019). *Banks lose out on revenue to mobile money*. Retrieved from https://www.the-star.co.ke/business/kenya/2019-04-20-banks-lose-out-on-revenue-to-mobile-money/

Moore, G. C., & Benbasat, I. (1991, September). Development of an Instrument to Measure the Perceptions of Adopting an Information Technology Innovation. *Information Systems Research, 2*(3), 192–222. doi:10.1287/isre.2.3.192

Mugambi, F. K., & Wanjohi, J. M. (2018). Factors affecting the implementation of Revenue Collection Systems in county governments in Kenya, A case of Meru county. *International Journal For Research In Business, Management And Accounting, 4*(8), 9-30.

Mugo, M. & Kilonzo, E. (2017). *Community – Level Impacts of Financial Inclusion in Kenya with Particular Focus on Poverty Eradication and Employment Creation*. Academic Press.

Muhammad, T., Dauda, S. A., & Mamman, D. (2018). The Contemporary Islamic Banking System (Jaiz Bank) in Tackling Financial Exclusion in Nigeria. *Uluslararası İslam Ekonomisi ve Finansı Araştırmaları Dergisi*, *4*(1), 24–40. doi:10.25272/j.2149-8407.2018.4.1.02

Muiruri, J., & Ngugi, J. (2014). The effects of financial innovation on the financial performance of commercial banks in Kenya. *International Journal of Humanities and Social Science*, *4*(7), 51–57.

Munda, C. (2019, Jan 24). *Business Daily Africa*. Retrieved July 07, 2019, from businessdailyafrica.com: https://www.businessdailyafrica.com/economy/Sh4trn-mobile-phone-deals-move-half-Kenyas-GDP/3946234-4948816-tg94g1/index.html

Muriu, M. D. (2016). Strategy Implementation and Performance of Mobile-Commerce in Kenya's Commercial Banks. United States International University - Africa.

Museve, R. K. (2014, April). *The Legal Implications of Mobile Money Transfer Services to the Economy in Kenya: The Need for Regulatory Reform*. Nairobi, Kenya: University of Nairobi.

Muthiora, B. (2015). *Enabling Mobile Money Policies in Kenya: Fostering a Digital Financial Revolution*. GSMA Mobile Money for the Unbanked. Available.

Nazari, M., & Alidadi, M. (2013). Measuring credit risk of bank customers using artificial neural network. *Journal of Management Research*, *5*(2), 17–27. doi:10.5296/jmr.v5i2.2899

Ndahiro, R. (2017). *Digital Financial Services can reduce worries on how to pay school fees*. Retrieved from: https://www.uncdf.org/article/

Ndiaye, O. K. (2014). Is the success of M-Pesa empowering Kenyan rural women? *Feminist Africa*, *18*, 156–161.

Nduku, E., & Tenamwenye, J. (2014). *Corruption in Africa: A Threat to Justice and Sustainable Peace* (Vol. 14). Focus. Retrieved from https://www.amazon.com/Corruption-Africa-Threat-Justice-Sustainable/dp/2889310175

Newman & McNally. (n.d.). *Identity Theft Literature Review*. U.S. Department of Justice Document No.: 210459. Available at https://www.ncjrs.gov/pdffiles1/nij/grants/210459.pdf

Ng'ethe, V. (2018). *How many young Kenyans are unemployed? A look at the numbers*. Retrieved from https://africacheck.org/2018/10/08/analysis-how-many-young-kenyans-are-unemployed-a-look-at-the-numbers/

Ngugi, B., Kamis, A., & Tremaine, M. (2011, Summer). Intention to Use Biometric Systems. *e-Service Journal*, *7*(3), 20-46.

Njeri, W. (2018). *Digital Payments in Zimbabwe Removing the Hassle from School Fees Payments*. Retrieved from: https://cellulant.com/blog/

Njeru, G. (2018). *Relationship between financial innovations and inclusion among the Commercial banks in Kenya*. University of Nairobi.

Nupur, A. (2019). *Will It Backfire? Why Indian lenders are giving loans to risky customers with low credit scores*. Available at https://qz.com/india/1641387/indian-banks-nbfcs-fintech-firms-are-looking-over-cibil- scores

Nyathira, N. (2012). *Financial innovation and its effect on financial performance of commercial Banks in Kenya*. University of Nairobi.

Nzayisenga, A. (2017). *Effect of Mobile Lending on the Financial Performance of Commercial Banks in Kenya*. Nairobi: University of Nairobi.

Obaidullah, M., & Latif, A. (2007). Enhancing Islamic Financial Services for Micro and Medium sized Enterprises. *Conference Proceedings*. Presented at the First International Conference on Inclusive Islamic Financial Sector Development, Negara, Brunei.

Ochenge, R., & Tiriongo, S. (2018). Gapss from the Cap: Implications for Financial Inclusion in Kenya. *KBA Centre for Research on Financial Markets and Policy Working Paper Series 23.*

OECD. (2019). *Money Laundering and Terrorist Financing Awareness Handbook for Tax Examiners and Tax Auditors*. OECD. Retrieved from www.oecd.org/tax/crime/money-laundering-and-terrorist-financing-awareness-handbook-for-tax-examiners-and-tax-auditors.pdf

Office of Fair Trading. (2013). *Payday Lending Consultation on a market investigation reference*. Available at https://assets.publishing.service.gov.uk/media/532ad541e5274a226800039f/oft1482.pdf

Ogedebe, P.M. & Jacob, B.P. (2012). E-Payment: Prospects and Challenges in Nigerian Public Sector. *International Journal of Modern Engineering Research, 2*(5), 3104-3106.

Ojijo, P. (2014). *26 Legal Issues in Mobile Money Transactions*. Kampala: LawPronto Limited. Paul Francis (06/05/17) Mobile App Development Process BHW Group. Available at https://thebhwgroup.com/blog/mobile-app-development-process

Ojong, C. M., Anthony, O., & Arikpo, O. F. (2016). The impact of tax revenue on economic growth: Evidence from Nigeria. IOSR. *Journal of Economics and Finance*, *7*(1), 32–38.

Okifo, J., & Igbunu, R. (2015). Electronic Payment System in Nigeria: Its Economic Benefits and Challenges. *Journal of Education and Practice*, *6*(16).

Okuttah, M. (2011). *PesaPal launches school fees payment platform.* Retrieved from: https://www.businessdailyafrica.com/magazines/

Oladeji, K. (2014). *Integrated Personnel and Payroll Information Systems (IPPIS) for Universities and other Higher Institutions of Learning. A Paper Presentation at Northwest University*, Kano, Nigeria.

Oliveira, T., Faria, M., Thomas, M. A., & Popovič, A. (2014). Extending the understanding of mobile banking adoption: When UTAUT meets TTF and ITM. *International Journal of Information Management, 34*(5), 689–703. doi:10.1016/j.ijinfomgt.2014.06.004

Onyango, P., & Tostensen, A. (2016). *Situation of youth and children in Kibera*. Retrieved from https://www.cmi.no/publications/file/5527-the-situation-of-youth-and-children-in-kibera.pdf

Oromo, M. A. (2015). *The Relationship Between Mobile Money And Loans Issued By Commercial Banks In Kenya* (Master's dissertation). University of Nairobi.

Orrell, D., & Chlupatý, R. (2016). *The Evolution of Money*. Columbia University Press. doi:10.7312/orre17372

Owuor. (2019). *Mobile-based lending is a double-edged sword in Kenya—helping but also spiking personal debt*. University of Colorado. Retrieved from https://qz.com/africa/1722613/mobile-money-lending-in-kenya-helps-but-also-spikes-debt/

Pan, Y. (2019, June 9). *Jing Daily*. Retrieved July 29, 2019, from jingdaily.com: https://jingdaily.com/wechat-social-commerce/

Parasuraman, A. (2000). Technology readiness index (TRI): A multiple-item scale to measure readiness to embrace new technologies. *Journal of Service Research*, *2*(4), 307–320. doi:10.1177/109467050024001

Parasuraman, A., & Colby, C. L. (2014). An updated and streamlined technology readiness index: TR 2.0. *Journal of Service Research*, *18*(1), 59–74. doi:10.1177/1094670514539730

Parasuraman, A., & Grewal, D. (2000). The Impact of Technology on the Quality-Value-Loyalty Chain: A Research Agenda. *Journal of the Academy of Marketing Science*, *28*(1), 168–174. doi:10.1177/0092070300281015

Pasti, F. (2018). *2018 State of the Industry report on Mobile money*. London: GSMA.

Paul, G., & Totolo, E. (2018). Digital Credit. In *Kenya:Evidence from demand-side surveys*. FSD Kenya.

Pavlou, P. A. (2003). Consumer acceptance of electronic commerce: Integrating trust and risk with the technology acceptance model. *International Journal of Electronic Commerce*, *7*(3), 101–134. doi:10.1080/10864415.2003.11044275

Peace Child International. (2018). *Youth unemployment causes and solutions*. Retrieved from https://peacechild.org/youth-unemployment-causes-and-solutions/

Peiffer, C., & Rose, R. (2018). Why Are the Poor More Vulnerable to Bribery in Africa? The Institutional Effects of Services. *The Journal of Development Studies*, *54*(1), 18–29. doi:10.1080/00220388.2016.1257121

Pesapal. (2019). Retrieved from: https://www.pesapal.com

Pham, T. T. T., & Ho, J. C. (2015). The effects of product-related, personal-related factors and attractiveness of alternatives on consumer adoption of NFC-based mobile payments. *Technology in Society*, *43*, 1–16. doi:10.1016/j.techsoc.2015.05.004

Phonthanikitithaworn, C., Sellitto, C., & Fong, M. (2015). User Intentions to Adopt Mobile Payment Services: A Study of Early Adopters in Thailand. *Journal of Internet Banking and Commerce*, *20*(1), 1–29.

Porteous, D. (2006). *The Enabling Environment for Mobile Banking in Africa*. DFID.

Pousttchi, K. (2008). A modeling approach and reference models for the analysis of mobile payment use cases. *Electronic Commerce Research and Applications*, *7*(2), 182–201. doi:10.1016/j.elerap.2007.07.001

Pramis, J. (2013). *Number of Mobile Phones to Exceed World Population by 2014*. Available online at: http://www.digitaltrends.com/mobile/mobile-phone-world-population-2014

Pratt, J. W., & Zeckahuser, R. (1991). *Principals and Agents: The Structure of Business*. Harvard Business School Press.

PWC. (2015, Dec. 12). *Bank of the Future: What bank customers want to experience by 2020.* 2015 Ghana Banking Survey.

Ram, S., & Seath, J. N. (1989). Consumer resistance to innovation: The Marketing problem and its solutions. *Journal of Consumer Marketing*, *6*(2), 5–14. (accessed on 9th July, 2019) doi:10.1108/EUM0000000002542

Rao, C. H. H. (2008). Achieving Inclusive Growth; Recent Experience and Challenges Ahead. *Chandra Shekar Memorial Lecture, I*(3), 16. Retrieved from http://isid.org.in/pdf/NLv01i3.pdf

Rao, Y. (n.d.). *Big Data Algorithm Applied to Credit Risk Assessment Model.* School of Finance, Dongbei University of Finance and Economics. DOI doi:10.5013/ IJSSST.a.17.42

Ratha, D., De, S., Kim, E. J., Seshan, G., & Yameogo, N. D. (2019). Migration and Movement: Recent Developments and Outlook. *Migration and Development Brief*, (31), 1–29. doi:10.1016/B978-0-12-409548-9.10596-2

Ratha, D., Eigen-Zucchi, C., Plaza, S., Wyss, H., & Yi, S. (2013). Migration and Remittance Flows: Recent Trends and Outlook 2013–2016. *Migration and Development Brief*, (21), 1–29. Retrieved from http://scholar.google.com/scholar?hl=en&btnG=Search&q=intitle:Migration+and+Remittance+Flows:+Recent+Trends+and+Outlook,+2013-2016#0

Rathore, H. S. (2016, April). Adoption of digital wallet by consumers. BVIMSR's. *Journal of Management Research*, *8*(1), 69–75.

Rea, S. C., & Nelms, T. C. (2017). *Mobile Money: The First Decade. Institute for money, technology and financial inclusion.* Working Paper 2017-1.

Reaves, B., Scaife, N., Bates, A., Traynor, P., & Butler, K. R. (2015). *Mo(bile) Money, Mo(bile) Problems: Analysis of Branchless Banking Applications in the Developing World. In 24th USENIX Security Symposium* (pp. 17–32). Washington, DC: USENIX Association. Retrieved from https://www.usenix.org/conference/usenixsecurity15/technical-sessions/presentation/reaves

Rizan, M., Warokka, A., & Listyawati, D. (2014). Relationship Marketing and Customer Loyalty: Do Customer Satisfaction and Customer Trust Really Serve as Intervening Variables? *Journal of Marketing Research & Case Studies*, *2014*, 1–12. doi:10.5171/2014.724178

Robertson, T. S., & Myers, J. H. (2004). Personality correlates of opinions leadership and innovative buying behavior. *JMR, Journal of Marketing Research*, *6*(2), 164–168. (accessed on 9th July, 2019) doi:10.1177/002224376900600204

Rogers, E. M. (1983). *Diffusions of Innovations* (3rd ed.). London: The Free Press Collier Macmillan Publishers.

Rogers, E. M. (1995). *Diffusion of innovations* (4th ed.). New York, NY: Free Press.

Rolfe, A. (2017, July 5). *Is mobile money a haven for money launderers?* Retrieved October 15, 2019, from PaymentsCM: https://www.paymentscardsandmobile.com/is-mobile-money- a-haven-for-money-launderers/

Rolfe, A. (2018). *The Rise of Digital and Mobile Wallet: Global usage statistics from 2018.* Payments Cards & Mobile. Retrieved from https://www.paymentscardsandmobile.com/mobile-wallet-global-usage-statistic/

Rolfe, A. (2019). *Mobile money transactions equivalent of half of Kenya's GDP.* Retrieved from: https://www.paymentscardsandmobile.com/

Rome, F. A. O. (2010). *The average rate of female agricultural land ownership is less than 20% in developing countries*. Rome: FAO.

Rosenberg, J., & Morawczynski, O. (2008). *Why has M-Pesa become so popular in Kenya?* Retrieved from https://www.cgap.org/blog/why-has-m-pesa-become-so-popular-kenya

Saborido, R., Ruiz, A., Bermúdez, J., Vercher, E., & Luque, M. (2016). Evolutionary multi-objective optimization algorithms for fuzzy portfolio selection. *Applied Soft Computing*, *39*, 48–63. doi:10.1016/j.asoc.2015.11.005

Safaricom PLC (Kenya). (2019). *Financial Statements for the year 2018.* Author.

Safaricom. (2019). *Safaricom.* Retrieved from: https://www.safaricom.co.ke/

Sangeetha, C. & Kapul, K. (2018). *Catalyst for financial inclusion. Bank the unbanked with Digital channels*. Academic Press.

Sarker, S., & Wells, J. D. (2003). Understanding mobile handheld device use and adoption. *Communications of the ACM*, *46*(12).

Sarma, M., & Pais, J. (2011). Financial Inclusion and Development. *Journal of International Development*, *23*(5), 613–628. doi:10.1002/jid.1698

Says, O. H. (2018, March 2). *Banking + Fintech Collaboration: More Important Than Ever.* Retrieved November 12, 2018, from The Financial Brand website: https://thefinancialbrand.com/71050/banking-fintech-collaboration-bigtech-trends/

Scharwatt, C., & Williamson, C. (2015). *Mobile Money Crosses Borders: New Remittance Models in West Africa*. GSM Association. Retrieved from https://www.gsma.com/mobilefordevelopment/wp-content/uploads/2015/04/2015_MMU_Mobile-money-crosses-borders_New-remittance-models-in-West-Africa.pdf

Scharwatt, J. F. (2016). *Mobile money facilitates 1.7 million school fee payments in Côte d'Ivoire*. Retrieved from: https://www.gsma.com/mobilefordevelopment/english/

Schierz, P. G., Schilke, O., & Wirtz, B. W. (2010). Understanding consumer acceptance of mobile payment services: An empirical analysis. *Electronic Commerce Research and Applications*, *9*(3), 209–216. doi:10.1016/j.elerap.2009.07.005

Scott, S. V., Reenen, J. V., & Zachariadis, M. (2017). The Long-Term Effect of Digital Innovation on Bank Performance: An Empirical Study of SWIFT Adoption in Financial Services. The Centre for Economic Performance.

Scott, R. III., & Steven, P. (2011). A Double Squeeze on the Middle Class. *Journal of Economic Issues*, 45(2), 333-341.

Sefiane, S., & Benbouziane, B. (2012). Portfolio selection using genetic algorithm. *Journal of Applied Finance and Banking*, *2*(4), 143–154.

Senge, P. M. (1990). *The Fifth Discipline. The Art and Practice of the Learning Organization*. New York: Currency Doubleday.

Shachmurove, Y. (2002). The Behavior of Secondary European Stock Markets to Positive and Negative Shocks. *International Journal of Business*.

Shatskikh, A. (2013). *Consumer acceptance of Mobile Payments in Restaurants* (Master Thesis). University of South Florida, Department of Hospitality Administration.

Sheppard, B. H., & Sherman, D. M. (1998, July). The Grammars of Trust: A Model and General Implications. *Academy of Management Review*, *23*(3), 422–437. doi:10.5465/amr.1998.926619

Shorouq. (2010). Neuro-Based Artificial Intelligence Model for Loan Decisions. *American Journal of Economics and Business Administration*, *2*(1), 27-34.

Simpson, J. A. (2007, October). Psychological Foundations of Trust. *Current Directions in Psychological Science*, *16*(5), 264–268. doi:10.1111/j.1467-8721.2007.00517.x

Sinclair, P. S. (2001). Financial Exclusion: An Introductory Survey. *Economic Journal (London)*, *95*, 21–41.

Singh, S. (2016, December 20). As India braces for digital payments future, how secure are banks from cyber attacks? *Economic Times*. Retrieved 2016, from Economic Times: http://economictimes.indiatimes.com/tech/internet/as-india-braces-for-digital-payments-future-how-secure-are-banks-from-cyberattacks/articleshow/56073576.cms?from=mdr

Slade, E. L., Williams, M. D., & Dwivedi, Y. K. (2013). Mobile payment adoption: Classification and review of the extant literature. *The Marketing Review*, *13*(2), 167–190. doi:10.1362/146934713X13699019904687

Society for International development and Kenya Bureau of Statistics. (2013). *Exploring Kenya's Inequality. Pulling apart or pooling together*. Author.

Solin & Zerzan. (2010). Mobile Money Methodology for Assessing Money Laundering and Terrorist Financing Risk. In *Mobile Money: Methodology for Assessing Money Laundering and Terrorist Financing Risks*. GSMA Discussion Paper.

Sousa, R., & Voss, C. A. (2006). Service Quality in Multichannel Services Employing Virtual Channels. *Journal of Service Research*, *8*(4), 356–371. doi:10.1177/1094670506286324

Spinello, R. A. (1997). *Case studies in information and computer ethics*. Prentice Hall.

Spread the Love. (2018). *School fees to be paid through mobile*. Retrieved from: https://newspublictrust.com

Staff Reporter. (2018). *Digitizing Uganda's Education Sector with Mobile Payment Platform*. Retrieved from: https://paymentsafrika.com/payment-news/

Straub, E. T. (2009, June). Understanding Technology Adoption: Theory and Future Directions for Informal Learning. *Review of Educational Research*, *79*(2), 625–649. doi:10.3102/0034654308325896

Subex. (n.d.). *White Paper Preventing Mobile Money Frauds with Appropriate Countermeasures*. Retrieved October 18, 2019, from Subex: https://subex.com/pdf/Whitepapers/Mobile-Money-Whitepaper1

Suri, T. (2017). Mobile Money. *Annual Review of Economics*, *9*(1), 497–520. doi:10.1146/annurev-economics-063016-103638

Svensson, J. (2005). Eight Questions about Corruption. *The Journal of Economic Perspectives*, *19*(3), 19–42. doi:10.1257/089533005774357860

Tamara, C., & Claudia, M. (2015). *How M-Shwari Works: The Story So Far. Access to Finance Forum Reports by CGAP and Its Partners*. Academic Press.

Tan, G. W.-H., Ooi, K.-B., Chong, S.-C., & Hew, T.-S. (2014). NFC mobile credit card: The next frontier of mobile payment? *Telematics and Informatics*, *31*(2), 292–307. doi:10.1016/j.tele.2013.06.002

Taylor, S., & Todd, P. (1995). Assessing IT Usage: The Role of Prior Experience. *Management Information Systems Quarterly*, *19*(4), 561–570. doi:10.2307/249633

Templeman & Moniz. (2019). *Quantify geopolitical risk with alpha-DIG*. Deutsche Bank Research.

Teo, A. C., Tan, G. W. H., Ooi, K. B., Hew, T. S., & Yew, K. T. (2015). The effects of convenience and speed in m-payment. *Industrial Management & Data Systems, 115*(2), 311–331. doi:10.1108/IMDS-08-2014-0231

The Economist Intelligence Unit. (2018). The 2018 Government E-Payments Adoption Ranking (GEAR). *The Economist.*

The Glossary of Education Reform. (2015). *Unique Student Identifier.* Available at https://www.edglossary.org/unique-student-identifier/

The International Telecommunication Union (ITU). (2016) *Regulatory & Market Environment Digital financial services: Regulating For Financial Inclusion— An Ict Perspective.* Available at https://www.itu.int/dms_pub/itu-d/opb/pref/D-PREF-BB.REG_OUT02-2016-PDF-E.pdf

The Lunchbowl Network. (2011). *Facts and information about Kibera.* Retrieved from https://www.lunchbowl.org/

The New Dawn. (2019). *Lonestar Cell MTN launches University fees payment via Mobile Money.* Retrieved from: https://thenewdawnliberia.com/

The World Bank. (2014). *Global Findex (Global Financial Inclusion Database).* Development Research Group, Finance and Private Sector Development Unit: World Bank. Retrieved 2016, from databank.worldbank.org/data/reports.aspx?source=global-findex-(global-financial-inclusion-database)

The World Bank. (2018). *Addressing the Youth Employment Crisis Needs Urgent Global Action.* Retrieved from http://www.worldbank.org/en/news/press-release/2015/10/13/addressing-the-youth-employment-crisis-needs-urgent-global-action on 31/03/2019

The World Bank. (2018). *Poverty incidence in Kenya declined significantly but unlikely to be eradicated by 2030.* Retrieved from https://www.worldbank.org/en/country/kenya/publication/kenya-economic-update-poverty-incidence-in-kenya-declined-significantly-but-unlikely-to-be-eradicated-by-2030 on 02/04/2019

Thomas, H., Jain, A., & Angus, M. (2013, September). *Cashless Journey.* MasterCard Advisors. Retrieved from MasterCard Web site: https://newsroom.mastercard.com/wp-content/uploads/2013/09/Cashless-Journey_WhitePaper_FINAL.pdf

Thompson, E. A. (2007). *Misplaced Blame: Islam, Terrorism and the Origins of Hawala.* The Hague: Koninklijke Brill N.V.

Thompson, R. L., Higgins, C. A., & Howell, J. M. (1994). Influence of Experience on Personal Computer Utilization: Testing a Conceptual Model. *Journal of Management Information Systems, 11*(1), 167–187. doi:10.1080/07421222.1994.11518035

Times of India. (2016, December 13). *None of mobile payment apps in India fully secure, warns Qualcomm.* New Delhi, India: The Times of India. Retrieved 2016, from http://timesofindia.indiatimes.com/business/india-business/None-of-mobile-payment-apps-in-India-fully-secure-warns-Qualcomm/articleshow/55967778.cms

Tolofari, S. (2005). New Public Management and Education. *Policy Features in Education*, 75-89.

Tonui, C. (2018). *Kenya's Mobile Phone Penetration Surpasses 100% Mark*. Retrieved from: https://kenyanwallstreet.com

Trafimow, D., Brown, J., Grace, K., Thompson, L. A., & Sheeran, P. (2002, Autumn). The Relative Influence of Attitudes and Subjective Norms from Childhood to Adolescence: Between-Participant and Within-Participant Analyses. *The American Journal of Psychology*, *115*(3), 395–414. doi:10.2307/1423424 PMID:12221916

Transparency International – GCB. (2019). *Citizens speak out about corruption in Africa*. Retrieved from https://www.transparency.org/news/feature/citizens_speak_out_about_corruption_in_africa

Trust, F. (2011). *Finscope, 2010. FinScope South Africa 2010. Finscope, 2011. FinScope South Africa 2011*. Retrieved from Finmark Trust website: www.finscopeafrica.com

Tschannen-Moran, M., & Hoy, W. K. (2000). A Multidisciplinary Analysis of the Nature, Meaning, and Measurement of Trust. *Review of Educational Research*, *70*(4), 547–593. doi:10.3102/00346543070004547

Tsilizani, E. N. (2016, November 2). *University of Bolton Institution Repository*. Retrieved October 19, 2019, from University of Bolton: http://ubir.bolton.ac.uk/id/eprint/960

Ulwodi, D. W. (2017). *Financial Inclusion and Welfare: Evidence from the Global Findex and Financial Access Surveys*. Nairobi, Kenya: University of Nairobi.

UN. (1999). *International Convention for the Suppression of the Financing of Terrorism*. New York: General Assembly of the United Nations.

UNDP. (2015). *United Nations Development Program*. Retrieved from: https://www.undp.org/content/undp/en/home.html

UNESCO Institute for Statistics. (2011). *Financing Education in Sub-Saharan Africa Meeting the Challenges of Expansion, Equity and Quality*. UNESCO Institute for Statistics. Available at http://uis.unesco.org/sites/default/files/documents/financing-education-in-sub-saharan-africameeting-the-challenges-of-expansion-equity-and-quality-en_0.pdf

UNESCO. (2016). *Leaving no one behind: How far on the way to universal primary and secondary education?* Montreal: UNESCO.

UNESCO. (2019). *Education in Africa*. Retrieved from: http://tcg.uis.unesco.org/country-profile/

UNESCO. (2019). *Meeting Commitments: Are countries on track to achieve SDG 4?* Montreal, Paris: UNESCO.

United Nations Development Programme. (2018). Retrieved from http://www.ke.undp.org/content/kenya/en/home/countryinfo.html

United Nations Economic Commission for Africa -UNECA. (2016). *Measuring corruption in Africa: The international dimension matters - African Governance Report IV*. Retrieved from https://www.uneca.org/sites/default/files/PublicationFiles/agr4_eng_fin_web.pdf

United Nations. (2016, January 1). *Sustainable Development Goals*. Retrieved October 16, 2019, from United Nations: https://www.un.org/sustainabledevelopment/sustainable- development-goals/

USAID. (2010). *Mobile Financial Services Risk Matrix*. Available https://www.gsma.com/mobilefordevelopment/wp-content /uploads /2012 /06/ (accessed on 1st July ,2019)

ValuePenguin. (2019, April 14). Retrieved July 29, 2019, from Valuepenguin.com: https://www.valuepenguin.com/personal-loans/average-personal-loan-interest-rates

Van Reisen, M., Fulgencio, H. T., Van Stam, G., & Otieno, A. (2016). mMoney Remittances: Contributing to the Quality of Rural Health Care. In AfriCOMM (pp. 1–17). Academic Press.

Varnali, K., Yilmaz, C., & Toker, A. (2012). Predictors of attitudinal and behavioral outcomes in mobile advertising: A field experiment. *Electronic Commerce Research and Applications*, *11*(6), 570–581. doi:10.1016/j.elerap.2012.08.002

Vedapradha, R., Hariharan, R., & Shivakami, R. (2019). Artificial Intelligence: A Technological Prototype in Recruitment. *Journal of Service Science and Management*, *12*(03), 382–390. doi:10.4236/jssm.2019.123026

Vedapradha, R., & Ravi, H. (2018). Application of Artificial Intelligence in Investment Banks. *Review of Economic and Business Studies*, *11*(2), 131–136. doi:10.1515/rebs-2018-0078

Venkatesh, V., & Davis, F. (2000). A theoretical extension of the technology-acceptance model: Four longitudinal field studies. *Management Science*, *46*(2), 186–204. doi:10.1287/mnsc.46.2.186.11926

Venkatesh, V., Morris, M. G., Davis, G. B., & Davis, F. D. (2003, September). User Acceptance of Information Technology: Toward a Unified View. *Management Information Systems Quarterly*, *27*(3), 425–478. doi:10.2307/30036540

Venkatesh, V., Thong, J., & Xu, X. (2012). Consumer acceptance and use of information technology: Extending the unified theory of acceptance and use of technology. *Management Information Systems Quarterly*, *36*(1), 157–178. doi:10.2307/41410412

Vital Wave. (2014). *Digital Payments for Education in Uganda*. Uganda: Vital Wave.

Vodafone. (2013). *Tokyo-drift-how-japan-leads-the-way-on-m-payments*. Retrieved from http://www.vodafone.com/business/globalenterprise/tokyo-drift-how-japan-leads-the-way-on-m-payments-2013-08-13

Vorster, J. M. (2012). Managing corruption in South Africa: The ethical responsibility of churches. *Scriptura*, *109*(1), 133–147.

Wachira-Keriri. (2012). *Competitive Advantage of the Use of Credit Reference bureaus By Commercial Banks In Kenya* (Master's dissertation). The University of Nairobi.

Walker, R. F., Haasdijk, E. W., & Genets, M. C. (1995). Credit Evaluation Using a Genetic Algorithm. *Iin Intelligent System for Finance and Business. John Wiley and Sons.*

Wallace, L. G., & Sheetz, S. D. (2014). The adoption of software measures: A technology acceptance model (TAM) perspective. *Information & Management, 51*(2), 249–258. doi:10.1016/j.im.2013.12.003

Wan, G., & Che, P. (2004). Chinese air travelers' acceptance towards electronic ticketing. *Proceedings of Engineering Management Conference.* 10.1109/IEMC.2004.1407118

Wang, G., Dou, W., & Zhou, N. (2008). Consumption attitudes and adoption of new consumer products: A contingency approach. *European Journal of Marketing, 42*(1/2), 238–254. doi:10.1108/03090560810840998

Wang, W. T., & Li, H. M. (2012). Factors influencing mobile service adoption: A brand-equity perspective. *Internet Research, 22*(2), 142–179. doi:10.1108/10662241211214548

Wan, W. N., Luk, C. L., & Chow, C. W. C. (2005). Consumers' adoption of banking channels in Hong Kong. *International Journal of Bank Marketing, 23*(3), 255–272. (accessed on 12th October ,2019) doi:10.1108/02652320510591711

Watkins, E. (2013). Mobile payment has hotel applications. *Hotel News Now.* Retrieved from http://www.hotelnewsnow.com/Article/12378/Mobilepayment-has-hotel-application

Wayne, W. (2019). *Diffusion of Innovation theory.* Boston University.

WB. (2016). Feminization of agriculture in the context of rural transformations: What is the evidence? WB.

Wechsler. (2019). *Mobile Money Transfers Suspected of Financing Dusit D2 Terror Attack.* The DFS Observatory.

Westin, A. F. (1967). *Privacy and freedom.* Athenaeum.

White, D. (2012). *The Social and Economic Impact of M-PESAon the Lives of Women in the Fishing Industry on Lake Victoria.* Independent Study Project (ISP) Collection. Paper 1246.

WHO. (2016, July 21). *One Health and the Sustainable Development Goals.* Asunción, Paraguay: World Health Organization.

World Bank and InfoDev. (Ed.). (2012). Maximizing Mobile: 2012 Information and Communications for Development. Washington, DC: World Bank : InfoDev.

World Bank Press Release. (2018). *Accelerated remittances growth to low- and middle-income countries in 2018.* Retrieved from: https://www.worldbank.org/en/

World Bank. (2003). *Reaching the Rural Poor: A Renewed Strategy for Rural Development.* Washington, DC: Author.

World Bank. (2014, January 13). Retrieved July 28, 2019, from databank.worldbank.org: https://databank.worldbank.org/reports.aspx?source=1228

World Bank. (2016). *Digital Dividends* (World Development Report No. 102725). Retrieved from The World Bank website: www.worldbank.org

World Bank. (2019). *Credit Reporting Knowledge Guide 2019*. Available at documents.worldbank.org/curated/en/262691559115855583/pdf/Credit- Reporting-Knowledge-Guide-2019.pdf

*World Inequality Report*. (2018). Academic Press.

World Population Review. (2019). *Nairobi Population 2019*. Available at http://worldpopulationreview.com/world-cities/nairobi-population (accessed on 12th October ,2019)/

Worlu, C. N., & Nkoro, E. (2012). Tax revenue and economic development in Nigeria: A macroeconometric approach. *Academic Journal of Interdisciplinary Studies*, *1*(2), 211–223.

Wu, J. H., & Wang, S. C. (2005). What drives mobile commerce? An empirical evaluation of the revised technology acceptance model. *Information & Management*, *42*(5), 719–729. doi:10.1016/j.im.2004.07.001

Xinhua. (2019). *Kenyan schools embrace mobile money fee payment*. Retrieved from: https://www.khmertimeskh.com

Xinhua. (2019, January 30). Retrieved July 20, 2019, from xinhuanet.com: http://www.xinhuanet.com/english/2019-01/30/c_137787614.htm

Yaghoubi, N.-M., & Bahmani, E. (2010, September). Factors Affecting the Adoption of Online Banking An Integration of Technology Acceptance Model and Theory of Planned Behavior. *Journal of Business and Management*, *5*(9), 159–165.

Yang, A. S. (2009). Exploring adoption difficulties in mobile banking services. *Can. J. Admin. Sci.*, *149*(2), 136–149. doi:10.1002/cjas.102

Yang, S., Lu, Y., Gupta, S., Cao, Y., & Zhang, R. (2012). Mobile payment services adoption across time: An empirical study of the effects of behavioral beliefs, social influences, and personal traits. *Computers in Human Behavior*, *28*(1), 129–142. doi:10.1016/j.chb.2011.08.019

Yiu, C. S., Grant, K., & Edgar, D. (2007). Factors affecting the adoption of Internet Banking in Hong Kong—Implications for the banking sector. *International Journal of Information Management*, *27*(5), 336–351. doi:10.1016/j.ijinfomgt.2007.03.002

Yunus, M., & Alan, J. (2003). Banker to the Poor: Micro-Lending and the Battle Against World Poverty (Rev. ed.). New York: Public Affairs.

Zarmpou, T., Saprikis, V., Markos, A., & Vlachopoulou, M. (2012). Modeling users' acceptance of mobile services. *Electronic Commerce Research*, *12*(2), 225–248. doi:10.100710660-012-9092-x

Zhang, G. P. (2004). Neural Networks in Business Forecasting. Idea Group Inc. doi:10.4018/978-1-59140-176-6

# About the Contributors

**Thaisaiyi Zephania Opati** is currently the Head of Department and a lecturer at the Riara School of Business. He has published two books "Personal Branding –King Solomon's way" (2012) and "The Terrorist in the boardroom" (2014). He has also published "Characteristics of the African Buyer's Purchase Behaviour in conjunction with Olamide Shittu and Uchenna Uzo as a chapter In Indigenous Management practices in Africa –A guide to practitioners (2018) Uchenna Uzo and Abel Kinoti (Eds) Emerald Publishing. He has also published a Chapter "USA Economic Nationalism and the Second-Hand Clothes Industry in Sub-Saharan Africa (2019) in International Firms' Economic Nationalism and Trade Policies in the Globalization Era Harish C. Chandan and Bryan Christiansen (Eds). He has taught in Riara University and Jomo Kenyatta University of Agriculture and Technology. He has consulted for United Nation Volunteer Association and Global Village Publishers as a business writer. He has presented a paper in Lagos Nigeria about "Effects of Foreign Advertising on The Kenyan Millennials" at Lagos Business School in August 2016; He also in conjunction with Dr. Margaret Oloko he presented a paper that looked at "The critical factors that determine brand loyalty of children to the adulthood" at "Africa Rising" at Riara University in August 2014. He has also presented a paper "Branding to Children - the adults becoming" in the International Commerce Advertising, Marketing and Retail Conference (INCOMAR) Maleka Malaysia in 2010. He has also conducted the "Campus Climate Survey study" at University Technology Mara Malaysia. His master's paper thesis was focused on "Strategic fit of the diversification of the KFC and Pizza Malaysia." of the two outlets. He is a Commonwealth Scholar, a member of the Charted Institute of Marketers (UK) and a member of Academy of International Business. His interest is in Branding, Strategy, Consumer Behavior and International .

* * *

**Sayed Fayaz Ahmad** is a Certified Professional in Engineering Management (CPEM) from the American Society of Engineering Management (ASEM) and a

Certified Project Director (CPD) from the Global Association for Quality Management (GAQM). He is working as Assistant Professor and Coordinator MPhil/Ph.D. Business Management programs. He holds a Ph.D. in Engineering Management from Gomal University (GU) and holds M.S. in Telecommunication Engineering Management from the University of Engineering and Technology (UET) Peshawar. In addition, he holds BS-Telecommunication Engineering from Baluchistan University of Information Technology, Engineering, and Management Sciences (BUITEMS) Quetta. He has a vast experience in research and has conducted many types of research in Public and Private Sector organizations of Pakistan. In his Doctorate research, Mr. Sayed Fayaz Ahmad created a Model for Knowledge Management and Strategically Suitable Decision Making in Telecommunication Sector Organizations.

**Olayemi Abdullateef Aliyu** is the Group Manager for Postgraduate Business Programs at the Faculty of Business Management and Legal Studies, Toi Ohomai Institute of Technology, New Zealand. Dr Aliyu's core expertise is in Marketing, with a focus on quantitative analyzes of business performance. He holds a PhD in Marketing, Masters in Economics, Postgraduate Diploma in Financial Management, Postgraduate Diploma in Adult Teaching and Professional Certificate in International Contact Center Management. He is also a full member of the Chartered Institute of Marketing London UK.

**Chris Niyi Arasanmi** is a senior lecturer at the Faculty of Business Management, Toi Ohomai Institute of Technology, Rotorua, New Zealand, where he teaches strategic management, IT Management, Business Intelligence and Analytics, Digital Business and Research Method. Chris received a PhD in Business Information Systems from Auckland University of Technology (AACSB accredited), Auckland, New Zealand. His research interests are in enterprise information systems, ERP training, Information systems implementation, IS adoption, digital commerce and mobile learning.

**Samuel M. Ekundayo** is a Senior Lecturer at the School of Computing at the Eastern Institute of Technology, New Zealand. His expertise range from Educational technology to Software development, Social Media to Activity theory. He holds a PhD in Business Information Systems from Auckland University of Technology, New Zealand, a Masters degree from Nanyang Technological University, Singapore and a Bachelors (Hons) degree from Coventry University, United Kingdom. Prior to becoming an academic, Dr Samuel was a Business Analyst.

**Albert Juma** is a teaching focused lecturer of Physics at La Trobe University since January 2019, prior to which Juma was a teaching associate at Monash University and Research Assistant at Deakin University. Dr. Juma has taught Physics for over five years in several countries but now with a new focus on contemporary teaching methods for science subjects. He holds a PhD in experimental physics from Free University Berlin in Germany, having studied charge transport and atomic diffusion in nano-composite heterostructures for new generation photovoltaic devices. After one year postdoc research experience in Estonia, he lectured in Botswana for two and half years before moving to Melbourne. He also has a keen interest in contributing towards improving the education system in developing countries and to support the young and ambitious students seeking opportunities for further studies.

**Palak Kanojia** is currently working as Assistant Professor in University of Delhi. Presently, she is a doctoral scholar in Department of Commerce, Delhi School of Economics. She has done her master of philosophy on customer adoption of electronic payment systems. She has published six research papers in journals and contributed two chapters in edited books. She has presented several research papers in the National and International conferences in University of Delhi. She has attended more than twelve faculty development programs and seminars. She has organised around three academic seminars and programs for faculty. Her research interests include marketing, consumer psychology, behavioural studies, e-commerce and digital technologies.

**Rehema Kiarie** is a lecturer in Riara University. She teaches marketing and management courses. She has a multifaceted approach in relation to her professional career which involves interacting with both international and local parties that has been a great inspiration to her career. Her hobbies are reading, travelling and swimming.

**Madan Lal** is a passionate academician and scholar in the area of International business and marketing. He teaches papers in the area of International Economics, International trade, Research Methodology and Marketing. He has taught in the Institute of Management Studies(IMS), Banaras Hindu University (BHU), and presently working as Professor in the department of commerce, Delhi School of Economics, University of Delhi. Dr. Madan Lal earned his Doctor of Letters (D.Litt.) degree from IMS, Banaras Hindu University. He did his MA economics and MBA-IB from Punjab University Chandigarh. and Ph.D. Degree from H. P. University Business School, HPU Shimla, Himachal Pradesh. Dr. Lal has done two major research projects in the area of marketing and international trade. He has authored and edited three books and published more than two dozen research papers in national and international journals. He has coordinated about fifteen FDPs/ QIPs, workshops and conferences of national and international level and delivered lectures at various academic platforms including in-house and corporate training and capacity building programs. Dr. Lal's professional service includes editorial roles, affiliation to various boards/committees, conference participation as Chair/ Co-chair/key note speaker and student advising.

**Joy Mueni** is a senior lecturer and Chair of the communication and multimedia journalism department at Riara University, Kenya. She has distinguished herself as a competent media scholar with interests in the interplay between communication and media and issues relating to gender, children and popular culture.

**Eric Niyitunga** is a lecturer at the University of Johannesburg, school of Public Management, Governance and Public Policy. He holds a PhD in Political Studies from the same University. His philosophy in lecturing and supervising students at Masters and Doctoral levels is informed by the need to pass on knowledge to the next generation as a way to eradicate poverty and violence, particularly in Africa. His research interests include research methods in international relations, critical cases in governance, international diplomacy, democratising service delivery, international peace and security, and ethics in mediation. He has published 10 peer-reviewed articles in social sciences journals and two book chapters in social sciences reference books. Dr Niyitunga has presented papers at a number of local and international conferences and events across the globe. He conducted research methodology and article writing workshops at selected universities in Africa, China and United Kingdom. He was selected as a United Nations Humanitarian Peace Ambassador (2018-2019) and attended a UN conference on humanitarian peace that took place in Thailand. He continues his role as a peace ambassador and educator by being part of the peace education organisation, an organisation that seeks to educate young people for peace in Southern Africa region. He has successfully acted as a non-assessing chair for Master's and doctoral students on a number of occasions for different higher education institutions. He is also an alumni of the African Leadership Centre, a think tank that located in Nairobi, Kenya.

**Gilbert Oyoo** is passionate about working with organizations and governments to protect themselves and the wider financial system from abuse by people and entities intending to cause harm to others through financial crime. His areas of interest include Sanctions screening and Anti-Money Laundering (AML/CFT), Enterprise Risk Management (ERM), Know Your Customer (KYC) and Customer Due Diligence checks, Third Party Risk Management, Regulatory Change Management (RCM) and Internal audit solutions for governments and non-government entities. He is currently the Risk Solutions Specialist covering East and West Africa regions. Prior to this he served as a Senior Consultant, Risk Advisory East Africa where he led teams during training sessions, corporate governance reviews, internal controls audit engagements and development, testing and implementing governance plans. He has delivered Financial Crime / AML / CFT, Enterprise Risk Management and Business Continuity Management and Internal Controls training to government and private sector practitioners in East and West African countries. He has also served as the Chair to ISACA Kenya Board Committee on communications. His academic background includes a Bachelor's Degree in Business Information Technology, Certification in Information Systems Audit (CISA), and Certified in Oracle Database Design as well as an on-going Master of Science in ICT Policy and Regulation and Certification as a Certified Fraud Examiner (CFE).

**Fayaz Ahmad Sayed** is a Certified Professional in Engineering Management (CPEM) from the American Society of Engineering Management (ASEM) and a Certified Project Director (CPD) from the Global Association for Quality Management (GAQM). He is working as Assistant Professor and Coordinator MPhil/Ph.D. Business Management programs. He holds a Ph.D. in Engineering Management from Gomal University (GU) and holds M.S. in Telecommunication Engineering Management from the University of Engineering and Technology (UET) Peshawar. In addition, he holds BS-Telecommunication Engineering from Baluchistan University of Information Technology, Engineering, and Management Sciences (BUITEMS) Quetta. He has a vast experience in research and has conducted many types of research in Public and Private Sector organizations of Pakistan. In his Doctorate research, Mr. Sayed Fayaz Ahmad created a Model for Knowledge Management and Strategically Suitable Decision Making in Telecommunication Sector Organizations.

**Muhammad Shahid** is working in Professorial rank at HCT, UAE. He has worked as Associate Professor at UOL and ICT, PTCL-Etisalat. He has rich industry experience and has worked as Telecom Consultant. He has number of publications in reputed journals and conferences.

**Gladys Wanjiku Thuita** is a lecturer in Riara University, school of business taking accounting and finance. She also handles the docket of student affairs, in the school. She is the current elected Membership secretary, AIB SSA. In addition she holds an MBA in Finance, Bachelors in Business Administration (Accounting and Finance) and a Certified Public Accountant (K). She is coupled with over 10 years working experience in Accounting and Finance from a wide number of corporation which include the multinationals. She has published in peer-reviewed journals. With personal attributes such as being pro-active, self-driven, result-oriented, excellent technical, analytical and planning abilities, Gladys is set to add value in the academic field especially in the areas of research and lecturing.

# Index

# S



# T

www.ingramcontent.com/pod-product-compliance
Lightning Source LLC
LaVergne TN
LVHW061547290926
849162LV00004B/940
* 9 7 8 1 7 9 9 8 2 3 9 8 8 *